EUROPEAN
BUSINESS
CUSTOMS & MANNERS

EUROPEAN
BUSINESS
CUSTOMS & MANNERS

MARY MURRAY BOSROCK

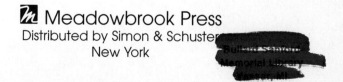

Meadowbrook Press
Distributed by Simon & Schuster
New York

Library of Congress Cataloging-in-Publication Data

Bosrock, Mary Murray.
  European business customs & manners : a country-by-country guide / by
Mary Murray Bosrock.
     p. cm.
  Includes bibliographical references and index.
  ISBN 0-88166-497-9 (Meadowbrook)   ISBN 0-684-04001-8 (Simon &
Schuster)
  1. Business etiquette—Europe. 2. Corporate culture—Europe. 3.
Intercultural communication—Europe. 4. National characteristics, European.
5. Europe—Social life and customs. I. Title: European business customs and
manners. II. Title.
  HF5389.3.E85B67 2006
  395.5'2'094—dc22
                              2005023343

Editorial Director: Christine Zuchora-Walske
Editor: Megan McGinnis
Editor and Researcher: Catherine A. H. Walker
Proofreader: Angela Wiechmann
Editorial Assistant: Alicia Ester
Production Manager: Paul Woods
Graphic Design Manager: Tamara Peterson
Desktop Publisher: Danielle White
Index: Beverlee Day
Cover Photo: Val Escher; Globe in image © 2006 by George F. Cram Co.,
    4719 W. 62nd Street, Indianapolis, IN 46268, 800.227.4199 x 3715

© 2006 by Mary Murray Bosrock

Published by Meadowbrook Press, 5451 Smetana Drive, Minnetonka,
Minnesota 55343

www.meadowbrookpress.com

BOOK TRADE DISTRIBUTION by Simon and Schuster, a division of Simon
and Schuster, Inc., 1230 Avenue of the Americas, New York, New York 10020

10 09 08 07 06   10 9 8 7 6 5 4 3 2 1

Printed in the United States of America

To Ron, who has given me the world: our sons, Matt and Steve.
To Matt and Steve, who have given me my girls: Monique, Leslie,
Alyssa, Isabella, Juliana, Alexandra, and Anna.

CONTENTS

Preface ix
Acknowledgments xiii

Part I: Getting Started

1. How to Go International 3
   Avoid Generalizations 3
   Don't Be the Ugly American 3
   Show Consideration and Respect 5
   The Ten Commandments of Visiting Europe 6

2. The European Union (EU) and the Euro 7
   The Facts of the EU 7
   The Euro 10
   Challenges Facing the EU 11
   The Newest EU Nations 15

3. General Rules: What to Know and How to Behave 19
   Basic Facts and Statistics 19
   Meeting and Greeting 20
   Names and Titles 21
   Language 23
   Dining 36
   Drinking 39
   Toasting 40
   Entertaining European Guests 40
   Tipping 41
   Manners 42
   Dress 44
   Gifts 46
   Punctuality 50
   Pace 51
   Corporate Culture 52
   Especially for Women 57
   Safety and Health 59
   Holidays and Festivals 61
   Interfaith Etiquette 61

Part II: Country Information

Austria 71
Belgium 85
Bulgaria 97
Cyprus 107
Czech Republic 119
Denmark 131
Estonia 143
Finland 153
France 165
Germany 179
Greece 195
Hungary 209
Ireland 223
Italy 235
Latvia 251
Lithuania 265
Luxembourg 277
Malta 287
Netherlands 299
Norway 313
Poland 325
Portugal 339
Romania 351
Slovakia 365
Slovenia 377
Spain 389
Sweden 403
Switzerland 415
Turkey 427
United Kingdom 441
    England 454
    Scotland 458
    Wales 462
    Northern Ireland 466

Resources 470
Index 471

PREFACE

The world is not globalizing—it's already global. To many, globalization has meant that old systems and ways of thinking no longer work. Goods, money, and people now cross borders at astonishing speeds. While globalization didn't create many of today's economic problems and cultural clashes, it made us aware of them, which has made many people feel helpless to solve them.

This book will help you gain control as you do business internationally. It's not about manners, etiquette, or how to hold your fork. It's about survival—for our companies, economy, and way of life. To survive, we must compete in a global economy. And to compete effectively, we must understand other countries, cultures, and ways of doing business. Intercultural understanding was once a luxury for the idle rich, but no longer. Ignoring cultural differences isn't innovative or clever; it's arrogant and bad for business.

In Europe, economic change isn't eliminating differences of history, language, culture, and work habits that have defined people for centuries. Instead, as the European nations move toward an economic and political alliance in which they make many decisions collectively and share a common currency and legal structure, each country is trying harder than ever to preserve its identity—which means you need to respect each country's unique culture and customs to ensure business success.

This book includes information everyone should know when interacting with Europeans, whether as a host or guest. When you're the host, you expect your European guest to know your country's basic customs; the more knowledgeable your guest, the more favorably you view him or her. Similarly, the more you know about your European host's culture, the better the impression you'll make and the faster you can discuss business.

Although it's designed as a resource for businesspeople, this book is also helpful to leisure travelers, students, teachers, travel and hospitality professionals, and hosts who regularly entertain European visitors. Keep this book on your desk or tuck it in your suitcase. I've organized it with your busy schedule in mind.

In Part I, I discuss the most basic rules for communicating with someone from another culture. I also include information about the European Union and the euro as well as important customs that are practiced in nearly every European country. In Part II, I provide details on communication and behavior in thirty European nations. Before you meet or talk with a European, you can quickly learn or review important facts about his or her culture that'll help you communicate clearly.

The information in this book isn't just "nice to know." It's vital to your success and that of your company if you want to do business in Europe or with Europeans. Knowing this information can lead to increased earnings for your company. In short, what you learn in this book will go straight to your bottom line.

The World According to Me

As you read this book, please understand that it reflects my experiences as an international businessperson. I'm simply telling it as I see it. All of us personalize our observations, no matter where we are in the world. A half-dozen people on a street corner in Dayton, Ohio, will tell six different stories about the traffic accident they just witnessed. A half-dozen people in Delhi will do the same.

I base my discussion of each country not only on personal observations but also on meetings with people from that country: diplomats, doctors, lawyers, businesspeople, teachers, and students. My goal is to pass on what I've learned and what other people with significant international experience have deemed important to know about Europeans.

Letter from Europe

Over the past several years, as I collected information for this book, I asked Europeans for their views of Americans and what they'd like to tell Americans planning to visit Europe. The following is a compilation of their more significant comments.

Dear American Friends:

You may have heard we are anti-American. We are not. How can we be? Many of us have family members and friends who are American citizens. Some of the best and brightest leaders shaping Europe's future have been educated in your colleges and universities. Efforts to fight terrorism in our countries and world wide require our solidarity. We share too many common values not to work together.

There is, however, a big difference between liking Americans and agreeing with your government. We feel, as longtime friends and allies, it is our right and responsibility to disagree when we feel you are wrong. In the past we worked together to defeat our common enemies. The future will require the same kind of cooperation without either of us giving up our independence and self-determination.

We know you love your country. We love ours. We do not mind that you say, "America is the greatest country in the world." The vast majority of you, however, have never set foot outside your country and have not learned much about the rest of the world, even in your schools. Your lack of knowledge about the histories, cultures, and people outside America is not only appalling but also insulting.

You say September 11, 2001, changed your country. We all mourned that day. Remember, though, it did not happen just to you. People from twenty European nations (including sixty-seven Brits) also died that tragic day. The terrorism you experienced came from outside your country. Too often, ours comes from within. Most of us have lived with terrorism and war in our homes. Many of us have been tortured and killed for worshipping the wrong god—or the right god in the wrong way. It is rare to find someone in Europe who has never lost a relative to war or terror.

We do not dislike America or Americans, but we are not preoccupied with you, either. We need to invest our time and talents in our own countries and our new union. We are more concerned about the challenges we face in bringing our countries together. We have worked hard to put aside border disputes and memories of war. This has not been easy. While we share an economic union, we struggle to put bitterness behind us and accept each others' cultures. It has been sixty years since the end of World War II, and we desperately want to avoid war and maintain peace. Please recognize and support this challenging effort. Our world will be a better place if the European Union is successful.

We are not quaint, backward, simple people. While we preserve and cultivate some traditional customs, we are a modern, computer-literate, well-educated society. Many of us enjoy a higher standard of living than our counterparts in the United States. We delight in your exuberance, optimism, simplicity, and desire to be told how wonderful you are. But we do not appreciate your trying to teach us the "truth."

When you come to Europe, take the time to learn about us and our customs. Leave your baseball caps, sneakers, and sweat suits at home. Lower your voice, and try to speak our language. Sample our food, enjoy our landscapes, visit some of our museums. We are proud of our homes, countries, and traditions and would like you to respect them.

Please visit us, but please come informed and with an open mind. We want to get to know you before we do business with you.

Respectfully,

Your European Friends

P.S. Especially to those of us who lived behind the Iron Curtain, America is more than a place—it is a universal dream, the land of the free and the home of the brave. Please keep the United States true to its values and beliefs—not only for you, but for us as well.

ACKNOWLEDGMENTS

For their valuable contributions, I'd like to thank the following people:

Manfred Adami

Marc Al, Honorary Consul of the Netherlands

Phyllis E. Bakke, Honorary Consul of Sweden (retired)

Heino Beckmann, Honorary Consul of the Federal Republic of Germany

Gina Bertolini

Magdaline Bovis

Katie Bowen, Executive Assistant to HM Consul General, British
  Consulate-General, Chicago

Kirsten Andersen Braun

Jurgita Dapkute, Third Secretary, Cultural and Education Affairs, Lithuania

Inga Domka, External Relations Manager, The Latvian Institute

Jan Doubrava

Raimonds Dzelme

Liana Eglite, Information Officer, Embassy of Latvia

Hubert Feichtlbauer

Anna Mazzucchi Freiman

Agnes and Laszlo Fulop

Michael Gergely

Don Grubich

Paul R. Heinershceid, Honorary Consul of Luxembourg

Kerstin Stråmark Johansen

Thor Stein Johansen, Consul General of Norway

Dorothea Johnson

Kerstin Johnson

Erika Kahler

Herb Kahler, Honorary Consul of Austria

Bruce Karstadt, Honorary Consul General of Sweden

Daniel Karvonen

Elisabeth Kehrer, Austrian Ambassador to Malta

Jasmine Z. Keller, Honorary Consul of France (retired)

Wendy Moore Kelly

Gabriele Klimaite

Patrick W. Ledray, Honorary Consul of Romania

Urs Lindenmann, Honorary Consul of Switzerland

Gris Livieri, Secretary, Embassy of Estonia

Annina Luck

John J. Luknic, Honorary Consul of the Slovak Republic

John Marshall, OBE

Melinda Mate

William McGrann, Honorary Consul of the United Kingdom of Great Britain

Jane Calabria McPeak, Honorary Consul of Italy

Livija Medne

Joseph A. Mestenhauser, Honorary Consul of the Czech Republic

Joseph Y. Micallef, Honorary Consul General of Malta

Dimitar Mihaylov, Embassy of Bulgaria

August J. Molnar, American Hungarian Foundation

Edel Moore

Tim Odegard

Fiona O'Donovan

Fred and Sally O'Donovan

John Omorean

Mark A. Pace, First Secretary and Consul, Embassy of Malta

Linda Pederson

Nancy Peters

Kevin Ries, Consular Agent for Luxembourg

Anelise Sawkins, Honorary Consul of Denmark

Maria Schweikert

Jacque Stassart, MD

Lydie Stassart, Honorary Consul of Belgium

Gloria Steine, Honorary Consul of Bolivia

Vaidas Taucius, Secretary, Lithuanian Embassy

Sean Timmins, International Trade Specialist, Central and Eastern Europe Business Information Center, Washington DC

Magdalena Walendowska, Information Officer, Embassy of Poland

Marianne Wargelin, Honorary Consul of Finland

Senol Whaley

Evan Williams

Kenneth Zapp, former Honorary Consul of the Republic of Slovenia

Laura Zeigler, MD

Special thanks to my husband, Ronald M. Bosrock, Honorary Consul General of Austria, and to Dermot Moore of Dublin, who have supported this book in many ways from its inception.

And to all the others who helped and encouraged me in ways large and small, my sincere thanks.

Mary Murray Bosrock

Mary Murray Bosrock
Saint Paul, Minnesota

Part 1

GETTING STARTED

HOW TO GO INTERNATIONAL

Avoid Generalizations

Just when you're tempted to generalize about a European, you'll meet a gregarious Finn, a humorless Irishman, a Hungarian who doesn't care about food, a rude Englishwoman, or a lethargic German—and all your generalizations will go out the window.

Even though people from the same country often look alike, speak the same language, eat the same foods, and practice the same religion, each one is different. Uniqueness is what makes international travel so much fun. I've listened to people of the same nationality debate a particular custom or behavior—and they rarely agreed. Women disagreed with men. Older people disagreed with younger ones. Sometimes there was general disagreement. Each person had a unique way of behaving and unique way of interpreting others' actions, which often led to miscommunication.

If people who share a culture sometimes have trouble communicating, then is communication *impossible* for a business traveler? Certainly not. Although you'll probably never meet a Swede who has every quality I describe in the chapter on Sweden, my quarter-century's experience in Europe has shown that there are certain common customs and characteristics you'll encounter when dealing with people from a particular country. Knowing these commonalities will help you understand Europeans and feel more comfortable with them. It'll help you avoid misunderstandings and communicate clearly and effectively so you can establish productive business relationships—and possibly friendships.

There isn't a country I've worked or traveled in that I haven't enjoyed. Regardless of how dynamic the business environment or how beautiful the countryside, it's always the people—the thousands of individuals I've met—who hold my interest and eventually win my heart.

Don't Be the Ugly American

The term *the ugly American* was introduced as the title of a 1958 novel by William J. Lederer and Eugene Burdick about an ignorant, incompetent

U.S. ambassador to a fictional Southeast Asian country. The term became widely known after the film based on the novel was released in 1963, and it quickly became an epithet for rude, self-centered people who roamed the world with utter disregard—even disdain—for other cultures.

Many of the Americans I work with and meet on my travels aren't ugly—just uninformed. They want to understand and appreciate other cultures, but they have little experience or exposure to customs different from their own. In the continental United States, we can travel thousands of miles in several directions without encountering significant cultural or linguistic differences. In Europe, a journey of a few hundred miles can take you through several countries, cultures, and languages. It's no surprise that international travel can befuddle Americans!

Most of us don't have the time or ability to learn the numerous languages and customs of cultures around the world. So how can we begin to communicate with our international business associates? By being willing to make mistakes. Sensitive imperfection can be endearing.

For example, an ambassador I know says his wife always learns the language of a country faster than he does. Why? Because she tries to speak the language as she shops, tours, visits, and dines—and she doesn't worry when she makes mistakes. Her earnest attempts to speak the language charm the local people, who encourage her communication efforts. The ambassador—with an official position to uphold—never speaks the language unless he's certain he can speak it correctly. He doesn't get the practice and encouragement his wife does, and thus he doesn't learn the language as quickly.

Be aware that there are good mistakes and bad mistakes. Good mistakes, like those the ambassador's wife makes, clearly convey the message "I care, I'm trying, I'm sorry if I got it wrong." Bad mistakes, like dressing sloppily or asking inappropriate questions, shout, "I don't care, I won't try, and I'm not one bit sorry if I don't understand you." These are mistakes that give international visitors a black eye.

Approach international travel as if it were an invitation to a party at your boss's home. At such an event, you'd behave with the goal of a raise or promotion in mind. You'd be sensitive, dress appropriately, and bring a suitable gift. When visiting a host country, adopt the same attitude and take the time beforehand to learn the customs and behaviors that'll make you a gracious guest.

Show Consideration and Respect

Consideration and respect are the qualities you need most for successful international travel. I base every suggested behavior in this book on these qualities. You can't show others respect and consideration without first learning about them and their culture.

But doing your homework before you visit a country is just part of the task; once you're in the country, you must keep learning. You can learn a lot about appropriate behavior by observing, asking, listening, and—the best method—trial and error. Trying shows your vulnerability and humanity, and it can excuse numerous communication errors. We all make mistakes when communicating in our own culture, so we certainly can't expect perfection when communicating in another.

When interacting with Europeans, ask yourself, "Are my actions considerate and respectful?" Following are the most important ways you can learn appropriate behavior so your consideration and respect won't go unnoticed or misinterpreted:

- Observe how the local people behave. This is one of the easiest, safest ways to learn appropriate behavior. Note what others wear, how they greet one another, how they eat. Follow their example, and you'll usually be correct.
- Whenever communication or expected behavior is unclear, quietly and politely ask your host or business associate, the hotel concierge, or a shop clerk what to do or say. You may feel foolish, but people will appreciate that you're trying to learn. Here's information you'll want to ask about if it's not absolutely clear:
  * What's the expected attire for an event?
  * What's the proper pronunciation of a name?
  * What tip is expected?
  * What's an appropriate gift for the occasion?
  * What's the proper way of wrapping and presenting a gift?
  * What flowers are appropriate for an occasion?
  * When and where may I smoke?
  * What time does an invitation really mean?

Listen carefully and write down necessary information. For example, when a person says his or her name, listen carefully to the pronunciation and write the name phonetically. Note any titles given.

- During meetings or presentations, listen closely to your hosts and take careful notes. Doing so signals your sincerity. If your hosts speak English as a courtesy to you, remember that English may be their second or third language, and you may need to listen even more closely. (If you get impatient, be empathetic. Think how well *you'd* express yourself in your second or third language.) If you're not sure what's been said or what's expected of you, politely ask for clarification. It's better to ask a question than risk misunderstanding.

- At social functions, listen carefully to what local people say to you and to one another. Ask informed questions; your genuine interest will always be appreciated. What you learn about a country and culture from these exchanges will come in handy in future conversations.

Showing consideration and respect will never steer you wrong, and even small gestures carry a lot of weight. Try to speak a few words of the host country's language, taste the local food, greet people properly, learn from others' behaviors, and you'll successfully build business relationships and friendships.

The Ten Commandments of Visiting Europe

1. Recognize and respect uniqueness. Each country—and each of its residents—is unique.
2. Do your homework. A basic knowledge of each country's culture and history will greatly benefit you.
3. Make the effort to build relationships.
4. Never compare countries to one another or to your country.
5. Never judge another country's political or social system.
6. Take your time and be patient. The pace of life and business may be very different from your country's.
7. Be flexible. Adapt to the environment. Don't expect others to adapt to your style.
8. Always be sincere.
9. Ask, look, and listen! Europeans are proud of their cultures and history. They'll enjoy teaching you about their ways.
10. Assume the best about people and their actions. Most behavior is rational once we understand its rationale.

THE EUROPEAN UNION (EU) AND THE EURO

The Facts of the EU

Brief History

In the 1950s and '60s, Belgium, France, Italy, Luxembourg, the Netherlands, and West Germany established three economic unions to pool resources, abolish tariffs, and promote free trade. In 1967, these organizations merged to form the European Community (EC), and in 1968 the EC established a customs union (a free-trade zone with a common external tariff) among member states. In the late 1970s, the nations worked to manage their currency exchange rates. By 1986, Denmark, Ireland, the United Kingdom, Greece, Portugal, and Spain became EC members. In 1987, the Single European Act went into effect; its goal was to remove remaining barriers and increase harmonization among EC countries, thus increasing the competitiveness of member nations.

In 1992, the EC nations signed the Treaty on European Union in Maastricht (commonly known as the Maastricht Treaty) to form the European Union. Primary goals were to form a common currency, a central bank, and a closer political union. The Maastricht Treaty took effect in November 1993, and in 1995 three new nations joined the EU. In 2004, ten new countries joined, bringing EU membership to twenty-five nations. Bulgaria and Romania are working to fulfill the conditions of membership and expect to join the EU in 2007. Albania, Bosnia-Herzegovina, Croatia, Macedonia, Serbia, Montenegro, and Turkey hope to join in the following years.

Qualifications for EU Membership

To qualify for EU membership, applicant nations must uphold the following economic and political standards, which were outlined during the 1993 EU summit held in Copenhagen and became known as the Copenhagen criteria:

- Politics: The nation must be a stable democracy with a commitment to the rule of law, human rights, and the respect and protection of minorities.

- Economy: The nation must have a stable and functioning market economy, capable of competing in the EU's internal market and coping with market forces and competitive pressures.
- Administration: The nation must meet the obligations of membership and implement and enforce EU law, which it must adopt in its entirety.

Timeline of the EU	
1952	The Treaty of Paris takes effect, and Belgium, France, Italy, Luxembourg, the Netherlands, and West Germany establish the European Coal and Steel Community (ECSC).
1958	The Treaties of Rome take effect, and the six ECSC countries establish the European Economic Community (EEC) and the European Atomic Energy Community (Euratom).
1967	The Merger Treaty takes effect, and the three communities become the European Community (EC).
1973	Denmark, Ireland, and the United Kingdom join the EC.
1981	Greece joins the EC.
1986	Portugal and Spain join the EC.
1992	Switzerland applies for membership, but to date has not advanced the application.
1993	The Maastricht Treaty takes effect, and the EC becomes the European Union (EU).
1994	Norway chooses not to join the EU.
1995	Austria, Finland, and Sweden join the EU.
2004	Cyprus, the Czech Republic, Estonia, Hungary, Latvia, Lithuania, Malta, Poland, Slovakia, and Slovenia join the EU.
2007	Bulgaria and Romania expect to join the EU.

Population of the EU

About 457 million people reside in EU nations; this is about 7.1 percent of the world's population and ranks behind China (20.3 percent) and India (16.8 percent) but ahead of the United States (4.6 percent) and Japan (2 percent).

Objectives of the EU

The EU is meant to be a place where political borders aren't as important as the common economic and political interests of the member states. The EU endeavors to guarantee free movement of goods, services, labor, and capital—the pillars of a single market. Its primary economic goals are to:

- Lower trade barriers
- Increase economic activity
- Work as a bloc to form a global economic entity

There are other considerations beyond economics. Europe endured terrible wars during the first half of the twentieth century, and its residents looked to the economic unions to end bitter rivalries, build peace among former enemies, and create a new order based on shared interests. The eight former Communist nations that joined the EU in 2004 saw membership as a way to achieve the economic and social standards of living that their western counterparts have enjoyed.

Common law and equality among all nations are the EU's political goals. To that end, the EU set up the following five institutions to pool resources and work for peace and prosperity:

- European Parliament (elected by residents of member states)
- Council of the European Union (represents member states' governments)
- European Commission (EU executive body; proposes and enacts legislation)
- Court of Justice (ensures compliance with the law)
- Court of Auditors (controls lawful management of the EU budget)

Culture Preservation

Although European countries share a common heritage of basic values, each has a unique national culture and several local cultures. Uniformity isn't the goal of the EU, which recognizes the importance of preserving each country's identity. The common interest of the EU must be balanced with national interests and respect for diversity.

As political borders drop, cultural borders rise. People are more determined than ever to hold on to their cultural distinctness (language, food, religion, and customs), even as they enjoy and anticipate the benefits of EU membership. For example, before Spain joined the EU, its government had been poised to abolish bullfighting. Since becoming an EU member, however, Spain dropped that plan and instead chose to embrace bullfighting as part of Spanish culture. In fact, a new generation of matadors has gained celebrity status.

The Euro

The euro is the common currency used by participating EU member states. Its purpose is to make doing business across borders easier by providing stability, uniformity, and simplicity. Increasingly, the euro is used for international payments and reserve currency; it's competing with the American dollar to become the world's most important currency.

In 2002, twelve of the then-fifteen EU member states replaced their sovereign currencies with the euro. (Denmark and the United Kingdom chose to keep their own currencies, and although technically required by its EU membership to convert to the euro, Sweden has not pursued conversion.) Nations with euro currencies are part of the Eurozone (or euro area). The ten nations that joined the EU in 2004 are working toward joining the Eurozone by the following years:

Estonia, Lithuania, and Slovenia	2007
Cyprus, Latvia, and Malta	2008
Slovakia	2009
Hungary and the Czech Republic	2010
Poland	no target year

To convert to the euro, a country must be a member of the Exchange Rate Mechanism (ERM II) for at least two years. It must also must meet a number of conditions, including:

- Price stability
- Absence of excessive government deficit
- Exchange rate stability
- Long-term interest rates

The euro symbol is €. There are one hundred cents in a euro. Euro bank note denominations are €5, €10, €20, €50, €100, €200, and €500. Coin denominations are €2, €1, 50 cents, 20 cents, 10 cents, 5 cents, 2 cents, and 1 cent. Each country mints its own euro coins, with one common side and one national side. Coins can be used anywhere within the Eurozone, no matter where they were issued. Monaco, San Marino, and Vatican City have adopted the euro as their national currency (these places also mint their own coins), and it's the de facto currency in Andorra, Kosovo, and Montenegro.

Challenges Facing the EU

Immigration and Integration

Immigration and immigrants aren't new to Europe, but globalization has increased the flow of immigrant workers across borders. Many of them hail from Russia, the Balkans, Turkey, and sub-Saharan Africa, and they bring languages and cultures that are foreign to their new neighbors.

Largely because of its declining native population, Europe's economy couldn't remain competitive without immigrant workers. But the integration of new immigrants has been extremely challenging. And the smaller the country—with a smaller population, fewer resources, and less space—the more daunting the challenge.

Ireland, for example, had been a homogeneous nation of only four million people. But since joining the European Community in 1973, it has had to accommodate immigrants from Nigeria, Romania, and the Congo. By comparison, Germany and France have dealt with immigration for generations, and their larger geographical areas with much larger native populations can more easily accommodate immigrants.

In general, Europeans don't ascribe to the largely American view that diversity and multiculturalism enrich society. Most strongly believe that immigrants should completely adopt the cultures of their new homes. Those who won't—or can't—most often live in virtual ghettos, where housing is substandard, well-paying jobs are scarce, and opportunities severely limited. Immigrants and their offspring seldom live among native Europeans.

Once immigrants settle in an EU nation, they can't work until the host country formally processes and approves their applications. In the meantime, they receive generous welfare benefits—and many citizens grumble when they see immigrants seemingly enjoying the life of leisure while they must go to work. Conversely, when immigrants do gain employment, some complain that their native neighbors want them to do their jobs during the day and then somehow disappear at night.

The vast majority of immigrants obey the law, but younger generations have begun to resent the economic and cultural discrimination they experience in EU countries. Their simmering anger has occasionally exploded into violence. In recent years, cultural clashes have led to assassinations, riots, and bombings all over the continent.

In addition, the spread of diseases like tuberculosis and AIDS (whose rates are unchecked in countries from which many immigrants come) is raising concern that immigration harms the social structure of the host countries. Fear and hate unite otherwise diverse right-wing nationalist groups. While the majority of the population doesn't share their beliefs, the groups' destructive actions toward immigrants have been widespread. (The fascist movements that tore Europe apart last century illustrate that point.)

EU nations must address the problems surrounding immigration if they're to uphold the objectives of peace and prosperity. Their future depends upon their abilities to support people of diverse cultures and to provide equal opportunities to all EU residents.

Religion and Secularism

Europe has been overwhelmingly Christian for many centuries, but Christianity's dominance hasn't prevented strife among religions or even among Christian sects. During the last thousand years, tensions between Eastern and Roman Christians, then between Catholics and Protestants, have led to massacres. The Holocaust provides a painful example of the bloody battles between European Christians and Jews over the centuries.

Official state atheism has been responsible for atrocities as well. In many former Communist countries, untold numbers of people were imprisoned and even killed for practicing their faith when public (and sometimes even private) worship was banned.

Today, religious practices vary widely among European countries, and each nation is trying to find a balance between tradition and tolerance—especially when Judeo-Christian ideals and other faiths exist side by side.

The Muslim faith isn't new to Europe (the Moors ruled Spain from the eighth to fifteenth centuries), but the influx of Muslim immigrants in the last few decades has inflamed religious tensions in Europe. Currently, Muslims compose between 3 and 5 percent of the EU population. But Europe's native population is declining, while Muslim birthrates are rising. If Turkey joins the EU, its population will give it as much clout as Germany, and there will be more Muslims than Protestants in the EU.

This potential shift in the religious makeup of the EU has member states asking how much they should accommodate a religious minority. For example, recently a teacher in Italy received attention across Europe after she removed a crucifix from the classroom wall to make a Muslim student feel more welcome.

Furthermore, the recent suicide attacks in Spain and England, assassinations in the Netherlands, and outbreaks of anti-Semitic violence in countries still recovering from the Holocaust have left the EU wondering whether to encourage or even compel Muslim immigrants to assimilate, as well as how to minimize the influence of Islamic radicalism—all while maintaining respect and tolerance for the Muslim faith.

Crime and Terrorism

In the last two decades, crime has increased in all European countries—from car theft in England and Italy to bicycle theft in the Netherlands to pickpocketing in Spain and Poland. Nations that once prided themselves on low crime rates are now struggling to identify the causes of crime. (Likely candidates include increased urbanization, mobility, abandonment of religion and moral codes, poverty and inequality, ethnic minorities, and drug use.) Europeans are keenly aware that crime reduction is a key to maintaining their high quality of life, and they're working toward implementing crime-reduction programs.

Terrorism in Europe is a problem with devastating consequences. Many European countries have lived with terrorism for decades—the Euskadi Ta Askatasuna (ETA) conflicts in Spain and the violence in Northern Ireland and London are but two examples. But the recent Islamic terrorist attacks in Europe have threatened all the countries. Gilles Kepel, a French scholar of radical Islam, said, "The most important battle in the war for Muslim minds during the next decade will be fought not in Palestine or Iraq but . . . in the outskirts of London, Paris, and other European cities, where Islam is already a growing part of the West."

With great courage and determination, Europeans are facing increased terrorism, and all of Europe has intensified security. Combating terrorism requires a united front, but the EU isn't a sovereign government and thus finds it difficult to form a single line of defense. Each nation has its own security system, and many nations worry about sharing security information across borders.

Nevertheless, each nation is attempting to secure its citizens' safety while working with the EU for the safety of all member states. Increased security has led not only to larger police forces, but also to new restrictions on streets and bridges and in train stations, airports, amusement parks, and so on. To many Europeans, this is an unfortunate but necessary price to pay.

Regionalism

It may be hard to believe, but Germany and Italy (as nation-states) are younger than the United States. Until the mid-1800s, people identified themselves as members of regional groups like Bavarians and Neapolitans, not as Germans and Italians. Even today, no European nation has just one culture. Shifting borders, alliances, and migration have placed different cultures within others. There are pockets of Hungarians in Romania, Russians in Latvia, and Germans in Poland—and each group retains its own culture and language while also assuming a national identity.

As a result, many EU residents may identify more strongly with their region than their country. Most Europeans not only don't want to move to another country, but they'll also resist moving to a different city or region within their own country. This resistance is becoming increasingly problematic because as jobs move, people must move.

Nationalism

The EU's guiding documents promise to celebrate, respect, and preserve each nation's identity and culture. Putting these documents into practice, however, hasn't been easy and never will be. Cultural and linguistic issues are complex, and seemingly small matters can explode into big problems.

One example that no one had anticipated arose when Hungary, Latvia, Lithuania, and Slovenia joined the EU in May 2004. In the 1990s, the EU members agreed on the spelling *euro*, except in Greek. (Greek doesn't use the Roman/Latin alphabet.) But in Hungarian, *euro* (as a shortened form of *Europe*) is spelled *euró*. In Slovenian it's spelled *evro*; in Lithuanian it's *euras*; and in Latvian it's *eiro*. In late 2004, as translators prepared the final draft of the European Constitution, these four nations balked. A Hungarian diplomat said, "We're not going to spoil the constitution because of an accent, but we don't like people telling us how to spell things in our own language." Latvia was more resolute in its opposition. After decades of Soviet-encouraged Russian immigration made Latvian a minority language in many parts of the country, Latvians grew especially protective of their language.

This example shows that joining the EU doesn't mean relinquishing national identity. On the contrary: People of EU nations fiercely protect their customs, cultures, and languages.

Declining Population

Currently, the net reproduction rate in EU countries is below zero. In 2005, the EU's overall fertility rate fell to 1.47 children per woman. For a population to grow by reproduction, its replacement level must be more than two to one—that is, on average each woman must bear at least two children.

For nations used to generous welfare benefits and retirement plans, the combination of a low birthrate and a longer-lived population (due to improved health and medical advances) brings new challenges. Each European nation is investigating the causes of its population crisis and debating whether cultural shifts, job instability, expensive housing, or lack of incentives (family benefits, parental leave, childcare, and equal pay) is exacerbating the problem.

Traffic

The traffic problem seems out of control in many European cities, which are densely populated and were built long before the invention of motorized vehicles. Cities from Dublin to Bucharest are struggling with clogged streets, air pollution, and scarce parking. (Parking is not only nearly impossible to find, but also extraordinarily expensive.) Some cities are limiting the number of vehicles on their streets, and drivers sometimes must pay fees before driving in certain areas. Despite these efforts to control traffic, the number of vehicles and their accompanying problems continue to grow.

Depending on whom you talk to, drivers in Portugal, Spain, or Italy are the worst in the world. Regardless of your location, beware when driving anywhere in Europe. In fact, avoid driving entirely, if possible. High speeds and (in some countries) sweeping disregard for road rules make driving hazardous. Use trains and mass transit systems, which are generally very good. If you do drive, know that cell phone use while driving is illegal in most European countries. And as in the United States, never drink and drive.

The Newest EU Nations

A New Beginning

On May 1, 2004, ten European nations celebrated their new membership in the European Union. These nations fought for autonomy—as well as for their languages and cultures—for centuries. At different times, the Ottoman Empire, the Russian Empire, the Austrian and then the Austro-Hungarian Empires, Germany, and the Soviet Union dominated different areas.

Malta and Cyprus have had their own unique struggles during the last century, but the other eight countries share a Communist past. The Czech Republic, Hungary, Poland, and Slovakia were part of the former Soviet Bloc, which also exerted influence on Slovenia. Estonia, Latvia, and Lithuania completely lost their status as independent nations and became Soviet republics.

Before the demise of Communism in the late 1980s and early 1990s, Communist governments owned and operated the land and controlled the people, means of production, taxes, and consumption; in some cases, they even controlled religious organizations. To accomplish anything, a person had to bribe or blackmail a party apparatchik, who was often too apathetic to act otherwise. Any activities outside the party could quickly arouse suspicion and censure.

Now these new EU countries' borders are open for travel and trade. Their residents have freedom of religion, privately owned land, a military answerable to them, and laws written by democratically elected officials. When doing business with people from these nations, however, remember that they, their parents, and their grandparents have seen world wars and genocide played out on their soil. They've seen borders shift depending on who was in power. They've seen their cities destroyed and rebuilt only to be destroyed again. They fought fiercely and watched friends and family die to secure the economic and political freedoms they enjoy today.

Economics and Business

Before World War II, Poland, Hungary, and the Czech Republic were market-driven economies. They did business with the rest of Europe and understood the fundamentals of capitalism. In fact, in the 1980s Hungary developed a hybrid market economy before it broke free of communist control.

Today, the economies of former Communist countries are changing at a breathtaking pace. But one shouldn't assume that people will instantly embrace capitalism and the free market. After living nearly forty years in an economy based on state-owned industries, central planning, and policies that limited potential, people's attitudes toward capitalism can't easily and quickly change. Older generations still view the Western countries through the lens of Hollywood, which has depicted capitalist societies as obsessed with money, sex, drugs, and violence. Plus, state propaganda against the United States and the West was pervasive and damaging.

But these attitudes are changing, even as the countries hold on to their traditions. In rural areas, for example, you may see a horse-drawn wagon with its driver listening to an iPod, or small cottages that sport satellite dishes. Cities are becoming modern and busy, and their people are proud that they work long days; some even work two jobs. They point out that they don't take the long holidays and work the short weeks that their counterparts in the other EU nations do.

Other nations are taking notice of the economic possibilities in these countries. Money that was once invested in Western European countries is now going to the Central European countries. These nations offer excellent opportunities to do business, and the prospects will get better and better as their economies catch up to those of the other EU nations—thanks to strong growth and tightened budgets. The geographic position of these nations is superb, and their people are well educated.

Business Tips

When doing business in former Communist countries, keep in mind that laws, business practices, and attitudes are still evolving. Here are some general points to consider:

- People may suspect that Americans intend to cheat them. Under Communist rule, people only became—and remained—wealthy if they were corrupt. That stigma lingers. To build a business relationship, you'll have to let people get to know and trust you.
- Be careful about doing business with people you don't know or for whom you can't get good references.
- Meet your prospective business colleagues face to face.
- Have your correspondence translated into your colleagues' language by a reputable translator. It's worth the expense.
- To make a deal, you may have to meet with government officials as well as business associates. Hire a savvy local person to help you navigate the bureaucracy and business regulations.
- Theft, racketeering, and weak judiciary systems are problems.
- As a result of Communism, people may fear telling the truth and may not share information easily.
- Many people face a shortage of startup capital.
- Competition, customer service, and prompt delivery of products are new concepts.
- Product quality may need improvement. (Communism emphasized quantity over quality.)
- Contracts may be considered statements of intent, not ironclad promises.
- While many people are modern and innovative, most don't have long business perspectives.
- People may not volunteer services. Under Communist rule, there was nothing voluntary in the government's request of its citizens to

"volunteer." People learned to do just what was necessary to get by and escape unwanted attention.

- Don't refer to countries as Eastern Europe or people as Eastern European. These terms are geographically incorrect. The region is Northern and Central Europe, and the people are Czechs, Poles, Hungarians, and so on.
- Don't lump people together, assuming that their cultures and experiences are similar.
- Don't treat people as though they're simple or backward—they're anything but. To survive and build lives for themselves and their families, they needed resourcefulness and creativity. Many of them are extremely well informed and well educated. Many speak several languages.
- When selecting gifts, never choose cigarettes, gum, or any gift that suggests modern consumer goods are unavailable.

GENERAL RULES: WHAT TO KNOW AND HOW TO BEHAVE

Basic Facts and Statistics

In 2002, the National Geographic Society conducted a survey that featured fifty-six multiple-choice questions on global geography. More than three thousand young adults in Canada, France, Germany, Great Britain, Italy, Japan, Mexico, Sweden, and the United States participated. Americans averaged twenty-three correct answers—only Mexicans fared worse. Almost 30 percent of the Americans couldn't find the Pacific Ocean on a world map, and 56 percent couldn't find India, the world's second-most populous country. Despite almost daily news about the Middle East, nearly 85 percent couldn't locate Afghanistan and nearly 80 percent couldn't find Israel.

Other countries often complain about Americans' ignorance. Americans seem to know nothing about the people and places beyond U.S. borders. What's worse, they don't demonstrate much interest in learning.

For international business success, you don't need extensive training or experience in foreign languages or cultures. You simply need to take the time necessary to develop a basic knowledge of your host country and its culture. Without this knowledge, you'll appear not only ignorant, but also arrogant.

Here are the basic facts you should know when visiting a country:

- Its official name
- The collective name of its people

> At a dinner party during the Cold War era, my dinner partner—a graduate of an elite East Coast university—asked, "Does your husband feel comfortable representing a Communist country?" My husband represents Austria, a multiparty democracy with a market economy, as an honorary consul general. How do you answer that question diplomatically?

- The language(s) spoken
- Its president's or prime minister's name
- Its political system
- Its currency
- Whether it belongs to the European Union (EU)
- Main events of the past century, including border disputes and recent allies and enemies (The more details you know, the better your conversation will be.)
- Current issues and events

Meeting and Greeting

First impressions are powerful! Good first impressions create the expectation of positive relationships. Bad first impressions require a lot of work and time to overcome—if such an opportunity even arises. When you've traveled thousands of miles and spent a lot of money in hope of developing a new business relationship, you need to make the best possible first impression.

Your chances of making a good first impression improve enormously if you know what to expect when meeting a person or group. Doing your homework lets you relax and project a positive attitude. In addition, exercising restraint, common sense, and good taste will help ensure that a relationship gets off to a good start. For example, avoid a knuckle-crushing, arm-pumping handshake in favor of polite reserve with an open, friendly attitude.

General Rules
- Most Europeans shake hands with everyone upon arrival and again upon departure. Shake hands with men, women, and children.
- In business, extend your hand to the most senior-ranking person first, regardless of gender.
- In social situations, shake hands with women before men. If you're a man, wait for the woman to initiate a handshake. There may be cultural or religious taboos against women shaking hands with men outside the family. If a woman nods, smiles, or otherwise indicates a greeting without extending her hand, do the same and consider yourself greeted.
- If you're a woman, extend your hand first when shaking hands. If you don't, European men may not extend theirs, and that may lead to misunderstandings. Don't be offended if a man declines to shake your hand. Some cultures have taboos against physical contact between the sexes.

- Shake hands at business and social functions.
- In offices, be sure to shake hands with administrative staff.
- In many countries, be prepared to give and receive a lighter, less firm handshake than you would in the United States.
- Be sure to stand before shaking hands.
- Always remove gloves before shaking hands.
- Never shake hands with one hand in your pocket.
- In some countries, a man (especially an older man) may kiss a woman's hand when meeting. Accept this greeting graciously; never giggle or act self-consciously. If you're a man, however, never attempt to kiss European women's hands.

Names and Titles

To Europeans, a person's name and title express a wealth of information about family history, education, profession, reputation, and personal achievement. Names and titles are sources of pride; foreign visitors must understand that the correct use of a person's name and title shows respect. Incorrect use is an insult.

In the United States, people shift from using last names to using first names almost immediately after meeting. Americans consider it warm and friendly to do so and think everyone believes the same—not true. Using first names makes many Europeans uncomfortable.

Traditionally, Europeans seldom addressed one another by first names—even among close friends. Today, name usage is changing. Younger people, people in the information technology industry, and people in some countries may use first names almost immediately. Visitors, however, shouldn't use first names until their hosts and colleagues explicitly invite them to do so.

Using names and titles correctly is one of the most complicated tasks for an international traveler, even an experienced one. Specifics about correct usage vary among countries; consult each country's chapter to learn the etiquette for name and title usage there. Knowing the specifics is worthwhile: Proper use of someone's name and title can lead to a successful negotiation, while misuse may end a business relationship.

General Rules

Think of the following rules as tools for establishing a cultural comfort zone. If you want to make your colleagues comfortable and amenable to doing business, respect their cultural comfort zone for using names and titles.

- Know each country's rules for name and title usage.
- When someone is introduced to you, listen carefully to the name's pronunciation. Ask for it to be repeated if you didn't catch it.
- As soon as possible, write down the name phonetically.
- Ask each person by what name he or she prefers to be addressed.
- Always use last names until you're invited to use first names, or until others repeatedly use your first name.
- Ask for a person's business card so you can see the correct spelling of the name and the correct title.
- When in doubt, use a title. Always use the title on someone's business card or the title used upon introduction.
- If someone has more than one title and you're uncertain which title to use, use the higher title. Err on the side of formality.
- When conversing or corresponding with someone in English, it's acceptable to use English professional titles (*doctor, professor,* and so on).
- Never give anyone a nickname.
- Younger people may use first names more quickly than older people; nonetheless, wait to be invited before using first names.
- Upon meeting people, say your name slowly and pronounce it clearly.
- If necessary, help the introducer or host with your name's pronunciation.

> Many of my Austrian friends, whom I've known for twenty-five years, still call me "Mrs. Bosrock." Many of my Irish friends have called me "Mary" since we first met. How friends address me says nothing about the sincerity of our friendship, only about their cultures and customs.

When to Use Miss

The use of the courtesy title *Miss* is in flux in Europe. *Fräulein, Mademoiselle,* and similar terms were once used to address all unmarried women, but today many European women don't want their marital status defining their identity.

The use of this title varies not only from country to country, but also from region to region within countries. To be safe, use *Miss* and its equivalents only when addressing girls younger than age eighteen. You won't insult an unmarried woman by addressing her as *Frau* instead of *Fräulein* or *Madame* instead of *Mademoiselle*. Listen to how your colleagues address female wait staff, shop clerks, and so on, and follow their lead. While some regions use *Miss* to address women in these occupations, others don't.

Language

Speaking a host country's language is the best way to win friends for yourself, your company, and your country. Nothing better conveys the message "I care about you, your culture, and your country" than taking the time to learn the native language. The warm appreciation and welcome you'll receive are incomparable.

Realistically, however, most of us don't have the time to become fluent in other languages—and what languages would we learn if we did? The European Union has twenty-one official languages, with more being added as more countries join the EU. In addition, some European languages are difficult for native English speakers to learn, with multiple inflections and tongue-twisting pronunciations.

So what's the best approach? Learn a few simple, polite phrases—enough to show you're trying. Learn how to greet and thank your hosts. Learn a short toast; you don't have to say it perfectly, and your hosts will greatly appreciate your effort. Remember: mistakes made from trying are good mistakes. When you speak at least a few words in your host country's language, you express a positive attitude toward the country and its people, especially in countries where native languages were once suppressed.

English as a Second Language

Due partly to Britain's colonial influence and partly to American postwar success, English is the most common second language spoken in Europe. Many to most businesspeople speak English; however, English is likely their second or third language. If your hosts speak English with you, they're probably doing so as a courtesy. Don't assume English is your hosts' native language, and don't take the arrogant "everyone should speak English" attitude. Instead, to avoid misunderstandings, do the following:

- Speak slowly and clearly.
- Use the simplest words possible.
- Never assume the listener understands your meaning; if there's any doubt, repeat what you said in different ways until you're sure the listener understands you.
- Never use slang terms, idioms, sports analogies, or colloquialisms, such as:
  * "I was tickled to death."
  * "We've got you covered."

* "You can count on it."
* "I got a kick out of it."
* "We're batting a thousand."
- Always be patient and leave room for error.
- Assume the best; never jump to conclusions.

Pronunciation

A friend told me that when he visits his native country after a long absence, his family sometimes has trouble understanding him when he speaks the native language. He, in turn, has difficulty understanding regional dialects from other parts of the same country.

If it's hard for my friend to properly pronounce the language he learned as a child, what hope is there for those trying to speak a few polite phrases learned as adults? The good news is that most people will be pleased with your attempts to speak the local language. Saying *hello*, *please*, and *thank you* in the host language will make you friends, even if you butcher the pronunciations (although the French might take exception to butchering).

For each country I discuss in Part II, I provide a list of basic phrases in the primary language of that country. Please understand, however, that pronunciations are approximate. Only by listening to fluent speakers can one know a language's true pronunciation.

Also, just as in the United States, regional dialects can greatly change a word's pronunciation. Imagine a person from Massachusetts making a pronunciation guide of English phrases; it'd differ considerably from the same guide made by a Texan.

How important is a person's native language? Extremely important to those from countries where the native languages were once suppressed, like Latvia, Poland, or Greece. In Ireland, where a minority of the population speaks Irish (*Gaeilge*) and nearly everyone speaks English, people are nevertheless fiercely attached to Irish. In fact, in 2005 several counties on Ireland's west coast passed a law forbidding the use of English on road signs and official maps. Proponents say the place names support local history and language—and non-Irish speakers will have to deal with it.

Finally, be aware that many European languages use letters that don't appear in the English alphabet, and many use diacritical marks, which the English language doesn't use.

Using Interpreters

You've hired an interpreter and you think your communication problems are solved. Watch out! Your problems may just be starting. Clearly communicating ideas in business negotiations is difficult, even when parties speak a common tongue. When using more than one language to conduct business, misunderstandings are inevitable, which means an effective interpreter is crucial for clear communication. Here are some tips for using an interpreter:

- Ask your interpreter to advise you on meeting protocol—punctuality, preliminary small talk, when to begin discussing major issues, identification of participants, and so on.
- Before a meeting, discuss with your interpreter the meeting's objective and the main points you plan to make.
- Never place the interpreter between you and your colleagues. Address your remarks to your colleagues, not the interpreter.
- Take your time; speak slowly and clearly.
- Keep language simple and direct.
- Pause frequently to allow for interpretation—after every verbal "paragraph" or, when the matter is especially important or complicated, after every sentence.
- As your discussion proceeds, ask your colleagues questions and get their feedback.
- Repeat main points.
- Assume your colleagues can understand English, even if they're using an interpreter; never say anything you don't want others to hear.
- Follow up with a written summary of what was said and agreed upon.

The European Union considers multilingualism sacred, so it decided to translate every official document into each of the twenty-one official languages. For practicality's sake, however, the EU internally conducts most of its business in English, German, or French. (Although many consider English the predominant tongue, cultural considerations prevent the EU from becoming officially monolingual or even trilingual.) Interpreters work in soundproof booths, translating the EU's words into the official languages.

To date, the cost of multilingualism has passed 1.3 billion U.S. dollars. In June 2005, the EU granted the Basque, Catalan, and Galician languages the benefits of official EU languages. Spanish citizens who speak these languages will now receive translated EU documents, but only because the Spanish government will pay for the translation costs.

The cost of translation is one obstacle to achieving multilingualism. Another hurdle is a lack of translators. When Malta joined the EU in 2004, the EU had to suspend its rule that it translate all legislation simultaneously into all official languages. With only 400,000 native speakers, it was too difficult to find qualified translators for Maltese.

Some translations have been humorous. In one, *frozen semen* was changed to *frozen seamen*. In another, when a British Member of Parliament used the word *gobbledygook*, interpreters simultaneously froze in their booths, bewildered. And technology doesn't always bridge the language gap: a computer program translated *out of sight, out of mind* to *invisible lunatic*.

Conversation

There's no better way to get to know people than to engage in warm, friendly conversation. In Europe conversation is an art, and Europeans pride themselves on their conversation skills. Most are well informed about U.S. current events and enjoy asking questions about the United States.

To help your conversation skills, brush up on history, art, literature, and culture so you can contribute intelligently when conversing with your European colleagues. And the best tip is to ask questions. People everywhere are proud of their countries and love to talk about them. (*Note*: Some cultures prefer quiet or little conversation at the dinner table. Take your cues from your hosts and the other guests.)

The following sections are general guides for acceptable conversation topics, unacceptable topics, and topics that require sensitivity.

Acceptable Topics

- History of the host country: Ask respectful questions and make only complimentary remarks.
- Art and architecture
- Music
- Beauty of the host country
- Holidays: Europeans take pleasure and pride in their holidays (vacations). They like to travel and enjoy sharing their experiences.
- Sports: Football (soccer) is generally popular. Read the sports pages of the local paper if possible. Know the names of local teams.
- Food and wine—local, regional, and global
- Music
- Cars
- Local attractions, places of historical interest, restaurants, and so on

Unacceptable Topics

- Business talk at social events, unless your European colleagues do so first
- Comparisons of anything in Europe to its American counterpart
- Personal questions: That is, don't ask about a person's:
    * Occupation
    * Income
    * Marital status
    * Education level
    * Place of residence
    * Health (Don't talk about your health, either.)
- Money, especially your money or your colleagues'
- Jokes: Jokes don't translate well, even if your colleagues speak English. Each culture has its own sense of humor. Also, jokes often depend on double meanings of words or phrases that don't exist in another language.
- Topics that use coarse language
- Insincere invitations: Never extend an invitation you don't intend to honor. It's an American custom to casually say "Let's have lunch sometime" with no intention (or obligation) of following through. If you make such an invitation to Europeans, they expect you to honor it.

Topics That Require Sensitivity

Each culture has its sensitive topics, those that can make emotions run high. For example, Europeans harbor strong feelings about World Wars I and II and their aftermaths. There hasn't been a war on U.S. soil for more than a century, and never a war of such destruction as the World Wars. Americans may not fully understand why the topic is so sensitive, and want to learn more about it.

When conversing with your hosts, the following topics may arise. If they do, ask sensitive, general questions, but don't offer your opinion unless you're extremely well informed. Your hosts may eagerly discuss these issues with you, but note their tone and body language. If they seem upset or uncomfortable discussing a topic, drop it and change the subject.

- World Wars I and II
- Nazism
- Communism
- Anti-Semitism
- The Holocaust
- Terrorism
- Politics
- Religion
- Ethnic tensions
- Immigration issues
- Class systems

Regional Terms

On page 3, I warn against generalizing people according to their culture. This warning extends to using regional terms. Europeans fiercely protect the customs that differentiate them from neighboring nations—even neighboring regions or cities. Europeans don't agree on the meanings of the following regional terms, so it's best if you don't use them.

- *Slavic*: Slavs are members of the Slavic-speaking peoples of Central and Eastern Europe. In Bulgaria, the Czech Republic, Poland, Slovakia, and Slovenia, the majority of people speak a Slavic language. Having the same linguistic roots, however, doesn't mean these cultures are interchangeable. There are East, West, and South Slavs. In addition, many cultures of Central and Eastern Europe aren't Slavic. For example, Hungarians are ethnic Magyars, and Romanians are descended from settlers hailing from the Roman Empire.

- *Balkan*: The nations that occupy the Balkan Peninsula are Albania, Bosnia-Herzegovina, Bulgaria, Greece, Macedonia, Serbia, Montenegro, and the European part of Turkey. These nations have vast cultural differences and great ethnic diversity. Don't use the word *Balkan* except as a geographical term.
- *Baltic*: Estonia, Latvia, and Lithuania are the Baltic nations, bordering the Baltic Sea. They do have some cultural similarities. But the Estonian language is unrelated to Latvian and Lithuanian, and Estonians are culturally similar to Finns. Most Lithuanians are Roman Catholic, Estonians are largely Lutheran, and a significant number of Latvians are Orthodox Christian. In short, there are as many differences as similarities among the three Baltic nations.
- *Eastern European*: Many nations that make up what Americans call Eastern Europe consider themselves to be in Central Europe (Hungary, the Czech Republic, Poland, Slovenia, and Slovakia) or Northern Europe (Latvia, Lithuania, and Estonia). These countries mistakenly became known as part of Eastern Europe when they were caught on the east side of the Iron Curtain during the Cold War. Don't use the term *Eastern Europeans* to refer to people from these countries; instead, use the terms *Central* or *Northern Europeans*.
- *Scandinavian*: The Scandinavian Peninsula includes Norway and Sweden. In the context of the European Union, Northern Europe includes Sweden, Norway, Denmark, Finland, and Iceland (sometimes Greenland, too). People in these countries don't use *Scandinavian* as an ethnic term; instead they refer to their nations as Nordic countries and call themselves Northern Europeans.

Written Communication
- Never base your opinions of your colleagues' intelligence on their English-language skills. Remember: English may be their second or third language.
- Try using your colleagues' language in salutations and closings. Use a personal closing.
- Be aware that your colleagues may judge a brief, to-the-point letter or e-mail as unimportant. A German professor once told me about a short e-mailed proposal an American had sent him. He said, "Obviously, this is not important information, if it can be summarized so simply." Meanwhile, I'm sure the American had congratulated himself on his brevity!

- Don't use acronyms (like FYI or ASAP) or abbreviations (like nite/night, 4/for, or U/you), especially in e-mails. North Americans regularly use these informal shortcuts in electronic communication, but Europeans may not understand them.
- If a message upsets you, calm yourself completely before responding—or telephone the sender for clarification. Verbal communication can help prevent "nasty-gram" correspondence.
- If in doubt, use a formal writing style rather than an informal one.
- Know an organization's hierarchy and who should receive copies of your letters and e-mail messages. Ask if you don't know. Don't use preset copy lists; send copies of correspondence only to people who should receive them.

Thank-You Notes

- Promptly write a thank-you note to anyone who hosted you for dinner, entertained you, or gave you a gift. Include a personal note about the gift or event.
- When you next write to or see someone who's given you a gift, mention or wear/display the gift. For example, wear the scarf a colleague gave you when next meeting with him or her, or display the crystal bowl prominently in your home when the giver visits.
- Your hosts (or those who give you gifts) will appreciate a thank-you note, but they won't necessarily expect one. Thank-you notes aren't as common in Europe as in the United States. Don't be offended if you don't receive one from a European colleague.

General Rules of Correspondence

Salutation
- Dear (Sir/Madam)
- Dear (title) + last name

Closing
- Yours truly
- Sincerely
- Yours sincerely
- Very truly

Envelope address
- Use an appropriate title (Mr., Mrs., Ms., or other) + first name + last name.
- Street number often follows the street name (Kipplingerstrasse 45).
- Postal code sometimes precedes city name (B-1020 Brussels).
- The bottom line is always the country name, spelled out in full in block capital letters.

Examples

Mr. Dermot Moore
Moore's China Shop
345 Rapidford Road
London SW6 5DZ
ENGLAND

Ms. Mary Wippermann
Avenue Louise 720 Bte 6
B-1020 Brussels
BELGIUM

Dr. Walter Steinbauer
General Director
The Allied Group Europe
Kipplingerstrasse 45
1010 Wien
AUSTRIA

Numbers
When writing numbers, some Europeans use a comma instead of a decimal point, and a period instead of a comma.

United States	Europe
€1.00	€1,00
€100.00	€100,00
€1,202.67	€1.202,67

Dates
In Europe, the day precedes the month.

United States	Europe
April 5, 2006	5 April 2006
4/5/06	5/4/06 or 5.04.06.

Time
Europeans generally use the twenty-four–hour clock: 2:00 PM, for example, is 14:00; 6:30 PM is 18:30; and 10:00 PM is 22:00. To get afternoon and evening times using this system, just add twelve hours to the time on your watch. Or to convert afternoon and evening times expressed in the European system to

the American system, subtract twelve hours. Both systems express morning times the same.

Europeans also sometimes express time orally and in writing differently than Americans do. In parts of Britain and Ireland, for example, 14:30 or 2:30 PM may be said "half two" (meaning half past two). In Germany, 2:30 may be said "*halb drei*" (meaning half before three).

Metric Conversion Chart

When you know	Multiply by	To find
inches	25	millimeters
feet	30	centimeters
yards	0.9	meters
miles	1.6	kilometers
centimeters	0.393	inches
meters	1.1	yards
kilometers	0.6	miles
ounces	28	grams
pounds	0.45	kilograms
grams	0.035	ounces
kilograms	2.2	pounds
fluid ounces	30	milliliters
pints, U.S.	0.47	liters
quarts, U.S.	0.95	liters
gallons, U.S.	3.8	liters
liters	2.1	pints, U.S.
liters	1.06	quarts, U.S.
liters	0.26	gallons, U.S.

Floors

In Europe, the "first floor" is generally a building's second level. The ground level is either not numbered or is labeled "0" or "ground floor." The second level is labeled "1," the third level is labeled "2," and so on.

Country/People/Language

Please note that I list each country's official languages in its respective chapter. These are the primary languages spoken by the majority.

Country	People	Major Language
Austria	Austrians	German
Belgium	Belgians	
Wallonia	Walloons	French
Flanders	Flemings	Flemish/Dutch
Bulgaria	Bulgarians	Bulgarian
Cyprus	Cypriots	Greek/Turkish
The Czech Republic	Czechs	Czech
Denmark	Danes	Danish
Estonia	Estonians	Estonian
Finland	Finns	Finnish
France	French	French
Germany	Germans	German
Greece	Greeks	Greek
Hungary	Hungarians	Hungarian
Ireland	Irish	English/Irish
Italy	Italians	Italian
Latvia	Latvians	Latvian
Lithuania	Lithuanians	Lithuanian
Luxembourg	Luxembourgers	Luxembourgish/French/German
Malta	Maltese	Maltese/English
Netherlands	Dutch/Netherlanders	Dutch
Norway	Norwegians	Norwegian
Poland	Polish	Polish
Portugal	Portuguese	Portuguese
Romania	Romanians	Romanian
Slovakia	Slovaks	Slovak
Slovenia	Slovenes	Slovenian
Spain	Spanish/Spaniards	Spanish
Sweden	Swedes	Swedish

Switzerland	Swiss	French/German/Italian/ Romansch
Turkey	Turks	Turkish
United Kingdom		
England	English/British	English
Scotland	Scots	English/Scottish
Wales	Welsh	English/Welsh
Northern Ireland	Northern Irish	English

Body Language

Eye contact; posture; placement of hands, feet, arms, legs—these body movements send positive or negative messages to other people. We misread these signals constantly within our own culture. Imagine the mixed signals we send and receive when dealing with another culture.

Behavioral scientists say people make seven hundred thousand signals through body language. What one person views as proper behavior, another may consider an affront. "Surely," you might say, "there must be some common ground. How about a smile? It's the universally understood gesture, right?" Not quite. Even a smile can be misunderstood.

It's true that smiling warms any environment, so smile if the occasion calls for one. But be aware that your smile may not be returned. In some cultures, people don't smile at strangers. Also, a smile has different meanings in different cultures. It can be a way to cover embarrassment, confusion, or anger. In some cultures, smiling at a person of the opposite sex may be interpreted as a sexual invitation.

General Rules

- Proper posture is a must. To Europeans, sloppy posture indicates a sloppy person. Sit with your back straight and your legs crossed at the knee or knees together. Don't sit with legs spread.
- Never mimic anyone's body language.
- Never mimic what you think is a national gesture.
- Never slap people on the back.
- Don't display affection in public.
- Keep your hands out of your pockets when speaking to or greeting someone.
- Never use toothpicks, nail clippers, or combs in public.

- Cover your mouth when you yawn.
- Don't chew gum in public.
- Never put your feet on furniture.
- Don't point or beckon with your index finger.
- Don't scratch in public.
- Men should rise when a woman enters the room. Remain standing until invited to be seated.
- Stand erect when a country's national anthem is playing. Never talk, laugh, or shuffle your feet.
- For mixed couples, each country has different rules about whether the man or woman should enter a restaurant first. Be prepared to follow the locals' example.
- Finally, don't be loud. A persistent worldwide criticism of Americans is that they're too loud and boisterous. Speak in a moderate tone and at a moderate volume.

Touching

In almost all European cultures, touching is a behavior reserved for friends and family members. Even Europeans considered "touchers" (those who hug and kiss their children, spouses, and close friends of the same or opposite sex) generally don't touch or want to be touched by strangers, people they meet occasionally, new business associates, or new acquaintances.

As you establish a relationship with European colleagues, be sensitive to the dos and don'ts of touching in their particular culture. If a colleague or friend gives you a hug or a kiss on the cheek, rejecting the gesture could be just as offensive as touching too soon.

A young woman was hired as a protocol officer for a large American city. One of her jobs was meeting and greeting foreign dignitaries. Having come from a family of Norwegian heritage, where kissing was done in private, she found her major challenge was graciously accepting the endless touching and kissing...left cheek, right cheek, left cheek again. She told me, "I kissed more strangers in my first year on the job than I had my mother, father, children, and husband during my entire life." Her remarks say nothing about her family relationships (she assured me she loves her family!), but they speak volumes about her comfort level when dealing with different cultures.

Common Gestures, Unexpected Meanings

Many gestures have different meanings in different countries. A gesture that may be appropriate in one country may be rude or have a completely different meaning in another. Such gestures include the "okay" sign, the nod, the thumbs-up gesture, and even the seemingly innocuous hand wave.

Because gestures can be so easily misunderstood, the best approach is to avoid them entirely if possible. Alternatively, learn in advance the local meanings of any gestures you consider essential to your business.

Dining

How you eat and respond to food are essential for diplomacy. Your table manners can quickly make or lose foreign friends. When your hosts offer a local delicacy or a national specialty, they're extending a sample of their culture as well as their friendship. If you reject the offering, which is often the best they have, you reject them, their culture, and their friendship—not an effective way to begin a mutually beneficial relationship.

Regardless of whether the food on your plate once swam, crawled, or flew, taste it. You may like it. Even if you don't, eat a reasonable portion anyway. I've eaten dozens of exotic dishes all around the world—a number of which I wouldn't choose to serve in my own home. And I survived. You'll survive, too. So try what you're served; tasting those brains or that tongue just might seal the big deal.

General Rules
- Lunch is generally noon to 1:00 PM
- Although lunch was once the main meal of the day throughout Europe, today most people, especially professionals, eat their main meal in the evening.
- Know and follow each country's rules on tasting.
- Sorbet or sherbet may be offered between courses to cleanse the palate.
- In some European countries, the salad course is served after the main course.
- Each country has its own rules about leaving food on your plate. In some countries, you'll insult your hosts if you don't eat everything you're served. Know the rules beforehand to ensure politeness—and prevent an upset stomach!
- Be aware of the number of courses served and pace your eating. Many of us have thought an appetizer was the main course. By the time the main

course arrived, we were too full to eat it. The courses of a full European dinner may include soup, fish or pasta, meat, salad, cheese and fruit, and dessert.

- After a meal at someone's home or after someone has bought you a meal, always write a thank-you note promptly.
- In restaurants, there may be a charge for each piece of bread or roll and/or butter.
- Don't ask for a doggie bag.
- Except for ice cream and chestnuts, don't eat while walking on streets.

> Before you book a table at a restaurant, check whether it accepts credit cards. Some don't accept any credit cards; others may accept ones from only one or two companies. This practice is true not only in small towns and villages, but also in larger cities including London, Paris, and Vienna.
>
> Also, call your credit card company before traveling to Europe to alert them that you'll be charging in foreign cities. Otherwise, your card may be refused. Credit card theft is a growing problem in Europe.

Table Manners

- Before sitting at the table, wait for your host to designate your seat and invite you sit.
- Men shouldn't sit until all the women have been seated.
- The host and hostess sit at opposite ends of the table. The female guest of honor is seated next to the host. The male guest of honor is seated next to the hostess.
- The guests of honor are served first.
- Eat only after the hostess has begun to eat. She'll do so after everyone has been served.
- Never put your elbows on the table.
- Rest your hands and wrists on the table, never in your lap.
- Try every dish served to you.
- If your knife and fork are in any way open on your plate (see left illustration), it means that you'd like more food or that you're not yet finished eating.
- When finished eating, place your knife and fork side by side on the plate so they're at the 5:25 position on a clock (see right illustration).

- Never smoke at the table without first asking your host and other guests for permission.
- Don't get up from the table until the hostess does.
- Never leave until coffee/dessert/cognac is finished.
- Thank the hostess before leaving the table.

Formal Dining
- Europeans eat continental style; that is, after using the knife to cut food and push it onto the fork, they keep the fork in the left hand to eat. Most Americans eat American style; that is, they hold the fork in the left hand (tines facing down) and the knife in the right. After cutting food, they lay down the knife and switch the fork to the right hand to eat. Many Americans can't eat continental style without clumsiness, so eating American style is acceptable with polite table manners.
- Forks are always placed to the left of the plate. Spoons and knives are always placed to the right of the plate. (If a fork is placed to the right of the spoons, it's a cocktail fork.)
- All silverware is arranged with the utensil to be used first laid on the outside, farthest from the plate. (Remember: Europeans may serve the main course before the salad.)
- The butter knife is laid on the butter plate.
- The fish course uses a fish fork and a fish knife. Make sure you use your fish knife to cut fish.
- Dessert silverware is provided as dessert is served. In some countries, however, it's placed at the top of the dinner plate.
- Occasionally, at less formal meals, Europeans don't use a bread plate. In that case, place bread directly on the table above your fork.

How to Eat Food You'd Rather Not
For the most part European food is marvelous to Americans, and most of us find limiting how much we eat abroad a major challenge. But many Europeans eat animal organs, some eat horse meat, others pork tartare—these and other dishes might be difficult for Americans to digest. If you have a weak stomach or dislike the food served, here are some helpful hints:
- Before you leave for the meal, prepare yourself mentally for the unexpected and take a dose of Pepto-Bismol.
- Never ask what a dish is until you've finished eating it.
- Cut the food into small pieces.

- Don't chew particularly unpleasant food, just swallow fast. Sometimes the texture is worse than the taste.
- Taste everything, and try to eat at least a little of it. If you just can't eat something, taking a taste is considered polite behavior.
- Never criticize, joke, or make a face about what's served.
- To distract yourself from the food and to pass the time until the next course is served, converse with your dining partners.
- When offered seconds of something you don't like, say, "Thank you, but let me finish this portion first." Then eat slower and talk more.

Drinking

While coffee and tea are popular beverages in Europe (many countries even have coffee- and tea-serving rituals—be sure to respect them), alcoholic drinks are staples. Many Europeans order beer or wine at lunch, and having a drink with friends or coworkers after work is customary in some countries.

In most European cultures, drinking is a social event that allows an opportunity for more personal connection. In addition, several regions produce distinctive beer, wine, or liquor. Their citizens are very proud of the local products and eager to share them with guests.

Try—or pretend to drink—beverages offered to you. Never flatly decline an offer for any beverage. Your refusal could insult the person making the offer.

Here are some other tips to consider:

- If you can't drink alcohol, tell your host ahead of time. Ask for a soft drink or fruit juice instead.
- Be careful when drinking alcoholic beverages in Europe. In some, the alcohol content is higher than in comparable drinks in the United States.
- Never drink and drive. The drunk-driving laws in many European countries are strict and the punishments severe.
- If you're hosting European guests, make sure to have nonalcoholic drinks available for those who don't drink alcohol for health, cultural, or religious reasons.
- Be aware that Turkish coffee is very thick and strong, and the coffee served in some countries can be extremely sweet.

Toasting

Use toasts to establish a closer, more friendly relationship. You should enjoy toasting and being toasted. It's an offer of friendship. Here are some tips for toasting:

- Know and follow each country's rules on toasting.
- If possible, make a toast in your host's or guest's language. Even if it isn't perfect, your European colleagues will enjoy and appreciate it.
- Make your toast short and make direct eye contact with the person you're toasting.
- Your colleagues will generally appreciate an accompanying story (short and in English), but don't tell jokes—they seldom cross cultural lines.

Entertaining European Guests

To Europeans, dining in your city's best restaurants can't compare to eating a meal served in your home. Visitors always enjoy seeing how you live, how you decorate your home, what music and art you enjoy, and—especially—meeting your family. An invitation to your home is a gesture your guests won't soon forget. Some points to remember:

- Check whether your guests have any dietary restrictions.
- Serve American food.
- Avoid huge, American-size servings of meat. Most Europeans (and others, too) eat much smaller portions of meat than Americans do.
- It's extremely important to always provide at least one vegetarian option when hosting an event. For religious, health, ecological, or animal-rights reasons, many Europeans are vegetarians.
- Don't offer guests a tour of bedrooms or other private areas of your home. They'll be more comfortable in "public" rooms like the living room, dining room, and den.
- Use the proper glasses for whiskey, wine, and beer. Never serve drinks in paper cups or serve food on paper plates with paper napkins.
- Don't offer guests root beer; it's not popular outside the United States.
- Always ask your guests if they'd like to experience a particular event while in your area. Some suggestions include:
  * Picnic or barbecue
  * Baseball or American football game
  * Concert or theater performance

* Museum visit
* Shopping
* Hiking
* Sightseeing
* Boating or sailing
* Playing golf or tennis

Tipping

Americans are among the most generous people on earth. When Americans visit another country and generously tip service people, they're trying to be kind and appreciative, not abrasive or arrogant. But they often create the impression that they're boorishly flaunting their wealth—or worse, trying to take over the country. Europeans say that overtipping is a sign of insecurity.

Everybody has a sense of personal worth, even if he or she isn't wealthy. You can violate that sense of worth by giving a tip that's inappropriately large or small. Tip too little, and service people are likely to feel cheated out of fair compensation for their work. Tip too much, and they can feel as though you consider them charity cases. But if you tip fairly and appropriately, they'll appreciate it without feeling demeaned.

Like everything else in Europe, tipping etiquette is changing. The key is to know both local customs and the value of what you're giving. Rules for tipping vary among countries, and inflation, fluctuating currency exchange rates, and rapidly changing local attitudes all affect appropriate tipping.

General Rules

Although Part II includes guidelines for tipping in each country, it's crucial to ask a local colleague or your hotel concierge for the current tipping practice for any service. This simple step can save you considerable embarrassment.
* Wait staff in Europe are generally professionals, not students working part-time. They're proud of their profession, and that makes tipping serious business.
* Keep in mind that service people are often from another country and may not speak English or the local language.
* Some hotels and restaurants in Europe include a 10 to 20 percent service charge. If you don't know if service is included, ask. You may leave an additional 5 percent gratuity if the service is exceptional, but it isn't mandatory.

- That said, it's worth noting that service personnel in hotels and restaurants that cater primarily to Americans may expect larger tips.
- Most restaurants are required to present you with an itemized bill; however, if the bill is in a language you don't understand, ask for an explanation, especially if the total is more than you expected.
- If someone has performed an exceptional service for you, discreetly give a reasonable tip to the person.

Manners

As prehistoric people began to interact with one another, they learned to behave in ways that made life easier and more pleasant. Over time, manners developed for practical purposes. For example, when two men met, they extended their right hands—and eventually shook them—to show that they weren't carrying weapons. A handshake served to demonstrate a lack of hostility, if not a display of friendship.

Although the manners used in much of the Western world have common roots, they've evolved in different ways in different places. The following are some general guidelines on European manners. (See Part II for information on manners specific to each country.)

Queen Elizabeth II hosted a dinner at Buckingham Palace in honor of a newly elected president from a former British colony in Africa. Nobility and leading Members of Parliament were invited.

That evening, the queen and the president entered the dining room with great ceremony. The president, who had risen through the army ranks, wasn't schooled in the English style of formal dining. The queen saw how ill at ease he was and attempted to make him feel comfortable.

But when the first course was served, the nervous president reached across his plate and began to sip from his finger bowl. Seeing the shocked faces of the other guests, the queen calmly reached across her plate and sipped from her own finger bowl. Then everyone else—nobility and Members of Parliament alike—reached across their plates and sipped from their finger bowls.

That was graciousness—and that's what manners are all about.

General Rules

- Show respect for others' habits and customs.
- Respect others' privacy and dignity at all times; when in doubt, put yourself in their place and act accordingly.
- Europeans always appreciate quiet, modest behavior.
- Always say "please" and "thank you"—in the local language, if possible—even if your hosts don't. (Keep in mind that some Europeans don't say "please" and "thank you," especially to service people.)
- Don't ask for a tour of someone's home, and never wander uninvited into bedrooms or other private rooms.
- On public transportation, men should stand until women are seated.
- Don't make noise, talk, or crinkle paper during an opera, concert, or play.
- Always ask to use anyone's phone in an office or home. In many countries, there's a charge for local calls as well as for long-distance calls. Offer to pay any charges your calls incur.
- Turn off your cell phone in restaurants, theaters, museums, places of worship, or anyplace else where cell phone use is disruptive.
- When answering your cell phone, speak quietly and excuse yourself to finish the call.

Smoking Etiquette

Attitudes toward smoking are changing world wide, as are the circumstances under which smoking is acceptable. Compared to Americans, Europeans smoke in large numbers. But they do know the health hazards associated with smoking and secondhand smoke, and more and more of them are taking the warnings seriously. If you smoke, follow these guidelines:

- Always be considerate of your European hosts or colleagues.
- Discreetly observe when and where others smoke.
- At meals, don't smoke at the table unless you see others smoking. Even then, ask the people around you whether they mind if you smoke.

If you don't smoke, more and more European hotels offer nonsmoking rooms, and more and more restaurants offer nonsmoking sections. Ask before you book a room or table whether nonsmoking areas are available.

Dress

Dressing appropriately and attractively has two rewards. First, your appearance should convey that you've made an effort; dressing properly creates an opportunity for you to project that you're someone with whom others want to do business. Second, and perhaps most important, your appearance affects your behavior. Dress well, and you behave well and project confidence.

Conversely, there's no worse feeling than sticking out because your dress and appearance don't conform to local standards. Calling attention to yourself makes you uncomfortable, and you'll generally project that discomfort to others.

Europeans say, "There are clothes to wear at home and those to wear outside the home," which means they dress up to go out. Europeans judge people on their appearance. They believe how you dress indicates your personality and social status. They expect Americans to dress as Americans—but within certain bounds of taste. So dress like an American—a clean, neat, pressed, polished one with classic, conservative tastes in styles and colors.

> I once attended a conference in Miami, Florida, hosted by an American company for its Italian affiliates. The conference chairperson invited everyone to attend the Friday meeting in casual attire.
>
> On Friday morning, all the Italian men arrived in designer shirts, pleated linen pants, and Italian loafers. Most wore fashionable sport coats as well. The Italian women wore lovely long skirts and beautiful silk blouses. As the meeting began, one of the North American managers arrived wearing athletic shoes, shorts, a college sweatshirt, and a baseball cap.
>
> Not a word was spoken, but it was difficult to assess who was most uncomfortable at that meeting.

General Rules

Dress in Europe is becoming less formal, but the following rules still apply.

- Don't go native. Nothing will make you look sillier or feel more self-conscious than trying to dress like a local and failing.
- Never wear sloppy, dirty clothing and shoes; always wear high-quality clothing and shoes. Europeans will judge you on the quality of your attire.
- Make sure your shoes are clean and polished. Never wear scuffed or unfashionable shoes.

- When in doubt, dress conservatively. Cover what's inappropriate to leave uncovered.
- Good grooming is vital. Make sure your nails are clean and manicured.
- For men, a dark suit and tie are always appropriate.
- For women, a dress or skirt is always appropriate. For evenings, the "little black dress" is appropriate to attend a dinner, the opera, the theater, or a concert. Accessories are important. Wear a high-quality scarf, jewelry, and shoes, and carry a stylish purse.
- Invitations specifying "formalwear" usually mean full eveningwear.
- Invitations specifying "informal" or "casual" mean "smart casual"—which means a nicely coordinated, stylish, elegant outfit. Men wear linen blazers, pleated pants, or stylish designer jeans. Women wear fashionable slacks or skirts and matching blouses.
- Wear shorts and jeans with caution. Always check beforehand to make sure they're appropriate for the occasion.
- Don't wear shorts, sundresses, or sleeveless tops when visiting a church.
- Unless you're engaging in athletic activities, avoid wearing athletic shoes and sweat suits. Never wear this attire in restaurants or shops, or for any business occasion. Europeans don't consider it casual wear.
- Avoid wearing:
  * Funny hats or T-shirts
  * Down vests
  * Country club attire (golf shorts, tennis clothes, and so on)
  * Any clothing in loud, flashy colors (brightly colored plaid pants or sport coats)
  * Any clothing in polyester and other synthetic fabrics (Stick with cotton and wool.)
- People working in information technology careers may dress more casually for business than those in other careers.

> Europeans separate nudity from sexuality. Except for perhaps the Irish and United Kingdom citizens, most Europeans are comfortable with nudity. In your European travels, you may encounter topless public beaches and swimming pools as well as saunas that forbid clothing. Be aware of the local clothing rules and know your comfort level. For example, Parisians consider men's swimming trunks sloppy and dirty, and have officially banned them from public pools. Spandex briefs are the only legal alternative—making many American businessmen decide they don't want to take a swim after all.

- Don't be surprised if a restaurant refuses to seat you when you're dressed inappropriately.

Finally, if your dress and appearance don't pass muster, relax. Note any errors for future reference, and then carry on with your business. If you conduct yourself with dignity, good taste, and consideration for others, your behavior will overcome any sartorial deficiency.

Gifts

Gifts are a symbolic way to show appreciation and strengthen relationships. A vital part of doing business in Europe is knowing what gift to give and to whom, when to give it and under what circumstances, and how to present it. Gift-giving customs vary among countries, and observing them is important. It'd be a shame to insult someone you're trying to impress, and a bad gift can ruin a business deal or a friendship.

In general, gifts should:
- Never be cheap or tacky.
- Be of high quality, but not ostentatious. Look for brand names with international prestige.
- Never be intimate items.
- Never be practical items.
- Never violate a tradition or religion (see pages 62–67 for gift suggestions for members of various religions).
- Never be vulgar or insulting.
- Be appropriate to the relationship and culture.
- Be comparable in value to the gifts you receive.

General Rules

While there's no detailed protocol for gift giving in Europe, you should know the following guidelines. Also, make sure you read in Part II the section on gifts for the country you're visiting and follow the advice.

When you receive a gift
- Accept it graciously. Refusing to accept a gift can insult the giver.
- Open it according to custom. In some cultures, people don't open gifts in the giver's presence.

- Always record the gift on the giver's business card, in your address book, or in a file.
- Wear or display the gift when you next meet with the giver. Comment on its usefulness or how much enjoyment it's given you.
- Write a thank-you note promptly.

When you give a gift
- Personalize a gift whenever possible. There's no nicer gift than one that shows you took the time to find something that reflects the recipient's tastes, interests, and personality.
- Always record a gift you give to prevent giving it to the same person again.
- Know the significance of a color. Some colors have certain positive or negative meanings in different cultures.

General gifts to consider giving
- High-quality liquor or wine, unless the recipient doesn't drink or the recipient comes from a nation or region known for its liquor or wine
- Good-quality chocolates (excellent for hostess and business gifts)
- High-taxed luxury items like whiskey, cognac, cigars, watches, and cigarette lighters (Many of these items are available in airport duty-free shops and sometimes on international flights.)
- High-quality, American-brand items (Lenox china, for example)
- Other high-quality American-made items:
    * Local or regional arts or crafts
    * Native American arts or crafts
    * Amish handmade products
    * Photo books about your city, state, or region
    * Framed photos of your state or region
    * Candy from a local candy maker
    * Maple syrup, wild rice, or other regional foods
    * California wine (unless the recipient comes from a nation or region known for its wine)
    * American cookbooks (if the recipient reads English and understands U.S. measurements)
    * T-shirts/sweatshirts from universities in your state (for younger people)
    * Small gifts for any children (toys, children's books from your country or home region, sweets), if visiting a colleague's home

General gifts to avoid giving

- Items that number thirteen (a taboo in many cultures)
- Sharp objects (knives, letter openers, and so on—they traditionally connote the severing of a friendship.)
- Handkerchiefs (connote grief)
- Products that are signature items in a region: For example, don't give beer in Germany, wine in France, and so on. Especially don't give a product if it was produced elsewhere; giving an Italian wine to a French colleague would be a terrible faux pas.

Hostess Gifts

When invited to someone's home, always bring a gift for the hostess. Here are some general suggestions:

Consider giving

- Wine—unless you're in a region that prides itself on its local wine
- Brandy, whiskey, and other liquor (Ask for advice at a liquor shop.)
- Pastries and high-quality chocolates
- Books and recordings of music

Don't give

- Clothing
- Perfume
- Jewelry
- Other personal items
- Any of the general gifts to avoid listed above

Flowers

In many countries, it's thoughtful to send flowers to the host's home on the morning of a dinner party. Ask a florist what flowers are appropriate for the occasion. While generally a lovely gift, the type, color, and number of flowers given can have symbolic meanings. For example:

A friend of mine, whose parents were born in Italy, told me her mother wept uncontrollably the day my friend was born because the mother received a mum plant from a well-meaning American acquaintance. In Italy, mums symbolize death. Today, my friend is fifty years old, and I think it's only now that her mother finally believes she'll survive.

- Mums and lilies are often given only for funerals and are widely associated with death.
- Red roses mean romance in every European country. Don't give them unless you have amorous intentions.
- An even number of flowers can mean bad luck in almost all European countries. Always give an odd number of flowers—except thirteen flowers, which Europeans also consider unlucky.

Business Gifts

Whether a gift is for an individual or a group, its value should match the level of the business relationship. Sometimes an expensive gift fits the occasion and circumstances, but other times an overly extravagant gift could create embarrassment if the recipient can't reciprocate. Here are other tips for giving business gifts:

- In Europe, business gifts generally aren't given at first meetings; in fact, some may consider the timing of such gift-giving crude.
- Tuck a wrapped gift in your briefcase. If you're unexpectedly given a gift, you can reciprocate.
- Always use good-quality gift-wrap.
- Don't include your business card with a gift.
- Don't initiate gift giving.
- If there are several people present, wait until the recipient is alone to give your gift. Or give a group gift or several individual gifts.
- If you're a man who's giving a gift to a European woman, tell her you're giving it on behalf of your wife, secretary, or other appropriate woman. Doing so says the gesture isn't a romantic one.

Consider giving

- Practical, high-quality office items
  * Fine pen and pencil sets
  * Business cardholders
  * Leather briefcases and portfolios
- Electronic items
  * Laser pointers
  * PDAs
  * Calculators

- Cigarette lighters (if you know the recipient smokes)
- Items that aren't noticeably inferior or superior to the gifts you've received, and are reasonably priced (Recipients may perceive overly expensive gifts as bribes.)
- Meals at highly recommended restaurants

Don't give
- Literature or artwork from a country with whom the host country has a strained relationship (for example, don't give a Polish colleague a gift from Germany)
- Items in colors that have negative meanings in the host country or are associated with political beliefs (for example, red for Communism)
- Obviously expensive items that your colleagues may interpret as bribes
- Any of the general gifts to avoid listed on page 48

Punctuality

In countries where punctuality is expected, lateness says you:
- Lack respect.
- Have sloppy, undisciplined personal habits.
- Are potentially unreliable as a business partner or supplier.

If you're an "Oh well, what's a few minutes late?" person, I suggest you become an on-time person when traveling abroad. In most European countries, being more than ten minutes late is unacceptable. Punctuality shows that you understand local customs and can follow them. But don't get angry or frustrated if Europeans from some countries (Spain, for example) are late for an appointment; they probably won't understand your anger and won't apologize for being late.

In Part II, I cover each country's general attitude toward punctuality. Follow this guide. Keep in mind what one country considers late, another may consider early. For example, a social engagement scheduled to start at seven o'clock begins at 7:00

Pope Benedict XVI, a German, met with some pilgrims from his homeland a week after his election as pope in April 2005. He apologized for his lateness, explaining that his previous meeting had run longer than expected. He joked, "The Germans are used to punctuality. I'm already very Italian."

on the dot in Germany, 7:15 in the United Kingdom, and up to an hour later in Italy, Greece, or Spain. If uncertain about an event's "real" start time, ask your host, a friend, or the hotel concierge. If you can't verify this information, err on the side of punctuality.

Traffic

Traffic is a major problem in all European urban areas. It may take you much longer to arrive at your destination than expected. Always allow extra time. Better yet, do what the Europeans do: take mass transit. You'll see many businesspeople of all levels using public transportation.

Time

As I mention on pages 31–32, always be aware of the different written and verbal ways Europeans express time. Not knowing this information could affect your punctuality.

Pace

One of the greatest challenges in doing international business is understanding and accepting the local pace—that sense of urgency (or lack thereof) with making or postponing decisions, keeping promises, meeting deadlines, and getting the job done. To foreigners, the local pace may be faster or slower than what they're used to; but to the locals, the pace is natural and reflects cultural habits and attitudes.

It's important to understand that one pace isn't necessarily better or worse than another—it's just different. If local colleagues aren't advancing a project as quickly as foreign colleagues would like, the locals' perceived slowness doesn't reflect malice or incompetence; they just operate more slowly in their culture. And the foreign colleagues must learn to understand and accept that fact.

Because Europe's history is much longer than the United States', Europeans (unlike Americans) feel less need to get everything done immediately. Their pace is a little slower than Americans', and their level of intensity a little lower. They believe it's important to spend time with their families and leisurely enjoy a good meal with a glass of wine.

This slower pace applies to business operations as well. Europeans look at business results with a long-term view. They don't focus nearly as much on the current quarter's results; they're more concerned about how all company stakeholders will fare in the long run. Also, Europeans aren't as concerned about growth as are Americans—a direct correlation, I believe, to the European sense of history. If a European company has been profitable for several hundred years—and has done well by its owners, employees, and customers—its managers don't necessarily think it has to grow 10 or 20 percent each year.

To many businesspeople, learning and adjusting to a different pace is more difficult than learning and adjusting to a different punctuality. Knowing a country's pace and exercising patience are vital to your business success—and your sanity.

Corporate Culture

Your company has asked you to go abroad. Are you lucky? You bet you are! Someone thinks you have a skill worth exporting or an ability to sell your company's services or products in another country. You're on your way to becoming an international business traveler, a role many businesspeople dream of but never get to play.

Are you nervous? I hope so. Nervousness means you won't be arrogant. Arrogance is the worst potential pitfall for the international business traveler. Acting arrogantly says, "I'll do it my way. I'm paying the bill; let them adjust to me."

> Peter Drucker, the management guru, said, "Be ready or be lost. If you don't think globally, you deserve to be unemployed and you will be."

Nervousness also means you might make the effort necessary to combine sound business practices with basic knowledge of the countries (that is, learning the basic facts of the countries you'll visit and a few basic phrases in their languages).

The European marketplace is diverse; its languages, cultures, and attitudes are all unique. Recognize and respect these differences; they affect every facet of business practice. Remember, people have fought wars over such differences. To ignore them is to risk offending your potential partner or customer and embarrassing yourself and your company.

Like everything else in Europe, corporate culture differs among countries. The following general facts, however, apply to most companies in most European countries.

- The individual is respected. A person generally works for his or her personal gain rather than for group goals.
- A clear hierarchy exists. The boss is the boss, and everyone knows it and responds accordingly.

- The organizational structure is generally vertical with decisions made at the top.
- Top managers dislike sharing information with subordinates.
- Communication from top to bottom is generally poor.
- Although rapidly becoming popular, participative management is still a relatively new practice in Europe and hasn't been widely adopted.
- Work life and private life are kept separate.
- In general, Europeans work toward developing relationships—not just doing business.

Note: The Nordic countries are the exception to many of these rules. Companies in these countries are relatively egalitarian, with a more horizontal organizational structure, shared responsibility, relatively open communication, and a more relaxed environment. They make decisions by consensus.

General Rules

- Don't attempt to Americanize the workplace. You'll be far more successful if you adapt to the local culture.
- Respect local customs, traditions, and work ethics.
- Seek to build relationships. Show a sincere interest in people.
- Be flexible and willing to operate within the existing business and political structures.
- Be prepared for perception gaps. Ways of thinking and approaches to life and business may differ from yours.
- Emphasize compatibility.
- Schedule appointments at least two weeks in advance.
- Avoid scheduling appointments for Friday afternoon, and never schedule appointments for Saturday or Sunday.
- Localize your marketing effort. What sells in Peoria doesn't necessarily sell in Paris, and what sells in Paris doesn't necessarily sell in Prague.
- Use a local sales force—you'll generally have more success this way. Local people understand the market better and have better connections than outsiders.
- Strive to improve the quality of your employees' lives and make them glad they work for you.

> Reading *The Economist* and *Financial Times* is essential for doing business in Europe.

Names and Titles

All general rules about using names and titles (see pages 21–22) apply
in business—only they're twice as important. Remember:

- Never use first names unless invited to do so.
- Learn correct pronunciation of names and use them often.
- Ask a person what name and title he or she prefers.
- Use a person's proper title.
- If possible, learn proper pronunciation and usage of names before you
  meet. Write down this information and underline the name you should
  use in conversation.

The Business Card

The business card is an important communication tool in Europe. It can
be one of your most valuable resources when meeting people. A typical
European business card tells you the following in the correct form and
with proper spelling:

- Company's name
- Person's name
- Person's corporate title (rank) and preferred professional title (European
  business cards may include several titles. Use the highest-ranking title.)
- Addresses of the company and person
- Phone, fax, and telex numbers, and e-mail address(es)

Your Business Card

- If possible, have your business card printed in the local language
  on one side and in English on the other side.
- Make sure your formal title appears on your card.
- If you hold any postgraduate degrees, include that information.
- If your company is more than fifty years old, put the founding year on
  your card. Longevity adds esteem.

How to Exchange Business Cards

Exchanging business cards is one of your first opportunities to make a positive
impression. Here's how to do it properly.

1. Walk to the person to whom you're presenting the card.
2. Shake hands and introduce yourself (if you haven't done so already).
3. Look the person in the eye and hand him or her your card with your right
   hand; be prepared to receive his or her card. Never pass out business cards
   as though you're dealing playing cards.

4   Treat your colleague's business card with respect. Don't shove it in your pocket or write on it in his or her presence. Writing on a business card (especially during a meeting) may offend people in some countries. Don't write information on a business card until after the meeting has ended.

5. Write the following important information on the back of the card as soon as you can after learning it. This information will come in handy when you write a thank-you note, speak on the phone, correspond, or visit the person months later. Your assistant also will appreciate knowing this information.
    - Phonetic pronunciation of the person's name
    - Spouse's name
    - Children's names and ages
    - Gifts given and received
    - Birthday
    - Special interests
    - School or university attended
    - Home address
    - Home phone number
    - Date of meeting(s)
    - Who introduced you to this person

Meetings

Here's some general information about meetings in Europe:
- The degree of formality in meetings varies among countries, as does the level of open communication, decision making, and information sharing among superiors and subordinates.
- A meeting's primary purpose may be to get to know and evaluate one another, to gain trust, or to check out the chemistry of participants. Know the meeting's purpose and come prepared.
- In some countries, meetings open with business discussions. In others, they begin with small talk.
- Take careful notes during meetings and presentations. Doing so signals your sincerity.

Presentations
- Learn a little about what your audience expects from a presentation. This knowledge will be invaluable.
- Dress professionally for a presentation. Europeans may consider informal clothing disrespectful. (See pages 44–45.)

- In the United States, speaking without notes shows a command of the subject. In Europe, however, it suggests you don't care enough to prepare. Europeans are comfortable with reading their presentations.
- In the United States, an enthusiastic presentation is almost required. In many European countries, such a presentation is considered phony or crude. When giving a presentation, be energetic yet professionally reserved.
- Be especially careful of your word choice in presentations, even if the audience understands English. During a presentation about the importance of exercise, an American doctor once told a group of British colleagues, "You have to get off your fanny!" The audience shifted uncomfortably; *fanny* is British slang for female genitalia.
- Don't expect Europeans to participate in audience activities. Be especially careful never to make anyone look foolish.
- Keep your hands out of your pockets and maintain good posture. To your European colleagues, sloppy body language indicates sloppy business practices.
- In the United States, we say, "There's no such thing as a stupid question." But Europeans won't ask a question that may make them look silly or ill informed, especially in front of a group. Keep this in mind during question-and-answer periods. Always answer questions seriously and respectfully.
- In many cultures, it's rude to respond to someone brusquely or contentiously. To attack a person's idea is to attack him or her personally. Be respectful at all times.
- Know how to graciously accept a gift (see pages 46–47) if you receive one at the end of the presentation.

Socializing

When establishing, renewing, or continuing a business relationship in Europe, be prepared to socialize. This is no time to decline invitations. Remember, most Europeans do business with people they know and trust. The time you spend socializing will pay big dividends.
- While working breakfasts are becoming common, Europeans prefer the business lunch. Some still consider a business breakfast uncivilized.
- Enjoy the local food—leave your diet at home as much as possible.
- If drinks are served, take one, even if you only sip it or pretend to drink it.
- Don't talk business at dinner unless your host initiates the conversation.
- Respect local dining and drinking customs.

- Be prepared for long evenings and late hours. Business deals may be made or broken during these hours.

Personalizing Relationships

In Europe, the "Hi, how are you? Let's sign the contract" approach rarely works. If you want to succeed in Europe, prepare to take the time to personalize your relationships. Here are some tips:

- Make it clear to people with whom you hope to do business that you're there for the long haul. Americans have a reputation for disappearing, so visit as often as possible.
- Stay in touch; phone, write, fax, and e-mail often.
- Contribute to local charities.
- Join appropriate associations in the local community.
- Spend time discussing local issues. (Be sure to brush up on them beforehand.) Any knowledge you show about the local culture will help build closer and stronger business relationships.
- Don't come on too fast or too strong. Maintain a low-key approach and adjust your pace, if necessary.
- Take time to build confidence.
- Be yourself—warm and friendly but initially more formal than you'd be at home.

Especially for Women

Around the world, more and more women are holding positions of power and prestige in business. These women have a lot in common. They struggle to meet the competing demands of family and career. Maternity leave, childcare, equal work for equal pay, and equal opportunity for raises and promotions—these are issues in Europe as well as in the United States. Some European countries are handling them better than others—in some cases, much better than the United States.

Attitudes toward businesswomen differ slightly among European countries, and prejudice still exists to some degree in several of them. But regardless of a country's attitude toward women, its citizens treat most foreign businesswomen politely. Local—not foreign—women bear much of the resistance toward women in business.

In fact, foreign businesswomen may have an advantage over their foreign male counterparts. Through a sense of courtesy and gallantry, European businessmen may grant initial meetings to foreign women that they wouldn't grant to foreign men.

Once Europeans recognize that you're a competent businessperson with the expertise and authority to make decisions, you can establish sound working relationships. What you do—not who you are—will determine your progress, so don't let gender stereotypes and prejudices stop you from pursuing opportunities. Do your homework, then step forward and request an international assignment.

General Rules

Europeans expect *both* men and women to use subtle, quiet manners in business situations. They disapprove of aggressive behavior. When doing business in Europe, you should:

- Research local customs toward women and respect them, even if you think they're silly or antiquated. Try not to be judgmental.
- Have your company send an introductory letter to your European colleagues. Make sure it states your title and qualifications as well as your authority.
- In countries with a less progressive view of women, have a respected local man introduce you to your new colleagues, clients, or customers.
- Define your role clearly and establish your position and ability immediately.
- Never lose your cool.
- Act womanly—that is, be refined and gracious, not aggressive or brusque.
- Enter meetings with confidence. Stand tall (even if you're not). Europeans will judge your expertise by your body language.
- Offer your hand first upon meeting or greeting a man.
- Respond gracefully when men open doors for you, stand when you enter a room, or otherwise exhibit chivalry. Gallantry is part of many cultures and isn't considered sexist.
- Don't be embarrassed or angry if someone kisses your hand or calls you *dearie* or another term of endearment.
- Do nothing that another could misinterpret as a sexual invitation. If you want to use a wedding ring to ward off advances, know that many European women wear their wedding rings on their right hands.
- Dress conservatively yet femininely—but never with sexual overtones.
- Be patient. It may be a new experience for some people to do business with women.

- Expect cultural misunderstandings. If you feel someone has insulted you, ask for clarification. Chances are, you've misunderstood the action or statement.
- Roll with the punches. If you're clearly dealing with someone incapable of working with a woman, consider asking a male colleague to join you or to handle that particular deal.

Safety and Health

Safety

When traveling abroad, take the same safety precautions you would when traveling in the United States. Follow these additional guidelines to keep safe when visiting Europe:

- See the list of resources on page 470 to help you plan a safe trip.
- The time to make important decisions is *not* after traveling seven to ten hours in a crowded plane. Jetlag—plus strange sights, sounds, smells, and customs—can confuse you, making it easier for others to victimize you.
- Always have a local escort.
- Know how to use public phones, and learn key phrases (such as "I need help.") in the local language so you can communicate with the police if necessary.
- At all times, have on hand the phone numbers and home addresses of your employer's local representatives, the nearest American embassy or consulate, and your principal business contacts.
- Always carry your passport, airline tickets, credit cards, and other valuables on your person—not in a briefcase or purse. Or leave them in a reputable hotel's safe.
- Don't carry documents or packages for anyone else, and store your own important papers in the hotel safe.
- Make photocopies of your passport's identification pages and keep one copy in a place separate from where you store your passport. Travel with several extra passport photos. The photos and copy of the identification pages will make it much easier to replace your passport if the original is lost or stolen.
- Don't carry papers that link you with the American government or the military. A terrorist could misinterpret even a card stating you're an "Honorary Kentucky Colonel."

- Don't wear a money belt or pouch outside your clothing or hung visibly around your neck. It could make you a target.
- Don't set your bag at your feet while checking schedules or using a phone. It might get snatched.

Hotel Safety

- Pack a small flashlight in case the hallways and stairwells are dark, or the hotel loses power.
- Take note of fire exits.
- Upon entering your room, make sure the phone line to the front desk works. Note emergency phone numbers.
- Keep your door locked at all times, even when you're in your room.

Driving

Driving in a foreign country is always difficult and nerve-racking. Large European cities have very heavy traffic, and their traffic rules differ from American cities'. In some areas, local drivers largely ignore the rules.

To avoid accidents, use public transportation (which is often excellent), take a taxi, or hire a driver. Remember that most European countries have stringent drunk-driving laws, and they're strictly enforced. If your socializing involves alcohol, take a taxi back to your hotel. Here are a couple of tips for hiring a taxi:

- Ask your hotel about reputable taxi companies. Hotel staff should also tell you how and where to get a taxi and the approximate cost to your destination. Generally, a hotel will phone a taxi for you. In many European countries, there are taxi companies that guarantee an English-speaking driver.
- Before you enter a taxi, verify the driver knows how to get to your destination and ask for the cost.

Health

- Check your health insurance policy before you travel. Make certain it covers emergency care in a foreign country. If it doesn't, buy a rider for coverage.
- For easier customs processing, keep medication in original, labeled containers.
- Take with you all prescription and nonprescription medication you may need.
- Pack a small first-aid kit.
- Take your physician's phone number with you.

Restrooms

- In some areas, you may find restrooms don't meet American standards. If you find a clean facility, use it. The next facility may not be so pleasant.
- Some restrooms in Europe display a sign requesting you place used toilet tissue in a bin rather than in the toilet bowl. For plumbing and sanitation reasons, it's important that you follow these directions.
- Carry facial tissues and premoistened towelettes with you in case neither is available.
- In Europe, you often must pay to use public toilets. Carry change with you.
- Men's restrooms may have female attendants. Don't act embarrassed.
- Always have small change available to tip restroom attendants.

Holidays and Festivals

Each European country and many regions within each country have holidays and festivals during which businesses are closed. Here's some general information you should know:

- Don't try to do business in July and especially in August, when many Europeans go on holiday. Some companies close for the entire month of August.
- Don't schedule appointments for the days around Easter or between Christmas and New Year's Day.
- Be aware of regional and local holidays and festivals. If you plan to visit customers or shop in the city, a little-known holiday could ruin your plans.
- Ask about school holidays. Many people travel with their families during these breaks, and cities may be more crowded.

Interfaith Etiquette

Traditionally, Europe has been Christian, but many people of other faiths live and work on the continent. Many non-Christian families have been European citizens for generations and have contributed significantly to the success and vitality of the European countries and their cultures. Today, many non-Christian newcomers are vital to Europe's economic growth.

General Rules

- Respect others' beliefs at all times. If you're invited to a service at a church, temple/synagogue, or mosque, ask about the correct protocol for dress and behavior. Each religion has rules that are sacred to its traditions.
- Women should carry a shawl or large scarf with them in case a house of worship requires a covered head and/or shoulders.
- Before planning an event, ask your guests whether they have any dietary requirements. When hosting a meal, it's important to always have at least one vegetarian dish available.
- Always learn and use the correct title for a clergy member or religious leader.

Christians

- Most Christians celebrate the Sabbath on Sunday.
- Most Christian churches welcome nonmember participation in their services. Ask before you take Communion. Some churches invite all participants to partake in Communion, and some allow only members of the faith to partake.
- Few Christian groups have dress restrictions or requirements for members. In Europe, however, all churches expect and appreciate modest dress. (That said, in the summer heat, churches can become cool refuges for the barely clad.)
- Most Christians don't have dietary restrictions except during Lent. Some Christian groups forbid consumption of alcohol or caffeine.
- In many European countries, Christians celebrate their name days (the days honoring the saints for which they're named) more than their birthdays. Name day celebrations include parties and gifts.
- Unless you know someone very well, it's best to avoid giving a Christian a religious gift.

Catholics

- Non-Catholics are invited to participate in every part of Mass except Communion. Only Catholics are allowed to receive Communion.
- If non-Catholics wish a priest's blessing, they should cross their arms across their chests and approach the altar with the communicants. A priest or deacon can administer a blessing, but a layperson distributing Communion can't.

- Catholics are required to abstain from eating meat only on Ash Wednesday and on Fridays during Lent. Ash Wednesday and Good Friday are also fast days, on which adults eat two small meals and one regular meal, and no food between meals. Some Catholics choose to abstain from eating meat on Fridays throughout the year.

At the Vatican

When visiting the Vatican, you may not wear shorts, miniskirts, or tank tops, and your legs and shoulders must be covered. You won't be allowed inside if you're not dressed appropriately. Vendors sell paper pants and shawls outside the Vatican.

Orthodox Christians

- Orthodox churches observe a different calendar than Western churches do. Some holidays fall on different dates, including Christmas and Easter.
- Easter is the most important day of the year. Services begin at midnight, when Saturday ends and Easter Sunday begins.
- All are welcome to celebrate the Divine Liturgy; however, only Orthodox Christians may take Communion.
- In worship, Orthodox men don't cover their heads. Women wear loose clothing that covers their arms and knees. Traditionally, women cover their heads when entering an Orthodox church, but many churches no longer follow this practice. Regardless, women should be prepared to cover their heads.
- There's no forbidden food in Orthodox Christianity, but there are special fasting periods throughout the year (like Great Lent) that require believers to abstain from eating meat, fish, wine, oil, and all dairy products. If you're entertaining an Orthodox Christian, ask whether he or she is observing a fast.

Hinduism

- Hindus worship as individuals rather than as a congregation.
- Hindus believe animals have souls and worship many animals as gods. Cows are the most sacred, but monkeys, snakes, and other animals are also sacred.
- Many Hindu temples don't allow leather. In a Hindu temple, don't wear leather shoes or belts, and don't carry leather purses, camera cases, and so on.
- Don't touch a Hindu statue or painting.
- If attending a Hindu funeral, wear white, not black.

Dietary Notes

Hindu dietary restrictions vary according to region, local custom, caste, and acceptance of outside practices.

- Orthodox Hindus prefer food that people outside their caste or religion haven't touched.
- Because the cow is sacred, beef is taboo.
- Because of Hindu doctrines of nonviolence, karma, and rebirth, orthodox Hindus shun all animal and fish products—except milk and honey, which orthodox Hindus consider pure because of their nonviolent connections to the cow and bee.
- Some Hindus eat eggs.
- While westernized Hindus may drink alcohol, most Hindus don't. Always offer fruit juices or soft drinks as alternatives, especially to women.
- When in doubt, ask for preferences. The question won't offend Hindus.

Gifts

- Present gifts with both hands. Never present a gift with only your left hand.
- Fruit and candy are good gifts.
- Don't use black or white gift-wrap; use yellow, red, or green gift-wrap.
- Don't give leather products, especially cowhide.

Judaism

- Sabbath begins Friday night at sundown and lasts until Saturday evening. It officially ends when three stars are visible in the sky.
- On the Sabbath, Orthodox Jews observe strict rules. For example, these rules prohibit driving, turning on and off electric lights, and pushing elevator buttons. (Some buildings program at least one elevator to make stops on every floor on the Sabbath so those who are observant don't have to push buttons.)
- When writing, some Jews spell *God* as *G-d*, because Jewish law forbids the destruction or defacement of the holy name.
- Some Jews don't pronounce *Yahweh* (the Hebrew name of God) outside of prayer or study.
- Following a tradition of modesty and propriety, Orthodox Jews generally don't touch people of the opposite sex. For this reason, let Orthodox Jews initiate handshakes.
- Dress modestly when meeting with Orthodox Jews.

Dietary Notes

- Food that Jewish laws sanction for consumption is called "kosher." People who observe these laws are said to "keep kosher."
- Generally, Orthodox Jews keep strictly kosher, Conservatives less so, and Reform Jews even less.
- Even within the same family, observance of kosher laws may vary. For example, some Jews might keep a kosher home but are less kosher outside the home.
- Kosher meat comes only from animals that a specially trained slaughterer kills according to ritual.
- Pork and fish without fins (including shellfish and eels) aren't kosher.
- To be kosher, Jews can't consume meat and dairy at the same meal or (more strictly) within six hours of each other. Orthodox Jews keep separate refrigerators and sets of dishes for storing, cooking, and serving meat and dairy.
- Many European Jews aren't strictly kosher, except possibly avoiding shellfish, pork, and pork byproducts. When in doubt, always ask Jews whether they're strictly kosher; the question won't offend them.

Gifts

- Don't give pigskin products to Jews.
- Don't give food as a gift unless you know it's kosher or you know for certain that the person doesn't keep kosher.
- If you give wine to Jews, it should be kosher. Shop at a kosher store to guarantee the wine is acceptable. Other types of alcohol aren't required to be kosher, so you can select a fine bottle of liquor for your Jewish colleague if he or she drinks.

Islam

- Muslims pray five times daily: at dawn, at noon, in the afternoon, in the evening, and at nightfall. While praying, they face toward Mecca.
- The faith expects its followers to attend noon prayers at a mosque on Fridays, the Muslim day of worship.
- Ramadan, the ninth month of the Muslim year, is a holy month of fasting during which the faithful may not eat or drink from dawn to sunset. Muslims joyfully celebrate the end of the fast in a three-day festival called Eid al-Fitr.

- Always pronounce *Muslim* "MUZ-lim," never "MOZ-lim." Don't use the spelling *Moslem*.
- Muslims don't worship Muhammad and are offended when Westerners call Islam *Muhammadanism* and its followers *Muhammadans*.
- Orthodoxy among Muslims varies just as it does among Christians and Jews. Not all Muslim women wear *hijabs*, not all Muslims refrain from drinking alcohol, and so on.
- When entertaining or hosting Muslims, discreetly ask whether they'd like time to pray. Prepare a quiet place for them to do so, and politely indicate which way is Mecca.
- When attending a Muslim service, men should wear long pants and women should cover their knees. Avoid wearing clothing that's too tight, too thin, or too revealing.

Body Language

- Many observant Muslims don't touch members of the opposite sex outside the family. If you're a woman, don't take offense if a Muslim man doesn't shake your hand.
- As a display of humility, devout Muslims may avoid looking into your eyes.
- Don't touch anyone, especially a child, on the head.
- To Muslims, the left hand is unclean. Don't eat, pass things, or gesture with your left hand, even if you're left-handed. You can use both hands when it's absolutely necessary (lifting something heavy, for instance).
- Be careful with your feet. The foot is the lowest part of the body and thus is unclean. Don't touch or move objects with your feet. Don't point or gesture at anything with your foot. Don't cross your legs or stretch your legs straight out in front of you. Keep your feet on the floor; never prop them on a desk or chair.

Dietary Notes

- Food that Muslims may eat is *halal*, meaning lawful. For meat to be *halal*, the animal must have been slaughtered in a certain way.
- Pork is not *halal*; avoid serving ham, bacon, pâté, hotdogs, or sausage. Avoid food prepared with lard—this can include piecrusts and other pastries.
- If hosting a banquet that includes Muslim guests, it's a good idea to avoid offering any pork dishes, because the other dishes might become contaminated in preparation or serving.
- Don't serve crab or lobster. Shellfish and fish without fins aren't *halal*. Fish with fins is an acceptable alternative.

- Observant Muslims don't consume alcoholic beverages.
- Avoid serving food cooked in alcohol, even if it has evaporated in cooking.
- For toasts, serve fruit juices to Muslims who can't consume alcoholic beverages.

Gifts

- Give and receive gifts with your right hand or with both hands.
- A high-quality compass makes an excellent gift for Muslims, who must face Mecca for prayers.
- Don't give alcoholic beverages or perfumes that contain alcohol.
- Don't give pigskin products or anything that contains pork.
- Don't give toy dogs or pictures of dogs. To Muslims, the dog is unclean.
- Don't give artwork depicting the human body, especially nude or partially nude females.

Part II
COUNTRY INFORMATION

AUSTRIA
REPUBLIC OF AUSTRIA

Greetings from Austria

Greetings from the small country with an erudite population. We Austrians are equally proud of our accomplishments in the modern world and our unique place in European history. Our contributions to civilization include Haydn, Schubert, Brahms, Bruckner, Klimt, Mahler, Mozart, Strauss, and Freud—to mention just a few.

We are not German, even though we speak the German language. We are a sovereign nation with our own culture. Please respect this fact. We also have fierce regional pride. People identify themselves as Carinthian, Burgenlandian, Styrian, Tyrolese, as well as others.

Our country has endured much change over the last century and a half. Vienna was the capital of the Austro-Hungarian Empire and thus was the focus for all that happened in our corner of Europe from 1867 to 1918. Once the center of imperial power, Austria became the small Republic of Austria after its defeat in World War I. In 1938, Nazi Germany annexed Austria.

After World War II, the Allies occupied our land. Our status as a nation remained in doubt until 1955, when the Austrian State Treaty ended the occupation, recognized our independence, and forbade reunification with Germany. As a condition for Soviet military withdrawal, Austria also ratified a constitutional law declaring its "perpetual neutrality." Since then, we have hosted numerous international peace conferences.

Vienna is a gateway between the East and the West. That position becomes even more important as the European Union expands, and many of us view the significance with mixed feelings. Some of us worry that the flow of immigrants to our nation from Hungary, Bulgaria, Romania, and the former Yugoslavia will "Balkanize" Austria.

Traditionally, though, we have absorbed new immigrants very well—just look at the number of foreign names in the Viennese telephone book. There are more than 735,000 foreigners living in Vienna and the rest of Austria, among them over 327,000 from the former Yugoslavia and nearly 131,000 from Turkey.

We see ourselves as contemporary and liberal. We revere education and the environment. We love nature and outdoor activities like hiking, skiing, and climbing.

The Viennese are more liberal and modern than those of us residing in the provinces. But many Austrians all over the country believe modern life and government legislation have weakened traditional family values. For example, the number of Austrian women working outside the home is one of the highest in the industrialized world—and the size of the Austrian family is one of the smallest.

Nonetheless, Austria is an ideal place for comfortable living and a wonderful place to visit. Have a look at the ball calendar. The Viennese Ball season traditionally runs from New Year's Eve to mid-February, but other balls are scheduled throughout the year. The balls are stunning, and attending them is a perfect way to waltz yourself into Austrian culture.

Vital Statistics

Population	8,184,691
Capital	Vienna
Area	32,380 square miles, slightly smaller than Maine
Government	Federal republic
Living Standard	GDP = US $40,320 per capita
Natural Resources	Oil, timber, iron ore, zinc, antimony, magnesite, tungsten, graphite, salt, lead, coal, lignite, copper, hydropower
Agriculture	Grains, potatoes, sugar beets, wine, fruit, dairy products, cattle, pigs, poultry, lumber
Industries	Construction, machinery, vehicles and parts, food, metals, chemicals, lumber and wood processing, paper and paperboard, communications equipment, tourism
Climate	Temperate; cold winters with frequent rain and some snow in lowlands and snow in mountains; moderate summers with occasional showers
Member of the EU?	Yes, since 1995
Currency	Euro (€)

Correct Name	noun: Austrian(s)
	adjective: Austrian
Ethnic Makeup	Austrians 91.1%, former Yugoslavs 4% (includes Croatians, Slovenes, Serbs, and Bosniaks), Turks 1.6%, Germans 0.9%, other or unspecified 2.4%
Languages	German (official nationwide), Slovene (official in Carinthia), Croatian (official in Burgenland), Hungarian (official in Burgenland)
Religions	Roman Catholic 73.6%, Protestant 4.7%, Muslim 4.2%, other 3.5%, unspecified 2%, none 12%

Meeting and Greeting

- An Austrian's handshake is firm, but not bone crushing. Maintain eye contact during handshakes.
- When greeting or departing, women may kiss one another—first on the left cheek, then on the right. Men don't kiss one another.
- Viennese men may kiss women's hands. Women should accept this tradition graciously. A foreign man shouldn't kiss an Austrian woman's hand.
- The most common greeting is *Grüss Gott* (groos goot), which means "may God greet you." Austrians use it in informal situations as well as very formal ones. They say it to everyone in the room, including wait staff, office staff, and salespeople.
- Austrian businessmen introduce themselves by last name only.
- In rural areas, people may greet strangers in public.
- Upon leaving, offer a handshake to everyone and say, "*Auf Wiedersehen*" (awf VEE-der-zay-un).
- Upon arrival and departure, Austrians often say the Viennese greeting *Servus* (SAIR-voos).

Names and Titles

- Austrians use first names only among very close friends and family members. However, there's a growing trend toward informality. Younger Austrians especially move quickly to using first names and *du*, the informal form of *you* (instead of the formal form *Sie*).

- Austrians are sensitive about their titles, especially in academia, and a person may have several titles. Someone's business card, for example, might list several titles, but the person might use only one or two when introducing him- or herself. Use whichever title(s) he or she uses. If you're not sure which title(s) to use, simply ask the person's preference. Be aware that academic titles confer status. Having a bachelor's degree warrants the title *Magister*, an engineering degree *Diplom-Ingenieur*, and the lauded PhD *Doktor*; people with these titles obtain privileges (like getting a table in a fully booked restaurant).
- The person who introduces you to an Austrian colleague should tell you whether he or she has an aristocratic title (for example, prince or countess). If a third party doesn't introduce you, pay attention to how others address the Austrian colleague; never ask someone about an aristocratic title. You can use an aristocratic title in conversation or personal letters, but not in official situations.
- When initially addressing a male professional, use *Herr* + professional title + last name.

  Example: *Herr Doktor Bauer*
- When initially addressing a female professional or a professional's wife, use *Frau* + professional title + last name.

  Example: *Frau Doktor Bauer*
- After the initial meeting, drop the last names and address people using *Herr/Frau* + professional title alone.

  Example: *Herr Doktor* or *Frau Doktor*
- A professor's wife may use the title *Frau Professor*.
- Even if you use first names with Austrians outside of work, in the office use only last names.

English	German	Pronunciation
Mr.	*Herr*	(hair)
Mrs./Ms.	*Frau*	(frow)
Miss (used only to address girls younger than age eighteen)	*Fräulein*	(FROY-line)

Language

- German is the official language, but each region has its own dialect. In some regions, there are minorities who speak Croatian, Slovenian, or Hungarian.

- Austria isn't an ideal place to learn German. German spoken in Austria differs in vocabulary, idiom, and pronunciation from German spoken in Germany. Austrian slang can frustrate people who speak some German.
- Many Austrians speak English, especially in Vienna. It's a required language in high school; however, most Austrians prefer to do business in German.
- Try to speak German; Austrians appreciate the effort.

Conversation
- Greet everyone formally before you begin a conversation. Austrians speak formally but directly.
- Austrians seldom give compliments, and they may receive them with embarrassment or even suspicion.
- Austrians find teasing unacceptable.
- Don't ask an Austrian "How are you?" unless you want a detailed answer. Austrians don't answer the question briefly, as Americans do.

Acceptable topics
- Classical music
- Opera
- Austrian art and architecture
- Sports
- Travel

Unacceptable topics
- Money
- Nazism (Never joke about Austria's Nazi past.)

Topics that require sensitivity
- Religion
- Anti-Semitism
- World War II

Body Language
Austrians conduct themselves with reserved, polite formality. Americans may misinterpret Austrians' body language as aloofness and unfriendliness.
- Austrians consider eye contact very important. Look people directly in the eye.

- In the past, Austrians didn't kiss, hug, or touch one another in public. Recently, especially in urban areas, more people are displaying affection.
- Staring at strangers is an Austrian pastime. Don't be offended or uncomfortable if Austrians stare at you.
- Austrians do queue (stand in line), but they may stand very closely to one another, touch their neighbors, and shove forward.

Phrases

English	German	Pronunciation
May God greet you	*Grüss Gott*	(groos goot)
Good day	*Guten Tag*	(GOOT-un taak)
Good morning	*Guten Morgen*	(GOOT-un MORG-un)
Good evening	*Guten Abend*	(GOOT-un AH-bent)
Please/You're welcome	*Bitte*	(BIT-ah)
Thank you	*Danke*	(DAHNK-uh)
Yes	*Ja*	(yah)
No	*Nein*	(nine)
Excuse me	*Verzeihung*	(fare-TSY-ung)
Goodbye	*Auf Wiedersehen*	(awf VEE-der-zay-un)
Pleased to meet you	*Sehr erfreut*	(zehr er-FROYT)
How are you?	*Wie geht es Ihnen?*	(vee gate es EE-nun)

Dining

Austrian cuisine incorporates the culinary expertise of many regions once part of the great Austrian empire.

Typical Foods

Wiener schnitzel: breaded and fried veal cutlet

Wild: venison

Knödel: bread or potato dumplings

Gulasch: paprika beef with *nockerl* (tiny dumplings)

Frittatensuppe: sliced crepe soup

Griessnockerlsuppe: semolina dumpling soup

Schweinsbraten: roast pork

Tafelspitz: boiled beef

Palatschinken: crepes

Salzburger Nockerln: soufflé from the Salzburg area

Marillenknödel: apricot dumplings

Apfelstrudel: apple strudel

Milchrahmstrudel: cream cheese strudel

Sachertorte: chocolate cake with apricot jam and chocolate icing

Melange: coffee with hot milk

Schlag: whipped cream (Viennese trademark served with coffee and on cake, strudel, and other desserts)

Drinking

- Austrians prefer drinking bottled mineral water.
- Austria is known for its wonderful *Wein* (wine), which is served with most meals. Austrians serve music, food, and local wine with abundant ambience in the *Heurigen*, the famous wine gardens in the Grinzing, Sievering, and Nussdorf suburbs of Vienna.
- Austrians also enjoy drinking the good *Bier* (beer) produced in their country.
- The Viennese *Kaffeehaus* (coffeehouse) is a cultural site. People sit for hours in one, reading papers, talking, and thinking. Some famous coffeehouse devotees were Sigmund Freud, Gustav Mahler, and Leon Trotsky.

> An American couple stopped in a Viennese coffeehouse, and the wife ordered a decaffeinated coffee. When the waiter came, he put down her cup and said briskly, "Oh, you're the hag." Insulted and incensed, the woman reported this rude comment to the restaurant manager, who politely explained that Haag is the most common brand of decaffeinated coffee in Austria.

Toasting

- Austrians use the toasts *Prost* (prohst), *Prosit* (PROH-zeet), and *Zum Wohl* (zuhm vohl) at formal and informal occasions.
- The host gives the first toast. Never drink before your host offers a toast.
- The guest of honor returns the toast later in the meal.
- Maintain eye contact during a toast.
- It's acceptable for women to propose toasts.

Tipping

- Restaurants: The word *Bedienung* indicates the bill includes a service charge. If the tip is included, the words *Bedienung Inclusiv* should appear at the bottom of the bill. If the tip isn't included, leave a 10 to 15 percent tip. Tip musicians €5 if making a request. Otherwise, there's no need to tip.
- Taxis: The fare includes the tip, but round up to the nearest euro when paying.
- Bellhops and porters: Tip one euro per bag.
- Hair stylists and barbers: Tip 10 percent of the bill.

Manners

Austrians expect proper manners at all times.
- Never eat until your host says, "*Guten Appetit*" (GOO-tehn APP-eh-teet).
- Never cut a dumpling with your knife. (Doing so implies that it's tough.)
- Break rolls with your fingers and eat them in small pieces.
- At a dinner party, don't leave any food on your plate.
- Austrians seldom entertain business guests in their homes. To them, the home is a private place. If someone honors you with an invitation to his or her home, don't ask for a tour; it's considered impolite.
- Leave a party by 11:00 PM.
- In restaurants, the person who extended the invitation pays the bill. Austrians won't appreciate a struggle over who pays.
- To beckon wait staff, raise your hand with your index finger extended. Do so quietly and never shout.
- In restaurants, you may be expected to seat yourself. Never sit at a table with a sign that reads *Stammtisch*, which means it's reserved for regular patrons.
- Men enter restaurants before women.
- Don't eat food while walking on the street; the only exceptions are ice cream and roasted chestnuts.
- Be quiet and orderly in public. Never be loud or boisterous.
- Greet salespeople when entering and leaving a shop.
- Don't extend an invitation unless you plan to follow through.
- Don't drop in on anyone. Call in advance to set up a meeting.

Dress

Austrians dress in European styles (see pages 44–45), sometimes with an Austrian touch (such as a brightly colored scarf). Their clothing is stylish, but never gaudy. In villages and mountain areas, *dirndl* and *loden* garments are common.

Austrians take pride in dressing well regardless of what they're doing or what position they hold. Austrians consider even running errands an event and dress appropriately for the occasion.

- Dress well (but not flamboyantly) for all occasions, and make sure your shoes are polished. Austrians will judge you by your attire.
- Business attire is conservative but elegant. Men wear dark suits, white shirts, and conservative ties. Women wear tailored suits with silk blouses; business dresses are also common, and elegant pantsuits are acceptable. Modest, understated accessories are common.
- At some balls, men wear tuxedos; for the Viennese Opera Ball, they wear white tails. Women wear floor-length gowns. For the opera and concerts, dark suits are more appropriate for men, and cocktail dresses for women.
- For casual occasions, men wear pants and shirts with sweaters. Women wear pants or skirts with sweaters, or casual dresses. Clean, fashionable jeans are acceptable.
- At upscale restaurants, business attire is appropriate. At beer and wine garden establishments, smart casual is more suitable (see previous bullet point).
- Athletic shoes, sweatshirts, and white socks are for the gym only. Many clubs and restaurants won't let you in without appropriate attire.
- Always bring warm clothes. Even in the summer, it can be cool, especially in the evenings.

Gifts

Austrians open gifts upon receipt.

Hostess Gifts

Consider giving
- Flowers, except red carnations (official flower of the Social Democratic Party), chrysanthemums or lilies (for funerals only), or red roses (connote romance): Give flowers in odd numbers only (even numbers connote bad luck, although a dozen is fine). Unwrap before giving them to the hostess.

- Pastries
- Chocolates
- Brandy
- Whiskey

Don't give
- German wine (Wines from other countries are acceptable.)

Business Gifts

Austrians generally don't exchange business gifts, but come prepared in case you receive one.

Consider giving
- Desk accessories
- Books
- Recordings of music
- Gifts from your home country or region

Don't give
- Gifts with sharp edges
- Gifts with your company's logo (unless very subtle)

Toilet Tips	
English	**German**
Restroom	*Toilette/WC*
Women's room	*Frauen*
Men's room	*Herren*
Hot water (red dot)	*Warm*
Cold water (blue dot)	*Kalt*

Helpful Hints

- Be aware that provincial Austrian culture differs dramatically from Viennese.
- To get a taxi, go to a taxi stand or ask the concierge to call one for you. Taxis aren't supposed to stop for anyone hailing them on the street.
- When riding public transportation, you'll hear *"Bitte, rechts stehen"* ("Please stand to the right"). The right side is for standing, and the left side is for

walking. Austrians strictly follow these rules. People will bump into you and demand you move over if you stand on the wrong side.

- Check your coat in the cloakroom at a theater or restaurant. Most theaters don't allow coats in the performance space.
- Don't ask to use the "bathroom" or "restroom." Ask for the "toilet" or "WC" (water closet).
- Don't pick up fruit or vegetables from a produce stand. Point to your selections and let the attendant place them in a bag.
- Don't jaywalk or cross a street against the light. Austrians respect authority.
- In shops and restaurants, sales taxes are included in the price and aren't added to the bill.
- Austrians love their dogs, which are allowed in almost all restaurants. They lie under the tables and are amazingly well behaved. Never pet a dog without the owner's permission.
- Austrians also love their cars. Mercedes-Benz, Audi, BMW: these vehicles are status symbols.

Punctuality

Austrians expect punctuality for business meetings. If you're delayed, call with an explanation.

Austrians insist on punctuality for social occasions, but there's a fifteen-minute grace period (the so-called academic margin). Never be late, however, for a concert or opera.

Corporate Culture

Structure

Austrian companies tend to have a vertical structure, with a small number of top people holding all real power. Those in authority expect (and receive) deference and obedience, and they're unlikely to appreciate criticism from subordinates or outsiders. Bosses criticize poor performance but seldom (if ever) compliment good performance.

Planning is cautious, conservative, and risk averse. With all this said, however, attitudes are beginning to change. With individualism on the rise in the European Union, Austrian business culture is starting to follow suit.

Meetings

Light conversation usually precedes the business discussion. Austrians run meetings efficiently, sticking to an agenda. Meetings aren't for brainstorming or for reaching a consensus.

Facts and figures help persuade Austrians. Decision making in Austrian companies is slow, with all facts thoroughly analyzed. Don't expect an answer to your proposal on the spot—be patient.

Communication

- Most businesspeople speak English, so you'll likely not need an interpreter.
- Austrians expect you to speak directly and formally, as they do.
- Correspond frequently by e-mail, fax, and letter; Austrian businesspeople like paper trails.
- On the phone or in letters, open and close with friendly comments to build personal relationships.
- Never call an Austrian colleague at home except in an emergency.

Business Cards

- Business cards in English are acceptable.
- Give your business card to the secretary upon arrival and to colleagues upon meeting.

Be Aware

- Try to have a respected third party introduce you. Whom you know is more important than what you know.
- Austrians may schedule their meetings weeks or even months ahead of time.
- Never cancel an appointment at the last minute; doing so will damage your relationship with Austrian colleagues.
- Rank and title are very important in Austrian business.
- Austrians may complain that they're overworked and can't accomplish a task by a given date. In reality, they're reliable, do high-quality work, and always meet deadlines.
- Traditionally, Austrian business people have carefully watched what they say. This attitude is relaxing, but be ready for your Austrian colleagues to guard what they say.

Socializing

- Austrians do most business entertaining in restaurants.
- Business breakfasts and lunches are common.
- After a relationship has developed, business dinners often include spouses.
- Reciprocate with a lunch or dinner invitation before you leave the country.

Especially for Women

Despite the culture's traditionally conservative attitudes toward women, more and more Austrian women are participating in politics and industry. Women make up nearly 40 percent of the Austrian workforce.

- A foreign woman won't have trouble doing business in Austria.
- A foreign woman won't have a problem inviting an Austrian businessman to dinner and paying the bill.
- Lunch is the most common setting for business discussions. A woman should stick to business lunches unless she knows her Austrian colleague well.

Holidays and Festivals

January	New Year's Day (1) Epiphany or *Heilige Drei Könige* (6)
March/April	Easter and Easter Monday
April/May	Feast of the Ascension (40 days after Easter)
May	May Day/Labor Day (1)
May/June	Whitmonday (day after Pentecost) Corpus Christi (about 8 weeks after Easter)
August	Feast of the Assumption (15)
October	National Holiday or Flag Day (26)
November	All Saints' Day (1)
December	Saint Nicholas Day (5) Christmas (25) Boxing Day or *Stephanstag* (26)

BELGIUM
KINGDOM OF BELGIUM

Greetings from Belgium

Greetings from the land of excellent beer, the world's finest chocolates, and more five-star restaurants than any other nation except France. You can get a taste of the world in Belgium.

Our central location attracts international organizations: Antwerp, Brugge, and Gent have been centers for global trade since the Middle Ages. The North Atlantic Treaty Organisation (NATO) is based in Brussels, our capital, as is the European Union (EU).

Like the EU, Belgium is a coalition of nations held together loosely by a weak central government. Less than one percent of our population lives in Eastern Belgium (within Wallonia) near the German border and speaks German. In the south and east regions, Wallonia makes up more than half of Belgium. While we Walloons speak French, we are not French! Do not treat us as quaint French people. We are reserved traditionalists, and may even appear aloof.

In the north and west, the people of Flanders speak Dutch. We Flemings consider ourselves reserved but open minded. We sometimes complain that the French-speaking Walloons look down on us.

Because we are linguistically split, Belgium is divided into three administrative communities; Wallonia, Flanders, and Brussels have separate legislative bodies and are largely autonomous. Constant compromising has made us flexible and capable of doing business in diverse settings.

We have two dominant cultures, but the cultural division stems more from pride of heritage than hostility toward the other culture. Walloons and Flemings love to work hard and play hard. We love eating good food, visiting cafés, and talking intelligently with friends. We are not loud or boastful, but we are proud of our excellent cuisine and our beautiful country. Strong families are vital to our society, and many of us settle in the towns where we were raised. Extended families often live on the same street, and our parents often help raise our children.

Walloons and Flemings both have international views and are eager to promote European integration. We are multilingual, cosmopolitan, and well prepared to work with the world. Come visit us—we are eager to meet you.

Vital Statistics

Population	10,364,388
Capital	Brussels
Area	11,787 square miles, about the size of Maryland
Government	Federal parliamentary democracy under a constitutional monarch
Living Standard	GDP = US $36,200 per capita
Natural Resources	Silica sand, carbonates
Agriculture	Sugar beets, vegetables, fruits, grain, tobacco, beef, veal, pork, milk
Industries	Engineering and metal products, motor vehicle assembly, transportation equipment, scientific instruments, processed food and beverages, chemicals, basic metals, textiles, glass, petroleum
Climate	Temperate; mild winters, cool summers; rainy, humid, cloudy
Member of the EU?	Yes, an original member from 1967
Currency	Euro (€)

The People

Correct Names	nouns: Belgian(s)
	    Walloons or French-speaking Belgians
	        (residents of Wallonia)
	    Flemings or Dutch-speaking Belgians
	        (residents of Flanders)
	adjectives: Belgian, Walloon, Flemish

Ethnic Makeup	Flemish 58%, Walloon 31%, mixed or other 11%
Languages	Dutch (official) 60%, French (official) 40%, German (official) less than 1%
Religions	Roman Catholic 75%, Protestant or other 25%

Meeting and Greeting

- Belgians shake hands lightly and briefly.
- Walloons may kiss or embrace close friends.

Names and Titles

- Professional titles aren't important to Belgians.
- Today, Belgians use first names more quickly than they had in the past. But they won't use first names with people of different ages or ranks. They'll also use last names with clients and customers.
- Some Walloons will introduce themselves by last name then first name. If you're unsure of the order of names, ask.
- Repeat your name when introduced.
- Flemings are more likely to use first names than Walloons.
- Be sure to address Flemings and Walloons correctly in the correct language, or use the English titles *Mr.*, *Mrs.*, *Ms.*, or *Miss*.

English	Dutch	French
Mr.	*Mijnheer* (muh-NAYR)	*Monsieur* (meh-SYUR)
Mrs.	*Mevrouw* (muhv-ROW)	*Madame* (mah-DAHM)
Miss	*Juffrouw* (yuf-ROW)	*Mademoiselle* (mahd-mwah-ZEL)

Note: Belgians rarely use *juffrouw* and *mademoiselle* except for very young girls or female wait staff and salesclerks.

Brief Sketches of Flemings and Walloons

Flemings

- A Belgian dialect of Dutch was once called Flemish, but now Flemings officially speak Dutch.
- Personal relationships are relaxed and low-key, but Flemings may be outwardly formal.
- Flemings use last names longer than the Dutch do.
- Flemish humor is mild and self-deprecating.

Walloons

- Walloons speak French, and most can't speak Dutch.
- Walloon etiquette is very traditional, and relationships are formal.
- Walloons use last names longer than the French do.
- Walloon humor is ironic and witty—usually at others' expense.

Languages

Dutch was once considered the language of servants and peasants, and French the language of the upper middle class—but no longer. In fact, Dutch-speaking Belgians (Flemings) make up more than half of the population, and French-speaking Belgians (Walloons) make up roughly a third of the population. Many Dutch speakers, however, use Flemish dialects.

Both Flemings and Walloons live in Brussels (located in Flanders), where French is the main business language. English (and sometimes French) is the language of choice for negotiators.

> Even the finch sings in two languages in this small country. *Vinkensport,* an ancient game in Flanders, tests how many songs a caged finch can sing in an hour. *Vinkeniers* want only birds that sound Flemish; when a finch sings with a French dialect from Wallonia, the song is disqualified.

Beware! If you're unsure which language to use, speak English. There's nowhere in Europe you can get in more trouble by using the incorrect language than Belgium. Many Belgians speak English, and speaking English is acceptable (and safe) in business and public places. But first apologize for not speaking your colleagues' language.

Conversation

Conversing with friends in cafés is a Belgian pastime.

Acceptable topics

- Sports: Football (soccer) is a national passion. Learn enough about the Belgian teams to ask your colleagues some informed questions.
- Vacations
- Belgian history
- Area of Belgium you're visiting
- Dining and drinking: Be sure to compliment the local food and beer.

Unacceptable topics

- Money (salaries, cost of things, and so on)
- Personal matters
- Health matters
- Linguistic divisions

Topics that require sensitivity

- Ethnic jokes: For example, Belgians tell jokes about the Dutch. Avoid joining in.

Body Language

- Belgians always maintain good posture.
- Don't snap your fingers.
- Never slap another's back.
- Keep an arm's length of space between you and another person.
- Try to sneeze and blow your nose in private.
- The "okay sign" (curling the index finger and thumb into a circle) means zero.

Phrases

See pages 170, 185, and 304 for French, German, and Dutch phrases.

Dining

Belgians are fond of saying that they cook their food with French finesse—and serve it in portions of German generosity. (With that said, portions in Belgian restaurants may be smaller than those served in American restaurants.)

Typical Foods

Moules (French) or *Mosselen* (Dutch): mussels

Moules Marinière: mussels steamed in white wine, garlic, and parsley, served with French fries

Anguilles: eels

Hochepot: stew of pork and mutton (a home-style dish)

Carbonnades Flamandes: beef cooked in beer

Civet de Lievre á la Flamandes: rabbit cooked in wine

Waterzooi: stewed chicken in rich broth

Horse meat: a delicacy served as a steak

Game

Fish

Cheese

Fruit

Drinking

- Be aware: Belgian beer has a much higher alcohol content than American beer.
- Belgians serve vermouth or Cinzano (a brand of Italian vermouth) before dinner. They serve beer and wine with meals.
- When you ask for whiskey, you'll get Scotch whiskey. *Scotch* is a brand of beer.

Toasting

- The Dutch toast *Op uw gezondheid* (op uv ge-ZOND-hite) means "to your health," and Belgians use it at formal and informal occasions. *A votre santé* (ah VO-truh sahn-TAY) is the French version of this toast.
- Wait to drink until your host offers the first toast.
- The guest of honor is generally expected to give a toast.
- In general, stand to toast.
- Woman may offer toasts.

Tipping

In general, tipping is not required in Belgium. Tip only if you're very happy with service. Here are guidelines if you wish to leave a tip:

- Restaurants: The bill usually includes a 15 percent service charge—*dienst inbegrepen* (Dutch) or *service compris* (French). Leave small change as an additional gratuity for exceptional service. If the bill doesn't include a service charge—*dienst niet inbegrepen* (Dutch) or *service non compris* (French)—leave a 15 percent tip.
- Taxis: The fare generally includes a tip.
- Cloakroom attendants: A sign stating tip suggestions is usually posted.
- Gas station attendants: A token tip is acceptable.
- Bellhops and porters: Tip one euro per bag.
- Maids and doormen: A tip is optional.

Manners

- Accept any drink your host offers. Don't ask for a drink not offered.
- Husbands and wives aren't seated together unless they're newlyweds.

- Belgians generally provide bread plates.
- Eat all the food on your plate. Belgians are thrifty and don't like waste.
- Belgians take great pride in their food, and meals are social and cultural events. Don't plan to dine quickly, and stay about one hour after the meal ends.
- Don't offer to clear the table or help in the kitchen.
- To beckon wait staff, raise your hand and make eye contact. Do so quietly and never call or shout.
- Always use a low, moderate tone when speaking. Don't be noisy or loud in public.
- Don't behave too casually. (Belgians consider casual behavior rude.)
- Don't flaunt wealth. Belgians appreciate modesty.

Dress

Belgians wear conservative clothing with an elegant French/Italian flair (newest trends, designer brands, very high quality).
- Businesspeople dress formally. Men wear dark suits, white shirts, silk ties, and polished shoes. Women wear elegant suits or dresses with tasteful jewelry and designer scarves.
- For formal occasions, men usually wear dark suits, and women wear cocktail dresses. Invitations will specify whether tuxedos and formal gowns are appropriate, but black-tie affairs aren't common.
- When attending an event at someone's home, attire should be smart casual: Men may wear sport coats (usually without ties), and women may wear elegant slacks or skirts with blouses.
- At most better restaurants, smart casual is appropriate. Dressy jeans are acceptable for more casual restaurants. (*Note*: Young Belgians wear jeans for casual wear, but adult Belgians don't often wear jeans.)
- Women don't wear athletic shoes in public, not even to the grocery store.
- Pack an umbrella, raincoat, and light sweater. Sunny days in Belgium can turn rainy quickly.

Gifts

Belgians generally open gifts upon receipt.

Hostess Gifts

Always give flowers in odd numbers (except thirteen). An additional small gift is also appropriate. Here are some suggestions:

- Books
- Recordings of music
- Liqueur
- Chocolates (Make sure they're Belgian.)

Send a thank-you note the day after a party. Consider also sending a basket of fruit or flowers.

Business Gifts

Belgian businesspeople generally don't exchange gifts, although it's common for Belgian companies to give small New Year's gifts (rather than Christmas gifts). If you haven't gotten to know a Belgian colleague well enough to learn his or her tastes, then you probably don't need to give a gift. Giving a small gift after a deal's completion is acceptable but not expected.

Consider giving
- Desk accessories
- Books
- Art from your home region

Don't give
- Gifts that feature your company logo

Toilet Tips		
English	**Dutch**	**French**
Restroom	*Toiletten/WC*	*Toilettes/WC*
Women's restroom	*Dames*	*Dames*
Men's restroom	*Heren*	*Hommes*
Hot water	*Warm water*	*Eau chaude*
Cold water	*Koud water*	*Eau froide*

Helpful Hints

- Don't ignore local tensions. The Walloons and Flemings coexist, but their rivalries dominate Belgian politics.
- Never drink, speed, or use cell phones while driving. Fines are heavy and foreign drivers may have to pay them on the spot.
- Belgian law requires everyone to carry identification at all times.
- Department stores and shopping malls are closed on Sundays.
- Belgian cities and streets may have both Dutch and French names. For example, the French names for Brugge and Gent (Dutch) are Bruges and Ghent.

Punctuality

Belgians expect punctuality for business meetings, and they insist on punctuality for social occasions. Call with an explanation if you're delayed.

Public transportation is excellent, but traffic in Brussels can be difficult. Allow plenty of travel time.

Corporate Culture

Structure

Flemish and Walloon companies differ sharply in structure and culture. Flemish companies tend to have a relatively horizontal structure with participative management. They prefer reaching decisions by consensus. Bosses are approachable, and perks are less important than pay.

By contrast, Walloon companies are much more formal and hierarchical. They consider rules and procedures important, and the boss makes the decisions. They take rank, job title, and office size and décor seriously.

Meetings

Initial meetings are for getting acquainted rather than serious discussion. Belgians want to get to know people before doing business with them. At subsequent meetings, Belgians tend to socialize for fifteen minutes before proceeding with business. They consider rushing into business rude. Formality is the general rule at meetings.

Especially in Wallonia, meetings are for the exchange of information and discussion of alternatives. Don't press for a decision.

Belgians are savvy, pragmatic businesspeople with a knack for negotiation. They look for practical solutions to issues or problems, so back your proposal with clear facts and figures.

Communication
- Belgians use English widely in business, so you most likely won't need an interpreter.
- Don't call a Belgian colleague at home except in an emergency.

Business Cards
- Business cards in English are acceptable.
- Present your business card upon meeting. It's often a time for discussing your company.

Be Aware
- Schedule appointments at least one week in advance.
- Flemish companies always have *NV* (public) or *BVBA* (private) after their names. Walloon companies use *SA* (public) or *SPRL* (private).

Socializing
- Belgians do most business entertaining in restaurants.
- Don't suggest business breakfasts. Belgians generally don't appreciate them; they prefer business lunches as a way to get acquainted.
- A business lunch could be several courses.
- Appointments made for 11:30 AM might include lunch.
- Business dinners may or may not include spouses.
- If someone entertains you, you should reciprocate.

Especially for Women

Belgians view women's roles conservatively, but many women are in the workforce. Traditionally employed as support staff, Belgian women are steadily acquiring higher-ranking positions.
- Foreign women won't have a problem doing business in Belgium.
- It's acceptable for a foreign woman to invite a Belgian man to dinner, and she won't have a problem paying the bill.

Holidays and Festivals

January	New Year's Day (1)
March/April	Easter (Friday–Monday)
April/May	Feast of the Ascension (40 days after Easter)
May/June	Whitsunday (Pentecost) and Whitmonday (day after Pentecost)
June	Corpus Christi (about 8 weeks after Easter)
July	Feast Day of the Flemish Community (11) Independence Day (21)
August	Feast of the Assumption (15)
September	Feast Day of the French Community (27)
November	All Saints' Day (1) Veterans Day (11) King's Day (15)
December	Christmas (24–26)

BULGARIA
REPUBLIC OF BULGARIA

Greetings from Bulgaria

Greetings from the land with an ancient musical tradition. Orpheus and the Muses, both important musical figures in Greek mythology, hailed from Thrace. We Bulgarians have kept that love of music alive, as we have all our traditions.

Over two thousand years ago, Bulgaria was the center of the Thracian civilization. (Spartacus, the slave who led a spectacular revolt against the Roman Empire between 73 and 71 BC, was from Thrace.) After the unification of Slavonic tribes in 681 AD, Bulgaria became one of the three most powerful states in Europe, and then was under Ottoman rule for nearly five hundred years.

Between the first and second powerful Bulgarian empires, the Byzantines ruled Bulgaria. But by the end of the fourteenth century, the Ottoman Empire gained control of our land. The formation of cultural centers and the spirit of the Christian religion kept us consolidated during the Ottoman rule. Our traditions and language supported us during the long struggle against foreign occupation.

A national revival in the nineteenth century was the final step towards liberation. Russia was an indispensable ally in this fight; two hundred thousand Russians died fighting for Bulgarian independence, along with numerous Romanians and Finns.

After liberation, we ratified the Tarnovo Constitution in 1879, one of the most democratic charters in Europe at the time. It established a constitutional monarchy controlled by a freely elected National Assembly. It also guaranteed equal rights to all subjects of the Bulgarian principality and stated that any slave from any nationality, race, or religion would immediately become free by just stepping on Bulgarian soil.

We began World War II allied with Germany, but the alliance did not last. In 1943, when the German-allied government attempted to export fifty thousand Bulgarian Jews to concentration camps, a storm of protest from key political and religious leaders stopped the action. We are very proud that we are the only nation in the region whose Jews were not decimated by the Holocaust. By the end of the war, we had switched sides to fight with our old ally, Russia. After the war, a Communist regime was installed.

Our agrarian economy was prosperous even under Communist rule (which allowed farmers to have their own plots), and industry grew strong. After the overthrow of the Communists in 1989, the transition to democracy has been difficult, but we are working hard. We joined the North Atlantic Treaty Organisation (NATO) in 2004 and look forward to European Union (EU) membership in 2007.

Bulgaria has well-preserved, centuries-old cultural treasures and astounding natural beauty. Relax on our beautiful Black Sea beaches and enjoy the excellent skiing and hiking in the Rila, Pirin, Vitosha, and Rhodope Mountains.

Our cuisine is superb; do not miss the chance to taste our excellent coffee and some of our traditional dishes, many of which feature yogurt. Yogurt originated centuries ago in Bulgaria (the organism used to ferment yogurt is named Lactobacillus bulgaricus).

We have so much to offer—come visit us soon.

Vital Statistics

Population	7,450,349
Capital	Sofia
Area	42,820 square miles, slightly larger than Tennessee
Government	Parliamentary democracy
Living Standard	GDP = US $3,990 per capita
Natural Resources	Bauxite, copper, lead, zinc, coal, timber, arable land
Agriculture	Vegetables, fruits, tobacco, livestock, wine, wheat, barley, sunflowers, sugar beets
Industries	Electricity, gas, water, food, beverages, tobacco, machinery and equipment, base metals, chemical products, coke, refined petroleum, nuclear fuel
Climate	Temperate; cold, damp winters; hot, dry summers
Member of the EU?	Applicant nation, hoping to join in 2007
Currency	Lev (BGL)

The People

Correct Name	noun: Bulgarian(s) adjective: Bulgarian
Ethnic Makeup	Bulgarian 83.9%, Turk 9.4%, Roma 4.7%, other 2% (including Macedonian, Armenian, Tatar, Circassian)
Languages	Bulgarian (official) 84.5%, Turkish 9.6%, Roma 4.1%, other and unspecified 1.8%
Religions	Bulgarian Orthodox 82.6%, Muslim 12.2%, other Christian 1.2%, other 4%

Meeting and Greeting

- Bulgarians shake hands with everyone when meeting and departing.
- They greet women before men, from oldest to youngest.

Names and Titles

When addressing Bulgarians, it's very important to use the titles *Gospodin*, *Gospozha*, and *Gospozhitsa*. Bulgarians rarely use first names except with family and very close friends. Omitting titles will sound awkward and might possibly offend your colleagues.

English	Bulgarian (phonetic)	Pronunciation
Mr.	*Gospodin*	(gohs-poh-DEEN)
Mrs. (Madam)	*Gospozha*	(gohs-poh-ZHAH)
Miss	*Gospozhitsa*	(gos-POH-zhit-sah)

Language

The Bulgarian language uses the Cyrillic (Russian) alphabet. If your stay is lengthy, it's a good idea to learn how to pronounce the alphabet phonetically.

Nearly everyone speaks Bulgarian—even the Turkish population, which speaks Turkish as a first language. Bulgarian is very similar to Macedonian, but the nation's Macedonian minority considers its language distinct.

Russian and German are common second languages. Under Communist rule, Russian was a required subject in school. English is a popular language to study today.

Conversation

Acceptable topics
- Global cultures, politics, and economies
- Current events, both local and international
- Sports
- Bulgaria's beauty (the Black Sea coast and the mountains)
- Bulgarian history: Asking intelligent questions about their history will impress Bulgarians.

Unacceptable topics
- Comparisons between Bulgaria and Romania
- Personal issues: marital status, children, and other family-related topics

Topics that require sensitivity
- Domestic politics
- Minority relations with the Turks and Roma (Gypsies)

Body Language
- In Bulgaria, nodding your head (once or twice) means "no" and shaking your head means "yes."
- Don't point with your index finger. Bulgarians consider the gesture rude.
- Female friends may link arms while walking on the street.

> An American family who adopted a young Bulgarian girl found the most difficult part of communicating with their new daughter was by nodding and shaking the head, gestures that have opposite meanings in Bulgaria. The miscommunication was both frustrating and amusing for a long time.

The Bulgarian language uses the Cyrillic alphabet. Below are the phonetic equivalents.

English	Bulgarian	Pronunciation
Hello	*Zdraveiteh*	(zdrah-VAY-teh)
Good day	*Dobar den*	(DOE-bar den)
Good morning	*Dobro utro*	(doe-BRO OO-tro)
Good evening	*Dobar vecher*	(DOE-bar VEH-chehr)
Please	*Molya*	(MOE-lyah)
Thank you	*Blagodarya*	(blah-goh-dah-RYAH)
You're welcome	*Hyama zashto*	(NYAH-mah zah-SHTOE)
Yes	*Dah*	(dah)
No	*He*	(neh)
Excuse me	*Izvinyavaite*	(izz-vih-NEH-teh)
Goodbye	*Dovizhdaneh*	(doe-VIZH-dah-neh)
Pleased to meet you	*Priatno mi eh da se zapoznaem*	(prih-YAHT-no mih eh dah she zah-pahz-NAH-yah zee vahs)
How are you?	*Kak steh?*	(kahk steh)

Dining

Turkey and Greece have influenced Bulgarian cuisine.

Typical Foods

Moussaka: casserole of pork or lamb with potatoes, tomatoes, and yogurt

Kufteta: fried patty of meat and bread crumbs

Sarmi: pork and rice stuffed into peppers or cabbage leaves

Banitza: baked cheese pastry

Pine honey: This traditional Bulgarian product now has to be labeled *pine jam*. According to EU restrictions, honey must be produced by honeybees from flowers, herbs, or leaves.

Dairy products, especially yogurt and cheese

Salads

Drinking

- *Rakia* is a grape and plum brandy.
- *Mastika* is an anise-flavored liquor.
- Bulgaria produces and exports high-quality red and white wines. Ask your host to recommend some local wine.

Toasting

- The toast *na zdrave* (naz-DRAA-veh) means "to your health" or "cheers." Bulgarians say it at formal and informal occasions. (They also say it after someone sneezes.)
- Bulgarians maintain eye contact while toasting.

Tipping

- Restaurants: The bill may include a service charge. If it doesn't, tip 10 to 15 percent of the bill.
- Taxis: Tip 10 percent of the fare.
- Bellhops and porters: Tip one dollar or the equivalent in leva.
- Hair stylists and barbers: Tip 10 percent of the bill.

Manners

Bulgarians will always make you feel welcome in their homes.
- Short speeches during dinner aren't popular in Bulgaria. But if you're invited to a Bulgarian home for dinner, make sure to briefly express your appreciation and compliment the hostess on the meal.
- Accept second helpings, if you can. Doing so will compliment your hostess.
- Bulgarians refill empty glasses and plates. If you're full, leave a small amount in your glass or on your plate.
- Be aware that Bulgarians may eat salads from a communal plate. In this case, use your own fork.
- Men should let women enter a room or building first.
- Don't leave a party early.

Dress

Bulgarian dress fashionably but not loudly. They always dress neatly in public. Their clothing is pressed—even jeans.

- For business, men wear suits and ties. Older Bulgarian men may wear trousers and sweaters. Women wear skirts, blouses, sweaters, and heels.
- For dinners, men wear suits, and women wear dresses or dress pants and blouses.
- For formal occasions, men wear dark suits, and women wear cocktail dresses. Black-tie events aren't common in Bulgaria.
- For casual occasions, men wear pants, shirts, and sweaters. Women wear dresses or sweaters and pants or skirts.

Gifts

Bulgarians may not open gifts if people other than the giver are present.

Hostess Gifts

Consider giving
- Flowers, except red roses (connote romance) or chrysanthemums (for funerals only): For special occasions (like the birth of a child), Bulgarians give flowers in odd numbers; they consider even numbers bad luck.
- Liquor (except to devout Muslims)
- Chocolates

Don't give
- Personal items

Business Gifts

Bulgarians exchange small business gifts at initial meetings. Present your gift at the end of the meeting, saying, "Here is a small souvenir from our country (or company)."

You may give your Bulgarian colleagues small gifts at Christmas, but they're not expected.

Consider giving
- Office items, like good-quality pen and pencil sets
- Wine (except to devout Muslims)
- Additional gifts for office staff (chocolates, coffee, tea, or office accessories)

Don't give
- Expensive items (may be interpreted as bribes)
- Anything that implies that modern consumer goods aren't available in Bulgaria (chewing gum, cigarettes, and so on)

Toilet Tips	
English	**Bulgarian**
Restroom	*Тоалетчата*
Women's restroom	*ЖЕНИ (Ж)*
Men's restroom	*МЪЖЕ (М)*
Hot water	(red dot)
Cold water	(blue dot)

Punctuality

Traditionally, Bulgarians weren't punctual for business or social occasions. But in today's rapidly changing business climate, they're starting to understand the importance of punctuality.

Rush-hour traffic may delay early-morning meetings in the big cities.

Corporate Culture

See pages 17–18 for more information on doing business with a formerly Communist nation. Here are some additional tips:
- Bulgarians exchange business cards immediately after shaking hands.
- Understand that Bulgarians may be suspicious of successful foreign businesspeople. Under Communist rule, people became—and remained—wealthy only if they were corrupt. To gain your Bulgarian colleagues' trust, you must be very open.
- It may take time to set up appointments, and you may have trouble making afternoon appointments, even though businesses are open.
- Be sure to confirm your meeting beforehand.

Especially for Women

Although Bulgarian law gives women the same rights as men, discrimination is common. On average, women earn less than men in similar jobs. They also shoulder most domestic duties, even if they work outside the home.

Bulgarians don't disapprove of women's working outside the home. Women (mostly urban) generally value such opportunities, not only because of the financial rewards, but also because of the independence and personal satisfaction they bring.

Since the fall of Communism, the proportion of women involved in high-level government offices has declined. Bulgarians debate whether the decline is due to gender discrimination or women's free choice in the market economy.

- Bulgarians accept foreign businesswomen.
- A foreign woman may have difficulty inviting an older Bulgarian man to a business dinner; however, he may accept an invitation for a business lunch, although he may insist on paying. Women who want to pay should make arrangements with the wait staff beforehand.
- Bulgarian men are courtly (pull out chairs for women, open doors for them, and so on). Women should gracefully accept this behavior; however, wearing a wedding ring may deflect unwanted attention, as will saying "I'm married." In general, women should prepare to attract attention if dining alone in restaurants.
- Women traveling alone are generally safe in Bulgaria, but always use common sense.

Holidays and Festivals

January	New Year's Day (1)
March	National Day of Freedom and Independence (3)
March/April	Easter and Easter Monday
May	Labor Day (1)
	Bulgarian Military Army's Day/ Gergyovden (St. George's Day) (6)
	Day of Bulgarian Enlightenment and Culture and of Slavonic Alphabet (24)
September	Unification Day (6)
	Independence Day (22)
November	National Day of the Bulgarian Revival Leaders (1)
December	Christmas (24–26)

CYPRUS
REPUBLIC OF CYPRUS

Because North Americans will most likely work with people from the Republic of Cyprus, this chapter focuses largely on the culture of Greek Cyprus. North Americans who will be working with Turkish Cypriots in the Turkish Republic of Northern Cyprus should also review the chapter on Turkey (see pages 427–39), as the cultures are similar.

Although the northern and southern cultures are much like the Turkish and Greek cultures, dialects and some customs differ significantly. Keep in mind, too, that Cyprus is a sovereign nation with its own identity, culture, and history.

Also, there are two important Sovereign Base Areas (SBAs) that the United Kingdom (UK) administers, polices, and governs. The bases are strategically invaluable for military aircraft and the communication facilities that are an important part of the UK's worldwide links.

Greetings from Cyprus

Greetings from our enchanting island. Our culture is one of the oldest in the Mediterranean. For ten thousand years, Cyprus has been a gateway between Europe and Asia, making the land a cultural, linguistic, and historic crossroads.

Our country has roots in several cultures. The Greek goddess of love, Aphrodite, was born in Cyprus. Saint Barnabas was born to Jewish parents in Cyprus, and some consider him to be one of the earliest Christian martyrs. During the Crusades, England's King Richard I married Berengaria of Navarre in Cyprus.

In 1960, Cyprus gained its independence from the United Kingdom, but the country was not united. A centuries-old conflict between the Greek majority and Turkish minority prevented unification, and the 1974 invasion of Turkish forces led to the displacement of nearly two hundred thousand Greek Cypriots in the north and a smaller number of Turkish Cypriots in the south, effectively establishing what is known today as the Cyprus Problem (always capitalized).

The animosity between the two cultures is inescapable, and there seems to be little desire to start fresh. Many Greek Cypriots assert that schools in Northern Cyprus brainwash their children to distrust Greeks—and many

Turkish Cypriots believe the schools in Southern Cyprus teach their children to distrust Turks.

As a result, Cyprus has had essentially two governments since 1974. The United Nations and all countries except Turkey recognize Cyprus as a single country controlled by the Republic of Cyprus, the Greek area in the south. Turkey recognizes the Turkish Republic of Northern Cyprus (TRNC), the Turkish area in the north. United Nations peacekeeping forces patrol a buffer zone around the Green Line, the boundary separating Greek and Turkish Cyprus. (Do not attempt to cross it at unauthorized points without permission; it is mined.)

The United Nations has worked for decades to reunite Cyprus under one government. But in April 2004, when both halves voted on reunification, the plan failed. Although 65 percent of Turkish Cypriots voted for reunification, 76 percent of Greek Cypriots voted against it.

Despite the decision to remain separated, relations between the north and south are thawing. In 2004, the Republic of Cyprus joined the European Union. Although Turkish Cypriots do not enjoy the benefits of EU membership equally with their southern neighbors, it is in their best interest to not further isolate themselves. In early 2003, the TRNC eased restrictions on entry into the Republic of Cyprus. Greek Cyprus reciprocated, and travel in both directions has become much easier (certain restrictions, however, still remain).

Cypriots displaced during the 1974 Turkish invasion were forced to abandon their land and properties, and the right for refugees to return to their vacated land and properties remains an important political issue today. In December 2005, the European Court of Human Rights ordered that the TRNC must begin paying reparations to Greek Cypriots who either fled or were forced out of the north during the invasion. Foreigners should be extremely careful when purchasing land and properties in Cyprus, as the titles may not be the current owners' to sell.

Our people generally regard themselves as either Greek or Turkish, not Cypriot. Greek Cypriots are very proud of their Hellenic heritage and its contributions to Western culture. They do not consider themselves Middle Eastern. They see Greece as a supportive "big brother," and more fly the Greek national flag than the Cypriot flag.

Many Turkish Cypriots are settlers (or children of settlers) from Turkey, who emigrated after the Turkish government encouraged settlement of "underpopulated" Northern Cyprus. The population is almost totally Muslim.

Putting aside our country's two contentious cultures, other nations have influenced Cypriot culture island wide. For example, the Syrians, Italians,

Lebanese, French, and especially the British have brought their recipes, many of which have become part of Cypriot fare. Our climate is ideal for agriculture, and using our native foodstuffs—figs, beans, herbs, olives, dates, and nuts—we have developed our own unique cuisine.

In the United Kingdom, Australia, North America, and elsewhere, there are sizable Greek Cypriot communities who communicate often with their homeland, giving Greek Cypriots a wide perspective of life in other countries.

In the south, we have enjoyed a flourishing economy with relatively low inflation and unemployment. The TRNC's economy, however, depends heavily on aid from Turkey, both in the form of direct aid to the TRNC government and in the form of low-interest loans to businesses in the TRNC.

Both the north and south welcome numerous tourists each year, especially honeymooners (who are fittingly drawn to Aphrodite's home). Many come to watch our various migratory birds. Others visit our astonishing archeological sites. It is a wonderful time to visit our land—come see us soon!

Vital Statistics

Population	780,133
Capital	Nicosia
Area	3,571 square miles (of which 1,295 square miles are in the TRNC), about 3/5 the size of Connecticut
Government	Republic
Living Standard (2004 estimate)	Republic of Cyprus: GDP = US $20,300 per capita TRNC: GDP = US $7,135 per capita
Natural Resources	Copper, pyrites, asbestos, gypsum, timber, salt, marble, clay earth pigment
Agriculture	Citrus, vegetables, barley, grapes, olives, poultry, pork, lambs, kids, dairy
Industries	Food and beverage processing, cement and gypsum production, ship repair and refurbishment, textiles, light chemicals, metal products, tourism, stone, wood and clay products
Climate	Temperate; Mediterranean with hot, dry summers and cool winters

Vital Statistics (*cont.*)

Member of the EU?	Yes, since 2004 (although EU laws don't apply to the TRNC)
Currencies	Republic of Cyprus: Cypriot pound (CYP); working toward converting to the euro by 2007 TRNC: Turkish lira (TRL)

The People

Correct Name	noun: Cypriot(s) adjective: Cypriot
Ethnic Makeup	Greek 77%, Turkish 18%, other 5%
Languages	Greek and Turkish (official), English
Religions	Greek Orthodox 78%; Muslim 18%; Maronite, Armenian Apostolic, and other 4%

Meeting and Greeting

- Cypriots shake hands warmly and firmly, with eye contact.
- Turkish Muslims may avoid looking into your eyes as a display of humility.
- Cypriots shake hands with elders first.
- Some Muslims may not shake hands with people of the opposite sex.
- Good friends may embrace and kiss.

Names and Titles

- Be sure to address Greek Cypriots and Turkish Cypriots correctly (in their language), or use *Mr.*, *Mrs.*, *Ms.*, or *Miss*.
- Professional titles are important to Cypriots. Use them if appropriate.
- See pages 197 and 429–30 for more information on Greek and Turkish names and titles.

Language

In written and formal communication, Cypriots use Standard Modern Greek, the language spoken in Greece. Informally, however, they use a Cypriot Greek dialect, which includes words and phrases not used in Greece. Many of these words are borrowed from Venetian, Arabic, English, and Turkish—cultures that have profoundly influenced the island over the centuries. In some ways, mostly due to the island's isolation from mainland Greece, Cypriot Greek is closer to Classical Greek than Modern Greek.

Cypriot Turkish varies from mainland Turkish in much the same way as Cypriot Greek differs from Greek. Cypriot Turkish has words not used in Turkish (many from Greek) and many words are pronounced in a slightly different way.

Many Cypriots (Greek and Turkish) speak English, especially businesspeople.

Conversation

Acceptable topics
- History
- Archaeology
- Cyprus's extraordinary beauty
- Cypriot cuisine
- Your family and business

Unacceptable topics
- Troubles between the Greek Cypriot and Turkish Cypriot populations: They're complicated and emotional. If your Cypriot colleague brings up the subject, remain politely neutral.

Topics that require sensitivity
- The Middle East, especially Israel and Palestine
- Local religious beliefs: Speak only respectfully of them.
- Turkey's relationship with the United States: Cypriots may be too polite to talk about what they consider America's mollification of Turkey. After a second bottle of wine, however, they may bring it up!

Body Language

See pages 198–99 and 431 to learn more about Greek and Turkish body language. Here's some general information:
- In Cyprus, there's little physical contact between men and women in public.
- Cypriots may stand closer to one another than Americans do.
- Don't touch a person's head.

- The following gestures are rude:
  * Waving your hand with the palm facing out and fingers spread
  * "Okay" gesture (index finger and thumb making a circle)
  * Thumbs-down gesture
  * Hand out, palm down, and middle finger extended down (means "up yours")
- The thumbs-up gesture means "okay."

Phrases

See pages 199 and 432 to learn Greek and Turkish phrases.

Dining

Cypriot hospitality is lavish, and sweets play an important part in entertaining. For more information on Cypriot dining and drinking customs, see pages 199–200 and 432–33.

Foods are similar to those served in Greece and Turkey (see pages 200 and 432–33), but there are local differences between dishes.

Typical Foods

Halloumi: white, semihard cheese, prepared from sheep's milk and mint (Cypriots have produced this traditional cheese for centuries. It's very versatile and used extensively.)

At a *taverna* (casual establishment), order a *meze* (MAY-zay). You'll receive up to thirty kinds of dishes, from savory to sweet. It's a complete meal, meant to be enjoyed slowly.

Kolokasi: root vegetable similar to a sweet potato (Tradition says King Richard I ate *kolokasi* at his wedding feast in Limassol in 1191.)

Loukanika: sausage that varies in flavor depending on where it's made (Coriander and other spices are mixed with the meat, then the sausages are soaked in red wine before being smoked.)

Meat: very fresh, not aged (You should be able to taste the difference.)

Fruit: abundant, delicious, and cheap

Drinking

- Coffee plays a big part in Cypriot culture, and it's impolite to refuse a cup. Cypriots add sugar before boiling the coffee, so you must specify whether you want your coffee sweet (very sweet), medium (somewhat sweet), or unsweetened.
  Cypriots serve three different kinds of coffee:
  * Instant coffee (*Nescafé*)
  * Filtered coffee: served in more expensive places and only upon request
  * Cypriot coffee (known as Turkish coffee everywhere else in the world): very popular, very strong, and always served with a glass of cold water (Watch out for coffee grounds at the bottom of the cup.)
- Cyprus produces spirits and beer, and it has produced wine for centuries. Even Northern Cyprus, although predominantly Muslim, produces wine. Be sure to sample different local varieties.

Toasting

See pages 201 and 433 for information on toasts in Greece and Turkey.

Tipping

- Restaurants: If the bill includes a 10 percent service charge, adding an extra 5 percent gratuity for exceptional service is appreciated. If the bill doesn't include a service charge, tip 10 percent.
- Bellhops and porters: Tip CYP1 per bag; in Northern Cyprus, tip the equivalent of one euro.
- Taxis: A tip of CYP1 is usually acceptable; in Northern Cyprus, tip the equivalent of one euro. For longer trips, tip more.
- Cloakroom and washroom attendants: Tip CYP1; in Northern Cyprus, tip the equivalent of one euro.
- Hair stylists and barbers: Tip 10 percent of the bill.

Manners

See pages 201–202 and 434–35 for more information on Greek and Turkish manners.

- In a person's home, it's impolite to refuse food or drink, and it's polite to finish everything on your plate.
- Never pass any items, especially food, with your left hand.
- Cypriots serve elders first at meals.
- Ask permission before taking photographs in places of worship.

Dress

Cypriots dress casually but neatly. Casual attire is similar to that worn in Western Europe. They dress formally for formal or high-level business or government functions.

- For business, men wear suits and ties. Women wear dignified attire (pantsuits, dresses, or skirts and blouses).
- For most formal events, dark suits are appropriate for men; black tie isn't common. Women wear cocktail dresses.
- Appropriate dress for restaurants varies: For outdoor and casual restaurants, smart casual is best. (See page 45.) For more elegant establishments, men wear suits, and women wear cocktail dresses. If you're unsure what attire is appropriate, ask a knowledgeable colleague or your hotel concierge.
- Even in warm weather, foreign men shouldn't remove their jackets or ties unless their Cypriot colleagues do so.
- When visiting monasteries or churches, men should wear trousers and shirts; women should wear clothing that covers their arms and legs completely.

Gifts

Cypriots generally don't open gifts in front of the giver. The recipient should thank the giver sincerely and put the gift aside to open later.

Hostess Gifts

Consider giving
- Chocolates
- Flowers, except white lilies (for funerals only)
- Pastries

Don't give
- Alcohol (if visiting a Muslim family)

Business Gifts

Greek Cypriots exchange business gifts as the Greeks do (see page 203). Turkish Cypriots, however, exchange business gifts as the Turks do (see page 436).

Consider giving

- Office items
- Good-quality pen and pencil sets

Don't give

- Personal items
- Knives or other sharp objects
- Alcohol, if the colleagues are observant Muslims: Although Muslim Cypriots are generally secular and many do drink alcohol, it'd be a faux pas to give alcohol to an observant Muslim.

Toilet Tips		
English	**Greek**	**Turkish**
Restroom	*Toaléta*	*Tuvalet*
Women's restroom	*Ginekón*	*Bayanlar*
Men's restroom	*Andrón*	*Baylar*
Hot water (red dot)	*Zesto nero*	*Sıcak su*
Cold water (blue dot)	*Kryo nero*	*Soğuk su*

Helpful Hints

- Stay away from cabarets. Many are bases for thugs and organized crime.
- Check your bar tab for inflated charges.
- Don't take photographs of anything that could be considered having military significance.
- Most of Nicosia is in the Republic of Cyprus, but part lies in the TRNC.
- Some monasteries exclude tourists who aren't Greek Orthodox. This restriction is usually posted.
- Extended families are very close and expect members to help one another.

Punctuality

Professional Cypriots are generally very experienced in international business and have adopted an "on-time" attitude. Tradespeople, however, may be an hour or two late for appointments; they call their lateness "operating on Cypriot time." Even if Cypriots are late, foreigners should be on time for business meetings.

For social events, arrive close to the time stated on the invitation, but don't come early.

Corporate Culture

Structure

There are relatively few large corporations in Cyprus. Companies are usually based on family structure, with the senior person (usually the father) calling the shots. Cypriots respect hierarchies. Show respect to people in authority, and don't try to go over someone's head.

Meetings

Meetings are to discuss and exchange ideas. The boss makes the decisions later. Cypriots are great talkers, and it's hard to keep business meetings short and to the point. Be prepared: meetings may be interrupted frequently.

Negotiations take time, and bargaining is important. Don't disagree with someone publicly, making them lose face, and never raise your voice or show emotion when speaking.

Communication

It takes time to build relationships. Cypriots want to meet you face to face and get to know you before doing business. They consider doing business over the phone or in writing too impersonal.

Business Cards

Always bring a large supply of business cards. Cypriots exchange them when first meeting someone.

Be Aware

- The economy in the TRNC is very curtailed because of insufficient diplomatic recognition. It depends heavily on economic support from Turkey.
- There's very little economic activity between Turkish and Greek Cyprus, although tensions are relaxing.
- Tourism is an important part of the Cypriot economy.
- Cypriots are loyal to people, not companies. If a company has to change representatives, the new person will have to build relationships all over again.
- Whom you know may be more important than what you know.
- Cypriots take contracts very seriously.
- Appointments are necessary. Never drop in for a meeting.
- To schedule initial appointments, always contact a potential client or customer in writing first, then follow up with a phone call.
- Offices and stores take a half-hour break at noon; in the summer months, they may also take a break from 1:00 to 4:00 PM.

Socializing

- Cypriots do most business entertaining in restaurants.
- If you're hosting, always immediately offer coffee, mineral water, or fruit juice to guests. Be sure to offer again if they initially refuse.
- Don't talk business at dinner unless your Cypriot colleagues do so first.
- Cypriots may invite spouses to dinners.

Especially for Women

Recently, there have been major changes in women's status in Cyprus. The Cypriot government has pledged to help female entrepreneurs and to designate women to key government posts. It has also passed legislation on equal pay for equal work. As a result, the number of Cypriot women working in business and commerce is increasing, especially among the younger generation.

Nevertheless, traditional views on the role of women are still widespread, especially among the older generation. A low percentage of Cypriot women work outside the home, and they're still underrepresented in elected office.

- Cypriots accept foreign businesswomen, but women may need to verify their qualifications and authority. Make sure your business card includes your full title and any postgraduate degrees.
- Women aren't allowed to visit some monasteries.
- Don't be offended if a Muslim man refuses to shake your hand.

Holidays and Festivals

Greek Cyprus

January	New Year's Day (1)
	Epiphany (6)
March	Green Monday (14)
	Greek Independence Day (25)
March/April	Orthodox Easter (Friday–Monday)
April	Greek Cypriot National Day (1)
May/June	Pentecost
August	Feast of the Assumption (15)
October	Cyprus Independence Day (1)
	Óchi Day (28)
December	Christmas (25–26)

Turkish Cyprus

January	New Year's Day (1)
April	Labor and Spring Holiday (1)
	National Sovereignty and Children's Day (23)
May	Atatürk Commemoration and Youth & Sports Day (19)
July	Turkish Intervention (20)
August	Social Resistance Day (1)
	Victory Day (30)
October	Republic Day (29)
November	Republic Day of Turkish Republic of Northern Cyprus (15)

Note: Some Muslim religious events are also observed.

CZECH REPUBLIC
CZECH REPUBLIC

Greetings from the Czech Republic

Greetings from the land with more castles and chateaux per square mile than any other country. Our capital, Prague, is one of the most beautifully preserved medieval cities in the world.

Although we suffered under dictatorships for much of the twentieth century, we are proud of our democratic tradition. Czechoslovakia was the only Central European country to remain a stable democracy between the World Wars. Our sovereignty was crushed in 1938 when the Munich agreement annexed the Sudetenland, an area with a mostly German population, to Nazi Germany. In 1939, Germany seized the rest of our nation. More than 350,000 of our people died in World War II; at least 250,000 were Jewish.

After the war, we chafed under Soviet domination. In our view, Czechoslovakia and East Germany were the most totalitarian of the Soviet Bloc nations. During the 1989 Velvet Revolution, largely peaceful protests ousted Communist rule and drew the admiration of the Western world. The revolution's leader, playwright and poet Václav Havel, rose to near rock star popularity. The first free elections took place in July 1990, and Havel became president of Czechoslovakia. On January 1, 1993, our country split, peacefully and upon mutual agreement, into the Czech Republic and Slovakia.

We are very proud of our cultural contributions, which are known world wide. (At one time, Prague rivaled Paris as the cultural center of Europe.) The composers Dvořák and Smetana were Czech. Alfons Mucha's famous paintings capture the mood of the late nineteenth century. Our puppet theater is legendary—even the Communist government approved it. If we invite you to the theater or an art exhibit, you should accept!

Although ours is perhaps the world's least religious country (largely because the Communists viewed the church as competition and therefore suppressed it), the Czech people paved the way for the Reformation of the sixteenth century. The work of Jan Hus, the most important fifteenth-century Czech Reformer, preceded Martin Luther's by a full century.

Despite our country's independence, we often have trouble thinking as an independent nation. Over forty years of Communist rule affected the way we think, solve problems, and reason—and those habits did not just disappear when we changed governments. Today, we debate among ourselves about who we are, and we struggle to achieve a new identity.

Nevertheless, we have one of the most vibrant and free economies in Central Europe, and our private sector is expanding. Communism interrupted our enterprise, but our spirit of innovation has always remained strong. We are proud that Škoda is one of only four companies in the world that have one hundred years' experience manufacturing vehicles.

Come to our country for business or pleasure. We will not disappoint you!

Vital Statistics

Population	10,241,138
Capital	Prague
Area	30,450 square miles, slightly smaller than South Carolina
Government	Parliamentary democracy
Living Standard	GDP = US $14,500 per capita
Natural Resources	Hard coal, soft coal, kaolin, clay, graphite, timber
Agriculture	Wheat, potatoes, sugar beets, hops, fruit, pigs, poultry
Industries	Metallurgy, machinery and equipment, motor vehicles, glass, armaments
Climate	Temperate; cool summers; cold, cloudy, humid winters
Member of the EU?	Yes, since 2004
Currency	Czech koruna (CZK); working toward converting to the euro by 2010

The People

Correct Name	noun: Czech(s) adjective: Czech
Ethnic Makeup	Czech 90.4%, Moravian 3.7%, Slovak 1.9%, other 4%
Language	Czech (official)
Religions	Roman Catholic 26.8%, Protestant 2.1%, other or unspecified 12.1%, unaffiliated 59%

Meeting and Greeting

- Mutual acquaintances should introduce people if at all possible.
- Czechs introduce women before men, from the eldest to the youngest.
- Czechs shake hands with everyone upon meeting and departing; however, if they meet someone later in the day whom they've already greeted, it's not necessary to shake hands again.
- Czech men greet one another with several quick, firm handshakes. Czech women shake hands more gently (with one another and with men).
- A man waits for a woman to extend her hand, unless she's his boss. Older Czech men may "air kiss" women's hands.
- Men should remove gloves before shaking hands, but women don't have to.
- Czechs may not smile when meeting strangers.
- When introducing themselves, Czechs first say their last names, then a greeting.
- Family and close friends hug one another upon greeting. "Air kissing" on the left cheek, right cheek, and the left cheek again is also common among family and close friends.

Names and Titles

- Czechs don't use first names until they're very well acquainted. Always use professional or academic titles and last names until invited to do otherwise.
- Czechs may preface a person's title with *Pán* or *Paní*. For people without professional or academic titles, use *Pán* and *Paní*.

  Examples: Professor Pavel Nemec *Pán* Professor Nemec

  Milada Emmerova *Paní* Emmerova

  Václav Klaus *Pán* Klaus
- Among one another, close friends may use *Pán* or *Paní* with a first name.

English	Czech	Pronunciation
Mr.	*Pán*	(pahn)
Mrs.	*Paní*	(PAH-nyee)
Miss	*Slečna* (used only for waitresses and girls younger than age eighteen)	(SLECH-nah)

Language

Czech is a Slavic language, related to Slovak, Polish, Croatian, and Russian. Czech and Slovak are similar enough that a Czech speaker can understand Slovak, and a Slovak speaker can understand Czech. The two largest regions, Moravia and Bohemia, speak dialects that differ slightly from each other.

Older Czechs may also speak Russian, while younger Czechs may also speak English and/or German. (Business and tourism have made German a popular language.)

> The word *robot* derives from the Czech word *robota*, which means "drudgery" or "servitude." Its current meaning became popular after Karel Čapek's science fiction play *R.U.R. (Rossum's Universal Robots)* about artificial workers premiered in 1921.

Conversation

Czechs often use jokes and parables in conversation, but they may view personal compliments as insincere.

Acceptable topics

- Czech beer: Compliment it often. You'll make friends if you say Czech Budweiser is much better than American Budweiser and apologize for Americans' theft of the label!
- Your life in the United States: Your hosts may ask you many questions about this topic, liberally injected with opinions.
- Your family
- Sports, especially ice hockey and football (soccer)
- Czech history, culture, and art: Ask lots of questions about these topics. Czechs especially appreciate a sincere interest in the Velvet Revolution and the subsequent transformation. But don't offer your opinions unless you're very informed.

Unacceptable topics

- Person's occupation: In social situations, don't ask people how they make a living, how much they earn, and so on. (You, however, may be asked these questions. Answer what you feel comfortable answering.)
- Health issues (yours or others)
- Personal or family problems: Czechs talk about such issues only with close friends.

Topics that require sensitivity
- World War II
- The Holocaust

Body Language
- Czechs consider eye contact and good posture important. Look a person in the eye when conversing and stand up straight.
- Czechs may stand closer to one another than Americans do; however, the more formal the relationship, the more distance between people.
- Good friends of the same sex may link arms when walking in public.
- When counting, the thumb means "one," that is, one (thumb), two (index finger), and so on.
- Flicking a finger against the neck is an invitation to have a drink of vodka (usually used only among men).

Phrases

Please note that the Czech language uses diacritical marks that aren't used in English. The Czech phrases below have been simplified for North American readers.

English	Czech	Pronunciation
Hello (informal)	*Ahoj*	(AH-hoy)
Good day	*Dobrý den*	(DOE-bree den)
Good morning	*Dobré ráno*	(DOE-breh RAH-no)
Good afternoon	*Dobré odpoledne*	(DOE-breh OHD-po-lehd-neh)
Good night	*Dobrou noc*	(DOE-breh nohts)
Please/You're welcome	*Prosím*	(PRO-seem)
Thank you	*Děkuji*	(dye-KU-yee)
Yes	*Ano*	(AH-no)
No	*Ne*	(neh)
Excuse me	*Promiňte*	(pro-MEEN-tay)
Goodbye (formal)	*Na shledanou*	(nah SKLAY-dah-noo)
Goodbye (informal)	*Čau (Ciao)*	(chow)
Pleased to meet you	*Těší mě*	(TYE-shee mnyeh)
How are you?	*Jak se máte?*	(YAHK-sheh MAH-teh)

Dining

- Czech cuisine doesn't include many vegetables and is heavy on meat and starches.
- Meals usually start with soup. Traditional Czech soups include meat broth, dried mushroom soup, and garlic soup.
- The Czech Republic has a surprising number of Mexican restaurants. There's even a blending of Mexican and Czech cuisines called "Czex-Mex."

Typical Foods

Knedliky or *zelo*: dumplings

Knedlo: sauerkraut

Vepřo: pork roast

Wild game: boar, venison, and hare (Czech game dishes are world famous.)

Sauces: Tomato sauce, dill sauce, and cream and butter sauces are important parts of Czech cuisine.

Potatoes, in many forms: potato pancakes, potato soup, potato croquettes, and so on

Pizza and hotdogs: You can buy both from street vendors.

Desserts: Many contain fruit.

Drinking

- Coffee: Very thick, strong Turkish coffee is the most popular. (Watch out for coffee grounds at the bottom of the cup.) American coffee is also available.
- Beer: World-famous Czech beer is the most popular alcoholic beverage. Pilsner beer originated in Pilsen. Czechs drink an average of 338 U.S. pints of beer per capita every year, one of the highest rates in the world. They believe: "Beer makes beautiful bodies."
- Wine: Moravia produces several fine wines.
- Friends socialize in pubs, coffeehouses, and wine bars.

Toasting

- The toast *Na zdraví* (nah ZDRAH-vee) means "to your health," and Czechs use it at formal and informal occasions.
- There are several toasts given throughout a meal. Don't forget to take your turn.

- If someone is toasting you, maintain eye contact with him or her during the toast.
- It's acceptable for women to offer toasts.

Tipping

- Restaurants: The bill may include a 10 to 12½ percent service charge. Feel free to add some small change for exceptional service. Give the tip to the cashier; don't leave it on the table.
- Taxis: Round up the fare to the nearest koruna.
- Doormen, porters, and bellhops: Tip the equivalent of one euro for each bag they handle.
- Hair stylists and barbers: Tip 10 percent of the bill.

Manners

- Always call ahead before visiting someone, even a close friend. Czechs consider unannounced visits impolite.
- When entering someone's home, remove your shoes if the host does so, or ask if it isn't clear what you should do.
- Men always rise when someone enters the room; women may or may not. Follow others' lead.
- Czechs serve the oldest woman or most honored guest first.
- It's polite to decline a second helping; however, when the hostess insists, you should accept.
- Compliment your hostess on the meal.
- Czechs always refill glasses. Keep your glass more than half-full if you don't want more, and don't pour for yourself. Refill your neighbors' glasses if needed.
- It's insulting to leave a party too early. Follow other guests' lead about when to leave.
- In restaurants, younger people may split the bill. Older people, however, will expect the person who extended the invitation to pay the bill.
- There may be little conversation at meals. Follow others' lead.
- Speak softly in formal settings. In informal settings (for example, pubs and private parties), loud voices are common.

- Beckon wait staff by raising your hand and extending the index finger, keeping it stationary. Address waiters and waitresses by *Pán* and *Slečna*. (*Note*: Czechs may find thanking the wait staff strange.)
- Smoking in public is generally acceptable, but first ask those around you for permission before lighting up.
- In public, men defer to women out of politeness.

Dress

After opening relations with Western Europe, Czechs began wearing European fashions. Business attire may be less formal than in Western Europe, but in general, the higher up the hierarchy, the better dressed the employee.

- For business, dress to reflect your position. Err on dressing more formally until you know the environment better. Men wear sport coats or suits. (Foreign men shouldn't remove coats or ties unless their Czech colleagues do so first.) Women wear conservative dresses or suits.
- For formal occasions, men wear tuxedos or dark suits. Women wear long formal dresses.
- For casual occasions, men wear pants and shirts with sweaters. Women wear pants or skirts with sweaters, or casual dresses. Clean, fashionable jeans are acceptable.
- For restaurants, business attire is appropriate for men and women. For more casual restaurants, casual attire is acceptable.
- Czechs don't wear shorts on streets.

Gifts

When given a gift, it's polite to ask the giver, "Shall I open it now?" especially if there are others present. The giver will ordinarily say yes. When visiting someone's home, bring small gifts for any children. The family will appreciate the gesture.

Hostess Gifts

Consider giving
- Flowers in odd numbers, except chrysanthemums (for funerals only)
- Wine
- Pastries
- Chocolate

Don't give
- Vodka or beer

Business Gifts

You may give business gifts at initial meetings, especially gifts from your home region or country; they provide an excellent opportunity to get acquainted. You may also give gifts at the end of a business deal. Exchanging small gifts at Christmas is appropriate, as long as you make it clear they're holiday gifts, not business gifts.

Be aware that Czechs may view business gifts as attempts to gain influence or instill a sense of obligation (a lingering effect of Communism in the Czech Republic). It may be prudent to ask knowledgeable contacts whether you should give gifts in certain situations or to certain people. If a recipient seems uncomfortable, say, "In the United States, giving a small gift in this situation is customary."

Consider giving
- Pen and pencil sets
- Books about the United States or your home region
- American gourmet food
- Good-quality American liquor

Don't give
- Vodka or beer
- Cheap items
- Obviously expensive items (may be considered bribes)

Toilet Tips	
English	**Czech**
Restroom	*Záchody/WC/Toalety*
Women's restroom	*Zeny, Dámy*
Men's restroom	*Muzi, Paní*
Hot water	*Teplá*
Cold water	*Studená*

Helpful Hints

- Ask your Czech hosts to show you their favorite outdoor recreation areas. (If you entertain Czechs in your home city, take them to local parks and arboretums.) Be prepared, though, if you have asthma or other breathing problems. The Czech Republic's air quality is poor.
- When you pay for items in stores, put your money on the counter instead of handing it to the cashier.
- In many establishments, people pay for their items first, get a receipt, and use the receipt to pick up their items. (In large supermarkets, however, people buy items in the same way as in the United States.)
- Stores aren't often open weekends and evenings, although some stay open Thursday evenings.
- Don't bargain in stores.
- Get an approximate fare before you get into a taxi. Some drivers try to cheat foreigners. Ask your host or hotel concierge for reputable taxi companies. Some guarantee English-speaking drivers.
- Always check your coat if possible.
- In restaurants, the wait staff will assume you want beer unless you indicate otherwise.
- Be sure to check your restaurant bill carefully. Restaurants must present a written statement, and don't hesitate to question unrecognized items. Keep in mind that many restaurants charge separately for a basket of bread or rolls.
- If you buy Czech crystal, make sure the piece features an oval sticker that reads "Bohemia Crystal—Made in the Czech Republic."

Punctuality

As Czechs begin to interact with their EU neighbors and the rest of the world, they're adopting a "time is money" attitude. Czechs try to be on time for social and business events. Foreigners should be on time, but be tolerant if Czech colleagues are late—they'll probably apologize for their tardiness.

City traffic is a huge problem and often causes lateness. The metro (subway) is the safest and fastest way to get around in cities.

Corporate Culture

See pages 17–18 for more information on working with businesses in formerly Communist countries.

Structure

Czech companies operate within strict hierarchies. To make progress in a Czech company, you must work with the high-level decision makers.

Meetings

Meetings may begin with small talk, but participants get down to business fairly quickly. Presentations should be clear, but don't have to be fancy. Make sure your brochures, handouts, and so on are accurately translated into Czech.

Communication

Although Czechs are direct, they take care not to hurt others' feelings or status. They communicate with emotion, but they base final decisions on facts and logic. Younger people may communicate more informally than their elders; however, all levels highly value protocol and etiquette.

Czechs may pledge more than they can deliver. Be cautious of promises until you've established some trust.

Be Aware

- While your Czech colleagues may not have their own business cards, they expect foreign businesspeople to have them. Have your business cards translated into Czech; don't give cards that have been translated into Czech *and* Slovak. Include your full title and any postgraduate degrees.
- Although Czechs welcome foreigners, they take their time building business relationships. They believe good business relationships require flexibility on both sides.
- When doing business with Czechs—more so than with other Central Europeans—what you know is more important than whom you know (but personal contacts are still important).
- While Czechs are modern and innovative, many don't have long business perspectives. Also, they may view contracts as statements of intent, not rule. (Contracts weren't honored under Communism.)
- After the Velvet Revolution, some people got rich quickly, and many others are trying to get rich quickly now. The business climate is stabilizing,

but be careful when doing business with people you don't know or for whom you can't get good references.

Socializing

- Czechs do most business and social entertaining in restaurants. An invitation to a person's home is a great honor.
- Business breakfasts are rare.
- At lunch or dinner, your colleagues may talk business.
- Czechs may invite spouses to business dinners, but rarely to lunches.

Especially for Women

Although most Czech women work outside the home, they're still largely responsible for household management and child rearing. Czech women hold mostly administrative and lower-level positions; however, workplace equality is growing and the cultural belief of women's subordination to men is disappearing.

- Foreign businesswomen should act professionally and always use an even tone when speaking. Czechs view loud, aggressive women negatively.
- Strangers may pay undue attention to women in public, although generally not in restaurants.
- In restaurants, foreign women may have difficulty paying when dining with men. (Local women can never pay.) If you want to pay, arrange payment with the wait staff beforehand—don't let the check come to the table.

Holidays and Festivals	
January	New Year's Day (1)
March/April	Easter and Easter Monday
May	Labor Day/May Day (1) Victory Day 1945 (8)
July	Saints Cyril and Methodius Day (5) Jan Hus Day (6)
September	Czech Statehood Day (28)
October	National Day (28)
November	Struggle for Liberty and Democracy Day (17)
December	Christmas (24–25) Saint Stephen's Day (26)

DENMARK
KINGDOM OF DENMARK

Greetings from Denmark

Greetings from the land where few have too much and fewer have too little. The Danish proverb "It is unassuming, but it is good" best describes our way of life.

We are very proud of our country and culture, even though we are modest by nature and never brag about our achievements. We value tolerance and diversity, and we highly regard the individual.

Our history of supporting the disenfranchised illustrates our compassionate national character. For example, during World War II we resisted the German occupation and not only smuggled nearly all of our 7,500 Jewish citizens to safety in Sweden, but we also operated their businesses and kept their homes clean. At the end of the war, we welcomed them home.

While our taxes may seem unbearably high to Americans, we accept paying them to support social welfare. All Danes enjoy free education, medical treatment, and hospitalization. We also provide an early-retirement pension if a citizen's ability to work is reduced, as well as a national pension large enough to live on when a citizen reaches age sixty-five. We are very proud of our excellent school system, where all students receive an outstanding cultural education. Danish laborers can easily converse with professors on a variety of subjects.

We are respected for our accomplishments in science, art, and architecture. Niels Bohr was one of the giants of atomic theory and a Nobel Prize winner. Søren Kierkegaard is widely considered the founder of existentialism. And what would our world be without Hans Christian Andersen, the poor Danish cobbler's son who gave the world wisdom, morals, and meaning in his captivating fairy tales? Written nearly two hundred years ago, his works—such as "The Little Mermaid," "The Emperor's New Clothes," and "The Princess and the Pea"—are still read and quoted world wide.

We value close, stable family lives. Most of our women work outside the home. Many couples live together before marriage and formalize the relationship when they have children (whom we respect as individuals).

In public, however, we are unexpressive and very low-key, preferring to be inconspicuous. As a result, we may appear unresponsive to foreigners. We are also uncomfortable chatting with strangers and forming instant friendships—and we do not liked to be touched. Please stand at least two arm's lengths from us.

We have to admit, we are a little pampered. Our little country grants us easy access to the good things in life. Take your time to travel across our small oasis. Country roads take you to grand castles, snug inns, beautiful forests, and sandy beaches. We have a well-organized road system and state-of-the-art bridges (as beautiful as they are practical) that link Denmark with the Scandinavian Peninsula and continental Europe.

> Every day, even during the German occupation, King Christian X went for a ride on his horse. One day a German soldier, observing the king on his daily ride, asked a bystander, "Where is the king's bodyguard?" The Dane turned to the German and said, "All of Denmark is his bodyguard."

Please remember, though, that we are a sovereign country. Do not call us Swedes or Norwegians. We are a separate people. Please learn our history, appreciate our culture, and visit our beautiful country.

Vital Statistics

Population	5,432,335
Capital	Copenhagen
Area	16,640 square miles, slightly less than twice the size of Massachusetts
Living Standard	GDP = US $51,610 per capita
Natural Resources	Petroleum, natural gas, fish, salt, limestone, chalk, stone, gravel, sand
Agriculture	Barley, wheat, potatoes, sugar beets, pork, dairy products, fish
Industries	Iron, steel, nonferrous metals, food processing, machinery and transportation equipment, textiles and clothing, chemicals, electronics, construction, furniture and other wood products, shipbuilding and refurbishment, windmills
Government	Constitutional monarchy
Climate	Temperate; humid and overcast; mild, windy winters and cool summers
Member of the EU?	Yes, since 1973
Currency	Danish krone (DKK): Denmark has chosen to use its own currency rather than converting to the euro.

The People

Correct Name	noun: Dane(s) adjective: Danish
Ethnic Makeup	Scandinavian, Inuit, Faroese, German, Turkish, Iranian, Somali
Languages	Danish (official), Faroese, Greenlandic (an Inuit dialect), German (small minority)
Religions	Evangelical Lutheran 95%, other Protestant and Roman Catholic 3%, Muslim 2%

Meeting and Greeting

- Danes give firm, brief handshakes with direct eye contact.
- *Goddag* (goh-DAH) means "good day" and is a common formal greeting.
- *Hej* (hey) means "hi" and is a frequent informal greeting.

Names and Titles

- Traditionally, Danes addressed only close friends and family by first names. Today, using first names is becoming more common, but don't use first names until your Danish colleagues do so.
- Use professional titles, especially with older people.
    Example: Professor Andersen
- If your colleague doesn't have a professional title, use *Herre* or *Fru*.

English	Danish	Pronunciation
Mr.	*Herre*	(hair)
Mrs.	*Fru*	(froo)
Miss	*Frøken*	(FRUH-ken)

Language

Danish is related to other Scandinavian languages, but it has undergone the most change from Old Scandinavian.

English is the predominant second language in Denmark. Eighty-five percent of Danes speak and/or understand English. Sixty percent of Danes speak and/or understand German.

Conversation

- Danes speak plainly and respect frankness.
- Danes sometimes express themselves contrarily. They may say, "It is wonderful weather," when it's pouring rain or, "It is a trifle chilly," when it's stifling hot.
- Don't ask a Dane "How are you?" unless you want a detailed answer. Danes don't answer the question briefly, as Americans do.
- Danes use *De* (dee), the formal *you*, for older people and strangers and use *du* (doo), the informal *you*, for younger people and friends.

Acceptable topics

- Danish history and culture
- Travel

Unacceptable topics

- Compliments, especially about a Dane's clothing: Danes seldom give compliments, and they may receive them with embarrassment or even suspicion.
- Topics that confuse Denmark with other Nordic countries
- Topics that Danes may consider boastful
- Personal issues, including religion and family (These issues may be discussed once a relationship has developed.)

Topics that require sensitivity

- Denmark's religious minorities and their place in Danish society

Body Language

- Danes don't show affection in public.
- Danes require more personal space than Americans do. Allow at least two arm's lengths of space.
- Don't touch Danes. For example, don't slap another's back or put an arm around another's shoulder.

Phrases

English	Danish	Pronunciation
Good morning	*Godmorgen*	(goh-MORN)
Good afternoon	*Goddag*	(goh-DAH)
Good evening	*Godaften*	(goh-AHF-tehn)
Please	*Vær sa venlig*	(ver-sah-VEHN-lig)
Thank you	*Tak*	(tahk)
You're welcome	*Velbekomme*	(VEL-beh-kom-meh)
Yes	*Ja*	(yah)
No	*Nej*	(nigh)
Excuse me	*Undskyld*	(OON-skewl)
Goodbye	*Farvel*	(far-VILL)
Pleased to meet you	*Gælder mig*	(GLAY-ah-dar my)

Dining

- Lunch breaks are generally short, and few Danes go out to lunch.
- A *Det store kolde bord* (literally, "the large cold table") is common for a formal lunch buffet.
- Dinner is generally long and slow (up to four or five hours) with much conversation. Formal dinners can serve up to seven courses.

Typical Foods

Smørrebrød: a Danish invention in which a piece of bread is spread with a thick, even layer of butter, then layered with fresh, savory, colorful, appetizing, and attractive complementary ingredients

Kogt Torsk: boiled cod

Flæskesteg med Rødka: roast pork with red cabbage

Røget Fisk: smoked fish (many kinds)

Engelsk Bøf: steak

Gule Ærter: soup of dried peas served with pork or sausage

Frikadeller: meatballs

Stegt Ål: fried eel

Rødspætter: sole

Sild: herring (most often pickled)

Lagkage: sponge cake with custard, strawberries, and whipped cream

Rødgrød: fruit compote

Drinking

- If you ask for *snaps* (a shot), you'll get a small, ice-cold glass of *akvavit* (or aquavit, a clear or slightly colored, very potent alcohol). Be careful not to drink too many *snaps*.
- *Akvavit* and *Øl* (beer) and are the national drinks. Ice-cold *akvavit* is an essential accompaniment to pickled herring and smoked fish. The Danes particularly like their local beers. They drink them with *smørrebrød* and to wash down *snaps*.
- Danes serve coffee only after the meal.

Toasting

- Toasting can be a very formal process.
- The toast *Skål* (skohl) means "cheers," and Danes use it at formal and informal occasions.
- Never sip your drink until the host says, "*Skål*."
- Never toast your hosts until they've toasted you.
- Never toast anyone senior to you in rank or age.
- Propose a toast by tapping your glass with a spoon.
- The person seated at the hostess's left (guest of honor) proposes a toast during dessert and gives a short speech to thank the hostess.
- It's not Danish custom for women to propose toasts, other than *Skål*. Nevertheless, you may see women proposing toasts.

Tipping

While tipping isn't customary, Danes appreciate a token tip.

- Restaurants always include a service charge of 12½ to 15 percent in the menu prices, but it's customary to round up the bill when paying.
- Taxi fares include tip.
- There's no obligation to tip gas station attendants, hair stylists, barbers, hotel maids, bellhops, or doormen. They all receive good salaries.

Manners

Use proper etiquette with Danes. They appreciate relaxed, polite manners.

- When arriving at someone's home, wait for your host to invite you inside.
- At formal dinners, each man may receive a card that features the name of his female dinner partner, who will sit to his right. He should escort her to the table.
- Danes love making speeches for their guests, for others, and for themselves.
- When Danes entertain at their homes, expect them to serve only half the prepared food. Danish families enjoy eating the leftovers for the next few days.
- Danes expect guests to eat all the food they've taken.
- Take a small portion of the first dish. It'll be served once or twice again.
- When you want food passed to you, say, "*Værsgo*" (VER-skoh), which means "please."
- Danes love conversation; plan to stay at least one hour after a meal ends to converse.
- Dinner parties can end as late as 1:00 AM. Some hosts don't consider the party a success if the guests leave before midnight.
- A visit to a Danish home after 7:30 PM generally doesn't include dinner.
- Danes may give lengthy, hearty handshakes after a meal while saying, "*Tak*" (thank you).
- After attending a party or event, you don't have to immediately extend a similar invitation to your hosts.
- Danes say *Tak* ("thank you") for everything, all the time.
- Summon wait staff by raising your hand, extending your index finger, and making eye contact. Never shout.

Dress

Danes normally dress in European fashions, and they never dress sloppily. They wear high-quality shoes that are always polished.

- Business attire is elegant but not ostentatious. Men wear dark suits with white shirts and conservative ties. Women wear modest but chic suits with heels.
- High-ranking executives may host black-tie affairs. Men wear tuxedos, and women wear evening gowns. For theater performances, ask your Danish colleagues or the hotel concierge about the expected dress.

- Dress for rain and cool weather.
- Topless bathing at beaches is common. Some beaches have sections for nude bathers.
- On Danish beaches, bathers wrap a towel around themselves to change clothes.

Gifts

Danes open gifts upon receipt.

Hostess Gifts

Consider giving
- Wrapped bouquet of flowers: Send the flowers before the event so the hostess doesn't have to care for them while other guests arrive.
- Liquor (very expensive in Denmark)
- Good-quality chocolates

Don't give
- Sharp objects
- Cheap or tacky gifts

Business Gifts

Danes don't normally exchange gifts at business meetings, but you may exchange small gifts at the successful conclusion of negotiations. Giving a Christmas gift to a Danish colleague is acceptable but not expected.

Consider giving
- Wine
- Chocolates
- Whiskey or other liquor

Don't give
- Cheap or tacky gifts

Toilet Tips

English	Danish
Restroom	*Toilet/WC*
Women's restroom	*Damer*
Men's restroom	*Herrer*
Hot water	*V*
Cold water	*K*

Helpful Hints

- Foreigners must register with local police within twenty-four hours of arrival. Hotels generally register for you. If not, obtain forms from the post office or local police.
- Treat everyone equally.
- Never call a Dane either a Swede or Norwegian.
- Don't act ostentatiously.

Punctuality

Danes expect punctuality for business and social occasions. Call with an explanation if you're delayed.

Corporate Culture

Structure

The structure of Danish companies tends to be functional and relatively horizontal. Competence earns authority, and everyone views the boss as the group leader. Authoritarian behavior, however, isn't acceptable. Companies make decisions after consulting everyone involved, but accountability lies with the individual.

Meetings

Danish informality is famous, and that trait definitely appears in business meetings. In most companies, meetings are frequent, and they begin and end punctually; however, Danes generally engage in fifteen minutes of casual conversation before proceeding with business.

Agendas are clearly defined, but companies encourage all participants to voice their opinions. Everyone knows in advance whether the meeting's purpose is to share information, discuss an issue, or make a decision.

Communication
- English is Denmark's business language, so you'll likely not need an interpreter.
- There's good horizontal communication between functional areas of Danish companies.

Business Cards
- Business cards in English are acceptable.
- Give business cards to everyone at a meeting.

Be Aware
- Danes care more about success than money, and more about abilities than titles.
- Although Denmark is a social welfare state, industry and agriculture are completely privately owned.
- Danes greatly admire independence and the entrepreneurial spirit.
- Danes dislike a hard sell and aggressive business tactics.
- To persuade Danes, you'll need straightforward facts and figures.
- Between visits, it's important to stay in touch by phone, fax, and e-mail.

Socializing
- Generally, Danes entertain informally in a cozy atmosphere.
- Danes usually do business entertaining in restaurants, even though they're very expensive.
- Business breakfasts aren't common. Business lunches are common, and Danes prefer them to business dinners. Business dinners are more social, but participants might discuss business.
- Danes don't commonly invite spouses to business dinners.

Especially for Women

Danes rarely discriminate against women, and foreign women won't have a problem doing business in Denmark. The percentage of Danish women who work outside the home is one of the highest in Europe. Many women hold managerial and professional positions. Plus, Denmark provides excellent maternity benefits, paternity leave, and childcare. Women generally return to work after having children.

- While it's acceptable for a foreign woman to invite a Danish man to a business dinner, an invitation to lunch is better. If a dinner invitation is necessary, the woman should extend it to include his wife.
- A traditional Danish man may insist on paying, but the younger generation has no problem letting a woman pay the bill.
- While women don't smoke on Danish streets, they smoke everywhere else. Some smoke cigars.
- It's acceptable for single men and women to patronize restaurants that offer dancing to meet members of the opposite sex.

Holidays and Festivals

January	New Year's Day (1)
March/April	Easter (Thursday–Monday)
April/May	Feast of the Ascension (40 days after Easter) Great Prayer Day
May/June	Whitsunday (Pentecost) and Whitmonday (day after Pentecost)
June	Constitution Day (5)
July	Industrial Holiday (most commonly, the first three weeks, although dates vary)
December	Christmas (24–26) New Year's Eve Day (31)

ESTONIA
REPUBLIC OF ESTONIA

Greetings from Estonia

Greetings from the land of nearly 1,500 lakes and over 1,500 islands. Estonia is the northernmost Baltic state. Ethnically, linguistically, and culturally, Estonians are related to Finns, but our culture is uniquely our own.

Beginning in the first century AD, our land has been ruled by a number of different powers, including the Vikings, Denmark, Germany, Sweden, Russia, and Nazi Germany. After World War II, the Soviet Union annexed our nation. Nearly eighty thousand native Estonians were deported between 1945 and 1953. During that time, Soviet policy encouraged ethnic Russians to relocate to Estonia and the other Baltic states. By 1991, Russian-speaking Estonians numbered nearly half the population.

In 1988, hundreds of thousands of Estonians gathered in public to sing patriotic songs and demand independence from the Soviet Union. The event became known as the Singing Revolution. We finally gained our independence in August 1991.

We have always referred to ourselves as the "Singing Nation." Our *regivärss* (rhythmic verse) dates back to the first millennium BC. There are written records of over a hundred thousand Estonian folk songs. Since 1869, our nation has organized a national song festival (*Laulupidu*); for the last few decades, we have held it every five years. In recent years, the festival has featured nearly thirty thousand performers and drawn audiences of three hundred thousand people. Estonia also holds periodic dance festivals (*Tantsupidu*).

We are proud of our traditions. Knitted gloves, mittens, socks, and hats have been part of Estonian folk costumes for centuries—and knitting continues to be a cultural pastime. Saunas are also part of our culture. After spending time in the sauna, some of us invigorate ourselves by plunging into icy lakes.

Estonians have revered education for centuries. Tartu University, founded in 1632, is one of Europe's oldest academic institutions. It is known for its scientific research; its library's collections of scientific publications number over three million.

Since gaining independence, our progress has been astounding. In 2006, the Heritage Foundation/Wall Street Journal *Index of Economic Freedom* ranked Estonia as the fourth-freest economy in Europe (after Ireland, Luxembourg, and the United Kingdom). To achieve this honor, we instituted low flat-tax rates and fostered a competitive business environment. Tallinn's Muuga Harbour is one of the Baltic Sea region's most modern cargo ports. In addition, Estonia has some of the world's highest-quality peat, and several of our European neighbors import our peat to use in horticulture.

We consider our Internet infrastructure among the most advanced in the world. Every Estonian school is connected to the Internet, including the most remote one-room schoolhouses. Over half our population uses the Internet. Do not be surprised to see a farmer surfing the Web with one hand while milking a cow with the other.

Because Estonia feels natural, not packaged or contrived, it is a popular vacation spot, especially with Finns. We are building shopping centers and roads at a breathtaking pace, but our traditional charm remains intact. A visit to Tallinn's Old Town, with its medieval architecture—some of the most well preserved in Europe—and excellent restaurants, is a must for any visitor. Be aware, however, that prices have risen significantly since we voted to join the European Union (EU). Inflation is a side effect of the economic reforms undertaken to qualify for EU membership.

Visit us to experience a wonderful combination of modernity and old-world charm. We welcome you!

Vital Statistics

Population	1,332,893
Capital	Tallinn
Area	17,462 square miles, slightly smaller than New Hampshire and Vermont combined
Government	Parliamentary republic
Living Standard	GDP = US $10,680 per capita
Natural Resources	Oil shale, peat, phosphorite, clay, limestone, sand, dolomite, arable land, sea mud
Agriculture	Vegetables, livestock and dairy products, fish
Industries	Engineering, electronics, wood and wood products, textiles, information technology, telecommunications
Climate	Maritime; wet, moderate winters and cool summers
Member of the EU?	Yes, since 2004
Currency	Estonian kroon (EEK); working toward converting to the euro by 2007

Correct Name	noun: Estonian(s) adjective: Estonian
Ethnic Makeup	Estonian 67.9%, Russian 25.6%, Ukrainian 2.1%, Belarusian 1.3%, Finn 0.9%, other 2.2%
Languages	Estonian (official) 67.3%, Russian 29.7%, other 2.3%, unknown 0.7%
Religions	Evangelical Lutheran 13.6%, Orthodox 12.8%, other Christian (including Methodist, Seventh-day Adventist, Roman Catholic, Pentecostal) 1.4%, unaffiliated 34.1%, other and unspecified 32%, none 6.1%

Meeting and Greeting

- Upon greeting and leaving, Estonians stand and shake hands firmly with both men and women, while maintaining eye contact.
- Men greet women first, and younger people greet elders first.
- Estonians rarely greet strangers in public.
- Estonians generally don't kiss one another in greeting, although many ethnic Russians do.

Names and Titles

- Don't use first names until your Estonian colleagues do so first.
- Always use the title on a person's business card, especially in written correspondence.

English	Estonian	Pronunciation
Mr.	*Härra*	(HARE-ah)
Mrs.	*Proua*	(PROW-ah)
Miss	*Preili*	(PREE-lee)

Language

During Soviet rule, Russian was the official language. Today, Estonian is the official language, and Estonians have reverted to using the Roman (Latin) alphabet.

After Estonia gained independence, many ethnic Russians stayed. To become Estonian citizens, they must pass an Estonian language exam—a requirement that has caused ongoing tension. Although many Estonians speak Russian, foreigners shouldn't use Russian to converse with them.

Some Estonians speak Finnish, and more understand it. Younger Estonians may speak English. English speakers should be aware that Estonian is a complex language that's difficult to learn.

Conversation

Estonians love to converse, but here are some tips to remember when conversing with them:

- Use a moderate tone when conversing; Estonians associate loud talking with drunkenness.
- Don't think Estonians are rude if they utter short exclamations or inject comments and questions when you're speaking.
- Avoid using sarcasm or irony.

Acceptable topics

- Estonia's historic and natural treasures: castles, cities, manor homes, islands, beaches, and forests
- Estonian Song Festival (*Laulupidu*) and Dance Festival (*Tantsupidu*)
- Estonian national basketball team

Unacceptable topics

- Personal topics: Never ask about someone's religion, job, political beliefs, and so on.

Topics that require sensitivity

- Russia (There's a long history of antagonism toward Russia.)
- The tensions between Estonians and the ethnic Russians who stayed after Estonian independence

Body Language

- Keep in mind that Estonians don't use many hand gestures when talking.
- Don't point with your index finger.
- The thumbs-up gesture is acceptable.

Phrases

Please note that the Estonian language uses many diacritical marks that aren't used in English. The Estonian phrases below have been simplified for North American readers.

English	Estonian	Pronunciation
Hello	*Tere*	(TEHR-eh)
Good day/afternoon	*Tere päevast*	(TEHR-eh PA-vast)
Good morning	*Tere hommikust*	(TEHR-eh HAW-mee-koost)
Good evening	*Tere õhtust*	(TEHR-eh EW-toost)
Please	*Palun*	(PAH-loon)
Thank you	*Tänan*	(TA-nahn)
You're welcome	*Võtke heaks*	(VEWT-ke hehks)
Yes	*Jaa*	(YAH)
No	*Ei*	(EH-ee)
Excuse me	*Vabandage*	(VAH-bahn-daj)
Goodbye	*Head aega*	(HEHD A-eh-ja)
Pleased to meet you	*Väga rõõmustav tuttavaks saada*	(VAH-gah ROW-ohm-uhs-tav TUT-tah-vahks SAH-ah-dah)
How are you?	*Kuidas käsi käib?*	(KOO-ee-dahs KA-see KA-eeb)

Dining

Estonian food is warm and hearty: meat, potatoes, root vegetables, mushrooms, bread, and soup. Visitors should also sample the many excellent fish dishes.

Typical Foods

Hernesupp: split pea soup (an Estonian favorite)

Mulgikapsad: pork and sauerkraut

Verivorstid: stew with cracked wheat and blood sausage

Kartulipannkoogid: potato pancakes, sometimes stuffed with mushrooms

Sült: jellied veal

Täidetud vasikarind: roast stuffed shoulder of veal

Rosolje: vinaigrette with herring and beets

Forrell: smoked trout

Braised goose stuffed with apples and plums (another Estonian favorite)

Fresh vegetables (rare out of season)

Horseradish sauce (very popular condiment)

Drinking

Ale, especially ale brewed on certain islands, is an Estonian specialty. Be warned: It's mild tasting, but very strong. Estonians also enjoy birch beer (fermented birch-tree sap), Saku (an excellent Estonian-brand beer), and *hõõgvein* (mulled wine).

Avoid any liquor that isn't in its original bottle or seems a suspiciously good bargain. Such liquor may contain methanol (wood alcohol), a poison that can cause blindness or even death.

Toasting

- Hosts usually make the first toast to express hospitality, gratitude, friendship, and good wishes. Guests should reciprocate with a toast to the hosts.
- The toast *teie terviseks* (TAY-ja TURV-es-ex) means "to your health," and Estonians use it at formal and informal occasions.
- The traditional toast *jätku leiba* (YAHT-koo LEE-bah) means "may your bread last," and Estonians use it at formal and informal occasions.
- Before beginning a meal, your hosts may wish you *head isu* (HAY-art EE-soo), which means "good appetite."
- Women may propose toasts.

Tipping

- Restaurants: The bill usually includes a 10 percent service charge, but feel free to include a small additional gratuity if the service is exceptional. If the bill doesn't include a service charge, tip 10 percent of the bill.
- Taxis: The fare may include a tip, but round up to the nearest EEK 10. If the fare doesn't include a tip, tip about 10 percent of the fare.
- Bellhops and porters: Tip the equivalent of one euro per bag.
- Doormen: Tip the equivalent of one euro.
- Hair stylists and barbers: Tip 10 to 15 percent of the bill.

Manners

- When dining with Estonians, wait for everyone to be served before eating, and wait for everyone to finish eating before leaving the table.
- During the meal, keep your hands above the table and be prepared to converse. Estonians appreciate conversation during meals.
- Asking for second helpings is a compliment to the cook. After the meal, always thank the cook.
- In public places or on public transportation, men offer their seats to women, and younger people offer their seats to their elders.
- Estonian men open doors for women; Estonian women expect the gesture.
- Always call before visiting an Estonian colleague. Never drop by unexpectedly.

Dress

Estonians dress similarly to Finns: conservatively and well. Even their children dress up when in public; they wear play clothing only at home. For their daily attire, Estonian women always wear makeup and often wear high heels with skirts or dresses, although younger women may favor slacks. Estonian men don't spend as much time on their appearance as women do, but they, too, never leave the house unless properly dressed.

- Never dress sloppily, even to make a quick trip to the market.
- Business attire is conservative and fairly formal for both men and women. Clothing and accessories should be of good quality, but brand names aren't important.
- For formal occasions, men wear suits and women wear cocktail dresses.
- Don't wear shorts, except on beaches.

Gifts

Estonians generally don't open gifts in front of the giver. The recipient should thank the giver sincerely and put the gift aside to open later.

Hostess Gifts

Consider giving

- Flowers (especially the first time you visit a home), in odd numbers only and except for white or yellow flowers (for funerals only): Flowers are also traditional birthday and graduation gifts for men and women.
- Wine or liqueur
- Candies or cakes

Don't give

- Potted plants

Business Gifts

Estonians don't expect business gifts, and they don't commonly give gifts at the end of negotiations.

You may give gifts, including at initial meetings. When you do, make sure they're small—more symbolic than valuable. For example, a pen or mug that features your company logo is appropriate.

Consider giving

- Gift items from your home region or country
- Recordings of music

Don't give

- Any food items
- Obviously expensive items (may be considered bribes)

Toilet Tips

English	Estonian
Restroom	*Tualett/WC*
Women's restroom	*Naistele*
Men's restroom	*Meestele*
Hot water (red dot)	*Kuum*
Cold water (blue dot)	*Külm*

Helpful Hints

- In summers, Estonian days are very long. Sunrise is at 3:00 AM and sunset is at midnight.
- Be aware that Estonians consider themselves Northern European. Never imply that they're Slavic.
- Don't spell *Tallinn*, Estonia's capital, with only one *n*. That's the Russian spelling, and it may arouse animosity.

Punctuality

Estonians expect punctuality for social and business occasions. They equate punctuality with reliability. If you're going to be late for an event or appointment, call with an explanation.

Corporate Culture

After gaining independence, Estonia has worked hard to achieve a free and open economy. In doing so, it has adopted a number of Western business models for strategic planning, accountability, and other processes—big changes from the Communist collectivist model.

In the Estonian workplace, employees have a great deal of autonomy. Supervisors give orders but let individuals decide the best way to accomplish a goal. Companies give credit to individuals; managers don't take credit for their subordinates' work.

In meetings, Estonians welcome debate. They view meetings as opportunities to explore different options and opinions. Subordinates feel comfortable sharing opinions with their managers and asking for feedback from them.

For more information about doing business in a formerly Communist country, see pages 17–18. Here are some additional tips:

- Try to have an established third party introduce you to potential colleagues and clients.
- Estonians prefer to make decisions by consensus.
- Estonians pride themselves for being hard working; many work overtime and weekends.
- Written agreements are essential to doing business in Estonia.
- Knowing some Estonian words and phrases will help you establish yourself, but it's not essential.
- Most businesses don't close for lunch.

Especially for Women

Every year, Estonian women's position in business improves. They still don't get paid as much as their male counterparts, but the salary gap is closing.

- While Estonians accept foreign businesswomen, it's important to act professionally and with reserve.
- Women can patronize bars and restaurants alone without harassment.
- After dark, don't walk alone; instead, take a taxi.
- Foreign women won't have a problem inviting Estonian men to business dinners.
- Women usually won't have trouble paying for a meal, but to be sure (and sophisticated), arrange payment with the wait staff beforehand.

Holidays and Festivals

January	New Year's Day (1)
	Epiphany (6)
February	Anniversary of the Tartu Peace Treaty (2)
	Independence Day (24)
March	Native Language Day (14)
March/April	Easter (Friday–Sunday)
May	Spring Day (1)
	Mother's Day (8)
May/June	Pentecost
June	National Flag Day (4)
	Day of Mourning and Commemoration (14)
	Victory Day (23)
	Jaanipäev (Saint John's Day)/Midsummer Day (24)
August	Day of Restoration of Independence (20)
November	All Souls' Day (2)
	Father's Day (13)
	Day of Declaration of Sovereignty (16)
December	Christmas (24–25)
	Boxing Day (26)

FINLAND
REPUBLIC OF FINLAND

Greetings from Finland

Greetings from the land of passion! While we Finns may lack expressive body language, we are certainly not without passion. We just display it differently than more physically demonstrative cultures. When we interact with you, we may not make eye contact, pat you on the back, or kiss and hug you. But as we say, "Even if we look at our shoes, we still like you."

One of our passions is coffee, and we drink a lot of it! Sharing coffee and lovely sweets with friends is an adored custom. Our coffee-drinking ritual is comparable to Japan's tea ceremony.

We are also passionate about our music, which is renowned for its quality and originality. Attend a concert in any Finnish town or city, big or small. In 2005, Musical America named Osmo Vänskä, a Finn and current music director of the Minnesota Orchestra, international conductor of the year. He is also music director of the Lahti Symphony Orchestra, a provincial Finnish orchestra that has won worldwide acclaim through its touring and its collection of groundbreaking Sibelius recordings.

We love our tango, which differs from the Argentine tango only in style. Each year, we elect a tango king and queen at the Seinäjoki Tango Festival. Sorrow, love, nature, and countryside are themes of our tango lyrics. We do not take the tango lightly. It belongs to us just as much as skiing and saunas. In 1997, we even issued a postage stamp commemorating the Finnish tango.

We fervently love our land. Our environment is one of the cleanest in the world, and we intend to keep it that way. We are Europe's seventh-largest country, and forests cover three-fourths of our land. Our winter nights are long, but the sun always shines in the summer.

We are devoted to equality for every person regardless of race, religion, ethnicity, or gender. In public places, you may hear announcements made in Finnish, Swedish, English, and Russian. While Russians are our largest immigrant group, we also have minorities of Somalis, Vietnamese, and Iraqis.

We refer to ourselves as Nordic; however, Finland is not a Scandinavian country. We will not get angry if you call us Scandinavian, but we may correct you politely.

We were never part of the Soviet bloc, but we are proud to have been the bridge between the Soviet Union and the West during the Cold War. In the 1990s, however, we fell into a recession when the Soviet empire collapsed. The Soviet Union had been our primary trade partner, and its demise left us facing an economic slump and a sudden rise in unemployment.

These events challenged our generous social security payments, and the pressure on our government finances was almost intolerable. Fortunately, the European Union assisted us, and today our economy is recovering nicely.

While we have provided cell phones to the world, we are not big talkers. We are quiet, simple, and reserved people. We appreciate others respecting our privacy. A cottage by a lake and a sauna to relax in—and maybe a bit of vodka—are all we need to make us happy.

If you love art or architecture, you will find Helsinki a paradise. If you love the outdoors, ski across our vast frozen lakes, hike in our amazing forests, visit our medieval castles, then relax in a sauna. We will provide the fragrant birch branches, the vodka, and, if necessary, a towel.

Do not come to Finland looking for fast food or fast friendships. Accept an invitation to a sauna or coffee party, and let us get to know you.

Vital Statistics

Population	5,223,442
Capital	Helsinki
Area	130,559 square miles, slightly smaller than Montana
Living Standard	GDP = US $37,550 per capita
Government	Republic
Natural Resources	Timber, iron ore, copper, lead, zinc, chromite, nickel, gold, silver, limestone
Agriculture	Barley, wheat, sugar beets, potatoes, dairy cattle, fish
Industries	Metal and metal products, electronics, machinery and scientific instruments, shipbuilding, pulp and paper, foodstuffs, chemicals, textiles, clothing
Climate	Cold; potentially subarctic but comparatively mild because of moderating influence of the North Atlantic Current, Baltic Sea, and numerous lakes
Member of the EU?	Yes, since 1995
Currency	Euro (€)

The People	
Correct Name	noun: Finn(s) adjective: Finnish
Ethnic Makeup	Finnish 93.4%, Swedish 5.7%, Russian 0.4%, Estonian 0.2%, Roma 0.2%, Sami 0.1%
Languages	Finnish 92% (official), Swedish 5.6% (official), small Sami- and Russian-speaking minorities
Religions	Lutheran National Church 84.2%, Finnish Orthodox Church 1.1%, other Christian 1.1%, other 0.1%, none 13.5%

Meeting and Greeting

- Finns shake hands firmly, with eye contact. Even children shake guests' hands upon meeting.
- Upon introduction, Finns say their first and last names while shaking hands. Foreigners should do so as well.
- The common Finnish greeting *Hyvää päivää* (HOO-vah PIE-vah) means "have a good day."

Names and Titles

- Finns commonly use first names during a first meeting, but they're aware of status.
- In written correspondence, Finns always use academic and professional titles instead of *Mr.*, *Mrs.*, or *Miss*.
    - Examples: Professor Nieminen
    - General Director Jokela
- Foreigners may use *Mr.*, *Mrs.*, or *Miss*, but Finns appreciate attempts to use *Herra/Rouva/Neiti*.

English	Finnish	Pronunciation
Mr.	*Herra*	(HAIR-rah)
Mrs.	*Rouva*	(ROW-vah)
Miss	*Neiti*	(NAY-tee)

Language

Although Finns are culturally similar to Scandinavians, Finnish differs distinctly from the Scandinavian languages. Most Finns are bilingual; many speak English.

Conversation

Finns tend to be quiet, reserved, unemotional, and sincere. They value their privacy—and silence. Never strike up a conversation with a stranger. Finns don't like invasions of privacy.

Acceptable topics
- Finland's culture and history
- Sports, especially skiing and ice hockey
- Music
- Travel

Unacceptable topics
- Any topic that implies Finland is the same as other Nordic countries
- Personal topics: religion, job, political party, and so on

Topics that require sensitivity
- Finland's relationship with the Soviet Union during the Cold War

Body Language

Although Finns' reserved body language is famous, they're nonetheless very friendly to foreigners.
- Don't kiss, hug, or touch in public. Finns don't— even among very close friends and relatives.
- Men remove their hats when meeting or talking and when entering an elevator, church, or home.
- Finns maintain eye contact when conversing.

In a country where body language is extremely reserved, the tango has captured Finns' bodies and souls since the 1930s. Finland has more than two thousand tango dance halls that men and women of all ages patronize.

Unlike the hot and heavy Latin dance, the *Tango Finlandia* is more like a waltz. The music is sad and melancholy, featuring songs about lost love. Finns would find an upbeat tango unthinkable. Dance halls flash "ladies' choice" or "men's choice" signs to help the Finns overcome their shyness.

Phrases

English	Finnish	Pronunciation
Good morning	*Hyvää huomenta*	(hoo-VAH WHO-o-men-tuh)
Good afternoon	*Hyvää ilta päivää*	(hoo-VAH EEL-tuh PIE-vah)
Good evening	*Hyvää iltaa*	(hoo-VAH EEL-taa)
Please	No Finnish equivalent—*pyydän* means "I ask"	(POOH-dahn)
Thank you	*Kiitos*	(KEY-tohs)
You're welcome	*Ole hyvä*	(OH-leh hoo-VAH)
Yes	*Kyllä*	(KEWL-lah)
No	*Ei*	ay (rhymes with *day*)
Excuse me	*Anteeksi*	(AHN-take-see)
Goodbye	*Näkemiin*	(KNACK-eh-meen)
How are you? (formal)	*Kuinka voitte?*	(KWIN-kah VOYT-teh)
How are you? (informal)	*Kuinka voit?*	(KWIN-kah voyt)
Pleased to meet you	*Hauska tavata*	(HOW-skuh TAH-vuh-tah)

Dining

Finnish cuisine combines traditional fare with modern, continental-style cooking.

Typical Foods

Voileipäpöytä: cold table or smorgasbord
Kesäkeitto: summer vegetable soup
Karjalanpiirakka: rye pastry with rice
Perunapiirakka: rye pastry with mashed potatoes
Merimiespihvi: beef chunks with onion, potatoes, and beer (family dish)
Poronliha: reindeer meat
Lohi: salmon
Kiisseli: fruit pudding
Rahkapiirakka: a dessert similar to cheesecake
Berries and whipped cream (most popular dessert)
Liver
Mushrooms
Herring
Soups, both meat and fish

Note: Many dairy products are lactose free. Roughly a quarter of Finns are lactose intolerant.

Drinking

- Finns love *sahti* (home-brewed beer), and they drink a lot of home-distilled hard liquor. They also often drink *kalja* (beer) or *olut* (low-alcohol beer).
- At home, Finns serve milk, water, and *sahti* with meals.
- At dinner parties, vodka, *kalja*, and aquavit (a clear, hard liquor) are favorite drinks. Vodka, however, is Finns' beverage of choice.
- *Marskin ryyppy* are *snaps* (shots) of aquavit or *Koskenkorva* (a popular brand of unspiced vodka), filled to the rim.
- Finns drink *viini* (wine) occasionally, but the beverage is becoming more popular as contact with the rest of Europe increases.
- *Marjalikööri* (berry), *mesimarja* (arctic bramble) and *lakka* (cloudberry) liqueurs are unique to Finland. Make sure you try them.

> Finns are among the biggest coffee drinkers in the world, and coffee plays a large role in their entertaining. They serve coffee (always in china cups) between meals or after dinner, with cookies and cakes.
>
> Serving the coffee is ceremonial, and you should never refuse a cup (although you may request tea). When you entertain Finnish guests, always serve them good-quality coffee in china cups.

Toasting

- Finns generally make toasts with *snaps* of vodka, aquavit, or *Koskenkorva*.
- The informal toast *kippis* (KEEP-pees) means "cheers." The popular Swedish toast *skål* (skohl) means the same thing.
- The formal toast *maljanne* (MAHL-ya-neh) means "your glass," and *terveydeksi* (TER-veh-oo-deck-see) is a formal toast used in business settings that means "to your health."
- Don't drink until your host proposes a toast.
- A guest should propose a toast to the host or hostess.
- It's acceptable for women to propose toasts.

Tipping

Tipping isn't widespread; most bills include a service charge.

- Restaurants: The bill almost always includes a 15 percent service charge; you can leave small change as an additional gratuity for exceptional service. If the bill doesn't include a service charge, leave a 10 to 15 percent tip.
- Taxis: A tip is optional. If you choose to tip, round up the fare.
- Bellhops and porters: Tip one euro per bag.
- Restroom attendants, hair stylists, and ushers don't require a tip.

Manners

- Finns behave very informally at home, and an invitation to a Finnish home is a great honor—but don't ask for a tour. Finns consider the request impolite.
- Don't eat anything with your fingers, except crayfish and shrimp.
- Don't offer to share your food or your beverage with anyone.
- Finns consider it bad luck to pass salt from hand to hand. Set the shaker on the table and let the next person pick it up.
- Take second helpings when offered, but know that Finns consider it rude not to eat all the food on your plate.
- There may be little or no conversation during a meal, but conversation may continue for an hour or two after dinner.
- Compliment the hostess, and thank her before saying goodbye to other guests.
- To beckon wait staff, wave your hand and make eye contact.
- Speak quietly in restaurants.
- Expect that restaurant hosts may seat strangers at your table if the restaurant is crowded (but not in upscale establishments). You don't need to talk to them. In fact, they may consider it an invasion of privacy if you do.
- Finns never split the bill at restaurants. The person who extended the invitation pays the bill.
- Don't show emotion in public.
- Don't eat while walking on the street.

Dress

Finnish fashion is of a very high standard. Finns dress conservatively and fairly formally, and they avoid wearing bright colors.

- For business, dress isn't strictly formal. The degree of formality depends on the industry and business. In general, women wear stylish suits. Men wear white or colored shirts with suits or sport coats. In summer, foreign men may remove jackets if Finnish colleagues remove theirs. (Finns often don't wear jackets in summer.)
- For casual occasions, dress is always smart casual. (See page 45.) Fashionable, pressed jeans are appropriate for very informal occasions.
- For formal occasions, men wear dark suits (Finns seldom wear tuxedos), and women wear cocktail dresses.
- Except in summer, better restaurants require jackets and ties.
- If visiting in the winter, bring very warm clothing. If visiting in the summer, bring lightweight clothing as well as a sweater, raincoat, and insect repellent.

Gifts

Finns open gifts upon receipt.

Hostess Gifts

Consider giving
- Cut flowers in odd numbers only, except for white or yellow flowers (for funerals only): Flowers are for sale throughout the country, and tulips are a Finnish favorite. You can also send flowers as a thank-you gift.
- Wine
- Chocolates

Don't give
- Potted plants

Business Gifts

Finns don't normally exchange gifts at business meetings, but you may exchange small gifts at the successful conclusion of negotiations. Giving a Christmas gift to a Finnish colleague is acceptable but not expected.

Consider giving

- Books
- Cognac and liquor (very expensive in Finland)
- Local/national gifts from your home country
- Recordings of music
- Art

Don't give

- Any excessively expensive items (may be considered bribes)

Toilet Tips	
English	**Finnish**
Restroom	*WC*
Women's restroom	*Naiset*
Men's restroom	*Miehet*
Hot water	*Kuuma vesi*
Cold water	*Kylmä vesi*

Helpful Hints

- Observe all hiking, fishing, and hunting rules.
- Malls, grocery stores, and department stores are closed on Sundays.
- Grocery stores close at 6:00 PM on Saturdays.
- Don't call Sami people *Lapps*, which is incorrect and offensive.
- Don't lump Finns with Swedes and Norwegians. Also, just because someone speaks Sami, Norwegian, or Swedish doesn't mean that he or she isn't Finnish.

Punctuality

Finns expect punctuality for business and social occasions. Call with an explanation if you're delayed.

Corporate Culture

Structure
The managing director makes the decisions.

Meetings
- Departments hold meetings to convey ideas to managers.
- Finns don't make small talk in meetings; they proceed directly to business.
- Know that two- to three-minute pauses are common; don't interrupt silence.

Communication
- Most Finns speak English, so you shouldn't need an interpreter.
- It's acceptable to call a Finnish colleague at home for important business.

Business Cards
- Finns exchange business cards upon meeting.

Be Aware
- Finland is a liberal society without class distinctions. Bricklayers and managers may socialize.
- Doing business in Finland takes time and patience.
- Finns have rigorous work and play ethics: they work at work, play at home.
- Finns strongly support labor unions.
- On days preceding holidays, most businesses close at 1:00 PM.

Socializing
- Finns do most business entertaining in restaurants. Since restaurants are expensive in Finland, know that an invitation to a restaurant means your hosts take you seriously.
- Your Finnish colleagues may invite you to a *voileipapöyta* (smorgasbord), a buffet-style meal that's popular for business. At a smorgasbord, take cold foods first, followed by hot, then the dessert. Once you have taken food from the tray, be sure to eat all of it.
- Business breakfasts aren't common. Finns commonly discuss business over lunch.

- A sauna may precede or follow a business lunch, but it's preferable to sauna before lunch. A sauna may also precede or follow dinner.
- Finns discuss business only after coffee—never during dinner.
- Finns often include spouses in business dinners, but they don't discuss business when spouses are present.
- Finns often include their children in dinner parties.

Especially for Women

Finns have a long tradition of treating women as equals to men in both business and at home. In 1906, Finland was the first European country to grant women the right to vote, and in 2000, Finland elected its first female president, Tarja Halonen. Today, 70 percent of women work outside the home.

Sauna Etiquette

Taking saunas is a venerated Finnish tradition, and most businesspeople are invited to a sauna at some point in their visit. Here are some tips for taking saunas gracefully:

- There are separate saunas for men and women.
- All Finns take a sauna in the nude, but you don't have to (although Finns will consider it strange if you don't). You'll be too hot in a bathing suit, but you may wrap a towel around yourself.
- Shower before entering the sauna.
- Allow the host to throw water on the hot rocks.
- Feel free to leave when you've had enough. Don't overdo it.
- Don't chat while in the sauna. It's a quiet place. (Although Finns may discuss business.)
- Finns generally serve beer, sausage, bread, and cheese during and after the sauna.
- The host may invite a guest to sit in a sauna with him or her. This is a special honor; never refuse except for health reasons.

- Foreign businesswomen may invite Finnish men to dinner and pay for the meal without difficulty.
- Women can safely go to bars or restaurants alone, but after dark women should take a taxi.

Holidays and Festivals

January	New Year's Day (1)
	Epiphany (6)
March/April	Easter (Friday–Monday)
April	May Day Eve—not an official holiday but widely observed (30)
April/May	Feast of the Ascension (40 days after Easter)
May	May Day (1)
May/June	Whitsunday (Pentecost) and Whitmonday (day after Pentecost)
June	*Juhannus* (Midsummer's Eve and Day) (Friday and Saturday between June 19 and 26)
October/November	All Saints' Day (Saturday between October 31 and November 6)
December	Independence Day (6)
	Christmas (24–25)
	Boxing Day (26)

FRANCE
FRENCH REPUBLIC

Greetings from France

Greetings from the land of elegance, style, and impeccable taste.

It may not be politically correct, but we know we are the most civilized people in the world. In anything that matters—fashion, art, music, literature, food, wine, perfume, architecture, politics—we are experts. Everyone else is a dilettante.

We are snobs about where we shop, eat, play, dance, holiday, even worship (that is, the 10 percent of us who do worship). We are comfortable with our snobbery because we base it upon having good taste rather than inherited wealth.

Our behavior is formal and rigid. Always remember that *etiquette* is a French word, and the word *casual* is not in our vocabulary. We have strict codes and established order for everything (established, of course, by us)—except driving, parking, smoking, and where men urinate. (Foreigners never cease to be amazed by where and in front of whom French men will urinate.) Many of our foreign neighbors think we are not just bad drivers—we are criminally dangerous drivers.

It is true we can be rude, Parisians especially. When the situation demands it, we feel rudeness is our obligation. According to our strict code, certain things are not done in public—such as asking for catsup. The French parliament even once debated whether a gentleman in a *pissoir* (a public urinal located on the street) should lift his hat to a female passerby.

We are traditionalists, and we resist outside influences that threaten our culture. We worry that American products and values are seducing our young people; McDonald's (*chez McDo*) has proliferated too well for our comfort.

At the same time, however, we find current products and trends irresistible. We love the latest clothing, films, and gadgets. We have given the world not just wine, poetry, and philosophy, but also groundbreaking medical and pharmaceutical research, telecommunications, software, and space technology.

Today, we face several new challenges. Many of us are not enthusiastic about the European Union (EU). In a referendum vote in 2005, we voted against the proposed EU constitution, even though our former president, Valéry Giscard d'Estaing, chaired the committee that drafted it. We have, however, accepted the concept of the EU because it is in our self-interest to do so.

We are working hard to maintain the quality of life we hold dear for all our citizens. While we cherish our culture, we have tried to welcome people of all races and religions into our country. Compared to other European countries, our population has the largest percentage of Muslims and the most Jews.

In the immediate postwar period, France was the only

> The history and friendship between the United States and France goes back over two hundred years. The French not only gave the United States the Statue of Liberty, but they also helped Americans gain independence. Both cultures share the same values: freedom and respect for the individual—however, just because the two countries are good friends doesn't mean they have to always agree.

European nation to encourage permanent immigration. We have welcomed immigrants, but we do not think it is too much to ask that the people who want to live in France *become* French. Immigrants must abandon their cultures and assimilate completely.

We are impatient with American visitors who insist on speaking English— loudly—and patronize only American restaurants. If you stop one of us on the street and demand, "Where's the Louvre?" we probably will not become friends. But if you learn a little about our culture and history, we will soon find common ground.

Vital Statistics

Population	60,656,178
Capital	Paris
Area	211,200 square miles, slightly less than twice the size of Colorado
Government	Republic
Living Standard	GDP = US $37,500 per capita
Natural Resources	Coal, iron ore, bauxite, zinc, potash, uranium, feldspar, fluorospar, gypsum, arsenic, fish, timber
Agriculture	Wheat, cereals, sugar beets, potatoes, wine grapes, beef, dairy products, fish

Vital Statistics (*cont.*)	
Industries	Machinery, chemicals, automobiles, metallurgy, aircraft, electronics, textiles, food processing, tourism
Climate	Generally cool winters and mild summers, but mild winters and hot summers along the Mediterranean; occasional strong, cold, dry, north-to-northwesterly wind
Member of the EU?	Yes, an original member from 1967
Currency	Euro (€)

The People	
Correct Name	nouns: French, Frenchmen, Frenchwomen adjective: French
Ethnic Makeup	Celtic and Latin with Teutonic, Slavic, North African, Indochinese, Basque minorities
Languages	French (official) 100%; rapidly declining regional dialects and languages (Provençal, Breton, Alsatian, Corsican, Catalan, Basque, Flemish)
Religions	Roman Catholic 83%–88%, Protestant 2%, Jewish 1%, Muslim 5%–10%, unaffiliated 4%

Meeting and Greeting

- The French shake hands with everyone. They don't start work until those who haven't seen one another that day shake hands. It's extremely bad manners, however, to shake hands with the same person twice on one day.
- A handshake may be quick with a light grip.
- A man may initiate a handshake with a woman.
- Frenchmen may kiss women's hands; accept this gesture graciously. Foreign men, however, should never kiss a woman's hand.
- The French kiss very formally: left cheek, right cheek, left cheek. Kissing is between family and close friends only.
- If you don't speak French, approach strangers with *"Bonjour! Parlez-vous anglais?"* (bone-ZHOOR PAHR-lay voo ahn-GLAY). Don't begin by speaking English, which the French consider rude.

Names and Titles

English	French	Pronunciation
Mr.	*Monsieur*	(meh-SYEUR)
Mrs.	*Madame*	(mah-DAHM)
Miss	*Mademoiselle*	(mahd-mwah-ZEHL)

- The French usually use first names only with close friends and family.
- Colleagues of the same rank generally use first names in private, but they always use last names in public. In any relationship, let the more senior person (in rank or age) suggest the use of first names.
- Address people as *Monsieur/Madame/Mademoiselle* without adding last names.
- Use *Madame* for all women, married or single, age eighteen or older (except for waitresses, whom the French address as *Mademoiselle*).
- Academic and professional titles are very important to the French, and they'll expect you to know them and use them properly. Here are some common examples:

English	French	Pronunciation
University professor	*Madame la Professeur*	(mah-DAHM la pro-fess-YOO)
Lawyer	*Maître*	(MEH-tehr)
PhD	*Monsieur le Docteur*	(meh-SYEUR leh dock-TYOO)
MD	*Docteur*	(dock-TYOO)

Language

No nation has fought harder to preserve its language than France. An entire academy works to ensure the French language's purity, ruthlessly plucking out new words. The Académie Française recently decided that the proper French word for *e-mail* is *courriel*.

Although French is the official language, many French people speak English. Unless your French is perfect, use it only for greetings, toasts, and occasional phrases. When speaking French, don't be offended if someone corrects your grammar or pronunciation.

When writing, be sure your grammar and usage are perfect. The French view proper writing as a sign of education and breeding.

Conversation

- Begin every conversation with strangers—salespeople, police officers, tour guides, and so on—with *bonjour* (bone-ZHOOR). It's rude to start talking without a greeting.
- The French don't tell or like to hear jokes. They prefer intelligent and satirical humor and appreciate funny stories about real-life situations.
- The French love a good debate to show off their logic skills and knowledge. To them, debate is an art form. They value intelligence in all matters. Join in only if you are knowledgeable.
- The French may interrupt, especially during a spirited conversation about history and politics. This isn't considered rude; rather, it shows their interest and engagement.
- The French use *vous*—the formal *you*—even after a twenty-year relationship. In any relationship, let the more senior person (in rank or age) suggest the use of *tu*, the informal *you*.

Acceptable topics
- Art
- Travel
- History (Brush up on your history before your visit.)

> Shortly after national hero Charles de Gaulle's death, Noel Coward was asked what he thought God and de Gaulle would talk about. Coward replied, "That depends on how good God's French is."

Unacceptable topics
- Personal issues (Never violate the French people's privacy!)
  * Occupation
  * Salary
  * Age
  * Marital status
  * Children
  * Health
- Criticisms of Napoleon

Topics that require sensitivity
- World War II
- The Nazi occupation
- Politics: Never ask about a person's political leanings, or how he or she voted.

Body Language

The French invented body language. Their eyes, hands, lips, and bodies express a full range of emotions. They are at ease with their bodies. Sex is part of life, and sex appeal and seduction are art forms.

- The French tend to stand close to one another, and may even touch your shoulder or pat your arm.
- The French don't smile at strangers and never smile unless they mean it. (They don't consider a smile a sign of approval or a greeting.)
- Stand or sit up straight. The French consider good posture a sign of breeding.
- Maintain eye contact.
- Sneeze or blow your nose as quietly as possible, using a handkerchief or tissue. If possible, leave the room.
- Don't slap your open palm over a closed fist. The French consider the gesture vulgar.
- The "okay" sign (curling your index finger and thumb to make a circle) means "useless" or "zero."
- Point only with your whole hand, never your index finger.

Phrases

English	French	Pronunciation
Good morning/day/ afternoon	*Bonjour*	(bone-ZHOOR)
Good evening	*Bon soir*	(bone-SWAR)
Please	*S'il vous plaît*	(seel voo PLEH)
Thank you	*Merci*	(mare-SEE)
You're welcome	*De rien*	(duh ry-EHN)
Yes	*Oui*	(wee)
No	*Non*	(no)
Excuse me	*Pardon*	(par-DOHN)
Goodbye	*Au revoir*	(o reh-VWAHR)
How are you?	*Comment allez-vous?*	(kom-oh-tah-lay-VOO)
Pleased to meet you	*Enchanté*	(ahn-shahn-TAY)

Dining

French food is not only fresh and well prepared, but also eye appealing. The French believe enjoying food is a spiritual experience. Watch how much time a shopkeeper will take to wrap a *tarte* or sweet. The box and the ribbon are gorgeous, and they are handled with flair.

Despite their rich diet (*créme fraîche*, butter, cheese, and extravagant sauces), French obesity rates are far lower than Americans'. The French credit their trimness to regular sit-down meals made from fresh ingredients. With this said, however, fast food is becoming more common as the French eat on the run—and obesity rates are climbing proportionally.

Always give proper respect and attention to your food and wine (an art in France). But don't overindulge in either.

Typical Foods
Patisseries (pastries) and *pain* (bread)
Vin (wine) and *fromage* (cheese)
Pâté: goose and/or duck paste
Quiche: pastry filled with bacon, eggs, cream, and cheese
Crêpes: paper-thin pancakes with filling
Escargots: snails in garlic butter
Bouillabaisse: seafood stew
Omelette: eggs fried with meat, vegetables, and cheese
Les Truffes: truffles
Horse meat: a delicacy served as a steak

Drinking

Only Luxembourgers drink more than the French. Beer, whiskey, and—of course—wine are all popular. The French believe they have the best wine in the world.

- Don't ask for a martini or whiskey before dinner—the French believe they numb the palate.
- The French may offer Pernod (a brand name of pastis, a licorice-flavored liqueur), kir, champagne, or vermouth before dinner. They always serve wine with meals (along with mineral water).
- The French often serve cognac, Grand Marnier, or other liqueurs after dinner. They serve fruit juice at the end of formal dinners.

Toasting

- The toast *a votre santé* (ah VO-truh sahn-TAY) means "to your health," and the French use it at formal and informal occasions.
- The host offers the first toast.
- Before drinking, wait until everyone has been served and the toast has been given.
- It's acceptable for women to propose toasts.

Tipping

- Restaurants: The bill usually includes a 10 to 15 percent service charge (*service compris*). You can leave small change on the table as an additional gratuity for exceptional service. If the bill doesn't include a service charge (*service non compris*), leave a 10 to 15 percent tip. If you're unsure whether a bill includes a tip, ask.
- Taxis: Tip 10 percent of the fare.
- Bellhops and porters: Tip one euro per bag. (Airport and railway porters charge by the item.)
- Restroom attendants: A sign stating a suggested tip is usually posted.
- Hair stylists and barbers: Tip 10 percent of the bill. Tip the shampoo person one euro.

Manners

The French are traditional, formal, and appreciate good manners.
- The French enter a room and are seated by rank.
- The French cut and eat almost all food with a knife and fork, but don't use these utensils to cut your salad. Fold your salad onto your fork with your knife. Also, never cut bread; break bread with your fingers.
- The French use bread to eat gravy and to help push food onto the fork (but not at a formal restaurant or party). They don't usually use bread plates. Put bread on the table next to your dinner plate above your fork.
- Never eat fruit whole; peel and slice it before eating. (Remember, use your fork and knife as much as possible.)
- Cut cheese vertically. Don't cut off the point.
- To signal that you'd like more food, leave your knife and fork open on your plate (see illustration on page 37).

- Eat all the food on your plate. The French consider leaving food on your plate impolite.
- Don't add salt or pepper to your food, and don't ask for condiments. Doing so implies the food isn't properly seasoned.
- The spoon and fork above the plate are for dessert.
- If you don't care for more wine, leave your wineglass almost full.
- Don't ask for more wine; it's the host's responsibility to make sure the guests are served. If you're the host, keep an eye on your guests' glasses and offer wine accordingly.
- Don't smoke between courses.
- Conversation is a vital part of dinner in France. Be prepared to converse.
- The modern way to beckon a waiter is to quietly say, "*Monsieur*" or "*S'il vous plaît*" rather than "*Garçon.*" Say "*Mademoiselle*" to summon a waitress.
- Always speak in a moderate tone, and always behave graciously.
- Close doors behind you when entering or leaving a room.

Dress

The French are the world's fashion leaders. Dress is conservative and understated, but always elegant and fashionable. Be clean and well dressed at all times.

- For business, men may wear colored, white, or striped shirts with conservative suits. Women should dress well but conservatively for business meetings. In general, women wear skirts or dresses more often than slacks.
- Men should keep suit coats on in offices and restaurants.
- For most formal occasions, men wear dark suits, and women wear cocktail dresses. Invitations will indicate whether black tie is necessary.
- Dress jeans are fine for weekends or the country; otherwise, the French wear high-style casual attire (high-quality designer clothing that's well fitted and tastefully coordinated and accessorized).
- Casual or informal occasions can mean a coat and tie for men, and better restaurants require men to wear a coat and tie. If you're unsure what attire is appropriate, ask a knowledgeable colleague.
- Casual attire is inappropriate in French cities.
- You may change into a swimsuit on the beach by holding a towel around yourself. Be aware, though: nude and topless bathers are common.

Gifts

The French usually open gifts upon receipt, but they may not open them if people other than the giver are present.

Give high-quality gifts that are elegant or unique (or both). Gifts should have intellectual content and be aesthetically pleasing. They should be beautifully wrapped.

Hostess Gifts

- Always bring a small gift for the hostess when invited to someone's home.
- A hostess probably won't unwrap a gift immediately (unless no other guests are present or expected).
- Always send a handwritten thank-you note the day after a dinner party. Consider sending it by messenger with flowers or a basket of fruit.

Consider giving
- Candy
- Cookies
- Cakes
- Flowers, except mums (for funerals only): If possible, send flowers the morning of the party (a popular gesture in Paris).

Don't give
- Gifts in odd numbers, especially thirteen
- Wine, unless it's of exceptional quality: The French pride themselves on their wine cellars and usually want to choose the wine themselves.

Business Gifts

- You may exchange small business gifts, but usually not at the first meeting.
- It's acceptable, but not expected, to give a Christmas gift to a French colleague.
- Never send a business gift for a French colleague to his or her home.
- Enclose a personal note—not a business card—with your gift.

Consider giving
- Recordings of music
- Art
- Books
- Office accessories

Don't give

- Items that feature your company's logo (The French consider such gifts garish.)

Toilet Tips	
English	**French**
Restroom	*Toilettes/WC*
Women's restroom	*Dames/Femmes*
Men's restroom	*Messieurs/Hommes*
Hot water	*Eau chaude*
Cold water	*Eau froide*

Helpful Hints

- Show knowledge of history, politics, and French culture.
- Don't expect a thank-you when you compliment someone. The French may appreciate compliments, but they usually receive them with denial.
- Don't select fruit or vegetables from stands. The vendor serves you. Vendors are likely to become angry if you touch their produce.
- The French consider rank more important than wealth.
- Tread lightly unless you're certain of the proper behavior, speech, or action. Etiquette mistakes are culturally unacceptable.
- Take the opportunity to shop in France—it's not cheap, but it's definitely an experience.
- The French regard normal body odor as natural. To them, body odors are sensuous; they prefer them to the scent of soap. They view Americans' obsession with hygiene as unhealthy and abnormal.
- Physical humor is popular. The French love the humor of Jerry Lewis and Buster Keaton. Frenchman Marcel Marceau made clowning and miming internationally famous.
- The French know how to focus on what they consider to be the good things in life. They celebrate holidays with verve but ignore the duties and burdens of religion.

Punctuality

The French consider punctuality a sign of courtesy. Call with an explanation if you're delayed.

Arrive fifteen minutes late for a house party, but be on time at a restaurant.

Corporate Culture

Structure

French business organization is modeled after the military. Organizations are highly centralized with a powerful chief executive, who's never wrong and never accepts the blame for anything.

Most companies have a vertical structure with a rigid chain of command, and middle management is multilayered. Everyone follows set rules and procedures, and the team approach among different ranks is rare. Companies admire technical competence and encourage rivalry and competition. They highly value loyalty; as a result, job-hopping is uncommon.

Employees complete tasks through a network of personal relationships and alliances. This subculture is flexible, informal, and energized to get the job done. Spontaneity and creativity take place at lower levels among peers who trust one another.

Meetings

Meetings generally have an established format and a detailed agenda. They're an opportunity for the boss to assert authority, and their purpose is to brief or coordinate and to clarify issues, not to discuss or debate—although participants sometimes offer suggestions.

The French get down to business quickly but make decisions slowly and only after much deliberation. They give presentations with great style and drama. Yours should be well prepared, well written, comprehensive, and informative, and presented in a formal, rational, and professional style that appeals to the intellect.

Communication

- Many French people speak and understand English, so an interpreter probably won't be necessary. Nevertheless, it's always a good idea to check ahead of time.

- Communications exist on two levels: formal and informal, corresponding respectively to the hierarchy and the working subculture.
- In a debate, respond with calm logic. Don't get emotional or irrational.
- Don't call a French businessperson at home except in an emergency.

Business Cards
- Print business cards in English or French. Include any academic degrees and/or professional titles.
- Carry a good supply of business cards. The French exchange them often.
- Give business cards to the receptionist or secretary upon arrival.
- Give business cards properly to each person you meet. (See pages 54–55.)

Be Aware
- There are close links between government and business; both public and private sectors are strong.
- Business people tend to be formal and conservative, and business relationships are proper, orderly, and professional. Don't discuss your personal life with French businesspeople. The French keep their personal lives separate from their business relationships.
- The French are astute economic planners, and that quality carries over into business, where economic plans are detailed and far reaching.
- Make appointments at least two weeks in advance.

Socializing
- The French do most business entertaining in restaurants.
- Reservations are necessary for most restaurants.
- The French still consider lunch a private time; however, the business lunch is becoming more common. (Business breakfasts are still rare.)
- Business lunches are formal and include appetizers, a main course, cheese, dessert, and coffee.
- The French consider dinner a social occasion and a time to enjoy good food, wine, and conversation. They don't like to discuss business during dinner. Be prepared to discuss French culture, heritage, and government.
- Senior managers socialize only with those of equivalent status.
- The French don't include spouses in business lunches; however, they may include spouses in business dinners.

Especially for Women

An increasing number of women in France hold management jobs in retail and service sectors, law, finance, and personnel; however, considerable bias exists toward women in industry. Women in management positions are better accepted in the major cities than in the provinces.

- The French generally accept foreign business-women, although they may flirt with them on occasion.
- A foreign woman may invite a Frenchman to a business lunch or dinner and shouldn't have a problem paying the bill.

> Frenchwomen are chic and elegant, and their great looks don't diminish as they age. Each dresses and coifs herself impeccably to her last day. Frenchwomen demand equal pay and equal access to jobs and education, and they're not shy about being sensual.

- Women should inquire about an area's safety before making reservations at a hotel or restaurant.
- After dark, women should avoid using the Paris Metro and take a taxi instead.
- Women should be careful of petty theft, especially in Paris.

Holidays and Festivals

January	New Year's Day (1)
March/April	Easter (Friday–Monday)
April/May	Feast of the Ascension (40 days after Easter)
May	May Day (1) V-E Day (8)
May/June	Whitsunday (Pentecost) and Whitmonday (day after Pentecost)
July	Bastille Day (14)
August	Feast of the Assumption (15)
November	All Saints' Day (1) Armistice Day (11)
December	Christmas (24–26)

GERMANY
FEDERAL REPUBLIC OF GERMANY

Greetings from Germany

Greetings from the land of order, punctuality, diligence, cleanliness, and thoroughness. We Germans believe that tolerance is a duty, and we have a strong sense of community and social conscience as well as a great desire to belong.

We hate breaking rules. We will not cross even empty streets against the light. We are thrifty, hard working, and industrious. Our clocks tell correct time, and we expect people to be on time, too. Please respect our sense of order. We find knowing exactly what is expected very relaxing.

While we are known for our orderliness and strictness, we have a fun side, too. We have great enthusiasm for our cultural heritage. We celebrate our customs by preparing specific dishes, wearing traditional costumes, and playing special music. We love to celebrate at our famous beer gardens (often thousands of us at a time). In the summer, visiting beer gardens is a wonderful way to escape the city and enjoy the weather and one another.

We believe it is important to strive for perfection in all areas of business and private life. As a foreigner, you may encounter only our public life, since we keep our public and private lives very separate. Do not expect quick friendships. Once we offer friendship, however, you will find us warm, sincere, and fun to be with. We will maintain friendships much longer than in societies that are less committed to nurturing relationships.

While we love our country, we frown upon nationalism. Regionalism is very strong in Germany. People tend to be more loyal to their region than their country. With that said, however, we do take pride in being German. We are so proud of our language and want to keep it vibrant and useful. Spelling reform (*Rechtschreibreform*) has been a hot topic here.

We also fiercely protect our environment and recycle religiously. Our woodlands and forests cover more than 30 percent of our land. Their beauty is awesome, and we intend to keep it that way.

Last but not least, our food is wonderful, especially if you like pork. You could eat off our kitchen floors, they are so clean. If you bring children to a restaurant, we expect them to behave. Your dog is also welcome—we know dogs behave.

History is a difficult subject for us. We never want anything like World War II to happen again. People born in the last sixty years wonder how to respond properly to the atrocities and guilt. How do we honor tradition and the past without excusing the terrible wrongs committed in Germany's name? The German people will debate the possible answers to this question for years to come.

Immigration is also a contentious issue. New laws require all foreigners seeking permanent residence to take courses in German language, law, culture, and history. The goal is integration with mutual respect for cultural diversity. ("Learning from one another, living together" is our motto.) Despite this goal, we struggle with our relationship with foreign workers and fiercely debate whether and how to make immigrants integrate into German society.

Although the eastern and western halves of our country reunited over fifteen years ago, cementing the two nations has been difficult and costly. After World War II, Great Britain, France, and the United States heavily subsidized and invested in West Germany, while the Soviet Union extracted war reparations from East Germany. When East Germany became a communist state in 1949, the economic gap between it and West Germany widened even further. This gap is a main reason why reunification will not be complete for many years, even though Communism failed here in 1990.

Nonetheless, Germany is still the world's third-largest economy after the United States and Japan. We have an excellent central location, bordering nine other nations. We have been technological leaders for centuries: Germans invented the printing press, along with countless other innovations. Our luxury cars, manufacturing, and medical and technology industries are of the highest quality. We are proud of our excellent work ethic and well-educated people.

It is true that we have had several years of economic stagnation—over 10 percent unemployment and lack of investment have hurt us—but we are still the European Union's largest economy. We are adept at beating the odds, so don't count us out.

Come to Germany, and see why we are so proud of our history, culture, and society. Share our food and drink, and get to know us!

Vital Statistics

Population	82,431,390
Capital	Berlin
Area	137,800 square miles, slightly smaller than Montana
Government	Federal republic
Living Standard	GDP = US $36,290 per capita
Natural Resources	Iron ore, coal, potash, timber, lignite, uranium, copper, natural gas, salt, nickel, construction material, timber, arable land
Agriculture	Potatoes, wheat, barley, sugar beets, fruit, cabbages, cattle, pigs, poultry
Industries	Among the world's largest and most technologically advanced producers of iron, steel, coal, cement, chemicals, machinery, vehicles, machine tools, electronics, food and beverages, shipbuilding, textiles
Climate	Temperate and marine; cool, cloudy, wet winters and summers; occasional warm mountain wind
Member of the EU?	Yes; West Germany was an original member from 1967. When East Germany reunited with West Germany in 1990, the EU recognized Germany as a member.
Currency	Euro (€)

The People

Correct Name	noun: German(s) adjective: German
Ethnic Makeup	German 91.5%, Turkish 2.4%, other 6.1% (made up largely of Greek, Italian, Polish, Russian, Serbo-Croatian, Spanish)
Language	German (official)
Religions	Protestant 34%, Roman Catholic 34%, Muslim 3.7%, unaffiliated or other 28.3%

Meeting and Greeting

- *Guten Tag* (GOO-tun tahk) means "good day" and is the proper way to greet someone.
- In Bavaria, the greeting: *Grüss Gott* (grees gawt) means "may God greet you."
- When introducing yourself, never use your title. Introduce yourself by your last name only.

  Example: *"Guten Tag.* Schmidt" or just "Schmidt."
- There's no need to shake hands when meeting someone on the street.
- It isn't quite proper to greet Germans with *sehr erfreut* (sair air-FROYT), which means "pleased to meet you," because Germans generally prefer to determine whether they're pleased to have met you. Many Germans, however, do use the greeting.
- Unlike Americans, Germans say, *"Wie geht es Ihnen?"* (vee gate es EE-nun), which means "how are you?" only to people they know, as an invitation to begin a discussion. They never say it upon introduction.
- When answering the phone, Germans usually state just their last names instead of a greeting.

Names and Titles

- Even more so than other Europeans, Germans don't use first names. People who have worked together for decades still address one another as *Herr* and *Frau* plus last names. Friends may use first names outside the office, but never at work.
- Titles are very important to Germans. Never use titles incorrectly.

English	German	Pronunciation
Mr.	*Herr*	(hair)
Mrs.	*Frau*	(frow)
Miss	*Fräulein*	(FROY-line)

Note: Germans traditionally used *Fräulein* for women younger than age eighteen, but the title is going out of style—even for young women.

- Address Germans as *Herr/Frau* + title and/or last name.

    Examples:

    Herr Schmidt or *Frau* Schmidt

    Herr Doktor Schmidt or *Herr Doktor*

    Frau Direktor Schmidt or *Frau Direktor*

- If you're unsure of someone's title, use a higher title—never a lower title.
- Never address a married woman by her husband's title.
- When addressing a woman of status, it's always correct to address her as *Gnädige Frau* (ge-NAY-dig-ah frow), which means "Madam."
- A *Doktor* can be either a medical doctor or a holder of a doctorate.
- Germans call a university professor "*Herr/Frau* Professor" without the last name.

Language

Although German is the official language, regional dialects are strong and spoken in most regions. Many Germans understand and speak English, but all will appreciate your attempts to speak German.

Conversation

- Germans usually consider small talk (*belangloses Geplauder*) a waste of time. On the other hand, they value the art of conversation highly.
- When Germans talk about what they know—especially in the language of their foreign guests—they're not flaunting their intellect. They merely wish to have a meaningful conversation and appreciate the opportunity to hone their language skills.
- Germans seldom give compliments, and they may receive them with embarrassment or even suspicion.
- Germans find teasing unacceptable.
- Germans are blunt and direct. They won't say, "I am not sure you are correct about that." They'll say, "You are wrong." Don't be offended!
- Don't ask a German "How are you?" unless you want a detailed answer. Germans don't answer the question briefly, as Americans do.
- Germans almost always use *Sie* (the formal *you*) in conversation and always when addressing a professor, doctor, or someone with academic rank.
- Although Germans traditionally used *du* (the familiar *you*) only among close friends by mutual agreement, the younger generation is more frequently using the informal pronoun.

- The older or more highly ranked person initiates the use of *du*, and a ritual may mark this offer of friendship and symbolic entry into each other's private life. Never take this offer lightly.

Acceptable topics
- Sports: Football (soccer) is a national pastime.
- Travel
- Current events
- Work or your profession

Unacceptable topics
- Personal or family issues: Family and work are kept separate. Don't ask about your colleague's family unless you've established a personal relationship.
- Money, especially salaries

Topics that require sensitivity
- World War II
- The Holocaust

Body Language

Germans may appear reserved and unfriendly until you get to know them.
- The thumbs-up gesture means "one" (for example, to signal wait staff that you'd like one beer) or may signal appreciation or agreement.
- Making your hands into fists, thumbs tucked inside, and pounding lightly on a surface expresses good luck.
- Never make the "okay" sign (curling your index finger and thumb into a circle). Germans consider the gesture very rude.
- Don't point your index finger to your own head. This gesture is an insult.
- In academic settings, university-educated Germans applaud by knocking on tables. All others applaud by clapping.
- Give Germans plenty of personal space, but know that they don't queue (stand in line). They push into you to move forward—and they won't apologize.

Phrases

English	German	Pronunciation
Good morning	*Guten Morgen*	(GOO-tun MAWR-gun)
Good afternoon/day	*Guten Tag*	(GOO-tun tahk)
Good evening	*Guten Abend*	(GOO-tun AH-bent)
Please/You're welcome	*Bitte*	(BIT-uh)
Thank you	*Danke*	(DUNK-uh)
Yes	*Ja*	(ya)
No	*Nein*	(nine)
Excuse me	*Verzeihung*	(fare-TSY-oong)
Goodbye	*Auf Wiedersehen*	(owf VEE-der-zeyn)
How are you?	*Wie geht es Ihnen?*	(vee gate es EE-nun)

Dining

The world may have once considered German cuisine heavy and filling, but that perception is changing. Today, Germans eat half as many potatoes and twice as many fresh fruits and vegetables as they did fifty years ago.

Typical Foods

Würste: sausages (numerous varieties)

Kartoffeln: potatoes

Nudeln: noodles

Bratwurst: fried sausage

Leberwurst: liver sausage

Wienerschnitzel: breaded and fried veal

Knödel: dumplings made from stale *Semmel* (rolls) or *Kartoffeln* (potatoes), sometimes with *Leber* (liver) added

Torten: decorated cake

> Germans give restaurants a "schnitzel test": The menu price of schnitzel tells you how expensive the restaurant is.

In Bavaria

Züngerl: pig's tongue

Wammerl: pig's stomach

Schweinebraten: roast pork

Schweinshaxen: roast knuckle of pork

Weisswurst: white sausage served between breakfast and lunch

Spätzle: small, heavy egg noodles

Sauerkraut: shredded cabbage that has been soaked, pickled, or marinated in vinegar or wine

Zwetschenkuchen: plum cake

In Berlin

Eisbein: knuckle of pork

Erbsensuppe: (yellow split pea soup) served mostly with *Bockwurst* (venison sausage)

Gans: goose

Drinking

- While German white wines are famous, *Bier* (beer) is Germany's trademark. Germany has more breweries than the rest of Europe combined.
- Today, Germany's younger generation is drinking more wine and cocktails, and less beer.
- Germans serve cool (not ice-cold) beer, wine, mineral water, and lemonade (all without ice) with meals. They serve brandy after dinner.
- Cocktail hours are short.
- Germans drink a lot of strong coffee.

Toasting

- *Prosit* (PROH-zeet) means "may it be good for you" and is an informal toast.
- *Zum Wohl* (tsoom vohl) means "to your health" and is a more formal toast, although you can use it for all occasions.
- At a dinner party, don't drink until after your host has raised a glass to the woman on his right and toasted everyone's health.
- When toasting as a guest, clink your glass (holding only the stem) with everyone near you and say *"Prosit,"* then take a drink. Then look into someone's eyes at your table, lift your glass slightly, and bring your glass down to the table.
- Don't begin eating until the host says, *"Guten Appetit"* (GOO-tehn APP-eh-teet), which means "enjoy your meal," to signal that guests may begin to eat. Guests may respond, *"Guten Appetit"* or *"Danke ebenfalls"* (DUNK-uh AY-ben-falls), which means "thanks; likewise."

- Higher-ranked people initiate toasts to lower-ranked colleagues, who are expected to reciprocate later.
- A delegation's leader or the highest-ranking person returns the host's toast later in the meal.
- A woman may propose a toast if she's the highest-ranking person or a delegation's leader.

Tipping

- Restaurants: Bills usually include a 10 to 15 percent service charge (the word *Bedienung* appears on the bill), but round up one or two euro when you pay at the table. If bills don't include a service charge, leave a 10 to 15 percent tip.
- Taxis: Tip 10 to 15 percent, then round up to the nearest full euro. Tip more if you have luggage.
- Bellhops: Tip one euro per bag.
- Porters: Their salaries include tips. Extra is optional.
- Hair stylists, barbers, and maids: A tip is optional.

Manners

Socially, Germans are very formal and expect politeness and good manners.
- Germans seldom invite others to their homes or out to dinner, but when they do, the invitation is sincere. They expect you to accept the invitation as an honor.
- Never invite a German to your home or to dinner unless you intend to follow through.
- A dinner invitation is for the entire evening. Germans consider it rude to eat and run. Conversation takes place before and after dinner.
- Use only your fork to cut potatoes and dumplings—never use your knife. Use a knife and fork to eat most other food, including sandwiches and fruit.
- If you take a break during the meal but want to continue eating, or you want more food, cross your fork and knife on your plate.
- Don't take more food on your plate than you plan to eat. If possible, don't leave any food on your plate.
- Germans expect the honored guests to make the first move to leave.
- The day after an event, thank your hosts in person or by phone.

- Be aware that the restaurant host may seat strangers at your table if the restaurant is crowded. You don't need to talk to them.
- Wait staff brings the bill only upon request. To beckon wait staff, raise your hand, make eye contact, and nod your head slightly.
- When entering a public place, men precede women.
- Except in a business meeting, men rise when women enter a room.
- Stand when an older or higher-ranking person enters the room.
- A man or younger person should always walk at a woman's left side.
- Turn off lights when leaving a room.
- Always close inside doors behind you.
- Never enter a room without first knocking.
- At an opera, concert, or play, never make any noise—unwrapping paper, fingering through the program, opening your purse, and so on.

Dress

Germans dress similarly to Americans, but with a European flavor (see pages 44–45). They consider dressing well and appropriately very important. They frown upon casual, eccentric, or sloppy attire.
- For business, men wear suits and ties in dark colors. Women wear dresses, suits, pantsuits, or skirts and blouses.
- For casual occasions, men wear pants and shirts with sweaters. Women wear pants or skirts with sweaters, or casual dresses. Clean, fashionable jeans are acceptable.
- At the theater or opera, men wear suits and ties, and women wear dresses or dress pants.
- Ask your hosts or the hotel concierge what attire is appropriate for a particular event. For example, some restaurants are smart casual (see page 45) and some are very formal.

Gifts

Germans open gifts upon receipt.

Hostess Gifts
When invited to someone's home, always bring the hostess a small gift.

Consider giving

- Unwrapped yellow roses or tea roses in an odd number (but not thirteen): For a large party, consider sending the flowers on the morning of the party or the next day as a thank-you gift.
- Chocolates

Don't give

- Carnations (symbol of mourning)
- Calla lilies and yellow or white chrysanthemums (for funerals only)

Business Gifts

Germans don't normally exchange gifts at business meetings, but you may exchange small gifts at the successful conclusion of negotiations. Giving a Christmas gift to a German colleague is acceptable but not expected.

Consider giving

- Books
- Bourbon
- Recordings of classical music
- American-made gifts

Don't give

- Pointed objects like knives, scissors, umbrellas (considered unlucky)
- Personal items
- Extravagant gifts
- Wine (Germans are very proud of their wine cellars.)

Toilet Tips	
English	**German**
Restroom	*Toiletten/WC*
Women's restroom	*Frauen*
Men's restroom	*Herren*
Hot water	*Warm*
Cold water	*Kalt*

Helpful Hints

- Germans are more formal and punctual than most other cultures. They have prescribed roles and seldom step out of line.
- Don't be offended if someone corrects your behavior (for example, taking off your jacket in a restaurant or parking in the wrong spot). Germans see policing each other as a social duty.
- Understand and respect cultural, political, and economic differences among Germany's various regions.
- Don't flaunt power, money, or influence.

Punctuality

Punctuality is a German trademark. Germans consider tardiness thoughtless and rude. They expect you to be punctual for business meetings and social occasions. Call with an explanation if you're delayed.

Corporate Culture

Structure

A strict vertical hierarchy exists and everyone respects it. A small group at the top holds power. The corporate organization is logical, methodical, and compartmentalized; everyone executes procedures and routines by the book. Rank is important, and Germans never schedule meetings among people of different ranks.

Subordinates respect the boss for being strong, decisive, and working hard; they rarely contradict or criticize the boss publicly. The boss gives unequivocal direction and may make even minor decisions. He or she seldom praises subordinates' work. Never embarrass the boss, and always address him or her (and all higher-ranked people) as *Frau/Herr* + title + last name (example: *Frau Doktor* Schmidt).

Despite the boss's authority, subordinates hold considerable power, due to national labor laws and German companies' consensus approach to decision making.

Fast-track promotions are rare; Germans consider steady progress and job security more important than rapid promotion. One's vehicle, size of office, and holiday venues symbolize individual success.

Meetings

- Meetings are formal with a set agenda. Their purpose is to learn different opinions with the goal to make a decision. Germans will negotiate and debate an issue fervently.
- Germans schedule meetings weeks in advance, and they always begin and end at the stated times.
- A primary goal of first meetings is to let participants get acquainted and determine one another's integrity. Germans usually begin to discuss business after a few minutes of general discussion.
- Meeting participants come well prepared. They back reports, briefings, and presentations with numerous facts, figures, charts, and tables. Germans consider being unprepared disrespectful.

Communication

- Most Germans speak and understand English. You generally won't need an interpreter, but check in advance.
- State your wishes clearly and directly. Don't worry about sparing a person's feelings. Germans consider the truth more important than making a person feel good.
- Communication within German companies tends to flow from top to bottom, with colleagues sharing information on a need-to-know basis only. With this said, however, Germans write extensive reports to elaborate on and confirm discussions.
- Before your visit, send personal and company profiles to German colleagues to establish credibility.
- Never call a German colleague at home unless it's an emergency.

Business Cards

- Bring plenty of business cards and present business cards properly. (See pages 54–55.)
- Business cards in English are acceptable.

Be Aware

- Germans take business very seriously. They're competitive, ambitious, and hard bargainers. They respect perfectionism in business and private life.
- Germans work hard (levity isn't common in the workplace), but they work fewer hours than their fellow Europeans. They insist on going home at quitting time and always expect to be paid for overtime.

- Germans don't change jobs often. Many (perhaps most) Germans stay with a company for many years, often their whole working lives.
- Don't misinterpret a German's pride in ability and achievement as arrogance.
- Contacts are vital to business success. When possible, use a bank, German representative, or the *Industrie- und Handelskammer* (Chamber of Industry and Commerce) to provide introductions.
- Avoid hard-sell tactics and surprises. Don't try to appeal to emotion or rely on personal testimony.
- Don't try to simplify or summarize information; Germans believe that if things are easily understood, they aren't important.
- Never lose your temper in public—Germans consider doing so a sign of weakness. Keep your voice firm and controlled. Never shout.
- Always deliver information and products to German clients on time.
- Avoid rescheduling or canceling an appointment.

Socializing

Germans are very hospitable to foreign business partners. They like fine cuisine and wine, and they view dinner as an occasion to enjoy both with good conversation. If you hope to establish a good relationship with your German colleagues, follow suit.

- Germans usually do business entertaining in restaurants.
- You can schedule business breakfasts, but Germans usually prefer business lunches.
- A casual lunch with business colleagues generally includes social conversation, not business.
- When socializing, Germans are reserved around their bosses or superiors. Privately, and among close friends, they joke, laugh, banter, and have a good time (*Gemütlichkeit*).
- Older people tend to socialize with others of their own social level. The younger generation tends to socialize with anyone at any level.
- Germans generally don't include spouses in business dinners. If your spouse is traveling with you, you may ask whether he or she can join you for dinner.

Especially for Women

Traditionally, Germans (especially older Germans) haven't accepted businesswomen in positions of responsibility and power. Even though sex discrimination is illegal in Germany, such cases are difficult to pursue.

The younger generation, however, has fewer problems with women holding higher positions in the business world.

- To successfully do business in Germany, women—especially foreign women—must establish their position and ability immediately.
- A foreign woman shouldn't hesitate to invite a German man to a business dinner, and she won't have any problem paying the bill.

Holidays and Festivals

January	New Year's Day (1)
	Epiphany (6—celebrated in some regions)
March/April	Easter (Friday–Monday)
April/May	Feast of the Ascension (40 days after Easter)
May	Labor Day (1)
May/June	Whitsunday (Pentecost) and Whitmonday (day after Pentecost)
June	Corpus Christi (60 days after Easter—celebrated in some regions)
August	Feast of the Assumption (15—celebrated in some regions)
October	National Day (Day of German Unity) (3)
	Reformation Day (31—celebrated in some regions)
November	All Saints' Day (1—celebrated in some regions)
	Repentance Day (third Wednesday—celebrated in Saxony)
December	Saint Nicholas Day (6)
	Christmas (24–26)

GREECE
HELLENIC REPUBLIC

Greetings from Greece

Greetings from the land of hot sun, beautiful seas, and majestic mountains. But Greece offers so much more, and you don't have to be Greek to feel a sense of homecoming when you visit.

Greece is the cradle of Western civilization. It is the country where the value of a single citizen prevailed in voice and vote, and a government—however unfinished—was called a democracy. Today, you can still see the classic Parthenon on the hill of the Acropolis at Athens. When walking in the Agora, you can listen for muffled echoes of ancient animated conversations among car horns and other modern sounds.

Our contributions to science, philosophy, art, architecture, and especially literature are priceless and indisputable. From Homer to Nikos Kazantzakis (*Zorba the Greek* and *The Last Temptation of Christ*), our literature has been provocative for nearly three thousand years—and it is relevant even today. In the second century AD, Pausanias wrote *Description of Greece*, an invaluable guide to ancient ruins; it is still available in many languages, including English.

Greeks are very family oriented. We would never shame or dishonor our families, the center of our lives. We highly respect our elders, and we care for our aged parents. Parents discipline children firmly, but regardless of income, they spend a great deal to feed, clothe, and educate them. Our men consider it an honor and responsibility to care for their families.

The changes in Greece in the last two decades have been amazing, as our country has moved from the fringe of the developed world to modernity. In 1981 we joined the European Community (now the European Union or EU), and since admission, we have worked feverishly to improve our nation. We are determined to develop better relations with Turkey and to carry out the economic reforms and disciplined business practices required by EU membership. We have also made major strides in women's equality, including legally abolishing the dowry system.

We work hard and play hard. As our incomes have increased, we have been able to ski, sail, and travel more than ever before. In keeping with our Olympic tradition, we love sports, including football (soccer), basketball, swimming, and sailing. Hosting the 2004 Summer Olympic Games was our chance to show off our nation to the world, and we relished the opportunity to celebrate our history and highlight our modern accomplishments.

While we believe these massive changes are positive, we worry that Greece's charm will be lost as our economy becomes more investment oriented and our infrastructure expands. To protect our culture, we fiercely guard our traditions.

Come see how modern and timeless Greece is. We welcome you!

Vital Statistics

Population	10,668,354
Capital	Athens
Area	50,940 square miles, slightly smaller than Alabama
Government	Parliamentary republic
Living Standard	GDP = US $21,880 per capita
Natural Resources	Lignite, petroleum, iron ore, bauxite, lead, zinc, nickel, magnesite, marble, salt, hydropower potential
Agriculture	Wheat, corn, barley, sugar beets, olives, tomatoes, wine, tobacco, potatoes, beef, dairy products
Industries	Tourism, food and tobacco processing, textiles, chemicals, metal products, mining, petroleum
Climate	Temperate; mild, wet winters and hot, dry summers
Member of the EU?	Yes, since 1981
Currency	Euro (€)

The People

Correct Name	noun: Greek(s) adjective: Greek
Ethnic Makeup	Greek 98%, other 2%
	(*Note*: The Greek government doesn't officially recognize any ethnic minorities in Greece.)
Languages	Greek 99% (official), English, French
Religions	Greek Orthodox 98%, Muslim 1.3%, other 0.7%

Meeting and Greeting

- Greeks shake hands warmly and firmly, with eye contact.
- Contrary to a common cultural stereotype, Greeks are more likely to greet good friends, not acquaintances or strangers, with hugs and kisses.
- When answering the phone, Greeks say, *"Embros"* (em-BROS), which means "go ahead."

Names and Titles

English	Greek	Pronunciation
Mr.	*Kyrios*	(KEE-ree-ohs)
Mrs.	*Kyria*	(KEE-ree-yah)
Miss (used only for girls under age fifteen and for waitresses)	*Despinís*	(theh-speen-EES)

- Formal address is *Kyrios* or *Kyria* + last name.
- If someone has a professional title, use it. Greeks are proud of their titles, especially doctors and lawyers. Use professional title + last name.
- Common, less formal address is *Kyrios/Kyria* + first name + last name.
- If you don't know someone's name, use *Kyrios* or *Kyria* by itself.
- Greeks move quickly from formality to informality.

Language

Greek is the official language, but many Greeks understand French and English. More than 10 percent of English words have Greek roots.

The Greek language uses the Greek alphabet, not the Roman (Latin) alphabet. Today's Greeks can read ancient Greek texts—the written language has changed very little. (The exact pronunciation of the ancient words, though, is unknown.)

Conversation

Greeks greatly appreciate any attempts foreigners make to speak the language, and are very patient when conversing with foreigners.

Expect Greeks to ask personal questions such as, "Are you married?" or "How much money do you make?" They're not being rude; they're trying to get to know you. If you don't want to answer a question, politely say, "In my country, that would be a strange question!"

Acceptable topics
- Family: Praise any children.
- Host's food and home: Compliment both often.

Unacceptable topics
- Politics: Don't join in political discussions between Greeks, who are well informed but very partisan.

Topics that require sensitivity
- Relations with Turkey and Cyprus
- Fascist dictatorships of the twentieth century

Body Language

> Expect pushing and shoving in lines. Push back or you'll never get anywhere!

- Greeks' gestures to say yes and no differ from North Americans' gestures.

  > Yes = slight downward tilt of the head: This gesture alone isn't polite. Say "yes" in Greek as well.

  > No = slight upward toss of the head with a slight click of the tongue and lifted eyebrows

  Greeks, however, often use North American body language to say yes and no, which could cause confusion. To be certain everyone understands, say "yes" or "no" in Greek and ask for a verbal response.

- The following gestures are rude:
  * Waving with the palm out and fingers spread
  * Waving by raising index finger and keeping palm closed
  * "Okay" sign (index finger and thumb making a circle)
  * Thumbs-down gesture
- The thumbs-up gesture means "okay."

- Greeks kiss one another on each cheek. This gesture is sometimes called a "French kiss"—don't confuse it for what North Americans consider a French kiss!

Phrases

Because the Greek language doesn't use the Roman (Latin) alphabet, Greek words in this table are spelled phonetically.

In Greek, the pronunciation of the letter *chi* ("ch") is similar to the pronunciation of the sound in the Scottish word *loch*, but softer and less guttural. This pronunciation is often hard for Americans; ask a Greek colleague to help you.

English	Greek	Pronunciation
Good morning	*Kaliméra*	(kah-lee-MEH-rah)
Good evening	*Kalispéra*	(kah-lee-SPEH-rah)
Good day/evening/night	*Chérete*	([CH]EH-reh-teh)
Please/You're welcome	*Parakaló*	(pah-rah-kah-LOW)
Thank you	*Efcharistó*	(ef-[ch]ah-ree-STOW)
Yes	*Ne*	(neh)
No	*Óchi*	(OH-[ch]ee)
Excuse me	*Me sinchórite*	(may seen-[CH]O-ree-tay)
Goodbye (one person; also sometimes used as a greeting)	*Yia sou*	(YAH su)
Goodbye (two or more people; formal)	*Yia sas*	(YAH sahs)
Pleased to meet you	*Hareka poli*	(HAH-ree-kah pol-EE)
How are you? (formal)	*Ti kanatey*	(tee kah-neh-TAY)
How are you? (informal)	*Ti kanees*	(tee kah-NEES)

Dining

Greek cuisine is justly world famous. Unfortunately, as more continental and international restaurants appear, the *tavernas* (casual restaurants) and *ouzeries* (bars) aren't as common as they once were. Never pass up an opportunity to eat local food at an authentic Greek eatery.

It's almost unthinkable to Greeks to eat alone. They're extremely generous hosts, and meals are social events for close friends to share food in a very relaxed atmosphere. At restaurants, wait staff won't hurry you to leave, even if people are waiting for tables.

Dinners are especially social. They usually end about 11:00 PM, which may seem late to Americans. But the meal is light, usually followed by wine and fruit or sweets.

Typical Foods
Moussaka: eggplant with meat sauce and cheese
Tiropeta: cheese pie
Spanakopeta: spinach, feta, and herbs in phyllo
Dolmathes: grape leaves stuffed with ground meat and rice
Souvlaki: a shish kebab—small pieces of meat (usually lamb) and vegetables on a skewer
Gyros: ground meat mixed with spices and grilled on a vertical spit, sometimes served on pita bread
Arnáki: lamb
Kotópoulo: chicken
Psária: fish
Elies: olives
Tyri: cheese
Ryzi: rice
Olive oil: very light and used for much of the cooking—Greeks consider it the healthiest oil.
Bread: Greeks truly believe it's the staff of life.

Drinking

- Greeks serve *ouzo*, an anise liquor often mixed with water, with appetizers.
- They serve *krasi* (wine) or *bíra* (beer) with meals.
- *Retsina* (wine with pine resin added) is a traditional drink but an acquired taste. Be adventurous and try it.
- Be extremely careful of your alcohol intake. Greeks can handle their alcohol and may take advantage of your inability to do so.
- *Ellenikó kafé* (coffee) is thick and very strong. Start by requesting *metrion* (MET-ree-oon), which means "medium," then decide whether you want to add sugar or order a more bitter coffee next time.

Toasting

- *Stinygiasou* (stee-nee-YEE-ah-su) means "to your health" and is an informal toast given to one person.
- *Eis igían sas* (ees ih-YEE-an sahs) also means "to your health" and is a formal toast given to two or more people.
- *Kali epitihia* (kahl-EE eh-pee-tee-HEE-ah) is a toast to good luck and success.
- The host normally proposes the first toast.
- It's acceptable for women to propose toasts.

Tipping

- Restaurants: The bill usually includes a 10 percent service charge. You can leave another 8 to 10 percent as an additional gratuity for good service. In a *taverna* (a casual establishment, not a bar), leave the tip on the table. In a more formal restaurant, leave the tip on the plate that brought the bill.
- Taxis: Drivers appreciate a small gratuity.
- Bellhops and porters: Tip one euro per bag.
- Hair stylists and barbers: Tip 10 percent of the bill.

Manners

- Seat yourself in most restaurants. If you're unsure whether to do so, ask the wait staff.
- To beckon wait staff, raise your hand and quietly say, "*Parakaló*" (pah-rah-kah-LOW), which means "please." You may have to be assertive with some wait staff to get the service you desire.
- In a *taverna*, a group generally orders several different dishes to share. In a more formal restaurant, each person orders his or her own dish.
- In smaller, informal establishments, a guest may go to the kitchen, look into several different pots, and choose a dish.
- Greeks eat some foods, like appetizers, with their fingers. Follow your host's lead.
- Continental restaurants serve bread at every meal, but there's no bread plate. Put bread directly on the table.
- Greeks may share the bill with the host, but foreigners shouldn't try to do so. Generally, the person who extended the invitation pays the bill.

- When dining in a home, the host offers several helpings of each dish, first to the oldest guests.
- When entertaining at home, the hostess prepares everything. For small groups, plates come from the kitchen prepared. For large groups, guests eat from a buffet.
- Eating all you like compliments your host, but make sure to eat everything on your plate. If you can't, you must say it's too much food the moment you're served. At that time, either you'll receive a smaller portion or the hostess will insist that you eat what you can, which means you needn't eat everything.
- Always respect the elderly as well as the Greek flag and national emblem.
- Be warm and genuine. Greeks don't care for pretentious or standoffish behavior.

> Greek hospitality is exceptional. Ancient Greeks believed a stranger might be a god in disguise and, therefore, were especially kind to strangers.

Dress

Dress in Greece is more casual than in most European countries.
- For business, men wear suits or sport coats with ties. Traditionally, Greek women preferred dresses to slacks, but that's changing. Today, they wear pantsuits or dresses.
- In restaurants, men wear jackets and ties in winter, but usually more casual attire in summer. Women wear dresses or dress pants and blouses.
- For formal occasions, men wear dark suits or tuxedos; in summer, they may wear open-necked white shirts with tuxedo pants and a cummerbund. Women wear evening gowns.
- You may wear jeans for informal occasions if they're clean and neat. Don't wear jeans at business affairs unless you're absolutely certain they're appropriate. Even then, wear only designer jeans.
- Women should never wear pants or shorts in churches or monasteries.

Gifts

Greeks open gifts upon receipt.

Hostess Gifts

Make sure a gift is wrapped before giving it to the hostess.

Consider giving
- Expensive wine
- Brandy or whiskey
- Pastries
- Cut flowers, except irises (for funerals only): You may choose to send a flower arrangement ahead of time.

Don't give
- Inexpensive wine
- Knives or any sharp objects

Business Gifts

Greek business colleagues commonly exchange gifts. The price of the gift depends on the relationship. Closer, stronger relationships exchange more expensive gifts than weaker relationships do.

Consider giving
- Expensive wine
- Items for the home
- Handicrafts from your home region, but only if they're authentic and tasteful

Don't give
- Inexpensive wine
- Knives or any sharp objects

Toilet Tips	
English	**Greek**
Restroom	*Toaléta*
Women's restroom	*Ginekón*
Men's restroom	*Andrón*
Hot water	*Zesto nero*
Cold water	*Kryo nero*

Helpful Hints

- To better understand Greek culture, watch the film version of *Zorba the Greek*.
- If your host insists upon something several times (eat more, stay longer, and so on), the offer is sincere.
- In villages, avoid praising a specific item excessively—especially a handmade item—or your host may insist on giving it to you.
- Orthodoxy is deeply ingrained in Greek culture, and the vast majority belong to the Greek Orthodox Church. Although a much smaller percentage attend services regularly, always respect the religion.
- Try to join in traditional Greek dances. The locals will greatly appreciate your effort.
- Bargain in shops or at the market, but not in department stores.
- Get an approximation of the fare before you get into a taxi.
- Be careful on the streets! Although Athenian traffic flow has improved a great deal (thanks to preparations for the 2004 Olympics), navigating traffic is still very dicey. The hordes of motorcycles pose the most danger.

Punctuality

Punctuality hasn't traditionally been important to Greeks. But as they do more business with the rest of Europe, punctuality is becoming more common and expected. It's less important, however, in social situations.

- Even though Greeks may be late for business meetings, they expect foreigners to be on time.
- For a dinner party, arrive at least thirty minutes late. In Greece, an 8:00 PM start time on the invitation means after eight o'clock.

Corporate Culture

Structure

Company structure is narrow and vertical. The boss is the owner or the owner's trusted employee; he or she gives directives and takes complete responsibility. Subordinates are delegated specific tasks with little responsibility.

Meetings

Meetings are a forum to express opinions or to inform the group. They seldom have a formal agenda. They usually begin with a general discussion and evolve into spirited exchanges in which everyone may speak or argue.

Consensus is important, and Greeks believe that meetings end when everything has been addressed. To them, setting an end time is irrational.

During meetings, participants drink coffee, ice water, *ouzo*, or whiskey.

Communication

- Greeks commonly use English in business, but it's best to check in advance whether you'll need an interpreter.
- Greeks distrust written communications; their letters and memos are often stiff and formal.
- Don't telephone in lieu of a meeting. Face-to-face meetings are vital to Greek business. Greeks want to know you before doing business with you, and personal contact is the best way to gain trust.
- It's acceptable to call a Greek colleague at home.

Business Cards

- Business cards in English are acceptable. Give one to everyone involved in your business dealings.

Be Aware

- For business success in Greece, you'll need courteous, patient persistence as well as connections to the right people. You must not be pretentious or aloof. Never appear to exploit or dominate a relationship.
- Never be demanding or hostile when dealing with bureaucracy, no matter how frustrated you get. If you get antagonistic, bureaucrats will try to impede your progress at every turn. Remain calm and politely ask for help. If you can avoid confrontation, you're much more likely to receive help.
- Document everything meticulously. Make hard copies of all transactions and get the appropriate signatures.
- Keep contracts simple.
- The official workday starts at 8:00 AM and ends at lunch, although it may start again at 5:00 PM and end at 8:00 PM.
- Many businesses are closed Wednesday afternoons.

Socializing

- Greeks usually do business entertaining in restaurants.
- Business breakfasts are rare, and business lunches are generally only for business guests.
- Greeks often entertain friends in their homes. They socialize based on compatibility, not business opportunity.
- Business dinners are social occasions, and business discussions are limited. Follow your host's lead when discussing business.
- Greeks commonly invite spouses to business dinners.

Especially for Women

Although there are still inequities, women's status in Greece has improved in recent years. Despite some discrimination against women in companies, clubs, and groups, women are well represented in Greek politics and professions. Many Greek women continue to work after having children. Greece has excellent maternity leave but lacks childcare facilities. Grandparents usually help take care of the kids.

- Greece is a good place for foreign businesswomen. Their opportunities depend on their connections, the same as for men.
- Some Greek men may regard American women as "easy." Be sure to always behave professionally.
- It may be a problem for a foreign woman to invite a Greek man to a business lunch or dinner. Try to invite others along or, if for dinner, invite his wife. A Greek man will always try to pay, but if you're insistent, he'll probably let you pay—especially if you arrange payment beforehand.
- Especially in cities, Greeks consider men's verbal harassment of women a sign of admiration, and foreign women should ignore it. If dining alone, choose a good restaurant (not a *taverna* or *ouzerie*) to avoid verbal harassment.
- Watch your belongings at all times.

Holidays and Festivals

January	New Year's Day (1)
	Epiphany (6)
February/March	Shrove Tuesday
March	Independence Day (25)
March/April	Orthodox Easter (Friday–Monday)
April/May	Feast of the Ascension (40 days after Easter)
May	Labor Day/May Day (1)
May/June	Whitsunday (Pentecost) and Whitmonday (day after Pentecost)
August	Feast of the Assumption (15
October	No Day/*Óchi* Day (28)
December	Christmas (25)
	Gathering of the Virgin's Entourage (26)

Note: Each island, village, and city has its own holidays as well.

HUNGARY
REPUBLIC OF HUNGARY

Greetings from Hungary

Greetings from the land whose people are one of a kind. We in Hungary are very proud of our unique language and history. We are fiercely independent, especially when we feel our independence is threatened.

Although the rest of the world calls us Hungarians, we call ourselves Magyars. Our origins are unique. People who populated Hungary centuries ago had migrated from western Siberia. Some believe the same people also migrated east to what is now Korea.

Our unique language is something of an enigma. A few linguists place Hungarian in the same language group that includes Korean and Mongolian. Others conclude that Finnish is a distant cousin. These claims are controversial, but they highlight our language's mystery.

It is difficult to summarize Hungarian contributions to science. Ten of the twelve Hungarian Nobel Prize winners were scientists, including Dénes Gábor (discovered and developed the holographic method) and Albert Szent-Györgyi (first to isolate vitamin C). Physician Ignác Semmelweis promoted hand washing in chloride water before examining women in labor (thereby saving countless lives), and János Neumann (John von Neumann) is thought by many to have invented the modern computer.

Our unique contributions to art and culture have been prolific. Franz Liszt and Béla Bartók are two of Hungary's many famous classical composers. Liszt invented the symphonic poem, composing music as a single bold movement instead of several separate movements. Magyar folk songs inspired Bartók. Zoltán Kodály, a prominent composer and collaborator of Bartók, created a well-known method of teaching music to children. Music teachers from around the world come to Hungary to learn Kodály's system.

On a quirky note: In 1974 Erno Rubik, a professor of architecture, invented the Rubik's Cube, a pop-culture toy of the 1980s.

We are so proud of our dramatic history. The Magyar tribes, under the leadership of Árpád, left the Don River in Russia and settled in the Carpathian Basin in 896 AD. The tribes ruled the area (for the most part, tyrannically) for the next fifty years, until Emperor Otto I defeated them and quelled their belligerence. Two decades later, the tribes recognized the authority of their king (Árpád's great-grandson, Géza) before the authority of the tribes' chieftains and welcomed relations with western countries. In 1000 AD, Géza's son, King Szent István (Saint Stephen), converted his kingdom to Christianity.

In the fifteenth century, we became an influential power in Central Europe. Although the Ottoman Turks conquered our land in 1526, their rule lasted less than two hundred years. In the late 1600s, Austria gained control of Hungary, and for the next two hundred years, we pushed to participate in the rule. At last in 1867, we formed a dual monarchy with Austria and became the Austro-Hungarian Empire, a formidable world power.

Unfortunately, after World War I, Hungary was in such chaos that it took two years to sign a peace treaty with the Allies. The Treaty of Trianon in 1920 cut Hungary's territory by more than two-thirds, placing significant numbers of Hungarian minorities in other nations.

Caught between Germany and the Soviet Union as World War II approached, Hungary threw its lot in with Germany. In 1944, the German army invaded to ensure Hungary's loyalty. After the war, Communists (supported by the Soviet Union) seized control, and the People's Republic of Hungary became a socialist state.

Hungarians chafed under Soviet influence. In 1956, Prime Minister Imre Nagy removed state control of the media, promised free elections, abolished the one-party system, offered demonstrators amnesty, and withdrew Hungary from the Warsaw Pact, declaring Hungary to be a neutral country. Soviet troops soon suppressed the revolt, however, and thousands of Hungarians were killed. Nagy was arrested, tried in secret, and executed in 1958.

> Originally two cities (Buda and Pest) situated on opposite shores of the Danube River, the Hungarian capital, Budapest, is a lovely city, rich in culture and easy to navigate on foot.
>
> Although many of its beautiful buildings are marred with graffiti, the city offers the best libraries, museums, art galleries, orchestras, sports facilities, and theaters in Hungary.

In 1968, limited privatization began in industry. By the mid-1970s, liberalization led to our nation's becoming the most developed and richest in the region. In the 1980s, we developed a hybrid market economy that has served our economy well.

We became a key player in the collapse of Communist control in Eastern and Central Europe. In 1989, we opened our border with Austria, giving thousands of East Germans the opportunity to escape to the West. In 1990, the Communist party voluntarily gave up its power, Soviet forces left, and Hungary became a multiparty parliamentary democracy.

After joining the European Union in 2004, we have continued to demonstrate strong economic growth. Visit us for business or pleasure—we offer wonderful spas, lovely cities, and spacious parks (our Hortobágy National Park is famous for bird watching).

There is no place else on earth like Hungary, and its people are like no other on earth. We are not Slavic, Baltic, Balkan, Latin, or German—we are Magyars. Come and see what we mean!

Vital Statistics

Population	10,006,835
Capital	Budapest
Area	35,919 square miles, slightly smaller than Indiana
Government	Parliamentary democracy
Living Standard	GDP = US $12,100 per capita
Natural Resources	Bauxite, coal, natural gas, fertile soils, arable land
Agriculture	Wheat, corn, sunflower seed, potatoes, sugar beets, pigs, cattle, poultry, dairy products
Industries	Mining, metallurgy, construction materials, processed foods, textiles, chemicals (especially pharmaceuticals), motor vehicles
Climate	Temperate; cold, cloudy, humid winters; warm summers
Member of the EU?	Yes, since 2004
Currency	Forint (HUF); working toward converting to the euro by 2010

The People

Correct Name	noun: Hungarian(s) adjective: Hungarian
Ethnic Makeup	Hungarian 92.3%, Roma 1.9%, other or unknown 5.8%
Languages	Hungarian 93.6% (official), other or unspecified 6.4%
Religions	Roman Catholic 51.9%, Calvinist 15.9%, Lutheran 3%, Greek Catholic 2.6%, other Christian 1%, other or unspecified 11.1%, unaffiliated 14.5%

Meeting and Greeting

- Hungarian men shake one another's hands firmly and just once. Hungarian women shake hands more gently (with one another and with men).
- Upon meeting, Hungarians embrace only close family and friends, touching cheeks. They may also "air kiss" one another (on the left cheek, right cheek, and the left cheek again).
- Hungarians introduce women before men, oldest to youngest.
- Hungarians introduce themselves by saying their last names first, then their first names.
- Let a mutual acquaintance introduce you to strangers. Don't introduce yourself unless absolutely necessary.

Names and Titles

Saying *úr* after the last name means "Mr." Adding *né* to the end of a last name means "Mrs., " and saying *kisasszony* after the last name means "Miss." Note that when written, *úr* and *kisasszony* are separate words, while *né* becomes part of the last name.

English	Hungarian	Pronunciation
Mr.	*úr*	(oor)
Mrs.	*né*	(nay)
Miss	*kisasszony* (used only for girls younger than age eighteen or female wait staff and clerks)	(KISH-ass-sahn)
Examples:	Mr. Medgyessy	Medgyessy *úr*
	Mrs. Medgyessy	Medgyessy*né*
	Miss Medgyessy	Medgyessy *kisasszony*

- Address people by their professional titles (printed on business cards or given during introductions). Follow professional titles with *úr* or *né.*
- If you don't know a person's professional title, address him or her by last name followed by *úr*, *né*, or *kisasszony*.

- *Asszony* (AH-son) is a term of respect for distinguished women, comparable to "Madam." Use it to address a high-ranking woman whom you don't know well.

    Example: Medgyessy *asszony*
- Among close friends, Hungarians sometimes use *úr* or *né* with the person's first name.
- Hungarians use first names only with family and close friends. Don't use first names with your Hungarian colleagues unless invited to do so.
- Hungarians use *úr* or *kisasszony* to address wait staff, shop clerks, and so on.

Language

Hungarian (Magyar) is a Finno-Ugric language (as are Estonian and Finnish). Hungarians don't speak Slavic languages. If you use these languages to speak with Hungarians, you'll insult them.

Especially in tourist areas, many Hungarians speak German and slightly fewer speak English, which is the foreign language most studied in schools.

Conversation

Speak in a moderate tone when conversing with Hungarians. They generally speak more softly than Americans.

Acceptable topics
- Hungarian culture: Be sure to do your homework first so you converse intelligently.
- Hungarian food and wine
- Your family, especially children: Hungarians love children. Bring photos of your children to show your Hungarian colleagues.

Unacceptable topics
- Personal questions: Don't ask about someone's job, salary, marital status, health, and so on.
- Comparisons between Hungary and its Slavic neighbors

Topics that require sensitivity
- The Soviet era
- World Wars I and II
- Relations with the Roma (Gypsies)

Body Language

- Good posture is important to Hungarians. Don't slouch or lean against anything.
- Hungarians don't smile as casually as do Americans. They may not smile upon introduction.
- Hungarians may stand closer to one another than Americans do.
- Good friends of the same sex may walk together arm in arm.
- Men flick their fingers against their necks to invite another man for a drink. This is a rather impolite gesture, and Hungarians don't use it in formal situations.
- To wave goodbye, raise your palm to face outward and bend the fingers together.
- Waving your hand from left to right means "no."
- When counting on your hand, your thumb is "one," index finger is "two," and so on.
- Hungarians consider the following gestures rude:
    * Shaking your fist at someone
    * The thumbs-down gesture
    * Holding your fist with the thumb between the index and middle fingers
    * Pointing to your head with your index finger (indicates that someone is crazy)

Phrases

Please note that the Hungarian language uses diacritical marks that aren't used in English. The Hungarian phrases below have been simplified for North American readers.

English	Hungarian	Pronunciation
Hello (formal)	*Kívánok*	(KEE-vah-nahk)
	Jó napot kívánok	(YOH na-poht KEE-vah-nahk)
Hello (informal)	*Szia*	(SEE-ah)
Good morning (informal)	*Jó reggelt*	(YOH reg-gelt)
Good morning (formal)	*Jó reggelt kívánok*	(YOH reg-gelt KEE-vah-nahk)
Good evening (informal)	*Jó estét*	(YOH ESH-teht)
Good evening (formal)	*Jó estét kívánok*	(YOH ESH-teht KEE-vah-nahk)

Good night	Jó éjszakát	(yoh AY-soh-kaht)
Please	Kérem	(KEH-rem)
Thank you	Köszönöm	(KEH-seh-nehm)
You're welcome	Nincs mit	(NINCH mit)
Yes	Igen	(EE-gen)
No	Nem	(nehm)
Excuse me	Bocsánat	(BOH-chah-not)
Goodbye (formal)	Viszontlátásra	(VEE-sohnt-lah-tash-roh)
Goodbye (informal)	Szia	(SEE-ah)
Pleased to meet you	Örülök, hogy megismerhettem	(ER-ruh-lerk hodj MEHG-ish-mer-heh-tem)
How are you?	Hogy van	(HODJ vahn)

Dining

Hungarian food is very rich and spicy. For most Hungarians, lunch is the main meal of the day. For many Hungarians, it's common to meet friends at cafés in the late afternoon for a snack and conversation.

Typical Foods

Gulyás: goulash, a thick soup of meat, vegetables, and dumplings, flavored with onions and paprika (It's the most famous Hungarian dish.)

Pörkölt: a roast pork stew

Töltött káposzta: stuffed cabbage rolls

Palacsinta: crepes that may be stuffed with savory or sweet fillings

Not all goulash is the same. Hungarian *gulyás* is not American goulash, which is closer to Hungarian *pörkölt*. In Hungary, *gulyás* is more of a soup than a stew and is never served over noodles. It's made of beef, carrots, potatoes, and small dumplings (similar to German *spaetzle*), and is flavored generously with onions and paprika.

The word *gulyás* means "herdsman" in Hungarian (comparable to an American cowboy). Herdsmen traditionally made *gulyás* outside, in a large round cast-iron kettle that hung over an open fire.

Quality restaurants serve *bogrács* (kettle) *gulyás* in small replicas of the kettles. It's spicy, so you have to drink a lot of wine with it.

Bread: usually served without butter
Paprika: a common seasoning in Hungarian dishes that can be mild to spicy

Drinking

- Wine: Hungarians are proud of their many excellent wines. Tokai is one of the most famous.
- Liqueur: Unicum is a popular Hungarian-brand bittersweet spirit, made from spices and herbs. Hungarians serve it throughout the day.
- Mineral water: Hungarians generally serve it instead of tap water.
- Coffee: Hungarians generally drink Italian espresso. If you'd rather have American coffee, ask for a "large with milk."
- Tea: Many Hungarians drink tea.

Toasting

- The toast *kedves egészségére* (KED-vish EGG-aysh-ah-gah-reh) means "to your health," and Hungarians use it at formal and informal occasions.
- The toast *jó étvágyat* (YOH ate-vah-dot) means "*bon appétit*," and Hungarians say it before eating.
- Hungarians expect hosts and guests of honor to make toasts, which are generally short except for special occasions.
- If you've received a toast, you must reciprocate.
- Maintain eye contact while toasting and receiving a toast.
- It's acceptable for women to propose toasts.

Tipping

- Restaurants: The bill may include a tip; if it doesn't, tip 10 to 15 percent of the bill. Tell your server how much you want to include as a tip. Don't leave your tip on the table.

    If a Roma musical group plays exclusively for your table, tip the equivalent of one or two euros. Leave the tip on the dish provided.
- Taxis: It's usually not necessary to tip drivers; however, feel free to tip 10 percent of the fare for a long trip or if the driver handles your luggage.
- Bellhops, porters, and doormen: Tip the equivalent of one euro per bag.
- Hair stylists and barbers: Tip 10 to 15 percent of the bill.

Manners

Hungarians behave very formally. Be sure to act accordingly. Loud, aggressive behavior, especially in public, shocks and repels Hungarians.

- When you enter someone's home, ask whether you should remove your shoes, or follow your host's lead.
- Foreign men shouldn't remove coats and ties unless their Hungarian colleagues do so first.
- Hungarians serve the eldest or most honored guest first.
- Don't add salt and pepper before tasting your food. Doing so insults the hostess.
- Don't rest your hands in your lap during a meal.
- If you don't want your glass refilled, leave it more than half-full.
- Eat everything on your plate. If you can't, apologize to the hostess.
- If you don't want more food, you may have to graciously decline the hostess's offer several times. Conversely, if you're hosting a dinner party, be sure to urge your guests to have another helping.
- Compliment the hostess on the meal, her home, her hospitality (she'll likely downplay the compliments).
- Hungarians may smoke between courses. If you wish to do so, ask permission of those around you.
- Always check your coat in a restaurant or theater.
- In restaurants, the person who extended the invitation pays the bill; however, the guest should make an effort to pay.
- Men should walk at the left side of women and honored guests, and they should always rise when someone (male or female) enters the room.
- When entering a bar together, the man enters before the woman.
- Beckon someone by raising your hand, index finger extended. Say, "*Kérem*" (KEH-rem), which means "please," to summon wait staff.
- Hungarians respond to compliments with self-deprecation. If someone compliments you, you should respond in kind.
- Don't talk to someone with your hands in your pockets or with sunglasses on.
- When sitting, don't rest an ankle on the knee. Women should cross legs at the ankles.

Dress

Hungarian attire is generally similar to North American and Western European attire.

- For business, men wear suits and ties. Women wear pantsuits or dresses. Business dress among younger Hungarians, however, may have more color and flair than in the United States.
- At the theater or opera, men wear dark suits. Women wear cocktail dresses.
- At restaurants, men wear jackets and ties. Women wear business attire.
- For casual occasions, men wear clean, pressed jeans with a shirt or a jacket and tie. (Ask someone what attire is appropriate.) Women wear comfortable but stylish clothing.
- Hungarians will notice your shoes. Make sure they're clean, fashionable, and polished.
- Younger Hungarians wear jeans in informal settings. If you want to wear jeans, make sure they're clean and stylish.
- Always dress well to attend church services. Men should remove their hats before entering a church.
- Older Hungarians (particularly in rural areas) may wear black attire for one year when a close relative dies. (For other deaths, the mourning period is six weeks.)

Gifts

Hungarians generally don't open gifts in front of the giver. Thank the giver sincerely and put the gift aside to open later. Don't forget to send the giver a thank-you note.

When visiting someone's home, bring small toys or candy for any children. The family will appreciate the gesture.

Hostess Gifts

Consider giving
- Liquor or champagne
- Flowers, except chrysanthemums (for mourning only) or red roses (connote romance): Make sure you give an odd number, and have them wrapped.
- Pastries

Don't give
- Wine or beer (implies that the host isn't providing any)

Business Gifts

Hungarians don't expect business gifts. Either don't give any gifts or give each person a small one. It's better to give everyone the same token gift than give just the boss an expensive gift.

Foreign men doing business with Hungarian women should bring wrapped flowers to the first meeting.

Consider giving
- Small, useful office items (pen and pencil sets or other desk items)
- Foods from your home region
- American-made crafts
- Books about the United States, especially your region

Don't give
- Personal items
- Sharp items (knives, letter openers, and so on)

Toilet Tips	
English	**Hungarian**
Restroom	*Toalett/WC*
Women's restroom	*Nöi*
Men's restroom	*Férfi*
Hot water	*Meleg*
Cold water	*Hideg*

Helpful Hints

- Always be warm, dignified, and serious when working with Hungarians.
- Although Slavic nations surround Hungary, never equate Hungarians with Slavs. Hungarians are ethnic Magyars.
- A person's name day (the day honoring the saint for which he or she is named) may be more important than his or her birthday. Your Hungarian friends and colleagues will appreciate your remembering their name days.
- Avoid driving in Hungary. Hungarians don't follow American road rules (or, seemingly, any rules), and it's difficult to anticipate other drivers' actions.
- Hungarians rate restaurants on a scale from one to four, with "one" the highest and "four" the lowest.

Punctuality

Hungarians expect punctuality for business and social meetings. If you're delayed, call with an explanation.

Be prepared: Both business and social events may run later than expected.

Corporate Culture

For more information on doing business with a formerly Communist country, see pages 17–18.

Structure

Hungarians structure their companies in strict hierarchies.

Meetings

Hungarians view first meetings as opportunities for getting acquainted, not making decisions. Companies may hold first meetings in a hotel, with subsequent meetings in offices.

To persuade Hungarians, you'll need facts to back up your claims, as well as abundant energy and a strong delivery. You may make presentations in English, but make sure all printed information is in Hungarian.

Communication
- You may need an interpreter, especially outside of Budapest.
- You may write business letters in English. Hungarians appreciate flowery yet formal prose.

Business Cards
- Have your business card printed in English on one side and Hungarian on the other. Include your formal title and any postgraduate degrees.
- Give your business card to everyone you meet.

Be Aware
- Foreigners must prove themselves to be reliable and trustworthy before they can do business in Hungary.
- While Hungarians consider contracts important, they expect them to be flexible.
- If possible, stay in large, international hotels. They're likely to provide access to a fax machine, the Internet, and other business necessities.

- Schedule appointments several weeks in advance, and confirm them a week before the scheduled dates. Know that you can't schedule meetings for a Saturday, even if a business is open that day.

Socializing

- Hungarians do most business entertaining in restaurants.
- Business lunches are for discussing business, not socializing.
- Dinners are social occasions, which usually include spouses.
- Upon signing a contract or completing agreements, throw a party for your new associates.

Especially for Women

Although many women are in the Hungarian workplace, it's still rare for them to hold positions of authority. Even if they work outside the home, Hungarian women still perform most domestic duties.

Spas

Hungary is famous for its natural hot springs, and Hungarians view spas more as medical treatments than beauty treatments. If you visit a spa, be aware of the following information:

- The hot baths are for soaking, not washing or swimming.
- If you have an appointment, arrive a few minutes early. Lateness is very rude.
- Spas have separate areas for men and women. Ask where you should go so you don't wander into someplace you shouldn't.
- Shower or bathe in designated areas before entering the hot springs. You should bring your own towel and soap.
- Keep your voice low and don't stare at other patrons or invade their privacy.
- Some spas allow nude soaking; others don't. If you're unsure, ask before you undress. Even in spas that allow nude soaking, you may wear a swimsuit (your own) if you wish.
- It's acceptable to exit the hot springs at any time if you get overheated.
- After your soak, consider having a massage. Massage services are usually quite affordable.

- For business success in Hungary, foreign businesswomen must act professionally and formally, not aggressively.
- Although Hungarian custom dictates that the person who extended the invitation pays for the meal, Hungarian men may feel obliged to pay for a

woman's meal. If you want to pay for a business meal, arrange payment with the wait staff beforehand. Don't let the check come to the table.

- Women shouldn't patronize an alcohol-only establishment (*borozó*) alone.

Holidays and Festivals	
January	New Year's Day (1)
March	Anniversary of 1848 uprising against Austrian rule (15)
March/April	Easter and Easter Monday
May	Labor Day (1)
May/June	Whitsunday (Pentecost) and Whitmonday (day after Pentecost)
August	Feast of the Assumption (15) National Day/Feast of Saint Stephen (20)
October	Republic Day (23)
November	All Saints' Day (1)
December	Christmas (25–26) New Year's Eve (31)

IRELAND
REPUBLIC OF IRELAND/EIRE

Greetings from Ireland

Greetings from the European Union's greatest success story! We Irish are very proud of our country and its new image as a thriving business community.

Over the past decade, the Emerald Isle has attracted people and investments world wide, and we're thrilled to see our own return home. Many Irish—young and old—who left for economic reasons are returning to Ireland and its excellent jobs. We now enjoy one of the highest standards of living in the developed world, and we attribute that fact directly to our investment in our children's education.

Even though we're now a sophisticated business center, we try to maintain our old traditions. Outside the cities, you'll still find traffic-free roads, where the only obstacles are occasional sheep herds. You can find endless pints of Guinness throughout the land. If you look hard enough, you may even spot leprechauns and fairies.

We love to talk, laugh, and tell stories. We welcome enthusiastic debates on almost any subject, and we share our opinions with gusto. Most of us strongly identify with our county of birth, and we love to tell jokes about those from other counties.

We're known as fighters ("Is this a private fight or can anyone join in?" is a common Irish joke), but there's nothing we like better than enjoying a "bit of *craic*" (lively joking and conversation) in a pub. Pubs are an important part of Irish life, and many of us unwind at our local pub on the way home from work.

We enjoy singing and are proud of our contributions to modern music, from the more traditional Clannad and Enya, who incorporate Irish musical elements, to rock 'n' roll artists Sinéad O'Connor, the Pogues, and U2.

Our love of music undoubtedly has influenced our wonderfully rhythmic literature. Ireland has produced some of the world's most celebrated authors: Jonathan Swift, Oscar Wilde, William Butler Yeats, James Joyce, Samuel Beckett, Sean O'Casey, and Brian Friel are prime examples.

We honor the Irish language, and although only a small group of us speak it daily, we've made Irish an official language. Today, all schoolchildren learn Irish, and the language appears on official documents and on road signs.

We're extremely proud of our history. We endured years of suffering and fighting, especially with the British. But centuries of invasion and occupation were unable to destroy Irish culture. In 1801, the Act of Union took effect, and Ireland became part of the United Kingdom of Great Britain and Ireland. Even when England forbade the teaching of our language, beliefs, and religion, we kept them alive.

Finally, in 1922 the Anglo-Irish Treaty took effect, and we became an independent country again—although six northern counties remained part of the United Kingdom. Please remember that the Republic of Ireland and Northern Ireland are separate countries. While we're saddened to have our island divided, we support a peaceful coexistence with our northern neighbors. Most of us in the North and the Republic are too busy living our lives to back radicalism on either side.

Over 88 percent of us belong to the Catholic Church, which had been a major unifying force for many years. But today fewer people attend Mass. Couples may live together before marriage, and many have children before or without marriage. Yet despite the Church's declining influence, don't be surprised to meet a clergy member at a family function.

Along with the rest of Europe, we're dealing with an influx of immigrants. Our once homogeneous culture now has to interact with people who look, act, dress, believe, and behave differently from us. They live in our communities and receive government support—a sore point for many of us.

Nevertheless, we're some of the most outgoing, hospitable people in Europe. We love visitors and will welcome you into our amazing bed-and-breakfasts as if you were part of our family. (If you smoke, however, you'll need to leave your cigarettes at home. We're the world's first nonsmoking country— and the majority of us love living smoke free.)

To understand us better, learn a little about our history and struggles for independence. Be genuine, buy your round in the pub, slow down—and the Irish will welcome you.

Vital Statistics

Population	4,015,676
Capital	Dublin
Area	27,140 square miles, slightly larger than West Virginia
Government	Republic
Living Standard	GDP = US $52,940 per capita
Natural Resources	Zinc, lead, natural gas, crude oil, barite, copper, gypsum, limestone, dolomite, peat, silver
Agriculture	Turnips, barley, potatoes, sugar beets, wheat, beef, dairy products
Industries	Food products, brewing, textiles, clothing, chemicals, pharmaceuticals, metal and mineral mining processing, machinery, transportation equipment, glass and crystal, software, tourism
Climate	Temperate maritime; modified by North Atlantic Current; mild winters, cool summers; consistently humid; overcast about half the time
Member of the EU?	Yes, since 1973
Currency	Euro (€)

The People

Correct Name	nouns: Irish, Irishmen, Irishwomen adjective: Irish
Ethnic Makeup	Celtic, English
Languages	English is the language generally used; Irish (Gaelic) is spoken mainly in areas located along the western seaboard. Both are official languages.
Religions	Roman Catholic 88.4%, Church of Ireland 3%, other or unspecified 3.5%, none 3.5%

Meeting and Greeting

- The Irish are warm, hospitable people. They shake hands firmly, with eye contact.
- The common greeting *Céad míle fáilte* (kayd MEE-la FALL-chah) means "a hundred thousand welcomes."

- "Cheerio" or "God bless" are common farewells.
- When telephoning an Irish colleague, it's proper etiquette to first ask, "How is the weather there today?" before proceeding with business.

Names and Titles

- The Irish usually use first names shortly after introductions, but wait until your Irish colleagues begin using first names before using them yourself.
- The Irish use professional titles like *Dr.* and *Professor*. (*Note*: They address medical doctors [except surgeons] as *Dr.* and surgeons as *Mr.*)

Language

The Irish (Gaelic) language has sentimental and nationalistic importance. Although the English tried to suppress the Irish language, it was never lost. Today, Irish is an official language, even though only small groups (mainly those living on the western seaboard) speak it daily.

While most people speak English, government employees and teachers must pass an Irish proficiency exam as a condition of employment. Children learn Irish in school and also must pass a proficiency exam in order to graduate.

Conversation

Conversation is Ireland's national pastime. The Irish love to chat and will talk easily to strangers. They also love to *slag* (tease). Good-natured teasing is part of the fun of visiting with the Irish.

Acceptable topics
- Sports, especially Gaelic football, rugby, and football (soccer)
- Music
- Irish culture

Unacceptable topics
- Criticism of others: The Irish are self-critical, but you should never criticize another.
- Personal success: Don't brag or draw attention to your education or accomplishments. The Irish hate arrogance. They may *slag* you if they believe you're showing off.
- Ireland's "quaintness": Never comment on how small or quaint everything is in Ireland compared to your home country.

Topics that require sensitivity

The Irish love to debate, and topics like religion and politics aren't taboo. As a visitor, however, you should let your host bring up controversial topics. Participate in a debate on the following topics only if your opinions are educated and informed.

- Ireland's historical relationship with United Kingdom, especially Northern Ireland (Don't in any way imply that Ireland is part of the United Kingdom or the same as Northern Ireland.)
- The Catholic Church
- Immigrants

Many English words have unique meanings in Ireland.

Word	Meaning	Word	Meaning
jar	a couple of drinks	runners	athletic shoes
dither	slow	footpath	sidewalk
knocked up	awakened	bill	check
homely	pleasant	frock	dress
boot	car trunk	queue	line
bonnet	car hood	ladies/gents	restroom
press	cupboard		

- The suffix *een* means "small." For example, *bor* means "road"; a *boreen* is a small road.
- A driver offers you a lift, not a ride. To ask for a ride has a sexual connotation.
- Don't be surprised if someone invites you over for *craic* (pronounced "crack"). In Ireland, *craic* means fun and jokes.
- Feeling "peckish" means feeling hungry.

Body Language

- The Irish aren't physically demonstrative and aren't comfortable with public displays of affection or overly friendly behavior.
- The Irish respect reserved behavior. They don't appreciate aggressive, obnoxious, or arrogant behavior.
- The peace sign, when made with your palm facing you, is an obscene gesture.
- Never push ahead in queues (lines). Take your proper place.

Dining

Traditional Irish food is simple, hearty, and delicious. It features lots of fresh vegetables and high-quality meats.

Breakfast is the signature Irish meal. It can include cereal (hot or cold), juice, and a "fry up" (eggs, grilled sausage, bacon, tomatoes, black pudding, brown bread, and butter) followed by toast with marmalade.

Dining in Ireland has become continental. Most larger Irish cities have several restaurants, hotels, and castles that specialize in excellent continental cuisine. There are also many gourmet restaurants and several gourmet cooking schools.

Typical Foods

Colcannon: a mixture of potatoes, cabbage, and onion
that's usually served with
sausage and bacon

Mixed coddle: boiled bacon
and sausages

> The potato is king in Ireland! How can you not enjoy a country where two or three different styles of potatoes are served at the same meal?

Fish and chips: usually eaten with vinegar and salt

Seafood: oysters, trout, salmon, and Dublin Bay prawns

Boiled bacon and cabbage

Soda bread and wheaten (brown) bread

Potatoes

Drinking

Enjoy beer, whiskey, or wine with your Irish host or guest. Always buy your round of drinks. Refusing a drink is a major insult in Ireland. Even if you don't drink alcohol for cultural, religious, or health reasons, you may want to order a drink and pretend to drink it.

Traditionally, the Irish drank tea, tea, and more tea. Today, coffee is very popular. Most cities have many coffee shops.

Typical Drinks

Beer: Many consider Guinness stout the national drink. (If you want American-style beer, ask for lager.) Be aware that the Irish serve beer at room temperature.

Black Velvet: a mixture of Guinness and champagne

Irish Mist: brand of whiskey-based liqueur

Irish whiskey

Irish Coffee: coffee with whiskey, sugar, and cream

Poitin (POE-cheen): extremely strong liquor (moonshine) sold illegally—drink it with caution. The Irish drink it to cure everything. They even rub it on stiff joints to cure arthritis.

Shandy: mixture of beer and lemonade (sounds awful but is delicious)

Wine: currently very fashionable to drink

Toasting

- *Slainte* (SLAHN-chah) means "good luck" and is more formal than the toast "cheers," another common toast.
- It's acceptable for women to give toasts.

> We go to the pub in the winter for warmth and in the summer for shade.
>
> —an Irishman

Tipping

- Restaurants: The bill often includes a 15 percent service charge. No extra is expected. If the bill doesn't include a service charge, leave a 10 to 15 percent tip.
- Pubs: A tip isn't necessary. If you have table service, you may leave a small tip.
- Taxis: Tip drivers 10 percent of the fare.
- Hair stylists or barbers: Tip 10 percent of the bill.
- Bellhops and porters: Tip one euro per bag.
- Theaters: Don't tip ushers.

Manners

The Irish are more gregarious than the British, and their manners are less reserved. Their table manners are like British table manners, only a bit more relaxed. (See page 448 to learn more about British manners.)

- Don't ask for a tour of an Irish home.
- Place the peelings from boiled potatoes on the small plate next to the dinner plate.
- When dining at someone's home, it's polite to eat everything served to you.
- Don't eat at an American fast-food chain. Doing so disrespects the local culture.
- Always send a handwritten thank-you note for a gift or meal.

Dress

The Irish dress fashionably. Their clothing may be casual, but it's smart casual (see page 45). Young people don't wear tweeds (considered old-fashioned). They prefer wearing apparel that's continental style.

- Dress modestly, conservatively, and in subdued colors. Avoid wearing loud colors, especially kelly green. Also avoid wearing white pants, nylon running suits, and other apparel that stands out.
- For business, men wear suits or sport coats and ties. Women wear suits, dresses, or skirts and blazers. (Irish women wear pants less often than North American women do.)
- For nonbusiness occasions, dress is generally casual, but check in advance.
- For formal occasions, men wear business suits, black tie, morning coats, or tails. (Ask your Irish colleagues or the hotel concierge which attire is required.) Women wear cocktail or formal dresses.
- Except for five-star establishments, few restaurants outside Dublin require a coat and tie.
- Wear shorts only at the beach. (Weather is rarely warm enough for shorts.)
- You'll need a raincoat and umbrella year-round.

Gifts

The Irish open gifts upon receipt.

Hostess Gifts

Consider giving
- Flowers, except white flowers or lilies (for funerals only)
- Chocolates
- Wine
- Continental cheeses

Don't give
- Expensive or ostentatious gifts

Business Gifts

Exchanging gifts is unusual in Irish business settings, but you may exchange small gifts at the successful conclusion of negotiations. Exchanging small business gifts is common at Christmas.

Consider giving
- Pens
- Books
- Desk accessories
- Ties
- Paperweights

Don't give
- Obviously expensive gifts (The Irish may consider them vulgar.)
- Tacky knickknacks

Helpful Hints

- Road signs are in English and Irish. In some areas, they're only in Irish.
- Be aware that the Irish don't like to deny a request. They often say "maybe" or "we'll see," instead of "no."
- All workplaces and public places are nonsmoking. This includes all chauffeured cars, taxis, and buses. One can smoke only outdoors or at home.
- Assume family entertaining includes children.
- Don't hitchhike. It's no longer safe.

- James Joyce referred to "dear, dirty Dublin," but the city is working on cleaning up. Make sure you dispose of litter properly in Dublin and throughout Ireland. At a shop, you may have to buy plastic bags to carry your purchases (as part of a campaign to reduce litter).
- Don't rush the Irish; they enjoy a slower pace.

> Ireland is home to a culturally distinct group of people called Travelers or Itinerants. (Don't call them tinkers or gypsies.) Their history is unclear. Some say Travelers descended from bards or traveling tinkers; others say they descended from landowners who were displaced during Oliver Cromwell's military campaign in Ireland. Relations between Travelers and "settled" Irish are an ongoing problem in Ireland.

Punctuality

The Irish have a relaxed sense of time and may be a little late for business or social meetings. A foreigner should be on time for business meetings and social gatherings at restaurants, but may arrive fifteen to thirty minutes late for other social events.

Corporate Culture

Structure

The structure of Irish companies is similar to that of British companies, but the Irish have a more flexible approach. The boss is the managing director or general manager and is elected by the board.

Planning and strategy are relatively short term. The Irish prefer to improvise rather than follow a rigid plan. They favor systems and rules with a practical (rather than intellectual) approach to problem solving.

The Irish dislike bureaucracy and, while outwardly accepting authority, rebel against it inwardly.

Meetings

Initial meetings are often low-key. The golf course is the social and business hub of Ireland, and the Irish develop business relationships and make (or at least influence) business decisions on the links.

Communication

The Irish speak only English for business, so you won't need an interpreter; however, they write official documents in both English and Irish.

Business Cards

The Irish most often exchange business cards immediately upon meeting.

Be Aware

- The Irish are routinely named Europe's hardest workers. The workforce is well educated and (increasingly) technically skilled. They're also astute and tenacious negotiators; don't let their easygoing demeanor mislead you.
- The old-boy network is alive in Ireland. Whom you know is vital to business success. Have a well-connected third party initiate business contacts.
- Don't schedule business trips for the first week in May, which is when many businesses attend trade fairs.
- Remember, the Irish want to do things their way. The British tried unsuccessfully to change Irish ways; you won't succeed if you insist on doing things your way.

Socializing

- The Irish do most business entertaining in restaurants.
- Business breakfasts are acceptable.
- Business dinners are usually social occasions and good ways to develop relationships.
- Spouses may or may not be invited to a business dinner.

Especially for Women

While traditional, conservative attitudes remain toward Irish women in the workplace, more and more women are holding positions of power. Since 1990, Ireland has had a woman president: Mary Robinson from 1990 to 1997 and Mary McAleese from 1997 to the present.

As a result, the younger generation is more open to women in business than older generations. Remember, though, that Ireland requires any potential colleague to have good connections.

Ireland is a great place for working mothers. Irish law guarantees working "mums" paid breaks to nurse their babies. Companies believe this law pays off, because breastfed babies get sick less often and their mothers miss fewer days of work.

- A foreign woman may invite an Irishman to dinner, but to prevent his misinterpreting her intentions, a lunch invitation is best.
- A woman should state her intention to pay for a meal upon extending the invitation.
- The Irish consider it proper for a woman to order a glass (half-pint) of beer or stout rather than a pint.
- A woman may buy a round of drinks.
- Pickpockets and purse snatchers are problems. Watch your purse carefully at all times.

Holidays and Festivals

January	New Year's Day (1)
March	Saint Patrick's Day (17)
March/April	Easter (Friday–Monday)
May	Bank Holiday (first Monday)
June	Bank Holiday (first Monday)
August	Bank Holiday (first Monday)
October	Bank Holiday (last Monday)
December	Christmas Day (25) Saint Stephen's Day (26)

ITALY
ITALIAN REPUBLIC

Greetings from Italy

Greetings from the land of contradictions. Italy is home to the Catholic Church and the Mafia, advanced engineering and antiquated plumbing, enormous wealth and extreme poverty.

Despite these paradoxes, we are blessed to live in a country with a climate, landscape, culture, and lifestyle that all our European neighbors envy.

We love life and being in love. It seems as though 99 percent of all Italian songs are love songs. Hollywood has made countless movies about Italian lovers. We do not mind. We have a good sense of humor and can laugh at ourselves easily. With that said, however, we do aspire to a comfortable dignity and admire it in others.

We love family and belonging to groups. We scrupulously maintain personal relationships and highly value loyalty, especially in families. Strong ties bind our families together. Northern Italian families live in nuclear units. In the south, many generations live in the same town or even the same home. We especially love children and include them in all family functions and activities.

Beauty, fashion, and style are as essential to us as breathing. We believe that having an appropriate appearance and making a good impression show respect for our family, friends, and company.

Bella figura means "beautiful figure" and refers to someone who presents him- or herself well and displays impeccable taste in attire, homes, cars, music, art, manners—in every facet of life. Take care how you present yourself to us. We will notice your appearance and will judge your importance and level of success accordingly.

Italians do not live to work, but work to live. But do not let that attitude mislead you into thinking we lack business initiative. We have been international businesspeople for thousands of years. While we believe that cultivation is a social necessity and is our greatest source of pride, we are not backward looking. We prize inventiveness, imagination, intelligence, and education, and we are receptive to new ideas and fresh solutions.

Today, we enjoy a standard of living consistent with our position as one of the world's seven major industrialized countries. Most of us own two cars and live in lovely homes.

Ours may be one of the most pleasant countries in the world, but we are aware that our nation is having major problems. We have high unemployment, especially in the south. We know we cannot maintain our lifestyle without expanding our economy—we have to innovate.

Our population is also shrinking; our birthrate is one of the lowest in Europe. We anticipate a population drop of more than 20 percent by 2050. More women in the workforce, more couples delaying having children, and more demands on economic resources (for example, more older family members to support) have caused average family sizes to drop. Our government is trying monetary incentives to encourage families to grow.

Another problem is our treatment of one another. From region to region, language, diet, and habits differ drastically. Regionalism is strong and not always kind. Northern Italians view those to the south as lazy, corrupt, half-Arab peasants. They believe southerners tolerate the Mafia and live off the hard-working northerners.

Conversely, southern Italians view northerners as poorly educated and more Austrian and French than Italian. They believe northerners benefit by simply being born in the richer part of Italy.

Despite our internal troubles, we welcome foreigners and like to learn about their strange ways and habits. Visit us and prepare for long conversations without many pauses. We are very gregarious, passionate, and hospitable. Do not try to understand us, though; just enjoy our charm and warmth.

Vital Statistics

Population	58,103,033
Capital	Rome
Area	116,306 square miles, slightly larger than Arizona
Government	Republic
Living Standard	GDP = US $30,630 per capita
Natural Resources	Mercury, potash, zinc, marble, barite, asbestos, pumice, fluorospar, feldspar, sulfur, natural gas and crude oil reserves, fish, coal, arable land
Agriculture	Fruits, vegetables, grapes, potatoes, sugar beets, soybeans, grain, olives, beef, dairy products, fish
Industries	Tourism, machinery, iron and steel, chemicals, food processing, textiles, motor vehicles, clothing, footwear, ceramics

Climate	Predominantly Mediterranean; Alpine in far north; hot, dry in south
Member of the EU?	Yes, an original member from 1967
Currency	Euro (€)

The People

Correct Name	noun: Italian(s) adjective: Italian
Ethnic Makeup	Italian; small clusters of German-, French-, and Slovene-Italians in the north and Albanian-Italians and Greek-Italians in the south
Languages	Italian (official), German (parts of Trentino-Alto Adige region are predominantly German speaking), French (small French-speaking minority in Valle d'Aosta region), Slovene (Slovene-speaking minority in the Trieste-Gorizia area)
Religions	Predominately Roman Catholic, with established Protestant and Jewish communities and a growing Muslim immigrant community

Meeting and Greeting

- If possible, have a respected third party introduce you to Italians. They prefer such introductions. In Italy, whom you know is as important as what you know.
- Italians shake hands firmly, with eye contact.
- Friends, including men, may embrace upon greeting. They may kiss one another on each cheek. Acquaintances may also kiss cheeks.
- Before 1:00 PM, Italians say, "*Buon giorno*" (bwone JOR-noh), which means "good morning" or "good day." After 1:00 PM, they say, "*Buona sera*" (BWONE-ah SAY-rah), which means "good afternoon" or "good evening."
- *Ciao* (chow) means "hi" or "goodbye" and is an informal greeting/farewell used between friends only. Never say *ciao* to a stranger.
- Some Italian men may "air kiss" women's hands—that is, their lips don't touch the hand. Foreign men should never attempt to "air kiss" women's hands.

Names and Titles

- Italians working in Italian-run companies use titles and surnames, but Italians working in multinational companies move quickly to using first names. In general, younger Italians move to using first names more quickly than older Italians do.

- Italian women almost always use their maiden names in business and on legal documents. They generally use their married names or both family names outside of business.

- Use *Signor/Signora/Signorina* to address Italians, unless they're university graduates with professional or academic degrees. In that case, use the titles in the second table.

English	Italian	Pronunciation
Sir or Mr.	*Signor*	(see-NYOR)
Madam or Mrs.	*Signora*	(see-NYOR-a)
Miss	*Signorina* (used only for very young, unmarried women)	(see-nyor-EE-na)

English	Italian	Pronunciation
Doctorate or medical degree	*Professore*	(PROH-fess-or-ah)
Liberal arts degree	*Dottore*	(DOH-tor-ah)
Law degree	*Avvocato*	(ahv-voh-CAH-toh)
Technical degree	*Ingegnere*	(in-jen-YAIR-ay)

Note: Use *dottore* if you know that the person is a university graduate but you're unsure of the proper title.

Language

Although Italian is the official language, there are French- and German-speaking minorities. Many Italians are bilingual. In fact, three million people live on "linguistic islands," where they still speak languages other than Italian.

Standard Italian is based on Florentine Italian, although over the years it has picked up characteristics of Roman Italian. As a result, there are many different Italian dialects spoken throughout Italy, and speakers of some dialects can't understand certain other dialects.

Italians usually speak English in business, fairly often speak it in hotels and restaurants, and occasionally speak it in taxis.

Conversation

- There are few lulls in Italian conversation. Italians enjoy a lot of humor and can be self-deprecating at times.
- Italians use *lei* (lay), the formal *you*, for anyone on a professional level. They use *tu* (too), the informal *you*, for friends and family only. Younger Italians move to using *tu* more quickly than older Italians do.

Acceptable topics

- Italian culture, including architecture, art and films, food and wine, and opera
- Sports, especially football (soccer)
- Italy's beauty
- Your home country's culture, history, and current events

Unacceptable topics

- Criticisms of Italian business practices: Even when your Italian colleagues complain about taxes, inefficiency, nepotism, and so on, never join in.
- Negative Italian stereotypes—not even in jest
- Personal topics: Don't ask people where they live, what they do for a living, and so on.

Topics that require sensitivity

- Religion, including Vatican policies
- Politics
- The Mafia
- Taxes
- World War II

Body Language

Of all Europeans, Italians are known for using the most body language (although its use is declining somewhat). Italians view communicating without gestures or expression as bland. More refined Italians, however, don't use gestures and many even consider them rude.

- Never mimic Italian gestures! Italians are seriously offended by such imitation.
- Kissing the fingertips means "beautiful." Italians use it to show appreciation for food, art, a woman, and so on.
- Touching the fingertips together (the "hand purse") could be considered the Italian national gesture. It conveys various meanings: a question, something good, fear, to name just a few.
- Maintain eye contact while talking with Italians. Otherwise, they may think you're uninterested or are hiding something.
- People of the same sex may walk arm in arm in public.
- Italians' personal space is smaller than Americans'. People push and shove in crowded places, and queue-jumping (cutting in line) is common. Italians consider neither behavior rude.

Phrases

English	Italian	Pronunciation
Good morning/day	*Buon giorno*	(bwone JOHR-noh)
Good afternoon/evening	*Buona sera*	(BWONE-ah SAY-rah)
Good night	*Buona notte*	(BWONE-ah NOH-tay)
Please	*Per favore*	(pair fah-VOH-ray)
Thank you	*Grazie*	(GRAHT-see)
You're welcome	*Prego*	(PRAY-goh)
Yes	*Si*	(see)
No	*No*	(noh)
Excuse me	*Mi scusi*	(mee SKOO-zee)
Goodbye	*Arrivederci*	(ah-ree-va-DARE-chee)
How are you?	*Come sta?*	(KOH-may stah)
Pleased to meet you	*Molto lieto*	(MOHL-toh LEE-ay-toh)

Dining

Italian food is not all pizza and spaghetti. Each region features wonderful dishes, and you should try them all. Italians lovingly make their meals with great attention to quality and freshness, and serve them with panache.

Lunch is light and casual unless it's a formal business lunch. In southern Italy, however, especially for foreign guests, lunch may be more formal.

Dinner is the main meal. Italians serve it between 8:00 and 9:30 PM, and it may last two to four hours. Dinner may be later in southern Italy and during the summer.

Typical Foods

Mortadella: bologna-like meat that tastes nothing like American bologna

Prosciutto: air- and salt-cured ham

Tortellini: small, filled pasta

Gnocchi: dumplings, generally made of potatoes and flour, but sometimes of only flour

Pesto: generally refers to a sauce made of fresh basil, garlic, olive oil, Parmesan (or pecorino), and pine nuts

Cannelloni: tubular pasta filled with meat or cheese and topped with sauce (usually tomato) and cheese

Pizza: various regional styles (many unlike American-style pizza), generally with thin crusts and scarce toppings

Polenta: cornmeal porridge

Panzanella: pieces of crusty bread mixed with herbs, tomatoes, onions, garlic, olive oil, vinegar, and spices

Drinking

- Drinking without eating is rare in Italy.
- Italians generally serve *vino* (wine) with every course. They also serve beer, Scotch, grappa (an Italian brandy), mineral water, and soft drinks.
- Cocktails aren't common in Italy, and cocktail hours are short or nonexistent.
- Italians don't appreciate hard drinking. They consider even mild intoxication very ill mannered. Women, especially, should drink in moderation.

Toasting

- *Salute* (sah-LOO-tay), *alla salute* (ah-lah sah-LOO-tay), and *cin-cin* (chin-chin): all toasts mean "to your health" and Italians use them at formal or informal occasions.
- When the host toasts the guest of honor, the guest of honor should reciprocate.
- Women generally don't propose toasts.

Tipping

In general, tip anyone who provides you a service.

- Restaurants: Most have a cover charge. In addition, the bill always includes a 10 to 15 percent service charge. Servers expect small change as an additional gratuity.

  When you order coffee at a bar, pay at the register and get a receipt. Leave a tip on the bar with the receipt.
- Taxis: Tip 15 percent of the fare.
- Hair stylists and barbers: Tip 15 percent of the bill.
- Bellhops and porters: Tip one euro per bag.

Manners

Italians value good manners and social courtesy. Easy formality is the basis of Italian etiquette, with consideration of others its goal.

- Compliment your hosts. Italians pride themselves on their hospitality.
- Italians don't serve butter with bread, and they don't use bread plates. Break bread and place it on the table next to your plate.
- Use your fork to roll pasta against the sides of your pasta plate. Never use your spoon to help roll pasta.
- Use only a fork to eat salad; never cut salad with a knife.
- Eat fruit with a knife and fork, except for grapes and cherries.
- Use your knife—not your fingers—to pick up a piece of cheese and put it on your bread or cracker.
- Italians never serve grated cheese with a fish dish or with pasta that contains fish.
- When being served, take a small amount of food. Your hostess will offer a second helping, and it's impolite to refuse.

- Try to eat everything on your plate, but if you're full, you may leave some food on your plate.
- Let your host pour wine, and sip it slowly.
- Don't refuse wine. If you don't want your glass refilled, take a few sips (or pretend to take sips) and leave your glass nearly full.
- The person who extended an invitation to a restaurant pays for the meal.
- When you're finished with a meal at a restaurant, ask the server for the bill. He or she may not bring it without your request.
- To beckon wait staff, raise your index finger and make eye contact. You can also say, *"Mi scusi"* (mee SKOO-zee).
- The day after a party or meal, send a thank-you note and flowers or a gift to the host's home.
- Always send a handwritten thank-you note for a gift.
- Try not to yawn, but if you must, cover your mouth.
- Don't make impolite bodily noises in public.
- Never remove your shoes in public.
- Men should remove their hats when entering a building.

Dress

Italy is a major center of European fashion. Italians dress elegantly but conservatively. They're chic and wear the latest fashions. Even people in small towns spend a great deal of money on their wardrobes and dress well at all times. Italians don't appreciate those who wear old, torn, or dirty clothing, and you seldom see anyone wearing such poor attire.

Making a good impression matters deeply to Italians. Whether you're working, shopping, or sitting in a café, you must wear the right clothing and look fantastic. Italians will notice your appearance and judge you accordingly. They believe that life is a performance and you must look and act your part.

In general, dress formally in the cities. If you choose to wear shorts in the city, make sure they're smart, stylish Bermuda shorts. You shouldn't wear shorts, sundresses, or sleeveless tops to churches. Don't wear sweat suits except for athletic activities.

Business and Entertaining

In Italy, men and women dress conservatively and formally for business and entertaining.

Men

- Dark, well-cut suits or sport coats
- Expensive, sophisticated ties
- Accessories: cuff links, tie clips, and chic watches
- For the theater or opera: dark suits and ties

Women

- Dresses or feminine suits or pantsuits (Don't dress like a man.)
- Hosiery: Most Italian women don't wear hosiery in the summer.
- Accessories: Wear brightly-colored accessories to accent dark suits and dresses.
- For the theater or opera: cocktail dresses and pumps

Italian Casual

Italian casual clothing is elegant, smart, and stylish.

- Men: pants and shirts, sweaters, sport coats
- Women: pants or skirts, elegant silk blouses and sweaters
- Men and women: Jeans are acceptable if they're neat, clean, and stylish.

Gifts

- Give a high-quality, significant gift. Italians are very generous gift givers, and you'll be embarrassed if you give a cheap gift.
- Wrap gifts beautifully but not in black gift-wrap with a gold ribbon (a sign of mourning) or in purple gift-wrap (considered bad luck).
- When visiting an Italian colleague's home, bring a small gift for each child and pay attention to the children during the visit.
- Italians open gifts upon receipt.

Hostess Gifts

Consider giving

- Chocolates
- Flowers (in an odd number), except chrysanthemums (connote death) or red roses (connote romance): Pink or yellow roses and mixed bouquets are favorites.

- Pastries
- Vases

Don't give
- Cheap or practical items
- Knives or scissors (considered bad luck)

Business Gifts

Exchanging gifts is common in Italian business. Although Italians generally don't exchange gifts at initial meetings, pack a gift in your briefcase. That way, if your Italian hosts give you one, you can reciprocate. You may exchange gifts at negotiations, but not necessarily.

Consider giving
Gifts should be brand name, but small and not obviously expensive.
- Desk accessories
- Recordings of music
- Framed art
- Books
- Whiskey, cognac, or other high-quality liquor (especially from your home country)

Don't give
- Cheap or practical items
- Knives or scissors (considered bad luck)
- Personal items

Toilet Tips	
English	**Italian**
Restroom	*Toilette/WC*
Women's restroom	*Signore*
Men's restroom	*Signori*
Hot water	*Acqua calda (C)*
Cold water	*Acqua fredda (F)*

Helpful Hints

- Bargain in stores or markets. Shopkeepers may say no, but they won't be insulted if you bargain politely.
- Park your car in a reputable, attended lot or garage. Car thieves are common in larger cities.
- Leave valuables locked in a secure place and take precautions with those you carry. Pickpockets are a problem in Italy, especially in major cities.
- Don't eat on the street (ice cream is the exception).
- Italians prefer subtlety and grace. Don't be too direct or overtly purposeful or efficient.

Punctuality

Punctuality for business meetings is very important. Italians view deliberate lateness in business as sloppy. They expect foreigners to be on time, but they may keep you waiting. Call with an explanation if you're delayed. It's extremely impolite to break an appointment.

For an event at someone's home, arrive fifteen to thirty minutes after the start time stated on the invitation.

Corporate Culture

Structure

Organizational styles are widely diverse in Italian companies. Reporting lines often aren't clear, and personal alliances build most organizations. Businesses are often family owned and operated, and they keep power within the family.

The boss is generally the owner, chairman, or managing director. Employees respect the boss for his or her charisma, creativity, empathy, consistency, and reliability. A plan's or project's development and execution require a respected leader who's capable of establishing personal relationships in order to secure commitment and cooperation.

Companies do nothing of importance "by the book." Pragmatism and improvisation are keys to success. Italians ignore protocol, rules, and organization charts when they seem obstructive. Depending on the business sector, companies may view regulations either as guidelines they can adapt or completely ignore, or as requirements they must strictly follow.

Meetings

Meetings are usually unstructured and informal. Discussions generally begin after a few minutes of small talk.

Formal presentations aren't common, but when given, they're usually to display the leader's status, personality, and charisma. If you're giving a presentation, materials should be clear and straightforward, but presented with flair.

A meeting's purpose is to evaluate the mood or test colleagues' support. Less often is the purpose to make a decision. Italians often make decisions privately, before meetings. (Companies, however, may never implement such decisions.) They generally clear new ideas with everyone involved before presenting the ideas in meetings.

Communication

- Italians use English often in business, but check ahead of time to see whether you'll need an interpreter.
- Don't call an Italian colleague at home except in an emergency.

Business Cards

- Italians want to know they're working with someone important. Be sure your business card features your formal title.
- Italians use business cards only in business—not socially, unless requested.
- Don't give a business card to the same person twice. Exchange them only the first time you meet.
- In meetings, present a business card to each person (unless you've already given one to him or her at an earlier time).
- When receiving a business card, look at the name and title carefully, then set it on the table in front of you or put it in your briefcase.

Be Aware

- Establish personal relationships with Italians; they like to deal with people they know and trust.
- Italians love to make money, and they do so with panache.
- Italians keep their work and private lives separate.
- Although Italians generally believe in enjoying life and work, some work six days a week. Also, southern Italians approach work differently from their northern neighbors. In the south, people do business leisurely. In the north, people believe in getting business done without wasting time. Pace yourself accordingly and try to make business appointments well in advance.

Socializing

Socializing is an important part of Italian business etiquette. If you refuse an invitation, you'll insult your host and will harm your chances of making a deal.

- Italians view Americans as poor hosts. When you entertain Italians, serve elegant meals with style. Ask your Italian contact to help you with the guest list.
- Italians rarely hold breakfast meetings and never hold them outside of big cities.
- Italians do their business entertaining in restaurants. Lunches can last three hours, and dinners are social occasions for getting acquainted.
- Discuss business at social events only if requested to do so.
- If the entertaining is at a private home, Italians almost always invite spouses.

Especially for Women

Even though the culture dictates that men rule the roost and women should be subservient and quiet, Italian women do exactly as they please whenever they please. Women hold the real power in families—mainly because they're brilliant at letting Italian men look macho and appear to make decisions.

Many Italian women are in professions like law, medicine, and accounting. But except in family companies, few hold high-level managerial positions. The business community is definitely male dominated.

That said, women's employment rates are rising. They're playing an increasingly important role in the workforce while continuing to be the primary caretakers at home. Feminism exists in Italy, but its followers are more in the north than in the south.

- Italians interact with members of the opposite sex without reservation. Enjoy the fun flirtation that's part of Italian life.
- Don't expect Italian men to pull out your chair or help you with your coat.
- Don't walk alone at night, and stay in a first-class hotel when traveling alone.
- Don't hesitate to eat alone in northern Italy. In southern Italy, however, men may approach a woman eating alone if they believe her attire and demeanor suggest she wants company.
- It's better for a foreign woman to invite an Italian man to lunch rather than dinner. If a dinner invitation is necessary, it should include his wife.
- Italian men usually will try to pay for a meal. If a woman wishes to pay, she must make arrangements with the wait staff beforehand.

Holidays and Festivals

January	New Year's Day (1)
	Epiphany (6)
March/April	Easter and Easter Monday
April	Liberation Day (25)
May	Labor Day (1)
June	Republic Day (2)
August	Feast of the Assumption (15)
November	All Saints' Day (1)
December	Feast of the Immaculate Conception (8)
	Christmas (25)
	Saint Stephen's Day (26)

Note: Most cities celebrate a day honoring their patron saint's birth or death, during which time businesses may close.

LATVIA
REPUBLIC OF LATVIA

Greetings from Latvia

Greetings from the land of many natural wonders. Latvia has roughly three thousand lakes—some big enough to hold multiple islands—and seemingly endless beaches.

For thousands of years, people have wanted our beautiful Baltic amber for jewelry as well as for mystical and spiritual purposes. During the reign of Roman Emperor Nero, our area was the start of the Great Amber Route.

Our nation also boasts many manmade wonders. You will find lovely architectural styles, from medieval to Art Nouveau, across the land. In fact, our capital, Rīga (which in 2001 celebrated its eight hundredth birthday), is also the capital of Art Nouveau architecture. Several city blocks feature unique examples of this style.

We consider Latvia the cultural gateway between Northern and Western Europe. Several famous musicians, writers, and painters have lived and worked in Rīga, which many people have called (and are again calling) "Little Paris." Many Latvians love ballet, dramatic plays, and opera.

Singing, including choral singing, is a national pastime. We have a rich tradition of folklore, the best examples of which are *dainas* (short, versed folk songs about Latvian culture and myth). There are more than two hundred thousand of these Latvian folk songs, and people know many by heart.

Our history during the last few centuries has been dramatic. From the early eighteenth to the late twentieth centuries, Latvia struggled against alternating German and Russian occupations. During World War II, the Red Army first occupied Latvia, then the Germans drove out the Soviets from a third of the land.

After the war, the Soviet Union annexed Latvia and began massive deportations of native Latvians to northern Russia and Siberia. Then, to replenish the population, the Soviets instituted large-scale immigration from Russia and other parts of the Soviet Union. In four decades, the number of ethnic Latvians in Latvia dropped from three-quarters to just over half the population.

In September 1991, Latvia regained its independence. Although we are glad we joined the European Union in 2004, our experience as a Soviet republic makes us wary of being a small part of a large whole. We cling to our customs and language, because both came close to extinction during the Soviet occupation.

Our determination to retain our culture has strained the relationship between ethnic Russians and ethnic Latvians. For those whose Russian ancestors arrived in Latvia during the 1700s, there is often little conflict with native Latvians. Many of these ethnic Russians are well integrated into Latvian society, speak Latvian, and participate in Latvian culture.

Of those who immigrated to our country from Russia after World War II, many segregate themselves and their families from Latvian culture and still do not speak Latvian—actions that likely stemmed in part from the Soviets' establishment of separate Russian and Latvian schools.

These ethnic Russians are proud of the Russian language and see little need to learn Latvian. Their reluctance to learn the native language angers Latvians, who are extremely proud of their beautiful language. Most Russians who arrived in the last fifty years are not Latvian citizens because they cannot pass a language test, a requirement for citizenship.

In their defense, many ethnic Russians complain that Latvians are too intolerant of people who speak Latvian with an accent or improper grammar. They argue it is hard to learn a language when mistakes are not permitted. Today, many ethnic Russians do not trust Latvians, and believe the Latvians want them to leave, despite the government's attempts to integrate them into Latvian society.

Amazingly, despite the segregation of Latvians from ethnic Russians and the resentment each group feels toward the other, there are no significant differences in educational achievement, employment, salaries, and living standards between the two groups.

Our internal conflicts should not prevent your visiting our wonderful land. Just remember that while Russia has heavily influenced our history, we are not Russian. Do not speak Russian to us. We consider ourselves Northern Europeans, and we enthusiastically receive any attempt foreigners make to speak Latvian. Come see us soon!

Vital Statistics

Population	2,290,237
Capital	Rīga
Area	24,938 square miles, slightly larger than West Virginia
Government	Parliamentary democracy
Living Standard	GDP = US $6,110 per capita
Natural Resources	Peat, limestone, dolomite, amber, hydropower, wood, arable land
Agriculture	Grain, sugar beets, potatoes, vegetables, beef, pork, milk, eggs, fish
Industries	Buses, vans, street and railroad cars, synthetic fibers, agricultural machinery, fertilizers, washing machines, radios, electronics, pharmaceuticals, processed foods, textiles (*Note*: Latvia must import energy and raw materials.)
Climate	Maritime; wet, moderate winters; summers often cool and rainy
Member of the EU?	Yes, since 2004
Currency	Latvian lat (LVL); working toward converting to the euro by 2008

The People

Correct Name	noun: Latvian(s) adjective: Latvian (*Note*: You may hear the words *Lett* or *Lettish* to refer to Latvians and their language. While the terms [derived from German] aren't offensive, they're rarely used.)
Ethnic Makeup	Latvian 57.7%, Russian 29.6%, Belarusian 4.1%, Ukrainian 2.7%, Polish 2.5%, Lithuanian 1.4%, other 2%
Languages	Latvian (official) 58.2%, Russian 37.5%, Lithuanian and other 4.3%
Religions	Lutheran, Roman Catholic, Russian Orthodox

Meeting and Greeting

- Latvians introduce themselves by saying their first and last names.
- Latvians shake hands firmly, with eye contact.
- Good friends may kiss one another on the cheek.

Names and Titles

Latvian

The following courtesy titles follow a person's last name as separate words. They're not capitalized.

English	Latvian	Pronunciation
Mr.	*kungs*	(koongs)
Mrs.	*kundze*	(KOOND-ze)
Miss	*jaunkundze*	(YAUN-koond-ze)

- Latvian names change grammatical form when used with courtesy titles. Latvians don't expect people who don't speak the language to know these grammatical changes.
  Examples:

English	Correct Latvian	Acceptable Latvian
Mr. Kalvītis	*Kalvīša kungs*	*Kalvītis kungs*
Mrs. Vīķe-Freiberga	*Vīķe-Freibergas kundze*	*Vīķe-Freiberga kundze*

- Use *kungs*, *kundze*, and *jaunkundze* when introducing someone else, but not when introducing yourself.
- Latvians use first names among friends, but to express affection, or when talking to children, they add the following diminutives to the end of the names: *īts* or *iņš* for men and boys, *iņa* or *īte* for women and girls.
- Latvians take foreign words, especially names, and change them to fit their language. For example, men's and boys' first and last names end in *s*. Women's and girls' first and last names end in *a* or *e*. Thus, in Latvian *Bill Clinton* becomes *Bils Klintons* and *Hillary Clinton* becomes *Hilarija Klintone*.

Russian

- Russian names have three parts:
  1. The first name
  2. The father's first name followed by a suffix—*evich* or *ovich* (son of) or *evna* or *ovna* (daughter of)
  3. The family name
- For Russian women and girls, *a* follows the family name. Upon marriage, Russian women generally take their husbands' family name.

  Examples:

Name	Meaning
Stepan Arkadyevich Oblonsky	son of Arkady Dmitrich Oblonsky
Maria Nikolayevna Tolstoya	daughter of Nikolai Ivanich Tolstoy
Anna Arkadyevna Karenina	wife of Alexei Alexandrovich Karenin

Language

When the Soviet Union occupied Latvia in 1940, Russian became the official language. In 1988 (three years before gaining independence), Latvia reverted the official language to Latvian, one of the oldest Indo-European languages still in use. Along with Lithuanian, Latvian is similar to Sanskrit, an ancient language. It uses the Roman (Latin) alphabet with many diacritical marks.

As a result of Soviet migratory policies, only about 60 percent of Latvia's residents are ethnic Latvians. Most speak both Latvian and Russian fluently (although many Latvians use Russian only to curse). German and English are common second languages. Younger people in the cities often speak English, but few rural or older people do.

In 1996, the National Agency for Latvian Language Training (NALLT) began a ten-year program to encourage citizens to learn Latvian. In recent years, younger ethnic Russians have learned Latvian, but many older ethnic Russians haven't—a point of contention for many ethnic Latvians.

Latvians fiercely protect their language. Speaking a few words of Latvian will greatly please your Latvian colleagues. Never speak Russian with a Latvian unless you're absolutely certain the person is an ethnic Russian.

Conversation

Acceptable topics

- Sports, especially ice hockey, basketball, and football (soccer)
- Latvia's natural beauty

Unacceptable topics
• Relations with ethnic Russians

Topics that require sensitivity
• World War II
• The Soviet years: Especially in a foreign language, Latvians may have trouble explaining what people went through during the Soviet occupation.

Body Language
• When speaking with Latvians, maintain eye contact. Doing so is a sign of honesty.
• Don't be surprised if someone bumps into you without apologizing.
• Latvians don't smile as readily as Americans do, but when they do smile, it's sincere.
• Latvians may not acknowledge or smile at strangers on the street.
• Don't talk with your hands in your pockets. Latvians consider doing so rude.
• Latvians consider waving an index finger impolite.

Latvian Phrases

English	Latvian	Pronunciation
Hello	*Sveiki*	(SVAY-kih)
Hello (informal)	*Čau**	(chow)
Good day	*Labdien*	(LAHB-deen)
Good morning	*Labrīt*	(LAHB-reet)
Good evening	*Labvakar*	(LAHB-vah-kahr)
Please/You're welcome	*Lūdzu*	(LOOD-zuh)
Thank you	*Paldies*	(PAL-dees)
Yes	*Jā*	(yah)
No	*Nē*	(nay)
Excuse me	*Atvainojiet*	(AHT-vy-nah-yeet)
Goodbye	*Uz redzēšanos*	(OOZ red-zeh-shah-nahs)
Pleased to meet you	*Priecājos iepazīties*	(PREETS-ah-yohs EE-paz-ee-tees)
How are you?	*Kā tev iet?* (casual)	(KAH tev eet)

* Although clearly not a Latvian word, *Čau* is the most common casual greeting among friends, colleagues, and relatives.

Russian Phrases

The Russian language uses the Cyrillic alphabet. The following are phonetic translations.

Good day	*Dobriy dyen*	(DOE-bree dyen)
Good morning	*Dobroye utro*	(DOE-broy-eh OO-troh)
Good evening	*Dobriy vecher*	(DOE-bree VAY-cher)
Please	*Pozhaluysta*	(pah-ZHAL-yoo-stah)
Thank you	*Spasiba*	(spah-SEE-bah)
You're welcome	*Ne za shto*	(NAY zah shtoh)
Yes	*Da*	(dah)
No	*Nyet*	(nyet)
Excuse me	*Izvinite*	(iz-vin-EET-eh)
Goodbye	*Dosvidanya*	(dos-vee-DAHN-yah)
How are you?	*Kak dela?*	(kahk DEE-lah)

Dining

- German foods have heavily influenced Latvian cuisine.
- Rīga has a fairly broad selection of modern restaurants that serve a variety of foods. LIDO is a chain restaurant that serves traditional Latvian food and is definitely worth visiting.
- Most Latvian professionals eat dinner as the main meal.

Typical Foods

Latvian
Cūkas galerts: pork in aspic
Skābie kaposti: sauerkraut
Kāpostu zupa: cabbage soup
Pīrāgi: small glazed buns filled with minced meat or smoked bacon
(a common snack and a staple of *Jani*, the summer solstice holiday)
Siļķe: herring
Lasis: salmon (the most popular fish)
Zutis: eel (fried, smoked, or salted)
Rasols: potato salad with herring, beet root, and apple
Debessmanna or *buberts*: a fluffy custard, served chilled
Klingeris: a special-occasion cake

Bread: especially whole grain breads like *rupjmaize*, a dark rye that's sometimes sprinkled with nuts and raisins (Latvians serve bread with every meal.)

Russian
Borscht: beet soup
Soljanka: soup with vegetables and sausage (Sometimes called "Russian soup," every cook has his or her own recipe.)

Drinking

Drinking is a significant part of Latvian culture. The legal drinking age is eighteen, but compliance isn't heavily enforced.

In business settings, sharing a drink after work is customary, and declining an offer is a social faux pas.

- Beer and vodka (or vodka-based drinks) are the most common alcoholic beverages, although wine is becoming popular. While Aldaris is the most popular brand of Latvian beer, foreign and locally brewed beers are becoming mainstream. Russians prefer vodka to Latvian beer.
- Rīga Black Balsam is a smooth, velvety, 90-proof liquor made of twenty-four ingredients, including herbs and spices. Latvia has been producing the bittersweet beverage since the mid-1700s. It's a unique drink (many declare it an acquired taste) that Latvians sometimes serve in cocktails (with black currant juice or cola) or coffee, or with ice cream.
- Because Latvians once considered cold drinks unhealthy, they consumed beer and soft drinks at room temperature. This attitude is changing, and the younger generation tends to prefer chilled drinks. Still, Latvians use ice in drinks sparingly.

Toasting

- The toast *priekā* (PREE-kah) means "cheers," and the toast *uz veselību* (OOZ VEE-shee-lee-buh) means "to your health." Latvians use either at formal or informal occasions.
- During a toast, always make eye contact with everyone with whom you clink glasses. Not doing so shows lack of interest.
- Women may propose toasts.

Tipping

While tipping isn't common in rural areas, it's appreciated. Tipping is expected in Rīga.

- Restaurants: The bill usually includes a 10 percent service charge. If the bill doesn't include a service charge, tip 10 percent.
- Bellhops and porters: Tip the equivalent of one euro per bag.
- Taxis: Round up the fare to the nearest lat.
- Hair stylists and barbers: Tip 10 percent of the bill.

Manners

- When entering someone's home, ask whether you should remove your shoes, or follow your host's lead.
- In most circumstances, ordering wine or beer at a business lunch is acceptable. Follow your colleagues' lead.
- Latvians consider it rude for women to pour alcoholic drinks.
- Don't eat on the street. (Ice cream is the exception.)
- To summon wait staff (or any service person), say, *"Atvainojiet"* (AHT-vee-nah-yeet), which means "excuse me."

Dress

Latvians wear European fashions, and they (including younger people) prefer more formal attire to casual wear, even in informal settings. They dress fashionably but not loudly.

- For business, men wear suits, neatly pressed shirts, and ties. Women wear dresses or pantsuits with hosiery and high heels. Some newer information-based companies are embracing a more casual dress code, but observe how your colleagues dress before wearing this attire.
- Many women wear traditional Latvian silver and amber jewelry, but less so in business culture.
- For casual occasions, men wear dress pants, shirts, and sweaters. Women wear slacks or skirts, blouses and sweaters. They often wear high heels.

Gifts

Latvians generally don't open gifts in front of the giver. The recipient should thank the giver sincerely and put the gift aside to open later.

Giving flowers is a national tradition. As a visitor, you'll be showered with flowers. When visiting friends, family, or business colleagues outside the office, you must bring flowers (in odd numbers only) for the women. Latvians bring flowers for women at even the most casual get-togethers.

Hostess Gifts

In addition to flowers, you may want to offer another gift.

Consider giving
- Liquor
- Fruit
- Pastries or cakes
- Chocolates
- Photo books of your home region
- Other items from your home region (for example, barbecue sauce if you're from Texas)

Don't give
- Flowers in even numbers (for funerals only)
- Gum, cigarettes, or other items that imply modern consumer goods aren't available in Latvia

Business Gifts

In general, Latvians don't open business gifts upon receipt, unless they're in the presence of only very close friends. If the gift is wrapped so they can see that it's more symbolic than valuable (for example, a pen or mug that features your company logo), they may open it in front of everyone.

Latvians may exchange small token gifts at initial meetings. (Expensive gifts are inappropriate.) You may give small gifts to Latvian colleagues at Christmas, but they're not expected.

Consider giving
- Pens (including pens with your company logo)
- Fine wine or single-malt Scotch
- Photo books of your home region

- Other items from your home region (for example, barbecue sauce if you're from Texas)

Don't give
- Gum, cigarettes, or other items that imply modern consumer goods aren't available in Latvia

Toilet Tips	
English	**Latvian**
Restroom	*Tualete*
Women's restroom	*Dāmām*
Men's restroom	*Kungiem*
Hot water (red dot)	*Karsts*
Cold water (blue dot)	*Auksts*

Helpful Hints

- Because of Latvia's northern latitude, midsummer days are very long, while winter days can be very short (December days may have less than seven hours of daylight).
- At first, Latvians are very formal—even cold. After a relationship has been established, they'll warm up.
- Latvians enjoy ice hockey, basketball, and football (soccer), in that order. Show an interest in them, and you'll likely strengthen relationships.
- If you have the time, the Rīga Motormuseum is worth a visit. It's the biggest antique vehicle museum in the Baltic countries, with world-wide recognition.

Punctuality

Latvians are generally punctual for business occasions, especially if they work for an international company. Employees of government or state agencies, however, may be less punctual. For social occasions, Latvians arrive on time or a few minutes late.

Foreigners should always be on time for business and social occasions.

Corporate Culture

For centuries, Latvia was a center of international commerce. With additions and improvements to its roads and railways—as well as three of its ten ports ice-free all year—Latvia is again turning into a transit hub and Rīga a dynamic international city.

For more information on doing business in a formerly Communist country, see pages 17–18.

Structure

Latvian companies are organized with a very hierarchical structure. They need a clear consensus to make decisions.

Meetings

- Before a meeting, send a list of the names (and titles) of your people who'll be attending. Your Latvian colleagues will assemble a team with similar expertise and status.
- Meetings begin and end with handshakes.

Communication

- It's best to hire a local contact when doing business in Latvia.
- Be calm and rational. Facts and figures will persuade Latvians better than emotion.
- Latvians are comfortable with long silences. Don't start talking to fill gaps in conversation.

Be Aware

- Latvians do business formally. Make sure you know the proper way to make introductions, address people, exchange business cards, and so on.
- Since its introduction in 1992, the Latvian lat has had no major currency fluctuations.
- Be patient: It takes time to build trust with your Latvian colleagues.
- It may take time to set up meetings. Confirm meetings in advance and in writing.
- Latvians work long days; more than half of those employed full-time work more than forty hours a week.

- Celebrations that include food and alcohol are common in Latvian workplaces.
- The Latvian government is eager to have foreign investment.

Socializing

If possible, always graciously accept a Latvian's offer to entertain you. Such an offer is always genuine and is an attempt to personally connect with you. A strong personal connection will better your chances of business success in Latvia.

Especially for Women

Latvians advocate gender equality. Men and women have equal access to education, yet more women than men attain a higher educational level. In fact, women make up more than half of Latvian graduates in science and engineering.

Latvian women are well represented in the workplace; they make up 49 percent of the workforce. In 1999, Latvia elected its first female president, Vaira Vike-Freiberga. She was reelected for a second term in 2003.

- Latvians accept foreign women in business.
- Foreign women won't have trouble inviting Latvian men to business dinners and paying for the meals.

Holidays and Festivals	
January	New Year's Day (1)
March/April	Easter (Friday–Monday)
May	Labor Day/ Convocation of the Constituent Assembly of the Republic of Latvia (1)
	Declaration of Independence of the Republic of Latvia (4)
	Mother's Day (second Sunday)
May/June	Whitsunday (Pentecost)
June	*Ligo* Day (23) and *Jani* (24)
November	Proclamation of the Republic of Latvia (18)
December	Christmas (25–26)
	New Year's Eve (31)

LITHUANIA
REPUBLIC OF LITHUANIA

Greetings from Lithuania

Greetings from the land of outgoing people with prized hospitality. We love to chat with visitors and always give our best to guests. Unlike our Baltic neighbors, Lithuanians are not quiet people. With our expressive, energetic gestures and body language, we behave more like Italians.

Music is an integral part of our culture. We love to express ourselves with song. Many of our folk songs are *sutartinės*, an ancient polyphonic form of song. Starting in 1924, we have held a national song festival every four or five years, attracting hundreds of thousands of people. The festival has never been suspended, even during the Soviet occupation.

Lithuania has had long, turbulent histories with Poland, Russia, and Germany. In 1386, our grand duke Jogaila married the Polish queen as part of an alliance to repel Germanic invaders, and he became the king of Poland. Soon afterward, Jogaila formally introduced Poland's Roman Catholic faith to his Lithuanian-speaking subjects. (Lithuanians were the last pagan people in Europe.)

Within a decade, Jogaila and his cousin Vytautas (whom Jogaila made ruler of Lithuania) led the two leading powers of the region. For nearly the next four hundred years, Lithuania and Poland were united—loosely so, until 1569 when the two nations strengthened their bond by becoming a joint commonwealth.

In the late eighteenth century, Lithuania and Poland's political power began to decline, allowing Russian forces to invade. After 1795, Lithuania became part of the Russian Empire.

By late 1915, the German military occupied our land, and Germany encouraged our desire for independence. (The Germans hoped to make Lithuania a satellite country of their homeland.) Our nation declared independence in 1918, but the Red Army invaded Lithuania a year later. We drove out the Russians within months, but had tense relations with Poland, Russia, and Germany for the next twenty years.

The Soviets again conquered our land in 1940, but only for a short time. Germany invaded and occupied Lithuania from 1941 to 1944, killing more than 250,000 of our people including nearly all Lithuanian Jews. After World War II, the Soviet Union annexed Lithuania. Nearly a quarter million Lithuanians were deported to Siberia and Central Asia.

During the next forty years, Lithuania was a Communist state, but our people never stopped wanting independence. The Forest Brothers, Baltic guerillas who fought for independence, antagonized Soviet occupiers, who effectively quelled the saboteurs in the 1950s. In the early 1960s, more native Lithuanians than Russian imports became government officials. In the 1970s, our country produced more *samizdat* (unofficial, unsanctioned underground publications) per capita than any other Soviet republic. In August 1991, Lithuania finally regained its independence.

After years of struggle against Soviet and Nazi occupations, we are very excited to be members of the European Union (EU). In November 2004, we became the first nation to ratify the European Constitution.

On May 1, 2004, when we joined the EU, we turned on all our lights for a satellite photo and sang songs. For decades, we had sung protest songs and our national songs to reinforce our heritage. Now we proudly sing as a free people. We believe that our determination to preserve Lithuanian culture was the most important factor in reinstating our nation.

Ethnic Russians living in Lithuania number far fewer than those living in Estonia and Latvia. Unlike our Baltic neighbors, we have had few problems with our Russian residents. Although ethnic Russians did protest when Lithuania declared independence, there have been no significant tensions since 1991. Lithuanian law guarantees minority rights, and Russians are well represented in both government and business and are well integrated into Lithuanian society.

Our future looks bright, and we are eager to move our society and economy forward. Please visit us soon and see our progress.

In the early 1970s, a high-school student named Romas Kalanta wrote a school essay about his desire to become a Roman Catholic priest. The Soviet-run school made his life so difficult that he dropped out. On May 14, 1972, Kalanta set himself on fire in the city gardens of Kaunas to protest the Soviet occupation. His death caused a tremendous uproar; people all over the nation protested and staged demonstrations.

In an attempt to quell the protests, government forces stopped bus and train traffic to prevent people from attending Kalanta's funeral. Today, a memorial stands where Kalanta killed himself in the gardens (renamed Sacrifice Field) to commemorate the protest.

Vital Statistics

Population	3,596,617
Capital	Vilnius
Area	25,174 square miles, slightly larger than West Virginia
Government	Parliamentary democracy
Living Standard	GDP = US $7,780 per capita
Natural Resources	Peat, arable land
Agriculture	Grain, potatoes, sugar beets, flax, vegetables, beef, milk, eggs, fish
Industries	Metal-cutting machine tools, electric motors, television sets, refrigerators and freezers, petroleum refining, ship-building (small ships), furniture making, textiles, food processing, fertilizers, agricultural machinery, optical equipment, electronic components, computers, amber
Climate	Transitional, between maritime and continental; wet, moderate winters and summers
Member of the EU?	Yes, since 2004
Currency	Litas (LTL); working toward converting to the euro by 2007

The People

Correct Name	noun: Lithuanian(s) adjective: Lithuanian
Ethnic Makeup	Lithuanian 83.4%, Polish 6.7%, Russian 6.3%, other or unspecified 3.6%
Languages	Lithuanian (official) 82%, Russian 8%, Polish 5.6%, other or unspecified 4.4%
Religions	Roman Catholic 79%, Russian Orthodox 4.1%, Protestant (including Lutheran and Evangelical Christian Baptist) 1.9%, other or unspecified 5.5%, none 9.5%

Meeting and Greeting

- Generally, Lithuanians shake hands upon greeting and departing. In social situations, men shake hands but women may not. Men and women always shake hands in business situations.
- To greet people at a distance, men may raise their hats or nod.
- Lithuanian men may kiss women's hands instead of shaking them. Foreign men, however, should never kiss women's hands.
- Good friends may kiss cheeks as a greeting.

Names and Titles

English	Lithuanian	Pronunciation
Mr.	*Ponas*	(PAH-nuhs)
Mrs.	*Ponia*	(PAH-nih-uh)
Miss	*Panele*	(PUH-neh-leh)

- When addressing others, Lithuanians include professional titles before a person's last name. (Use the title printed on one's business card or given during introduction.) They address doctors and teachers, however, by title alone.
- Never address an adult Lithuanian by his or her first name unless invited to do so.

Language

Lithuanian and Latvian are the oldest surviving Indo-European languages. These Baltic languages are the only modern ones related to Sanskrit, an ancient language.

The Lithuanian language nearly became extinct in the seventeenth century, when Polish became the official language. (It survived only in rural areas.) Then between 1864 and 1904, when Lithuania was part of the Russian Empire, Lithuanian was banned as a written and spoken language. National pride helped the language survive during the Soviet occupation.

Today, Lithuanian is the official language. English and German are popular second languages. Younger people tend to speak English, while older businesspeople and civil servants tend to speak German. Many Lithuanians also speak Russian.

Conversation

Lithuanians enjoy talking about almost any subject—very few topics are taboo. With that said, however, avoid any conversation that your Lithuanian colleagues may interpret as bragging. Lithuanians appreciate modesty.

When conversing with Lithuanians, it's important to maintain eye contact and speak in a moderate tone.

Acceptable topics
- Music: Lithuanians especially admire American rock music.
- Basketball: Lithuania won its third (and first as an independent nation) EuroBasket title in 2003. Some people refer to basketball as their second religion. School tournaments are popular.

Unacceptable topics
- Comparisons between Lithuania and other Baltic nations

Topics that require sensitivity
- The Soviet era
- Lithuanian politics

Body Language
- While on public transportation or standing in line, Lithuanians stand closer to one another than Americans do. In other situations, personal space is roughly the same as in the United States.
- In general, gestures mean the same in Lithuania as they do in the United States.

Phrases

Please note that the Lithuanian language uses diacritical marks that aren't used in English. The Lithuanian phrases below have been simplified for North American readers.

English	Lithuanian	Pronunciation
Hello (informal)	*Laba*	(LAH-bahs)
Good morning	*Labas rytas*	(LAH-bahs REE-tahs)
Good day	*Labas diena*	(LAH-bahs DEE-en-ah)
Good evening	*Labas vakaras*	(LAH-bahs VAH-kah-ruhs)
Please/You're welcome	*Prašau*	(PRAH-shoh)
Thank you	*Ačiū*	(AH-chyoo)
Yes	*Taip*	(tape)
No	*Ne*	(NAY-ah)
Excuse me	*Atsiprašau*	(aht-sih-PRAH-shoh)
Goodbye	*Viso gero*	(VEE-soh GEH-roh)
Pleased to meet you	*Malonu susipažinti*	(mal-loh-NUH soo-see-pah-ZHEN-tee)
How are you?	*Kaip sekasi?*	(kayp sek-US-ee)

Dining

- Most Lithuanians grow much of their own produce in "kitchen gardens." For those living in urban areas, the gardens are located on the city outskirts.
- Vilnius has a wide variety of restaurants with international cuisine.
- Bread holds a sacred place in Lithuanian culture. Lithuanians serve it (most commonly rye bread) at every meal. An old ritual dictates that fathers slice the bread and distribute it in a specific order to the others at the meal.
- Recently, grains have been more common in Lithuanian cuisine than meat.
- Lithuanians don't eat baked sweets every day. For holidays, however, there are plenty of cakes and pastries.
- Lithuanian hospitality is famous. If you're invited to someone's home for a meal, food will be abundant. Your hostess may prepare some food for you to take home. (Lithuanians call this take-home food the "rabbit's cake.")

Typical Foods

Šaltibarsciai: cold beet soup

Cepelinai: potato dumplings filled with meat or mushrooms

Bulviu Blynai: potato pancakes

Kugel'is: potato pudding

Mišrainē: vegetable salad

Agurkai: raw cucumbers dipped in honey

Aguonų Pienas: milk simmered with poppy seeds and sweetened with honey

Meat: usually pork (Traditionally, Lithuanians served meat smoked or salted, but today fresh meat is more common.)

Skilandis: pork and spices smoked in a pig's stomach

Mushrooms: very popular to eat (Many people go mushrooming as recreation.)

Drinking

Lithuanians equate drinking with socializing. They drink slowly so the conversation lasts as long as possible. Sometimes a group shares a drinking glass. They pass the glass and the bottle counterclockwise around the table, giving greetings or making toasts as each person passes them to the next.

- *Krupnikas* (a spiced honey liqueur) and beer are popular beverages. Locally made beer is excellent. For weddings, families often hire a beer brewer.
- Be careful if you try *midus* (mead). It can be very strong, although less potent versions are available.

Toasting

- Toasting is common at lunch and dinner, regardless of whether guests are present.
- The host proposes the first toast, and guests should reciprocate at some point during the meal or event.
- Toasting protocol is rather informal: give a short speech or tell a short story, propose the toast, and everyone drinks.
- The toast *Būk sveikas* (BOOK SVAY-kuhs) means "cheers," and Lithuanians use it at formal and informal occasions.
- It's acceptable for women to propose toasts.

Tipping

Tipping hasn't been customary in Lithuania, but it's becoming common.

- Restaurants: The bill may include a 7 percent service charge. If the bill doesn't include a service charge, tip 5 to 10 percent of the bill.
- Taxis: Round up the fare to the nearest litas.
- Bellhops and porters: Tip the equivalent of one euro per bag.
- Doormen: Tip the equivalent of one euro.
- Hair stylists and barbers: Tip 10 percent of the bill.

Manners

- Lithuanians consider mealtimes sacred. Their behavior at the table is quiet, dignified, and reverent. Make sure you behave accordingly.
- Never start eating until the host urges you to do so.
- Eat everything you're served. It's impolite to leave food on your plate.
- Men are chivalrous and open doors for women, offer women their seats, and so on.
- Don't chew gum in public.
- Don't talk with your hands in your pockets.

Dress

Lithuanians often dress in European styles, although American styles are becoming popular. Quality is important to them, and they will notice the quality of your attire. Make sure you dress stylishly and neatly at all times.

- For business, Lithuanians dress conservatively and formally. Men wear suits, and women wear dresses and heels. Some workplaces are dressing more casually, but it's better for foreigners to overdress, especially for first meetings.
- For formal occasions, men wear suits, and women wear cocktail dresses or tailored suits.
- Casual attire should be neat and clean. Lithuanians don't leave their homes in sloppy attire.

Gifts

Lithuanians open gifts upon receipt. They love flowers and frequently give them as gifts. When invited to someone's home, even for brief visits, bring unwrapped flowers. Make sure you give an odd number of flowers (giving an even number is for funerals only).

Hostess Gifts

Consider giving
- Candy
- Wine or liquor

Don't give
- Chrysanthemums (for funerals only) or white flowers (for weddings only)
- Any item that implies modern consumer goods aren't available in Lithuania (cigarettes, chewing gum, and so on)
- Items of Russian origin

Business Gifts

When first meeting with foreign businesspeople, Lithuanians often give small token gifts, and foreigners should be ready to reciprocate. Exchanging gifts upon the completion of a deal isn't common; toasting with champagne is more likely. You may give small gifts to your Lithuanian colleagues at Christmas.

Consider giving
- Pens
- Wine, liqueur, or cognac

Don't give
- Knives (indicate bad wishes)
- Handkerchiefs (believed to bring sadness)

Toilet Tips

English	Lithuanian
Restroom	*Tualetas*
Women's restroom	*Moterų*
Men's restroom	*Vyrų*
Hot water	*Karštas (k)*
Cold water	*Saltas (s)*

Helpful Hints

- Many Lithuanians adore American rock music, especially the Grateful Dead and Frank Zappa. (There's a bust of Frank Zappa in the center of the capital, Vilnius.) If you know a Lithuanian colleague is a fan, rock T-shirts and related items make good gifts.

- Lithuanians' Roman Catholic faith has been part of their identity for centuries. During the Soviet occupation, when the public expression of religion was banned, Lithuanians protested by erecting crosses on the Hill of Crosses. Between 1961 and 1979 the government destroyed crosses—and bulldozed the hill many times—but people kept returning to put up more crosses.

- *Lugan* is a derogatory name that Americans have used for Lithuanian immigrants. Never use this term.

- Amber is known as "Lithuanian gold," and it's an important national symbol.

Punctuality

Lithuanians expect punctuality for social and business meetings. If you're delayed, call with an explanation.

Corporate Culture

See pages 17–18 for more information on doing business with a formerly Communist country.

Structure

Lithuanian companies are hierarchical, and it's important to show respect to those with authority. While it's acceptable for subordinates to make suggestions and give feedback, a high-ranking foreign executive should make initial contact with a Lithuanian company. Lithuanians consider it an insult for potential clients or associates to send a representative who isn't allowed to make decisions.

Meetings

Meetings are for generating ideas and expressing opinions, but the boss makes the final decision. Before a meeting starts, your Lithuanian colleagues will show you where to sit (near others of similar status) and offer beverages. Meetings begin with small talk.

Presentations should be professional and factual. Don't use emotion as a selling tactic. Have presentation materials translated into Lithuanian.

Communication

Business communication is formal. Etiquette and protocol are important, especially to older Lithuanians. Younger Lithuanians may behave more casually.

Business Cards

- Include your formal title and any postgraduate degrees. Experience and status impress Lithuanians. They don't want to work directly with people they perceive to be subordinates.
- Exchange business cards with a handshake.

Be Aware

- Hire a local contact to help with introductions, regulations, and other business protocol.
- Schedule appointments two to three weeks in advance. Confirm meetings in writing, and again by telephone the day before each meeting.
- Take the time necessary to build relationships with your Lithuanian colleagues. You must meet prospective partners face to face.
- Lithuanians don't rush into deals. If you show impatience, they'll use time as a negotiating tactic.

Socializing

If a Lithuanian colleague entertains you at his or her home or at a restaurant, be sure to reciprocate with a similar offer soon.

Especially for Women

Lithuanians have traditional views toward women, but these are changing. Today, it's against the law in Lithuania to discriminate on the basis of sex. Lithuanian women are very well educated and are making strides in business. Opportunities are emerging.

Nevertheless, women are still underrepresented in business and government. Plus, although the law mandates equal pay for equal work, women often make less than men in similar jobs.

Lithuania has an ongoing problem with prostitution. It's a hub for trafficking women among European countries.

- Lithuanians flirt with one another in the workplace. It's common for Lithuanian men to compliment women on their appearance. Foreign women should graciously accept any compliments; they shouldn't act insulted.
- A foreign woman may invite a Lithuanian man to a business dinner, but he'll feel obliged to pay. To pay for a meal, women should arrange payment with the wait staff beforehand.

Holidays and Festivals

January	New Year's Day (1)
	Epiphany (6)
February	Independence Day (16)
March	Day of Restoration of the Independence of Lithuania (11)
March/April	Easter and Easter Monday
April/May	Feast of the Ascension (40 days after Easter)
May	Labor Day (1)
	Mother's Day (first Sunday)
June	Midsummer's Day (24)
July	State Day (6)
August	Feast of the Assumption (15)
November	All Saints' Day (1)
December	Christmas (25–26)

LUXEMBOURG
GRAND DUCHY OF LUXEMBOURG

Greetings from Luxembourg

Greetings from the small country with a giant attitude. Luxembourg is smaller than Rhode Island, and its population is smaller than Wyoming's, the least populous state in the United States.

What we lack in size, however, we make up for in pizzazz. Our land has vibrant landscapes, dense forests, and crisscrossing rivers. We also have medieval castles that look as though they are straight from a fairy tale.

We are extremely proud of our nation. Our motto is "We want to remain what we are." We value modesty, friendship, and strong national pride. We cherish our independence and identity. Our pace of life is slower than in most Northern European countries, but our standard of living consistently rates as the highest in Europe.

We have worked hard to become a respected, contributing member of the international community. We were founding members of the Benelux Economic Union in 1958, which was the model for today's European Union (EU). We actively support the EU and advocate for the smaller EU countries.

Nearly one-third of our residents are foreigners, the highest ratio in the EU. We are multilingual; most of us speak Luxembourgish, German, and French fluently. Many of us speak English, especially in tourist areas. Our cuisine offers splendid French, Belgian, and German dishes with our own flair. We have our own excellent beer and exceptional white wines.

Wedged between France and Germany, our country was repeatedly occupied, destroyed, then occupied anew. We had to rebuild more than twenty times in four hundred years, and we held on to our culture through many conquests. (From 1795 to 1815, France ruled Luxembourg and called it the Department of Forests, not a nation!)

After the Treaty of London in 1867 reaffirmed our autonomy, we declared our neutrality. Nevertheless, Germany invaded us in World Wars I and II. Much of the Battle of the Bulge was fought in Luxembourg.

In 1949, we gave up our neutrality to join the North Atlantic Treaty Organisation (NATO), and we joined other economic, political, and military organizations in the years that followed. We have no navy or air force, but

NATO's fleet of Airborne Early Warning reconnaissance aircraft is registered in Luxembourg.

In 1850, the discovery of iron ore in our land catapulted us into a top position in the European economy. We still export steel today. We created favorable banking and tax laws that have brought in global investment, letting us transform our once industrial economy to a service one. We are the world's eighth-largest banking center and a model of international finance.

Because of the United States' strong military presence in Luxembourg during World War II, Luxembourgers view Americans fondly. If you have a chance, visit the U.S. Military Cemetery at Hamm. Nearly eight thousand American soldiers of World War II lie at rest there, including General George S. Patton. Luxembourg still considers Patton its liberator. You may also want to visit the General Patton Memorial Museum in Ettelbruck.

Luxembourg is the world's only grand duchy. Please respect our uniqueness and do not call us French, Belgian, or—especially—German. We enjoy a prosperity that many larger nations envy. If you are looking to ski, hike, drink wine, or do business, please visit us. You won't be disappointed!

Vital Statistics

Population	468,571
Capital	Luxembourg
Area	998 square miles
Government	Constitutional monarchy
Living Standard	GDP = US $58,900 per capita
Natural Resources	Iron ore, arable land
Agriculture	Barley, oats, potatoes, wheat, fruits, wine grapes, livestock products
Industries	Banking, iron and steel, food processing, chemicals, metal products, engineering, tires, glass, aluminum, information technology, tourism
Climate	Temperate; humid and damp in the fall and early spring; occasionally cold in the winter; cool summers
Member of the EU?	Yes, an original member from 1967
Currency	Euro (€)

Correct Name	noun: Luxembourger(s) adjective: Luxembourg
Ethnic Makeup	Celtic base (with French and German blend), Portuguese, Italian, Slavs (from Montenegro, Albania, and Kosovo), and other European (guest and resident workers)
Languages	Luxembourgish (national language), German (administrative language), French (administrative language)
Religions	Roman Catholic 87%, Protestants 13%, small groups of Jews and Muslims

Meeting and Greeting

- Luxembourgers are friendly but reserved. Good friends greet one another with a kiss on each cheek.
- Luxembourgers shake hands gently.
- English greetings are acceptable.

Names and Titles

- Use professional titles or *Mr.*, *Mrs.*, or *Miss*. Luxembourgers use first names only for close friends and family.
- When married, a Luxembourg woman often keeps her maiden name, or she uses both her maiden name and her husband's surname, hyphenating the two.

Language

Eighty percent of the population speaks Luxembourgish (a Frankish-Germanic dialect mixed with German and French words). Luxembourgers use it more for speaking at home and at social occasions than for writing. They take pride in speaking the language.

Luxembourgers across socio-economic classes speak French and German fluently. French is the language of civil service, law, and parliament. Newspapers are written both in German and French.

Nearly half of Luxembourgers are trilingual, and 40 percent speak three or more languages. Most company employees speak and write French,

German, and English. Many Luxembourgers speak English because it's a compulsory subject in secondary schools.

Luxembourgers greatly appreciate foreigners' attempts to speak the local dialect. Locals resent foreigners who have lived and worked in their country many years without learning at least some Luxembourgish.

Conversation

Luxembourgers are very cultured, and they enjoy good conversation.

Acceptable topics
- Art
- Architecture
- Music
- Travel
- Luxembourg's natural beauty and historical sites
- Local food and wine

Unacceptable topics
- Comparisons between Luxembourg and France or Germany (Luxembourgers become particularly upset when others confuse them with Germans.)
- Luxembourg's small size
- The money-laundering investigations of recent years

Topics that require sensitivity
- The European Union
- Luxembourg's place in history

Body Language
- Luxembourgish body language is similar to Belgian and French body language (see pages 89 and 170).

Phrases

See also French and German phrases on pages 170 and 185.

English	Luxembourgish	Pronunciation
Good morning	*Gudden Muergen*	(GOOD-en MOY-en)
Good evening	*Scheinen gudden Metteg*	(SHEEN-en GOOD-en MET-egg)
Please	*Wannechgelift*	(van-EESH-ge-leeft)
Thank you	*Merci*	(MARE-see)
You're welcome	*Ech bieden ierch*	(eesh BEE-den eersh)
Yes	*Yo*	(yo)
No	*Nee*	(nay)
Excuse me	*Entschoellecht*	(ent-SHOHL-lekt)
Goodbye	*Awuër* or *Aeddi*	(AH-vwar) or (ED-ee)
How are you?	*Wie get et?*	(VAY get et)
Pleased to meet you	*Et freet mech Enchanteiert*	(et freet mek ahn-shan-TAY-eert)

Dining

- Most restaurants serve German-, French-, and Belgian-style food, and most menus are written in both French and German.
- For its size, Luxembourg has an extraordinary number of Michelin Guide–starred restaurants.

Typical Foods

Freshwater fish and crustaceans: trout, pike, and crayfish

Sauerkraut: served only with sausages or smoked pork

Multiple stews of meat and vegetables

Cooked cheese: spread on dark bread with mild mustard

Treipen: pork gut (casing) filled with meat, blood, and cabbage, and cooked until black

Judd mat Gardebounen: smoked pork with fava beans

Quenelles: fish (most often pike) dumplings

Chocolates: some of the best in the world

Drinking

- *Wein* (wine) and *Bier* (beer) are the most popular drinks. Make sure to try Luxembourg's delicious white wines.
- Luxembourgers never serve coffee with a meal, only with or after dessert.

Toasting

- *Prost* (prewst) is an informal toast that means "cheers." *Op är Gesondheet* (ahp air ge-SAHND-heat) is a formal toast that means "to your health."
- Luxembourgers also give French or German toasts (see pages 172 and 186–87).
- The host gives the first toast.
- Women may propose toasts.

Tipping

- Restaurants: The bill always include a 15 percent service charge. Leave a small additional tip.
- Taxis: Tip 10 to 20 percent of the fare.
- Bellhops and porters: Tip one euro per bag.
- Cloakroom attendants: Signs stating suggested tips are usually posted.
- Hair stylists and barbers: Tip 10 percent of the bill. Tip the shampoo person one euro.

Manners

Luxembourg manners are similar to those in Belgium and France (see pages 90–91 and 172–73).
- Compliment the food.
- To signal that you're not finished eating or that you'd like more food, cross your knife and fork on the middle of your plate.
- Eat all you take. Luxembourgers consider leaving food on your plate impolite.
- Don't ask for a tour of your host's home. Luxembourgers consider the request impolite.
- Don't put your hands in your pockets while speaking to anyone.

- Cover your mouth when yawning or sneezing.
- If possible, blow your nose in private.
- Respect people's privacy; don't ask personal questions.

Dress

Luxembourgers dress much like Belgians (see page 91). Cleanliness and neatness are very important.

- For men, casual attire means sweaters or sport coats and shirts without ties. For women, it means fashionable slacks or skirts and matching blouses.

Gifts

Luxembourgers usually open gifts upon receipt, but they may not open them if people other than the giver are present.

Hostess Gifts

A hostess probably won't unwrap a gift immediately, unless no other guests are present or expected.

Consider giving
- Flowers, except chrysanthemums (for funerals only) or red roses (connote romance)
- High-quality liqueur (Ask a retailer to recommend one.)
- Chocolates

Don't give
- Wine: Luxembourgers prefer to choose their own wines.
- Any gifts in odd numbers

Business Gifts

Luxembourgers may exchange small business gifts, but usually not at the first meeting. You may exchange a Christmas gift with a Luxembourg colleague (although it's not expected), but never send it to his or her home.

Consider giving
- Books
- Recordings of music
- High-quality liquor

Don't give

- Gifts that feature your company's logo
- Cheap, tacky gifts

Toilet Tips	
English	**Luxembourgish**
Restroom	*Toilettes/WC*
Women's restroom	*Dames*
Men's restroom	*Messieurs*
Hot water (red dot)	*C (Chaud)*
Cold water (blue dot)	*F (Froid)*

Helpful Hints

- Don't be surprised to see dogs in restaurants. Many establishments welcome dogs but not children.
- When you want information, be sure to ask specific questions. Luxembourgers may not volunteer information, but they answer specific questions.
- The first (street level) floor in buildings is numbered 0 or *res-de-chausée*, and the next floor up is numbered 1.
- Be aware that toilets may have flushing mechanisms that differ from those in North America.
- Expect the pace to be less hurried than in most other Northern European countries.

Punctuality

Luxembourgers take punctuality for business and most social occasions seriously and expect that you'll do likewise; call with an explanation if you'll be delayed.

For dinners in private homes, arrive fifteen minutes later than the start time stated on the invitation. Be on time for dinner in a restaurant.

Corporate Culture

Structure
Newer companies are developing a participative management style. Older, more established companies traditionally have had a rigid hierarchy, but union representation on the board has become more common and a consensus-oriented management style is evolving.

Meetings
Meetings are brief. Luxembourgers skip the small talk and get right down to business. Executives and managers make major decisions privately, not in meetings.

Communication
- Companies commonly use French, German, English, and Luxembourgish in business. Chances are, you won't need an interpreter, but it's a good idea to check in advance.
- Don't call a Luxembourger at home unless you've arranged to do so in advance.

Business Cards
- Luxembourgers commonly exchange business cards.
- Business cards in English are acceptable.

Be Aware
- Many international banks and multinational companies base their European headquarters or distribution centers in Luxembourg.
- There have been no major labor strikes in Luxembourg since 1922. Absenteeism is low. One-third of the workforce is from Portugal, Italy, Belgium, France, and Germany.
- Never be assertive, critical, aggressive, or rude when working with Luxembourgers.

Socializing
- Luxembourgers do most business entertaining in restaurants.
- Business breakfasts are acceptable.

- Dinners are social occasions for enjoying good food, wine, and conversation.
- Luxembourgers may invite spouses to business dinners.

Especially for Women

Although the business community is male dominated, many Luxembourg women work outside the home. Some play prominent roles in local politics. For example, Luxembourg City had a female mayor for nearly twenty years.

Luxembourg offers women excellent maternity leave, and many often return to work after having children.

- A foreign woman shouldn't hesitate to invite a Luxembourg man to dinner.
- To pay for business dinners, women should make arrangements with wait staff beforehand.

Holidays and Festivals	
January	New Year's Day (1)
February/March	Shrove Tuesday/Carnival
March/April	Easter and Easter Monday
April/May	Feast of the Ascension (40 days after Easter)
May	May Day (1)
May/June	Whitsunday (Pentecost) and Whitmonday (day after Pentecost)
June	National Day (23)
August	Feast of the Assumption (15)
November	All Saints' Day (1)
December	Christmas (25) Saint Stephen's Day (26)

MALTA
REPUBLIC OF MALTA

Greetings from Malta

Greetings from the small, sunny land whose people are famously hospitable. Over the centuries, numerous foreigners have occupied Malta, and we Maltese had to learn to get along with them.

In 60 AD, Saint Paul, the Apostle, was shipwrecked on Malta and soon experienced Maltese generosity. He states in the Bible, "[W]e then learned that the island was called Malta. And the natives showed us unusual kindness, for they kindled a fire and welcomed us all." Paul soon began to convert his hosts to Christianity, and we have been Christians ever since.

Malta is ancient. Some of its structures date from about 3800 BC, among the oldest in the world. During the Stone Age or Copper Age, a fertility cult may have dominated Malta, erecting impressive rock-cut temples at Hagar Qim and Ggantija.

Beginning around 800 BC, the Phoenicians, Carthaginians, the Roman Empire, Byzantine Empire, Arabs, Norman Sicilians, the Spanish Empire, and the Holy Roman Empire each had a turn ruling our land.

In 1530, the Spanish king and Holy Roman emperor, Charles V, deeded Malta to the Order of the Knights of Rhodes, a religious and military order of the Roman Catholic Church. As "payment" for the deed, every year the knights gave Charles V a Maltese falcon, the legendary bird of prey, to reaffirm their role as protectors of Christendom. (Sadly, the falcons are now extinct.) These Knights of Malta protected the islands for nearly three hundred years, establishing a cosmopolitan presence that is still strongly felt today, especially at their spectacular fortress overlooking the Valletta harbor.

By 1814, Malta became a British colony, and its economy centered on military facilities and the dockyard. During World War II, the Axis forces declared Malta a prime bombing target, and our nation—against severe odds—deterred the attacks. On April 15, 1942, King George VI awarded the George Cross, Britain's highest civilian decoration, to the entire Maltese population.

After the war, we alternated between establishing self-government and reverting to colonial rule, finally obtaining independence within the British Commonwealth in 1964. Ten years later, we became a republic.

Arab, Italian, French, and British influences have shaped our culture, and many Maltese identify with these nationalities. Some consider themselves

Continentals, identifying with Italians and the French. Other consider themselves Anglophiles, identifying with the British and even supporting British football (soccer) teams.

We are proud of our British connection. Many of us attended schools patterned after English schools (Eton, for example). Many of today's Maltese political and business leaders were educated in the British system.

Our lovely nation has its own particular challenges. While we have some of the world's finest natural harbors and one of the leading shipping registries, we have very few freshwater resources. Desalination of seawater provides more than half of our drinking water.

In addition, Malta is one of the world's most densely populated nations, with roughly 1,260 people per square kilometer. (By comparison, the United States has fewer than thirty people per square kilometer.) Some of us strongly believe overbuilding is causing major environmental problems.

Despite these challenges, we are proud of our sizeable achievements, including joining the United Nations and the European Union. We are well-educated, sophisticated, and cosmopolitan people with a wonderful sense of humor. Our families are very important to us, and we visit one another weekly or even daily.

Come experience our famed hospitality. We may appear reserved at first, and we expect good manners and courteous behavior. Once you get to know us, however, you will find us charming, warm, and welcoming.

Vital Statistics	
Population	398,534
Capital	Valletta
Area	122 square miles, slightly less than twice the size of Washington DC
Government	Republic
Living Standard	GDP = US $18,200 per capita
Natural Resources	Limestone, salt, arable land
Agriculture	Potatoes, cauliflower, grapes, wheat, barley, tomatoes, citrus, cut flowers, green peppers, pork, milk, poultry, eggs
Industries	Tourism, electronics, shipbuilding and repair, construction, food and beverages, textiles, footwear, clothing, tobacco

Climate	Mediterranean with mild, rainy winters and hot, dry summers
Member of the EU?	Yes, since 2004
Currency	Maltese lira (MTL); working toward converting to the euro by 2008

The People

Correct Name	noun: Maltese (singular and plural) adjective: Maltese
Ethnic Makeup	Maltese (descendants of ancient Carthaginians and Phoenicians, with strong elements of Mediterranean stock or English stock)
Languages	Maltese and English (both official)
Religion	Roman Catholic 98%

Meeting and Greeting

- Maltese always shake hands upon meeting and departing.
- Rural people may pat one another's backs, shoulders, or arms after shaking hands.
- Young people may use English greetings.

Names and Titles

- Maltese always use titles. They appreciate foreigners addressing a man as *Sinjur* and a woman as *Sinjura*.
- In some villages, people are known by their family's nickname, not last name.

English	Maltese	Pronunciation
Mr.	*Sinjur*	(sin-YOOR)
Mrs.	*Sinjura*	(sin-YOOR-ah)
Miss	*Sinjurina* (used only for girls younger than age eighteen)	(sin-YOOR-een-ah)

Language

Maltese is a Semitic language, with roots tracing back to Phoenician occupation of the islands millennia ago. Its main influence, however, was a medieval Arabic dialect, stemming from Arabic control of Malta.

The successive waves of occupation and control have heavily influenced Maltese. Latin, Italian, French, and English words have made their way into the language. Maltese is the only Semitic language to use the Roman (Latin) alphabet.

Today, English is an official language and a required subject in schools. Most Maltese speak it, including businesspeople. Many also understand Italian, which was the official language until 1934. At home, people generally speak Maltese.

Different areas have different dialects, and those in the three major cities differ from one another. In the past, a person's dialect marked his or her educational level.

For those who don't speak Semitic languages, it's difficult to learn and pronounce Maltese. Even those raised in Malta make pronunciation mistakes when they've lived away from the islands for a time. Nevertheless, try to learn some polite phrases and a toast in Maltese.

Conversation

Acceptable topics
- Malta's rich culture and history
- Football (soccer), the most popular sport: Ask your Maltese colleague about his or her favorite team.

Unacceptable topics
- Any intimation that Malta is a British colony
- Abortion, which is illegal in Malta

Topics that require sensitivity
- World War II
- Overbuilding of Malta
- The Roman Catholic Church
- Politics: Malta is a very small country, and your colleague may be related to someone in power. Don't take sides.

Please note that the Maltese language uses diacritical marks that aren't used in English. The Maltese phrases below have been simplified for North American readers.

English	Maltese	Pronunciation
Good morning	Bonġu	(BON-joo)
Good evening	Bonswa	(BONS-wah)
Please	Joghgbok	(yek YOJ-bok)
Thank you	Grazzi	(GRAH-tsee)
You're welcome	M'hemmx imn'hiex	(memsh im-NEESH)
Yes	Iva	(EE-vah)
No	Le	(leh)
Excuse me	Skuzi	(SKOO-zee)
Goodbye (formal)	Saħħa	(SAH-ha)
Goodbye (informal)	Caw	(chow)
Pleased to meet you	Ghandi pjacir	(AN-dee PYAH-chir)
How are you?	Kif inti?	(keef IN-tih)

Body Language

Maltese body language is warmer than British body language (see pages 445–46) but more reserved than Italian body language (see page 240). Don't expect much kissing from the Maltese.

Dining

Maltese cuisine is rich in vegetables and fish. In the past, meat was scarce and fish became a main protein source.

British and especially Italian cuisine have influenced Maltese dishes. For example, ravjul (ravioli) and kannoli (similar to cannoli) are popular foods. Breakfast is usually British fare: cereal, tea, and toast. British dishes (turkey, fruitcakes, puddings) are also common at Christmas.

Most other dishes have a Mediterranean flavor; some dishes are Arabic.

Typical Foods

Lampuka: dolphin fish (Swordfish is also popular.)

Fenkata: stewed rabbit (a national dish)

Soppa ta' l-armla: "widow's broth," which always contains a round of *Gbejniet* (sheep's or goat's cheese)

Minestra: vegetable soup

Aljotta: fish soup with garlic, peppers, tomatoes, rice, and fresh herbs

Bigilla: a thick pâté of broad beans with garlic

Pastizzi: pastry filled with either peas or ricotta (a popular, filling snack)

Sourdough bread: crusty and chewy

Drinking

- Maltese wines are gaining attention in Europe. In addition to varieties of French grapes, Malta produces indigenous grapes: *Gellewza* and *Ghirgentina*. Be sure to sample these distinctive wines.
- The Maltese brewery Farsons (in operation since the early 1920s) produces tasty ales and lagers.
- Kinnie is a popular brand of soft drink made from bitter oranges and herbs.

Toasting

The Maltese don't follow any special toasting rituals.

- The toast *evviva* (ay-VEE-vah) means "to life," and Maltese use it at formal and informal occasions.
- Toasts in English are acceptable.
- It's acceptable for women to propose toasts.

Tipping

- Restaurants: The bill may include a 10 percent service charge. If the bill doesn't include a service charge, tip 10 percent.
- Taxis: Taxis aren't metered, and you must negotiate the fare with the driver before beginning the trip. When paying the fare, round up to the nearest lira.
- Bellhops and porters: Tip the equivalent of one euro per bag.
- Doormen: Tip the equivalent of one euro.
- Hair stylists and barbers: Tip 10 percent of the bill.

Manners

Maltese manners are proper, like British manners (see page 448), but warm like the manners of their Mediterranean neighbors, especially Italy (see pages 242–43).

- At dinner parties, guests should wait to sit at the table until the host designates their seats and invites them to sit.
- Men shouldn't sit until all the women have been seated.
- Don't begin to eat until your hostess does.
- Never leave the table until everyone has finished eating.

Dress

The Maltese are conservative, and their clothing reflects that fact. They believe appearance indicates status. Never appear sloppy, and take care to groom properly.

- Business dress is generally quite formal; casual clothing (even smart casual) isn't appropriate in the workplace. Men wear suits, and women wear dresses or tailored suits. Women often wear hats to church services and official business or government functions.
- For formal occasions, men may wear tuxedos, and women wear cocktail dresses or evening gowns. (If you're unsure about the appropriate attire, ask your Maltese colleagues.)
- Casual attire is always elegant. Men wear slacks and shirts, and women wear blouses and skirts.
- Dress modestly when visiting churches. Women should wear dresses that come below the knee, and make sure their shoulders are covered. Also, don't wear shorts, sleeveless tops, sandals, or open-toed shoes.
- During the winter, dress in layers. Maltese may not heat their homes and offices as warmly as Americans do.

Gifts

Most Maltese open gifts upon receipt.

Hostess Gifts

Consider giving
- Flowers (in odd numbers only), except red roses (connote romance)
- Good-quality chocolates
- Pastries

Don't give
- Personal items, like clothing or perfume

Business Gifts

Consider giving
- Books about or crafts from your home region

Don't give
- Practical items
- Knives or scissors (connote the ending of a relationship)
- Handkerchiefs (connote sadness)

Toilet Tips	
English	**Maltese**
Restroom	*WC/Tojlit*
Women's restroom	*Mara*
Men's restroom	*Ragel*
Hot water	*Shun*
Cold water	*Kiesah*
Note: Restroom signs are often in English.	

Helpful Hints

- Malta is very crowded, and privacy is difficult to obtain (and thus, highly valued). Respect your Maltese colleagues' privacy.
- Never compare villages or praise one village while visiting another. There are some strong—even antagonistic—rivalries among villages.
- Don't refer to Italian, French, or especially British connections unless you're certain your Maltese colleague appreciates those connections. Some Maltese still resent foreign dominance. For example, during Britain's occupations, people with British last names received special privileges—a sore spot with some Maltese.
- Although Roman Catholicism is the dominant religion, Malta's constitution guarantees freedom of worship.

Punctuality

Although Maltese may be late for business meetings, foreigners should arrive on time and be prepared to wait.

For social occasions, arriving fifteen to thirty minutes late is acceptable, but no later, especially for dinners. Later arrivals may be acceptable for cocktail parties.

Corporate Culture

The Maltese approach to business is pragmatic, but not anxious. Maltese businesspeople say that they're efficient, but not neurotic.

For information on Maltese business practices, see the section on British corporate culture on pages 451–53, but remember that Maltese attitudes are slower and more laid back than those of their British counterparts.

Here's additional general information:

- It's not necessary to have your business cards translated into Maltese. Businesspeople speak English.
- Maltese exchange business cards at the beginning of meetings.
- Maltese businesses aren't hierarchical.
- Meetings may not have set agendas. They're largely for sharing information.
- Malta encourages foreign investment.

- Networking is essential in Malta. In such a small society, everyone knows everyone else. If you make a poor impression, others will hear about it quickly.
- It's a good idea to hire a respected local contact. You must establish who you are and demonstrate your credibility before you meet with Maltese businesspeople. Once you've established a relationship, it's not difficult to navigate any bureaucracy.
- When meeting Maltese, they're reserved until they get to know you.
- Lunches and dinners with colleagues are for building relationships; don't discuss business.

Especially for Women

Malta has the European Union's lowest rate of women who work outside the home. The rate is increasing, however, as more women return to work full- or part-time once their children are grown. Younger women are more likely to work outside the home than older women are.

When they do return to work, Maltese women may face obstacles in the workplace. As recently as ten years ago, Maltese banks might have insisted that a woman's husband cosign a business loan for her business. Although such a requirement is illegal today, it hasn't been eradicated.

Although men traditionally head Maltese families, women wield a great deal of domestic influence.

- Foreign women won't have a problem working with younger Maltese men. Working with older men, however, may present some challenges. To better your success when working with older Maltese men, follow the general rules on pages 58–59.
- Foreign women may have difficulty inviting older Maltese men to business dinners. If a man accepts a woman's invitation and she wishes to pay for the meal, she must arrange payment with the wait staff beforehand.
- Village pubs may be open only to men, but those in the cities welcome men and women.

Holidays and Festivals

January	New Year's Day (1)
February	Feast of Saint Paul's Shipwreck (10)
March	Feast of Saint Joseph (19)
	Freedom Day (31)
March/April	Easter (Friday–Sunday)
April/May	Feast of the Ascension (40 days after Easter)
May	Workers' Day (Labor Day) (1)
June	*Sette Giugno* (7)
	Feast of Saints Peter and Paul (29)
August	Feast of the Assumption Day (15)
September	Feast of Our Lady of Victories (8)
	Independence Day (21)
December	Feast of the Immaculate Conception (8)
	Republic Day (13)
	Christmas (25)

Note: Each village holds a *festa* (celebration) on the day honoring its patron saint.

NETHERLANDS
KINGDOM OF THE NETHERLANDS

Greetings from the Netherlands

Greetings from the land of commerce. Centuries ago, the Amsterdam Bank of Exchange was the biggest commercial bank in the world, and our Dutch East Indian Company was a large, powerful trading company for two centuries.

Globalism is nothing new to the Dutch. Our prosperous, open economy depends heavily on foreign trade, and the Netherlands is Europe's trading hub. In the European Union (EU), Dutch-operated companies account for a quarter of all land transport of goods and nearly half of all water transport.

In our opinion, we Dutch also created the multinational company: Philips, Unilever, and Royal Dutch Shell are just a few examples of Dutch-based companies. The Netherlands was a founding member of the North Atlantic Treaty Organisation (NATO) and the European Community, which is now the EU. In 2002, we were among the first countries to trade our strong currency for the euro.

We strive to be an egalitarian, classless society. Even our queen, Queen Beatrix, supports our middle class values and goes to work every day; she is not a figurehead. We do not bow or curtsy to her, but we trust and respect her greatly, as we do all our politicians. We have dozens of political parties but a coalition government, which handles opposition through negotiation, not confrontation.

While we value the pursuit of wealth, we are frugal. Having money is good, but we frown upon flashy displays of wealth. Although not all of us are religious, we believe in the Calvinist values of tolerance, hard work, moderation, and frugality. You will find we run our businesses as we run our country—with teamwork, cooperation, and negotiation.

We have an amazing, unparalleled facility for languages. For centuries, Netherlanders have been at least bilingual, and knowing different languages has been a main reason for our global business success. Today, 91 percent of us are bilingual and many of us speak several languages. (The average Dutch person speaks English nearly as well as a Midwesterner.) We say what is on our minds, but do not let our bluntness offend you. We are opinionated and are glad to listen to your opinions. Feel free to join in our debates.

Tolerance is not a luxury for us. We are Europe's second-most densely populated country, and we must live very close to one another. If every person's eccentricities maddened us, we would be miserable—which is why we shocked the world when, in 2005, we proposed the following: banning the use of languages other than Dutch and Frisian in all communication between the state and citizens, scrapping the right to permanent settlement for accepted refugees, stripping foreign rights to vote in local elections, and reintroducing policed borders—to name just a few proposals (some of which have since become law).

We do not believe these proposals diminish our respect for the individual. Rather, we feel we need to actively address immigration issues that are out of control. Like most European countries, we have many new residents with different values and lifestyles. Surinamese, Indonesians, Turks, Moroccans, refugees from the Balkans, and others are testing our tolerance. Nine percent of the population is foreign born (mostly Muslim).

When compared to native Netherlanders, immigrants are three times as likely to receive some form of government assistance and over three times as likely to be unemployed. Immigrants also make up half our prison population.

We struggle to deal with these facts honestly and fairly while preserving our identity. Our high population density, combined with immigration and crime problems, has forced thousands of native Netherlanders to emigrate. For many years, Dutch farmers have left their homeland because of increasingly restrictive agricultural policies. Now, financially successful businesspeople and computer specialists are leaving the country as well.

Although all drugs are technically illegal in our country, the Netherlands is known as the gateway for drugs to Europe—a distinction we neither want nor tolerate. But we also believe that we cannot simply enforce our drug laws; we must handle drug usage realistically in order to keep our society safe. For example, because we distribute free needles to heroin addicts, the Netherlands has the lowest number of drug-related deaths per capita in Europe. We also allow marijuana sales in certain controlled areas.

Despite our social troubles, we nevertheless try to be tolerant and open minded. We believe in liberal abortion policies and legalized prostitution, which we think protects society from violence and diseases. (If sexuality embarrasses you, our prostitutes, who publicly display themselves, may shock you.) Feminists and human rights groups, not the law or religious groups, criticize prostitution the most.

Our country is a great place to do business, but it is also a wonderful place to visit. Rent a bike and explore our lovely villages and towns, where you will find dikes, windmills, blazing tulip fields, rosy-cheeked farmers, and fabulous cheeses. Come and see for yourself!

Vital Statistics

Population	16,407,491
Capital	Amsterdam (The Hague, however, is the seat of government.)
Area	16,030 square miles, almost twice the size of New Jersey
Government	Constitutional monarchy
Living Standard	GDP = US $41,720 per capita
Natural Resources	Natural gas, petroleum, peat, limestone, salt, sand and gravel, arable land
Agriculture	Grains, potatoes, sugar beets, fruits, vegetables, livestock
Industries	Agroindustries, metal and engineering products, electrical machinery and equipment, chemicals, petroleum, construction, microelectronics, fishing
Climate	Generally temperate; mild winters and warm summers, but unsettled and windy; driest in spring
Member of the EU?	Yes, an original member from 1967
Currency	Euro (€)

The People

Correct Name	nouns: Dutch, Dutchmen, Dutchwomen, Netherlanders adjective: Dutch
Ethnic Makeup	Dutch 83%, other 17% (of which 9% are non-Western: mainly Turks, Moroccans, Antilleans, Surinamese, and Indonesians)
Languages	Dutch and Frisian (both official)
Religions	Roman Catholic 31%, Dutch Reformed 13%, Calvinist 7%, Muslim 5.5%, other 2.5%, none 41%

Meeting and Greeting

- The Dutch respect a person's privacy and seldom speak to strangers. They'll likely wait for you to make the first move. Don't be afraid to do so.
- The Dutch shake hands warmly, with eye contact. Upon introduction, they say their first and last names as a greeting.
- Good friends may "air kiss" one another: first on one cheek, then the other, and then back to the first.
- The Dutch frequently answer the telephone by stating only their last names.
- Don't say "hi" to older people, strangers, or people in high positions. Greetings in these situations should be more formal (*good morning/afternoon/evening*, in Dutch).

Names and Titles

- Professional titles (including *lawyer*, *engineer*, *doctor*, and *professor*) are important to some Netherlanders, and you should use titles if appropriate. It's generally clear upon introduction whether titles are important to a person. If they're not important, use general titles (*Mijnheer*, *Mevrouw*, *Juffrouw*, or *Mejuffrouw*).

English	Dutch	Pronunciation
Mr.	*Mijnheer*	(muh-NAYR)
Mrs.	*Mevrouw*	(muhv-ROW*)
Miss	*Juffrouw* (used for girls younger than age eighteen and female teachers, regardless of marital status)	(yuf-ROW*)
Ms.	*Mejuffrouw*	(muh-yuf-ROW*)
		* rhymes with *how*

- In business, use last names until you're specifically invited to use first names. Know that younger colleagues at all levels move quickly to using first names and *jij*, the informal *you*.
- Formal written correspondence, especially for foreign service or business letters, requires correct titles.

Language

Most Netherlanders speak Dutch, but people in the northeastern province of Friesland speak Frisian.

Many Netherlanders speak English, German, and French. In fact, 91 percent of the population speaks at least one other language. (Seventy-eight percent of the population speaks English.)

Conversation

The Dutch aren't loquacious. They avoid using superlatives and tend to be negative. They welcome open-minded debates but don't like to be interrupted. They're frank and direct, and they seldom take offense; they expect the same from outsiders.

Foreigners needn't worry much about hurting Netherlanders' feelings. The Dutch believe a person who never criticizes is either simple minded or a liar.

Acceptable topics
- Politics: Learn about Dutch politics before your visit so you can discuss the topic with some knowledge.
- Football (soccer)

Unacceptable topics
- Money, including prices and salaries
- Comparisons between the Dutch and German languages: The Dutch harbor old, unresolved negative feelings toward Germany.
- Personal topics: Respect people's privacy.

Topics that require sensitivity
- Religion: Don't proselytize.
- The royal family: Don't joke or make derogatory comments about the royal family.
- Your achievements: Don't boast or show off.
- Others' achievements: Don't compliment a Netherlander until you know him or her well. The Dutch offer compliments sparingly; to them, "not bad" is praise.

Body Language
- The Dutch don't touch one another in public. Leave as much space as possible between you and another person. On buses, trams, and trains,

however, you may need to use your elbow, purse, or umbrella to push your way through or to maintain your space.

- Netherlanders hug or embrace only close friends and family. (Hugging is more common in the south; those in the north are more reserved.) Bear hugs, however, aren't appropriate.
- While the Dutch expect eye contact and facial expression when speaking with someone, they may view smiling as insincere.
- Circling your index finger around your ear means you have a telephone call. Tapping your index finger on the center of your forehead means "crazy"; the Dutch consider it a very rude gesture.

Phrases

English	Dutch	Pronunciation
Good morning	*Goeden morgen*	(HOO-duh MOR-hen)
Good afternoon	*Goeden middag*	(HOO-duh MIH-dag)
Good evening	*Goeden avond*	(HOO-duh avnt)
Please	*Alstublieft*	(AHLS-tew-bleeft)
Thank you	*Dank u*	(dahnk ew)
You're welcome	*Geen dank*	(hain dahnk)
Yes	*Ja*	(yah)
No	*Nee*	(nay)
Excuse me	*Pardon*	(pahr-DAWN)
Goodbye	*Tot ziens*	(tat seenss)
Pleased to meet you	*Aangenaam*	(AHN-he-naam)
How are you? (formal)	*Hoe gaat het met u?*	(who HAHT het met oo-ay)
How are you? (informal)	*Hoe gaat het?*	(who HAHT het)

Dining

Food isn't an important part of Dutch culture, and Dutch cuisine isn't a source of cultural pride. Their meals are plain and generally eaten only with family. Only in the last two decades have Netherlanders invited one another to their homes for meals.

Typical Foods

Rijsttafel (rice table): spicy Indonesian specialties with various meats, vegetables, sauces, and rice (Indonesian restaurants are popular in the Netherlands.)

Nieuwe haring: first herring of the year, eaten raw with raw onions

Verse oesters: fresh oysters

Broodjes: buttered rolls topped with anything from cheese to crabmeat

Frieten: French fries eaten with mayonnaise

Stroopwafels: caramel sandwiched between cookie wafers

Bitterballen: deep-fried spicy meatballs

Erwtensoep: thick, hearty, meaty pea soup usually eaten with thick slabs of rye bread

Flensjes or *Pannekoeken*: large Dutch pancakes, served with a great variety of toppings, from bananas to bacon

Ontbijtkoek: spice cake, usually served at breakfast

Rookvlees: smoked horse meat

Hotchpotch: boiled stew that fulfills the Dutch values of quantity and quality

Cheeses: Edam, Kernhem, and Gouda

Note: The Dutch usually don't serve bread at dinner.

Drinking

- Strong black coffee is the national drink. The Dutch often socialize over coffee at 10:00 AM or tea at 4:00 PM, not at meals. They serve cookies or pastries at morning coffee and afternoon tea.
- The Dutch drink enormous quantities of *bier* (beer).
- Before dinners in homes, the Dutch serve *bier, jenever* (a very strong liquor that's like gin and is often followed with a beer chaser), and dry sherry. They consider *jenever* a man's drink and dry sherry a lady's afternoon drink.
- The Dutch serve *wijn* (wine) with meals.
- *Advokaat* is a thick, pungent yellow concoction made from eggs, served with whipped cream, and eaten with a spoon.

Toasting

- The toast *proost* (prohst) means "cheers," and the Dutch use it at formal and informal occasions.

- To give the toast properly, say, *"Proost,"* take a sip of your drink, and say the toast again. Then catch each guest's eye, clink each glass, and set down your glass. In western Netherlands, say the toast while raising your glass, then acknowledge each guest and take the first sip.
- Women may propose toasts.

Tipping

In many ways, the Netherlands is a self-service country. You must handle your own luggage, weigh your own produce, and pump your own gasoline. The Dutch consider themselves stingy tippers. Tip what you feel comfortable giving, but know that extravagant tips are an insult.

- Restaurants: The bill may include a 15 percent service charge. As an additional gratuity, round up the bill to the nearest euro. If the bill doesn't include a service charge, tip 5 to 10 percent for excellent service. Give the tip to the server or bartender; don't leave it on the table.
- Taxis: Round up the fare to the nearest euro.
- Bellhops and porters: Tip one euro per bag.
- Hair stylists and barbers: Tip at your own discretion. (The Dutch usually don't tip them.)

Manners

The Dutch value modest, low-key, and refined behavior. They consider ostentatious behavior or making a fuss undignified. They're serious and rarely display anger or extreme emotion.

Dutch manners combine informality with strict adherence to basic etiquette. In general, their manners are frank and no-nonsense.

- Before eating, wait until your host or hostess says, *"Eet smakelijk"* (ate smah-KAY-lick), which means "eat deliciously."
- Take a small amount of every dish to start. You'll be offered second helpings, and it's polite to accept.
- With that said, the Dutch value moderation. They won't appreciate your eating large amounts of food or asking for second and third helpings.
- You may leave a small amount of food on your plate when finished eating.
- Use your knife and fork to eat everything, including sandwiches, fruit, and pizza.

- The Dutch consider it rude to leave the table for any reason during dinner.
- Parties may go late. Plan to stay at least ninety minutes after dinner.
- At restaurants, the Dutch make it clear who pays the bill. No one hesitates to "go Dutch" (split the bill). In that case, be prepared to pay your fair share.
- To beckon wait staff, raise your hand, make eye contact, and say *ober* (OH-ber) or *mevrouw* (muhv-ROW). These words indicate "waiter" and "waitress," respectively.
- Many areas are nonsmoking. Always ask permission before smoking.
- The Dutch generally queue (stand in line) by taking a number. If there aren't numbers, they use the honor system to determine who's next in line.
- When walking with a woman on a sidewalk, a man walks nearest the street.
- Don't be surprised if someone bumps into you without an apology. The Dutch don't say "excuse me" as often as Americans do.

Dress

Don't judge a Netherlander's status or wealth by his or her appearance—you won't see much glamour. Dutch attire is informal and subdued. But when the occasion calls for proper attire, the Dutch dress carefully.
- For business, men may wear sport coats, although those working for the government or certain businesses wear suits and ties. Women wear tailored suits or dresses.
- In the office, you may remove your jacket. Doing so means you're getting down to business. When leaving the office, put on your jacket. In a meeting, follow the chairperson's lead before taking off your jacket.
- Better restaurants require men to wear suits and ties. At the theater, either formal or informal attire is appropriate (except for opening night, which requires formal attire). For restaurants and theater performances, women wear dresses or skirts and blouses.
- Dressy jeans are acceptable for informal situations. (Ask your Dutch colleagues if you're unsure whether jeans are acceptable.)
- The Dutch don't wear sneakers in the office or at a party, even with jeans.
- Halter tops and shorts are for the beach only.

Gifts

The Dutch generally open gifts upon receipt.

Hostess Gifts

When invited to someone's home, always bring a gift for the hostess. (Sending flowers on the morning of or the day after a party is also appropriate.) Present your gift upon arrival; the hostess will open it upon receipt.

Consider giving
- Flowers
- Wine
- Chocolates
- Candy
- Books

Don't give
- Knives
- Practical items
- Expensive gifts (The Dutch find ostentation embarrassing. A grand gesture of generosity only makes them uncomfortable.)

Business Gifts

In business, the Dutch exchange gifts only after developing a close, personal relationship. You may exchange Christmas gifts with Dutch colleagues, but it's not expected.

Consider giving
- Books
- Art
- Wine or liquor

Don't give
- Knives
- Practical items
- Expensive gifts

Toilet Tips

English	Dutch
Restroom	*Toilet/WC*
Women's restroom	*Dames*
Men's restroom	*Heren*
Hot water	*Warm*
Cold water	*Koud*

Helpful Hints

- Ask for the restroom, toilet, or WC. Don't ask for the bathroom. If you do, your surprised colleague will take you to the shower.
- Don't call the Netherlands "Holland." Holland is a region within the Netherlands.
- The Dutch are the cleanest people on earth except when it comes to their dogs. Watch where you step!
- There's one bike for every person living in the Netherlands. Everyone, from students to corporate leaders to grandmothers, rides a bike. The parliament even has a bicycle mechanic on staff. Renting a bike is cheaper and more fun than taking the tram, but watch out: You can get arrested for drunk biking and lose your license.
- When being entertained at someone's home, don't expect a meal unless the invitation states the hosts will serve a meal. The Dutch invite guests for drinks, wine, cheeses, and hot savories (small finger foods or appetizers) at about 8:00 or 9:00 PM. Sometimes the hostess serves wine and cheese at midnight.

Punctuality

The Dutch take punctuality for business and social occasions seriously and expect that you'll do likewise. They believe lateness, missed appointments, and postponements indicate untrustworthiness. Call with an explanation if you're delayed, or risk damaging a relationship.

Corporate Culture

Structure

Autocratic management still exists in many companies, but others have moved toward a more horizontal structure and participative management style. The difference depends on age: The younger the age of top executives, the age of the company, and the age of the industry, the more horizontal the structure and more participative the style.

Meetings

Meetings are regular and frequent. They're held primarily for discussion and followed by decision making. Participants observe reserved but informal business manners. The Dutch tend to get right down to business.

Presentations should be practical and factual. Make sure you've researched the ideas well and present them clearly.

Communication

- The Dutch use English widely in business, so you likely won't need an interpreter, but check in advance.
- Communications between functions or departments are open and tolerant. Colleagues clearly communicate strategies to all levels.
- Managers take work home and don't mind being called at home.

Business Cards

- Exchange business cards during or after conversation. (There's no set protocol to follow.)
- Business cards in English are acceptable.

Be Aware

- If there's no one to introduce you at a business or social meeting, introduce yourself and shake hands. The Dutch consider it rude not to identify yourself.
- The Dutch are hard working and pragmatic, and they're open to new ideas.
- Negotiations may be fast paced, but the decision-making process in many companies is ponderous. After companies make a decision, however, implementation is fast and efficient.
- Dutch companies are frugal and profit oriented, but not obsessed with numbers.

- Companies attribute success to the team, not individuals. But they hold individuals accountable for decisions.
- Every region has a different vacation period; check the vacation schedule of the region you're visiting before scheduling your trip. Also, don't plan business trips for the summer and over Christmas.
- Make appointments well in advance. The Dutch carefully structure their schedules and stick to them. Keep in mind that they start and end the workday earlier in the summer than during the rest of the year. They also take longer vacations than Americans do, as long as two to three weeks at a time.
- The Dutch believe if you make a commitment, you should honor it. Don't promise anything or make any offer you can't deliver. If you make an appointment, keep it. Netherlanders consider it rude to reschedule an appointment at the last minute.
- Although nearly half the country isn't religious, there are separate Protestant and Catholic universities, trade unions, television stations, and political parties.

Socializing

While the Dutch generally go home promptly after work and eat dinner with their families, businesspeople do like to entertain and be entertained.

- The Dutch do most business entertaining in restaurants, but they increasingly entertain at home as well.
- Business breakfasts aren't common.
- It's appropriate to discuss business during a lunch.
- While the Dutch often include spouses in business dinners, ask your host whether yours should be included. Netherlanders discuss business at any time during the meal, except when spouses are present.
- To treat your Dutch colleagues to fine dining, take them to a French restaurant.

Especially for Women

Women's struggle for equality is just beginning in the Netherlands, although small strides have been made.

Women make up more than 40 percent of the Dutch workforce. Even though more women than men are university graduates, fewer than 5 percent of professors are women. Few married women have careers, and fewer currently hold managerial positions. Women usually stop working when they have children—one reason may be because the Netherlands doesn't offer many childcare options.

The percentage of women working full-time in the Netherlands hasn't increased since the 1970s (25 percent—one of the lowest percentages in Europe). The percentage of women working part-time, however, is the highest in the European Union.

- The Dutch have no trouble accepting foreign businesswomen.
- It's acceptable for a foreign woman to invite a Dutchman to a business dinner, and she'll have no problem paying for the meal.
- Women can dine alone in a bar or restaurant without hassle.
- For safety reasons, ask the hotel concierge which areas you should avoid, and take taxis when out alone at night. Watch your belongings carefully on buses and streetcars.

Holidays and Festivals

March/April	Easter (Friday–Monday)
April	Queen's Day (30)
April/May	Feast of the Ascension (40 days after Easter)
May	Liberation Day (5)
May/June	Whitsunday (Pentecost) and Whitmonday (day after Pentecost)
December	Christmas (25–26)

NORWAY
KINGDOM OF NORWAY

Greetings from Norway

Greetings from the world's best country to live in—a claim backed by the 2001 United Nations Human Development Report.

By nature, we Norwegians are modest, and we value tolerance, simplicity, and kindness to one another. But we are also proud of our accomplishments. We are wealthy, well educated, and long lived. We live in excellent housing and have low unemployment.

We are convinced that we are Europe's most egalitarian social democracy, and our society meets all our citizens' needs. We work tirelessly to insure equal opportunities to all regardless of gender, sexual orientation, race, or religion. Our socialized health care keeps everyone healthy, and our state-sponsored higher education gives everyone equal opportunity to learn. Men and women share authority in our homes. Our families are small, and families with children up to age sixteen receive financial support from the government.

If Americans wonder how anyone can love royalty, they should learn about ours. When King Harald, then crown prince, became engaged to a commoner, we loved them both. When King Harald and Queen Sonja sent their two children to public schools, we loved them even more.

While we do not want to isolate ourselves from the rest of Europe, we have chosen not to join the European Union. We are fiercely independent and do not take orders from Brussels.

Although Norway is a small country, we believe our natural resources and our oil reserves let us maintain our independence. Our independent small-scale farming and fishing businesses let us preserve our economy, and our whaling businesses let us preserve our culture. We are one of the top three seafood-exporting nations world wide.

Peace and progress are our goals. In his will, Alfred Nobel named our capital, Oslo, as the city from which to award the Nobel Peace Prize. One theory to explain Nobel's decision is that he believed our government's practical policies demonstrated our support of peaceful conflict resolution.

Norway's first inhabitants, the Sami, settled here over ten thousand years ago. Twenty thousand Sami live in the far north, and some still live a traditional nomadic life herding reindeer. Likewise, we contemporary Norwegians are

determined not to let modernization obliterate our elaborate
folk costumes, dancing,
singing, and storytelling.
Our architecture (which dates
back to the Viking Age) is
unique and renowned. Our
stave churches are among
the oldest wooden buildings
on earth.

Norway is not a frozen
tundra! We have dramatic
fjords, sunny beaches, rolling
farmlands, enchanting forests,
and wonderful wildlife including seals, walruses, and polar
bears. Nature is at the core of
our lifestyle. We treasure our
landscape and our outdoor

Although Norway tried to claim neutrality during World War II, as it had done during World War I, the German army occupied the land in 1940. The Norwegians fought tenaciously, and as a result almost every northern Norwegian town and village was razed. Even after Norway surrendered and its government went into exile, Norwegians continued acts of sabotage.

Most famously, Norwegian soldiers destroyed the production facilities of Norsk Hydro, where the Germans were produc-ing a chemical vital to the development of a nuclear bomb. Many Norwegian civilians gave their lives to destroy a supply of the chemical en route to Germany.

activities, like sailing and cross-country skiing. Many of us have modest
second homes (*hytte*) in the mountains.

If you want to see our land at its best and brightest, visit us in the summer
during the midnight sun. From mid-May through most of July, the sun never
drops below the horizon in Norway's northern areas. Even in southern areas,
there is daylight from 3:00 AM to 11:00 PM. Conversely, the sun does not rise
in the north from the end of November through most of January.

Please visit us. We are warm and welcoming, and if you stay long enough,
you may not want to leave!

Vital Statistics

Population	4,593,041
Capital	Oslo
Area	125,200 square miles, slightly larger than New Mexico
Government	Constitutional monarchy
Living Standard	GDP = US $70,400 per capita
Natural Resources	Petroleum, titanium, copper, natural gas, pyrites, nickel, iron ore, zinc, lead, fish, timber, hydropower

Agriculture	Barley, wheat, potatoes, pork, beef, veal, milk, fish
Industries	Petroleum and gas, food processing, shipbuilding, pulp and paper products, metals, chemicals, timber, mining, textiles, fishing
Climate	West coast has marine climate with cool summers and mild, rarely freezing winters, moderated by the North Atlantic Current; coastal rainfall can be as much as 2,000 millimeters (80 inches) a year. Inland summers are warmer, winters are colder, and there's less rain.
Member of the EU?	No
Currency	Norwegian krone (NOK)

The People

Correct Name	noun: Norwegian(s) adjective: Norwegian
Ethnic Makeup	Norwegian, Sami (20,000)
Languages	Two dialects of Norwegian, Bokmål and Nynorsk (both official); small Sami- and Finnish-speaking minorities
Religions	Church of Norway 85.7%, Pentecostal 1%, Roman Catholic 1%, other Christian 2.4%, Muslim 1.8%, other 8.1%

Meeting and Greeting

- Norwegians shake hands firmly and briefly.
- Only good friends greet one another with *hei* (hey), which means "hi."
- Norwegians say *morn* (morn) to greet one another, regardless of the time of day.

Names and Titles

English	Norwegian	Pronunciation
Mr.	*Herr*	(har)
Mrs.	*Fru*	(fruh)
Miss	*Frøken*	(FROO-ken)

- For formal occasions and first introductions, address people with *Herr*, *Fru*, or *Frøken* + first name + last name. Thereafter, skip the first name and use only *Herr*, *Fru*, or *Frøken* + last name.
- Norwegians most often address one another with the "good day" greeting, *God dag* (goo dahg) + last name. They'll likely ask you to do the same.
- Norwegians don't normally use occupational titles (*professor*, *doctor*, and so on). As a foreigner, you may want to use the title on a Norwegian's business card when first meeting, but more informal Norwegians will ask you to use only last names.
- Don't use titles to address lawyers or clergy.
- Use last names and appropriate titles until your Norwegian hosts or colleagues invite you to use first names.
- The traditional way to address a Norwegian married couple is *Herr* and *Fru* + the husband's first and last names or just the last name.
  Example: *Herr* and *Fru* Nils Johansen, or *Herr* and *Fru* Johansen
- A contemporary way to address a Norwegian married couple is *Herr* and *Fru* + both the husband's and wife's first names + the husband's last name.
  Example: *Herr* and *Fru* Nils and Inger Johansen
- Be aware that more Norwegian women use just their maiden names after marrying.

Language

The official Norwegian language has two dialects that differ subtly. Three-fourths of the population speak Bokmål, which is influenced by the Danish language and is the "book language" (that is, it's used for written communication and for broadcasting). People living in urban areas mostly speak Bokmål.

People living in rural areas generally speak Nynorsk, which is based on spoken rural dialects. Norwegian law requires a certain percentage of schools and broadcast media to use Nynorsk.

Norwegian schoolchildren study Norwegian, French, and English. In fact, many Norwegians across the country understand English.

Conversation

When speaking with Norwegians, be sincere but emotionally reserved. Norwegians consider Americans too glib and casual. For example, don't say, "Pleased to meet you" or "How are you?" Norwegians believe Americans use these phrases without sincerity. If a Norwegian were to ask, "How are you?" he or she would expect a long, detailed answer.

Acceptable topics

- Norway's history and culture
- Norway's natural beauty: Norwegians are proud of their landscape. Take the time to notice it, appreciate it, and comment on it.
- Norway's decision not to join the European Union

Unacceptable topics

- Personal topics, like income, social status, age, and so on
- Comparisons between Norway and America, especially to suggest that America is better

Topics that require sensitivity

- Oil wealth
- Absenteeism from work
- The welfare state
- Taxes

In general, there are very few topics you can't discuss with Norwegians. Just always remember the Norwegian rule of conversation: *Janteloven*, which means never acting superior. Every Norwegian follows this rule, even royalty.

Here's how the rule breaks down, according to Aksel Sandemose, a famous twentieth-century Danish writer:

- You shall not believe that you *are* somebody.
- You shall not believe that you are as worthy as *us*.
- You shall not believe that you are any *wiser* than us.
- You shall not imagine that you are any *better* than us.
- You shall not believe that you know anything *more* than us.
- You shall not believe that you are *more* than us.
- You shall not believe that *you* are good at anything.
- You shall not *laugh* at us.
- You shall not believe that anyone cares about *you*!
- You shall not believe that you can teach *us* anything!

Body Language

Norwegians rarely touch one another except among relatives and close friends. Don't slap anyone's back, and don't put your arm around anyone.

Phrases		
English	**Norwegian**	**Pronunciation**
Good morning	*God morgen*	(goo MORE-en)
Good day (formal)	*God dag*	(goo dahg)
Good day (informal)	*Morn*	(morn)
Good evening	*God kveld*	(goo koo-EHLD)
Please	*Vær så snill*	(vahr soh SNIL)
Thank you	*Takk*	(tock)
You're welcome	*Vær så god*	(VAHR soh goo)
Yes	*Ja*	(yah)
No	*Nei*	(nay)
Excuse me	*Omforlatelse*	(ohm-fah-LAHT-el-seh)
Goodbye (formal)	*Adjø*	(ahd-YER)
Goodbye (informal)	*Ha det*	(hahl duh)

Dining

Norwegian food is typically quite simple and plain. Fish dishes are abundant.

Typical Foods

Reinsdyr: reindeer steak with lingonberries

Reker: boiled shrimp

Tork: cod

Flatbrød: crisp, thin rye bread

Laks: salmon

Røkelaks: smoked salmon

Gravlaks: salmon cured with dill

Sild: herring

Fiskepudding: fish pudding with bread crumbs and cream

Smørbrød or *Snitter*: bread with a topping, like shrimp, salad, salmon, or roast beef

Lutefisk: lye-soaked, nearly gelatinous dried cod (Norwegians love it, but it's definitely an acquired taste. Start with a small portion.)

Cheeses: along with fish, staples of the Norwegian diet

Drinking

Norwegians typically serve:

- Sherry, Scotch, and champagne as cocktails
- Wine or *øl* (beer) with dinner
- Port and Madeira with dessert
- Cognac after dinner
- Aquavit (a very potent hard liquor similar to a spiced vodka) with food that has a high fat content: It's used to calm the stomach and usually followed with a beer chaser. It doesn't go well with wine. You can drink aquavit in one gulp, but be careful—it's strong.

Toasting

- The toast *skål* (skohl) means "cheers," and Norwegians use it at formal and informal occasions.
- The host makes a small speech and offers the first toast.
- For a formal toast, look into the eyes of the person being toasted, nod slightly, say, "*Skål*," then take a drink. Before putting down your glass, meet the person's eyes again and nod.
- In formal settings, the meal ends with the male guest of honor tapping his glass with a knife and toasting the hostess on behalf of all the guests by saying, "*Takk*" (tock), which means "thank you." A short story or joke may accompany the toast.
- It's acceptable for women to propose toasts.

Tipping

Norwegian service workers in all industries receive good salaries. Tipping isn't expected or required, although it has become more common recently.

- Restaurants: It's common to round up the bill to the nearest NOK10. For exceptional service, you may leave a small tip, about 5 percent of the bill.
- Taxis: The fare includes a tip, but round up the fare to the next NOK5 or NOK10.
- Bellhops and porters: Tip NOK10 to NOK20 per bag.
- Gas station attendants, hair stylists, barbers, maids, and doormen: No tip is necessary. All earn good salaries.

Manners

- When at someone's home, wait until your host invites you to sit before doing so.
- Don't pick up an open-faced sandwich to eat it; use a knife and fork.
- It's polite to eat everything on your plate. Norwegians don't like to waste food, but they don't expect you to stuff yourself.
- It's impolite to leave immediately after dinner.
- On public transportation or in public venues, men offer their seats to women, and younger people offer their seats to the elderly.
- To beckon wait staff, raise your hand with your index finger extended.
- Speak quietly and don't behave too casually.
- Cover your mouth when yawning.
- Never invite someone to a meal or suggest "getting together" unless you can follow through.

Dress

Norwegian attire is conservative and in the European style (see pages 44–45).
- For business, men wear suits or sport coats and ties. Women wear tailored suits, dresses, or dress pants and blouses.
- In restaurants, men wear suits. Better restaurants require ties. Women wear dresses or blouses and dress pants or skirts.
- For the theater or opera, men wear dark suits. (Tuxedos aren't common.) Women wear cocktail dresses. Some people wear casual clothes.
- Clean jeans and T-shirts (not torn or faded) are appropriate for very casual occasions.
- Because the climate is cool much of the year, warm clothing is necessary.

Gifts

Norwegians open gifts upon receipt.

Hostess Gifts

Consider giving
- Flowers, except carnations or bouquets of only white flowers (for funerals only): If invited to a dinner party, send flowers to the hostess on the morning of the event.

- Chocolates
- Wine
- Pastries
- Liquor (very expensive in Norway)

Don't give
- Wreaths (for funerals only—even at Christmas)

Business Gifts

Norwegians normally don't exchange gifts at business meetings, but you may exchange small gifts at the successful conclusion of negotiations. It's acceptable to give a Christmas gift to a Norwegian colleague, but it's not expected.

In general, there aren't any gifts to avoid giving your Norwegian colleagues. But you shouldn't give an excessive gift; your colleagues may consider it a bribe.

Consider giving
- Good-quality brandy or whiskey (but not too expensive)

Toilet Tips	
English	**Norwegian**
Restroom	*Toalett/WC*
Women's restroom	*Damer*
Men's restroom	*Herrer*
Hot water	*V*
Cold water	*K*

Helpful Hints

- Never lump Norwegians with Swedes or Danes. Recognize the unique, adventurous spirit of Norwegians.
- A *smørgåsbord* is a meal that's served as a buffet.
- Surnames that end *-en* are most likely Norwegian or Danish. Names that end *-on* are most likely Swedish.
- *Lett øl* (light beer) means reduced alcohol content, not reduced caloric content.
- You should never drink and drive, but especially not in Norway. The legal limit for blood alcohol content is only 0.05 percent, and one beer could put you over the limit.

Punctuality

Norwegians take punctuality for business and social occasions seriously. They expect that you'll do likewise; call if you're delayed. A start time of 7:00 PM means 7:00 PM.

Corporate Culture

Structure

Participative management is the norm in Norwegian companies. Consensus is a priority, but the boss makes the final decisions. Norwegians are familiar with American business practices (efficiency, punctuality, direct speech, and so on).

Meetings

Informality is the rule in meetings; participants mix casual conversation and jokes with business discussions.

Communication

- Most Norwegian businesspeople are fluent in English, and you likely won't need an interpreter, but check in advance.
- It's acceptable to call a Norwegian colleague at home before 10:00 PM.

Business Cards

- Business cards in English are acceptable, and Norwegians generally exchange them without much ceremony.

Be Aware

- Norwegians have both a strong work ethic and a strong interest in leisure activities. Most office workers finish their workdays at precisely 4:00 or 5:00 PM, but it's not unusual for managers to work into the evening.
- Norwegians don't flaunt their success, wealth, or material possessions, and they don't care for people who do.
- Schedule appointments well in advance.

Socializing

- Norwegians generally do business entertaining first in restaurants. After colleagues get to know one another, home entertaining is common.
- Breakfast meetings aren't typical.
- Business lunches are to discuss business.
- Business dinners are mostly social, but guests may also discuss business. Let the host open the discussion.
- Dinners are generally long, with three courses and much conversation.
- Norwegians usually don't include spouses in business dinners in restaurants.
- First-class restaurants are very expensive. Ask your Norwegian colleague to recommend a restaurant.
- Cocktail hours are generally short (thirty to forty-five minutes).

Especially for Women

In terms of equality for women, Norway is very advanced. It's a good place for businesswomen. Norwegian women hold positions in all levels of corporate and public life.

- It's acceptable for a foreign woman to invite a Norwegian man to dinner, and she won't have a problem paying the bill.
- A woman may go to a bar or restaurant alone without hassle.
- It's generally safe to walk alone at night in most areas, but use common sense.

Holidays and Festivals

January	New Year's Day (1)
March/April	Palm Sunday Easter (Thursday–Monday)
April/May	Feast of the Ascension (40 days after Easter)
May	Labor Day (1) Constitution Day (17)
May/June	Whitsunday (Pentecost) and Whitmonday (day after Pentecost)
December	Christmas (25–26)

POLAND
REPUBLIC OF POLAND

Greetings from Poland

Greetings from the land of some of Europe's proudest and bravest people.

Two facts have had marked effects on Poland's history: its proximity to hostile neighbors and its mostly flat terrain. (*Polska* means "land of fields.") Through centuries of war and invasion, we Poles have earned our reputation as valiant, tenacious fighters. Napoleon Bonaparte once said, "There should not be anything impossible for my Poles!" when he ordered a light horse brigade into an impossible charge. The Poles fought bravely—but were cut down.

Polish warriors have a place in American history, too. Several Poles fought with the Continental Army in the American Revolution. Tadeusz Kosciuszko and Kazimierz Pulaski were both distinguished military officers.

In the early days of World War II, Polish cavalry officers charged German tanks and trucks on horseback—a meaningless gesture to some, but to us, one of utmost pride. Although the officers knew they could not win, they would not give up.

One of the most famous Polish sites is not one of pride, but of grief. *Oświęcim*—more widely known by the German name *Auschwitz*—stands as a horrifying reminder of the genocide that occurred during World War II. Nearly one hundred thousand Poles died at the concentration camp. By the end of the war, more than six million Poles died, half of them Jews.

True to our nature, we fought fiercely during the war, many of us helping those with little hope of survival. One such person was Irena Sendler, who helped rescue 2,500 Jewish children from the Warsaw Ghetto. Right under Nazi noses, Sendler had the children smuggled out, given new identities, and adopted by others until the war was over. She buried records of the children's true identities in jars. When the Nazis discovered her operation, Sendler was tortured but never revealed the records to the Gestapo.

After the war, we continued to struggle against tyranny. In 1945, our government became a Communist one. Poles did not welcome Communism; we say Communism fit Poland the way a horse's saddle fits a pig.

In the 1970s, Lech Wałęsa led the Solidarity movement, a fight against Soviet domination that continued until the collapse of Communism and the dissolution of the Soviet Union. In 1990, Wałęsa was elected the first president of the Republic of Poland. We joined the European Union in May 2004, officially establishing our determination to become a viable market economy.

The Roman Catholic Church has been entwined in our lives since 966, when the duke of Poland converted to Christianity. We credit the Church with helping us retain our culture and identity over centuries of occupation. Today, about 90 percent of us consider ourselves Catholic (even though a quarter of those do not attend Mass regularly). Evidence of our Catholicism is everywhere, from breathtaking medieval cathedrals to tiny rural chapels. In October 1978, when Karol Wojtyla, the Archbishop of Krakow, became Pope John Paul II, he was the first non-Italian pope elected since 1522.

We are very proud of our fine tradition of education, dating back to 1364, when Jagiellonian University in Krakow was founded. During World War II, one function of the Polish Secret State was to manage an underground educational system that taught more than a million elementary and secondary students and over ten thousand university students.

There have been six Polish Nobel Prize winners, including Maria Skłodowska Curie. She was the first woman to win a Nobel Prize and the first person to win two Nobel Prizes (physics and chemistry). Lech Wałęsa won the Nobel Peace Prize in 1983.

We are obsessed with nurturing our traditions and language, believing that a culture

> Poles' sense of humor is an important part of their identity. They love to tell jokes, often ironic and self-deprecating, as a way to cope with challenges and adversity.
>
> Here's a prime example: When, after another invasion, an old Polish woman learned her home was now in Russia, she replied, "Thank God! I could not have stood another of those cold Polish winters."

of such strength and courage should live on. Our contributions to the arts and literature are well known. Polish folk songs inspired famous Polish composer Frédéric Chopin. Especially during Communism, our literature often used allegories, allusions, and symbols to make political and social commentaries that escaped censorship. Our carved wood sculptures (an old tradition) and amber jewelry are world famous.

Poland borders Germany, the Czech Republic, Slovakia, Ukraine, Belarus, Lithuania, and Russia. Our location has placed us in the middle of many wars, but today our central position is excellent for doing business. Visit us in our lovely cities. We will welcome you warmly!

Population	38,635,144
Capital	Warsaw
Area	120,728 square miles, slightly smaller than New Mexico
Government	Republic
Living Standard	GDP = US $8,260 per capita
Natural Resources	Coal, sulfur, copper, natural gas, silver, lead, salt, amber, arable land
Agriculture	Potatoes, fruits, vegetables, wheat, poultry, eggs, pork, dairy
Industries	Machine building, iron and steel, coal mining, chemicals, shipbuilding, food processing, glass, beverages, textiles
Climate	Temperate with cold, cloudy, moderately severe winters with frequent precipitation; mild summers with frequent showers and thundershowers
Member of the EU?	Yes, since 2004
Currency	Zloty (PLN); no target date for converting to the euro

The People

Correct Name	noun: Pole(s) adjective: Polish
Ethnic Makeup	Polish 96.7%, German 0.4%, Belarusian 0.1%, Ukrainian 0.1%, other and unspecified 2.7%
Languages	Polish (official) 97.8%, other and unspecified 2.2%
Religions	Roman Catholic 89.8% (about 75% practicing), Eastern Orthodox 1.3%, Protestant 0.3%, other 0.3%, unspecified 8.3%

Meeting and Greeting

- Polish men and young people greet one another with a handshake. Handshakes are firm between men, less so between women or between a man and a woman.
- Polish women may greet one another with a handshake, or they may simply nod slightly upon introduction. Shake a woman's hand only if she extends it.

- Close friends may greet one another with a kiss on the right cheek, then the left, then the right again.
- A Polish man may kiss a woman's hand, but only if the woman is clearly older or younger than he. Foreign men shouldn't kiss women's hands.
- Children often curtsy or bow upon introduction.

Names and Titles

English	Polish	Pronunciation
Mr. (Sir)	*Pan*	(pahn)
Mrs. or Ms. (Madam)	*Pani*	(PAHN-ee)
Miss	*Panna* (very old fashioned and rarely used)	(PAHN-nah)

- Use first names only after your Polish colleagues invite you to do so; however, always use last names and titles with people who are of higher rank or are older than you.
- In business and formal situations, Poles address people by *Pan/Pani* + professional titles only.
    Examples: *Pan* Doctor or *Pani* Professor
- On occasion, Poles use *Madam* for *Pani*.
- Poles sign their names last name first and first name second.

Language

Polish is a West Slavic language that uses the Roman (Latin) alphabet. Its grammatical structure is complicated, but its pronunciation rules are consistent. It isn't difficult to learn some basic phrases—despite the intimidating diacritical marks and strings of consonants.

The most common second languages are German and English, the latter more popular in urban areas and among younger people. There are small ethnic minorities, like the Silesians and Kaszubs, who maintain their own languages. Most Poles, however, speak only Polish.

Although during the Communist era Poles learned Russian in school, you shouldn't speak Russian to your Polish colleagues, even if they're likely to understand it.

Conversation

In private, Poles are outspoken. They consider themselves realists, which may cross into cynicism. Their sense of humor is well honed. Telling jokes was a way to poke fun at Communism and Soviet control.

In formal situations, Poles begin conversations with *prosze pana* (PRO-sheh pahn) or *prosze pani* (PRO-sheh PAHN-ee), which means "please, sir" and "please, madam" respectively.

Acceptable topics
- Poland's beauty
- Music
- Art
- Pope John Paul II

Unacceptable topics
- Any topic that implies Poland is part of Eastern Europe: Poles consider themselves Central Europeans, not Eastern Europeans.

Topics that require sensitivity
- World War II
- Anti-Semitism
- The Austrian and German occupations: Don't use the German names for Polish cities. For example, the Germans called Gdańsk "Danzig." Be sure to use the Polish names.

Body Language
- Poles use their hands when talking.
- Poles stand closer to one another than Americans do.
- Girls may hold hands when walking together.
- Blinking both eyes indicates romantic interest.
- Placing an index finger along side the nose means that what you've just said is a joke or isn't completely true.

Phrases

English	Polish	Pronunciation
Hello/Good day/ Good morning	*Dzień dobry*	(djen DOH-breh)
Good evening	*Dobry wieczór*	(DOH-breh VYEH-chor)
Please/you're welcome	*Proszę*	(PROH-sheh)
Thank you	*Dziękuję*	(djen-KOO-yeh)
Yes	*Tak*	(tahk)
No	*Nie*	(nyeh)
Excuse me	*Przepraszam*	(psheh-PRAH-shahm)
Goodbye	*Do widzenia*	(doh vee-DZEE-nya)

Pleased to meet you
  (to a man)
	Miło mi Pana poznać	(MEE-woh mee PAH-nah
		  POH-znach)

Pleased to meet you
  (to a woman)
	Miło mi Panią poznać	(MEE-woh mee PAH-nyom
		  POH-znach)

How are you?	*Co nowego?*	(tsoh noh-VEH-goh)

Dining

Nearly half of Poland is arable land, and it has been a breadbasket for centuries, importing only exotic food like citrus, coffee, and spices.

Poles eat breakfast (*sniadanie*) early, then a light "second breakfast" (*drugie sniadanie*) around 10:00 AM. They eat their main meal, *obiad*, which doesn't have an American equivalent, in the early afternoon. It usually consists of soup, a main course with side dishes, and dessert. Families eat a light meal together between 6:00 and 8:30 PM.

Polish hospitality is famous. Poles welcome everyone, friend or stranger, with food.

Typical Foods

Zupy: soups with vegetables, meat, or even fruit, served hot or cold (They're an essential part of Polish cuisine.)

Pierogi: dumplings stuffed with a variety of fillings, including fruit, cheese, sauerkraut, and ground meat

Gołąbki: cabbage rolls stuffed with ground meat and rice

Kiszka: sausage made with fresh pig's blood

Kapusta: sauerkraut, usually stewed with pork

Bigos: dish of meat, mushrooms, sausage, and sauerkraut (Each family has its own recipe.)

Bread: freshly baked (Many Poles buy bread daily, but they use stale bread to thicken soups and to garnish dishes, as well as for other uses.)

Polish hams: an important export item

Mushrooms: used as main courses, side dishes, and flavoring (They're an important part of Polish cuisine.)

Pickles: cured in brine (The Polish pickles sold in the United Stated are cured in vinegar.)

Horseradish, dill, marjoram, caraway seeds: popular flavorings

Drinking

- Vodka is Poland's national drink, and Poles claim they invented it. It's available in many varieties, from sweet to extra dry, and may be infused with fruit, juniper berries, or herbs. One variety, *żubrówka* ("bison grass" vodka) is a brand flavored with grass from the Bialowieza forest, on which bison feed.
- Poles consume beer and soft drinks at room temperature. They consider cold drinks unhealthy.

Toasting

- The toast *na zdrowie* (nahz-DROHV-yeh) means "to your health," and the toast *smacznego* (smahch-NAY-goh) means *"bon appétit."* Poles say either at formal and informal occasions.
- The host may toast a guest during the meal. It's polite for the guest to return the toast later.
- It's acceptable for women to propose toasts.

Tipping

- Restaurants: The bill may include a 10 percent service charge. If the bill doesn't include a service charge, tip 10 percent. In either case, round up the tip to the nearest zloty or two.

- Taxis: Tipping drivers wasn't common in the past, but this practice may be changing as more businesspeople travel in Poland. Round up the fare to the nearest zloty or two.
- Porters: Tip 50 cents to one euro per bag.
- Bellhops: For showing you to your room, tip the equivalent of one euro. For handling your luggage, tip fifty cents to one euro per bag.
- Hair stylists and barbers: Tip 10 percent of the bill. Tip assistants 5 percent.
- Cloakroom or restroom attendants: Tip small change.

Manners

- Poles appreciate a beautifully decorated table. No matter how poor the home, they believe the table should be lovely. Table linens are often family heirlooms. When invited to a Polish home, make sure to compliment the table setting.
- Poles may not converse much during the meal, but they may talk at the table after the meal. Be sure to join in.
- If you've had enough to eat, leave a little food on your plate.
- Poles believe it's insulting to leave a dinner party early.
- Polish men are courtly; they offer women their seats, open doors for women, and so on.
- Always call before visiting someone. It's rude to drop by unexpectedly, even at a friend's home.
- After someone has entertained you, always send a handwritten thank-you note the next day.

Dress

Poles dress conservatively but fashionably, and they're careful about their grooming. European fashions especially influence younger people.
- For business, people at every level dress formally. Men wear dark suits. Women wear dresses or pantsuits; they never wear revealing clothing.
- For formal occasions, men wear dark suits; women wear cocktail dresses.
- Casual dress is always smart casual. (See page 45.) Jeans are appropriate for some casual get-togethers (for example, when visiting with young people or at cafés), but they should always be neat and stylish.
- When visiting churches, dress conservatively.
- Shorts aren't acceptable for either men or women, except at the beach.

Gifts

Poles usually open gifts upon receipt. When visiting someone's home, bring small gifts for any children. The family will appreciate the gesture.

Hostess Gifts

Consider giving
- Flowers, unwrapped and in an odd number
- Wine or vodka
- Chocolates

Don't give
- Anything that implies that modern consumer goods aren't available in Poland (chewing gum, cigarettes, and so on)
- Personal items

Business Gifts

It's traditional to exchange gifts with your Polish colleagues upon first meeting and at the successful completion of a deal.

Consider giving
- Books about your home region or any kind of art book
- Crafts or food items from your home region.

Don't give
- Very expensive gifts (may be considered bribes)

Toilet Tips	
English	**Polish**
Restroom	*Toalety*
Women's restroom	*Damska*
Men's restroom	*Męska*
Cold water	*Żimna*
Hot water	*Czepła*

Helpful Hints

- If smoking bothers you, be prepared: Many Poles smoke, and they consider it very rude—even hostile—to ask them to stop or step outside. Your Polish colleagues may even smoke during business meetings.
- Always ask your Polish hosts to tell you about their city's highlights.
- Never compare one region of Poland to another. Poles are just as proud of their home regions as they are of their nation.
- There are still Poles, especially in some rural areas, who wear traditional dress every day. Never assume they're in "costume."
- A Pole's name day (the day celebrating his or her patron saint) is often more important than his or her birthday. Don't forget to at least call your Polish friends on their name days.

Punctuality

Poles have a rather relaxed sense of time. Your Polish colleagues may be late for meetings, and they'll expect your patience. Foreign businesspeople should always be prompt.

For social occasions, especially at a person's home, arrive a few minutes late. Don't arrive early.

Corporate Culture

After decades of external control, Poles cheered the end of the Soviet occupation and Communism. Today, they're wary of foreigners' commandeering their economy. Poles welcome foreign business partners, but foreigners must not appear to dominate or exploit the developing economy in any way. Foreign companies should hire local Polish managers to oversee operations.

The change to a market economy has been slow and often painful. Unemployment has been high for several years, as job security has disappeared. The change has left many feeling resentful, but has also spurred entrepreneurs.

For more information on doing business with a formerly Communist country, see pages 17–18.

Structure

Poles respect the chain of command. Never go over someone's head.

Meetings

- Initial meetings are formal, but they aren't tightly run. Subsequent meetings will have stricter agendas.
- Before a meeting begins, coffee and tea are offered. Participants may politely decline.
- Meetings may run longer than the time scheduled. Poles allow time for everyone to express his or her opinion and for brainstorming. Make sure to plan plenty of time between meetings.
- After a meeting ends, people stay to make small talk. Be sure to participate.
- Ask permission to audio- or video-record meetings.

Communication

- Initially, meetings with prospective Polish colleagues must be face to face.
- Have a reputable translator translate your correspondence into Polish. Doing so is worth the extra expense. Before meetings, send translated copies of your proposal, a proposal summary, meeting agenda, and supporting documentation. Allow time for your Polish colleagues to review the material. Follow up each meeting with a meeting summary and revised summary of your proposal.

Business Cards

- Have one side of your business card printed in English and the other side in Polish. Finding print shops in Poland isn't difficult.
- Hand a business card to each person upon introduction. Don't slide your cards across the table or deal them to people as you would playing cards.

Be Aware

- In most cases, expect to meet with potential colleagues several times before striking a deal; however, Poles will move quickly if circumstances demand speed.
- Polish businesspeople can be very aggressive. Keep your cool.
- Hire a *zalatwic sprawe*—that is, a "wheeler dealer," a Polish contact person who knows how to successfully work with the bureaucracy and business regulations.
- Make as many contacts as you can.
- Communism emphasized quantity over quality. That mindset is disappearing, but slowly.

- As Poles transition to a market economy, customer service is still a fairly new idea.
- To make deals, you may have to meet with government officials as well as business associates.
- Confirm all appointments in writing.
- Impromptu appointments are unusual but not unheard of.

Socializing

- Going out to eat and drink is part of doing business in Poland. Your Polish colleagues expect enthusiastic participation.
- You don't have to keep up with your Polish colleagues' drinking; it's acceptable to stop when you've had enough alcohol.
- If a Polish colleague takes you to an expensive restaurant, reciprocate at a similarly priced restaurant. To spend far more or far less on him or her is an insult.

Especially for Women

Mostly for economic reasons, both men and women generally work outside the home in Poland. Grandmothers often take care of children and household matters while mothers are at work. Regardless of whether they work outside the home, women still largely manage households and child rearing.

Polish women haven't been well represented in higher levels of business and government, and Polish men aren't used to female supervisors. But these facts are changing. Hanna Suchocka was the Polish prime minister from 1992–1993. Hanna Gronkiewicz-Walz was the president of the National Bank of Poland from 1992–2000, then became vice president for the European Bank for Reconstruction and Development.

- Poles accept foreign businesswomen more than they do Polish business-women, but foreign women will still have troubles being accepted. To gain acceptance, they should have a trusted local colleague introduce them. In addition, they must present their credentials immediately and act professionally at all times.
- Polish men don't drink with women, and important conversations and decisions likely occur during after-work drinks. Foreign businesswomen should make sure that a trusted male subordinate attends these occasions in her stead.

- Poles may interpret a woman's approaching a male stranger and talking to him—even to simply ask for directions—as flirting.

Holidays and Festivals

January	New Year's Day (1)
March/April	Easter and Easter Monday
May	Labor Day (1)
	Constitution Day (3)
May/June	Corpus Christi (about 8 weeks after Easter)
August	Feast of the Assumption (15)
November	All Saints' Day (1)
	Independence Day (11)
December	Christmas (25–26)

Note: For some families, Christmas Eve, or *Wigilia* ("to await"), may be just as important or more so than Christmas Day.

PORTUGAL
PORTUGUESE REPUBLIC

Greetings from Portugal

Greetings from Europe's new hot spot. People are discovering our rich seafaring past, superb beach resorts, nostalgic towns, and a landscape covered with olive groves, vineyards, and wheat fields.

After we hosted EURO 2004, a sixteen-nation football (soccer) championship, the international jet set has shown even more interest in us. People are not only holding swank parties here, but also buying villas, golf courses, and retirement homes.

Nearly forty years ago, the world considered Portugal a poor, backward country. From 1932 to 1968, prime minister António Salazar ruled our country as a dictator. While his reign sidelined our country's progress, it may have helped us maintain our traditions. We are a conservative people and do not quickly embrace change. The Catholic Church strongly influences our lives, and we take *romarias* (festivals honoring patron saints) very seriously, almost as seriously as local football matches.

Savoring life is our passion, and simplicity is at the heart of our culture. Our food is simple, delicious, and served in large portions. We dress much of it with our delectable olive oil. With meals, we serve good-quality *vinhos* (wines) or port—the sweet wine (fortified with brandy) that is synonymous with Portugal. Only wine from the Douro River Valley in northern Portugal can be called port.

Portugal is one of the world's most distinctive wine producers, having many native grape varieties and accomplished vintners. Of course, we always knew we had fabulous wine, but now many Portuguese businesspeople as well as foreigners have been investing in vineyards and developing their own labels.

Much of our architecture is in the unique Manueline style, known for its Moorish and Flamboyant Gothic flourishes (extravagant twists, turns, spirals, and nautical themes). Decorative glazed tiles known as *azulejos* grace many of our buildings. We are proud of our United Nations Educational, Scientific and Cultural Organization (UNESCO) World Heritage sites, and we think Lisbon is one of Europe's most relaxed, attractive, and affordable capitals.

Our arts have historical roots. Dramatist Gil Vicente and poet Luís de Camões (whose *Os Lusíadas* is our national epic poem) started Portugal's rich literary tradition in the sixteenth century. In the early twentieth century,

Fernando Pessoa became renowned for his heteronymic writing (when an author conceives a new personality and writes works from that personality). The melancholy *fado*, which sixteenth-century sailors may have first sung, is our best-known music.

We cherish folk festivals, and in rural towns we still love traditional folk dancing. We enjoy bullfighting, but unlike the bullfights in neighboring Spain, the bull is not killed here.

If doing business in Europe or Africa interests you, our location is the gateway to both areas. We are members of the European Union (EU), Organisation for Economic Co-operation and Development (OECD), International Monetary Fund (IMF), and the North Atlantic Treaty Organisation (NATO).

You will need to be patient, however, as we are a work in progress. We have spent much of the last twenty years trying to forge new ties with the rest of Europe and restructure our economy—all while struggling to maintain our national culture. In order to advance our productivity and economic growth, we are ready to improve our educational system.

Come enjoy a moderate climate, one of Europe's lowest crime rates, moderately low unemployment rates, and friendly, hospitable people. We would love to work with you!

Vital Statistics

Population	10,566,212
Capital	Lisbon
Area	35,672 square miles, slightly smaller than Indiana
Government	Parliamentary democracy
Living Standard	GDP = US $17,920 per capita
Natural Resources	Fish, forests (cork), tungsten, iron ore, uranium, marble, clay, gypsum, salt, copper, zinc, tin, silver, gold, arable land, hydropower
Agriculture	Grain, potatoes, olives, grapes, sheep, cattle, goats, poultry, beef, dairy products
Industries	Textiles and footwear, wood pulp, paper, cork, metals and metalworking, oil refining, chemicals, fish canning, rubber and plastic products, ceramics, electronics and communications equipment, rail transportation equipment, aerospace equipment, ship construction and refurbishment, wine, tourism

Climate	Mild and wet in winter; warm and dry in summer, with droughts in the south
Member of the EU?	Yes, since 1986
Currency	Euro (€)

The People

Correct Name	noun: Portuguese adjective: Portuguese
Ethnic Makeup	Homogeneous Mediterranean stock; fewer than 100,000 citizens of African descent (who immigrated to the mainland from Africa during decolonization), Eastern Europeans (since 1990)
Languages	Portuguese (official), Mirandese (official but locally used)
Religions	Roman Catholic 94%, Protestant less than 1%, Jewish very small percentage

Meeting and Greeting

- The Portuguese shake hands firmly and warmly, with eye contact.
- When meeting friends, men embrace and pat one another on the back, and women kiss one another on each cheek. Friends of opposite sexes shake hands warmly, possibly while using the left hand to grasp the other's right shoulder or forearm.

Names and Titles

English	Portuguese	Pronunciation
Mr.	*Senhor*	(seen-YOHR)
Mrs.	*Senhora*	(seen-YOHR-a)
Miss	*Menina* (used only for girls younger than age eighteen)	(mee-NEE-nah)

- The Portuguese use the title *Doutor* (male doctor) or *Doutora* (female doctor) for anyone they suspect has a degree. They also use the specific titles *Engenheiro/Engenheira* (engineer) and *Arquitecto/Arquitecta* (architect). They include the general title *Senhor* or *Senhora* to show deference.
- For very formal occasions, use *Senhor/Senhora* + professional title + last name or last two names.

  Examples: *Senhora Doutora* Brito

  Senhora Doutora Varela Brito
- For standard formal occasions, you may drop *Senhor/Senhora* to initially address a new acquaintance.

  Example: *Doutora* Varela Brito
- After initially addressing someone, you may drop the name(s) and simply use *Senhor/Senhora* + professional title.

  Example: *Senhora Doutora*
- Use last names and appropriate titles until your Portuguese colleagues specifically invite you to use first names. The Portuguese generally use first names with family and close friends only.

Language

Although Portuguese is the official language, French and English are common second languages. Most Portuguese businesspeople speak English.

While written Spanish and written Portuguese are similar, Portuguese pronunciation is difficult and very different from Spanish. The Portuguese understand Spanish, but they'll reply in Portuguese.

Mirandese is a Romance language spoken by approximately a hundred thousand people, mostly in small northern villages. The Portuguese government protects and promotes the language as a unique cultural component, but its number of speakers has been declining for more than forty years and will probably continue to do so.

Conversation

The Portuguese converse informally, but they don't like to be interrupted. They also don't like confrontation or directness. You must try to understand not only what's being said, but also what's *not* being said.

Acceptable topics
- Family
- Football (soccer)
- Portuguese history: The Portuguese are proud of their contributions to global exploration. Their power at one time extended to India, the Far East, Brazil, and Africa.

Unacceptable topics
- Personal topics, like social position, career, salary, and personal finances: Don't be nosy or overly inquisitive.
- Comparisons to Spain: Portugal isn't Spain, and the Portuguese aren't Spanish!

Topics that require sensitivity
- Compliments: Feel free to sincerely compliment Portuguese food, wine, and culture—but compliment only people with whom you've built a relationship; otherwise, the Portuguese may consider your compliments insincere.

Body Language

While the Portuguese appreciate relaxed behavior, they don't use a lot of gestures and don't care for overly demonstrative body language. Physical contact, however, is acceptable between family and close friends.
- The Portuguese stand closer to one another than do Americans and Northern Europeans.
- Beckon someone with your palm down and fingers or whole hand waving (as if patting someone on the head).
- Never point with your index finger.

Phrases

English	Portuguese	Pronunciation
Good morning/day	*Bom dia*	(bong DEE-uh)
Good afternoon	*Boa tarde*	(BOH-uh tard)
Good evening	*Boa noite*	(BOH-uh noyt)
Please	*Por favor*	(por fah-VOR)
Thank you (by man)	*Obrigado*	(oh-bree-GAH-doo)
Thank you (by woman)	*Obrigada*	(oh-bree-GAH-duh)
You're welcome	*De nada*	(day NAH-dah)
Yes	*Sim*	(seeng)
No	*Não*	(NAH-oo)
Excuse me	*Com licença*	(com lee-SEN-sah)
Goodbye	*Adeus*	(a-DAY-oosh)
Pleased to meet you	*Muito prazer*	(MWEE-toh prah-ZERR)
How are you?	*Como está?*	(KOH-moo shta)

Dining

The Portuguese consume the most fish per capita in Europe. Their food is generally grilled or boiled. Most meals include eggs.

Typical Foods

Sardinhas asadas: charcoal-grilled sardines

Açorda: minced bread, egg, olive oil, and aromatic seasoning (for example, cilantro, coriander, and pepper)

> Some older Portuguese men don't eat chicken because they believe the female hormones fed to chickens could feminize them.

Bacalhau: dried, salted cod, cooked more than a thousand different ways

Pasteis de Bacalhau: deep-fried mixture of cod, potatoes, onion, and parsley

Frango na Pucara: chicken in a pot

Cozido à Portuguesa: boiled beef, pork, chicken, various types of smoked sausages, along with cabbage, carrots, potatoes, turnips, and rice made with the stock used to boil all the ingredients

Caldeirada: seafood stew of several types of fish, sliced potatoes, tomatoes, onions, garlic, and several seasonings

Caldo Verde: soup made with purée of potatoes and onions, shredded dark
green cabbage, and slices of smoked sausage

Pudim Flan: crème caramel pudding

Figos Recheados: dried figs stuffed with chocolate and almonds and served with port

Drinking

- The Portuguese usually drink white port, Scotch, and gin and tonic.
- They serve *vinho* (wine) with lunch and dinner. After dinner, they serve *aguardente* (a very strong local brandy) or port.
- Women usually drink Cinzano (a brand of Italian vermouth).
- The Portuguese serve *berveja* (beer) in summer.
- *Bica* (espresso) is very popular as is mineral water.

Toasting

- The toast *á sua Saúde* (a swah sah-OOD) means "to your health," and the Portuguese use it at formal and informal occasions.
- The host always toasts the guest of honor, who should reciprocate with a toast of thanks.
- It's acceptable for women to propose toasts.

Tipping

- Restaurants: The bill usually includes a 15 percent service charge (*serviço*). If the bill doesn't include a service charge, leave a 10 to 15 percent tip. You can leave small change as an additional gratuity for exceptional service.
- Taxis: Tip 10 percent of the fare.
- Bellhops and porters: Tip one euro per bag.
- Hair stylists and barbers: Tip one euro.
- Ushers, cloakroom attendants, washroom attendants, and gas station attendants: Give small change.

Manners

- Don't join the hostess in the kitchen unless invited.
- The Portuguese generally serve dinners family style—the guest of honor serves him- or herself first and passes dishes around the table.

- Don't use your fingers to soak bread in gravy; use your fork.
- The Portuguese eat fish with a special knife and fork.
- To signal that you'd like more food, place your fork and knife as shown on page 37.
- It's okay to leave food on your plate if you're full.
- After a meal, fold your napkin and place it on the table beside your plate.
- Let your host open the door when it's time to leave.
- Your hostess will appreciate your reciprocating the invitation in the near future.
- Summon wait staff by raising your hand.
- Don't eat while walking in public places (except for ice cream).
- Defer to older people.

Dress

The Portuguese dress conservatively. There's little difference in dress between work and social life.

- Portuguese men base their attire on a coat and tie. Businessmen wear suits or sport coats and ties.
- Portuguese women most often wear dresses. Businesswomen wear dresses, suits, or pantsuits.
- Women wear dresses to restaurants, and cocktail dresses are appropriate for the opera or theater.
- In restaurants, men should check in advance whether a coat and tie are required, but they can't go wrong with a suit and tie at a restaurant, opera, or theater.

Gifts

The Portuguese open gifts upon receipt.

Hostess Gifts

Consider giving
- Elegant flowers, except chrysanthemums (for funerals only)
- Good-quality chocolates

Don't give
- Wine: The Portuguese are proud of their own tastes in wine.

Business Gifts

The Portuguese normally don't exchange gifts at business meetings, but you may exchange small gifts at the successful conclusion of negotiations or, more commonly, at Christmas.

Consider giving
- Pens
- Crystal
- Ashtrays
- Any item that relates to the business itself (for example, if you work for a technology firm, a computer item like a laptop case)

Don't give
- Knives or sharp objects
- Cheap items

Toilet Tips	
English	**Portuguese**
Restroom	*Casa de Banho*
Women's restroom	*Senhoras*
Men's restroom	*Homens*
Hot water	*Água quente*
Cold water	*Água fria*

Helpful Hints

- Be sure to visit the markets, which are full of fish, fruit, flowers, and warm, friendly people.
- Bargain only in craft shops, not in department stores, other shops, or food markets.
- Be prepared: the Portuguese are statistically among the worst drivers in Europe.

Punctuality

Punctuality for social or business meetings isn't important to the Portuguese. They're often fifteen to thirty minutes late, but they expect that you'll be on time. Keep a relaxed attitude about time, and call with an explanation if you're delayed.

Corporate Culture

Structure

Most Portuguese companies' organization is hierarchical, with subordinates having limited power and responsibility. Companies emphasize short-term strategic planning. Teamwork is a new concept.

There's extensive government involvement in larger companies, but privatization has been underway since 1989. Small- and medium-size companies have been and remain in the private sector. A few powerful families have traditionally dominated heavy industry, but a new breed of entrepreneurs—many educated in the United States—is emerging.

Bureaucracy complicates and lengthens procedures—any interaction takes a long time. To the Portuguese, contracts are just paper—they're not as binding as Americans consider them.

The Portuguese legal system, although not corrupt, is very slow, and it's not unusual for resolutions to take five to ten years.

Meetings

Meetings are chiefly for briefing or discussion. Decisions may require several meetings, or one that lasts into the evening. Don't expect clear, decisive results.

Agendas exist, but participants don't always adhere to them. Everyone is encouraged to contribute. The Portuguese are flexible and collaborative in private, but consider meetings a time for competitive self-assertion; they strongly express their opinions before seeking common ground. If you require agreement or support at a meeting, you must lobby participants privately beforehand.

Let your Portuguese colleagues initiate business discussions. They may offer refreshments and friendly conversation before getting down to business. Always accept a beverage—even if you don't drink it.

Communication

While many younger managers speak English, all Portuguese colleagues will appreciate your having documents translated into Portuguese before sending them. Plan on hiring an interpreter for business meetings.

It's acceptable and common to call a Portuguese colleague at home.

Business Cards

- The Portuguese exchange business cards frequently.
- Business cards in English are acceptable.

Be Aware

- To the Portuguese, business relationships are personal and informal, and trust and loyalty are important.
- Organizational procedures are often complex, but you can negotiate them.
- Nepotism, breaking rules, and taking shortcuts are very common.
- The Portuguese don't respect deadlines. If you expect your Portuguese colleagues to meet deadlines, you must carefully negotiate delivery dates and make sure they're clearly understood.
- Portuguese customer service is weak.
- Schedule appointments well in advance and confirm them as their dates approach.

Socializing

- The Portuguese do most business entertaining in restaurants.
- Business breakfasts are acceptable.
- Business lunches and dinners are often long, relaxed, and full of conversation.
- Dinners with business colleagues are social events. Don't discuss business at dinner unless the host raises the subject.
- Business colleagues may eat together at restaurants, but they seldom socialize otherwise.
- The Portuguese may include spouses in business dinners, but not always.

Especially for Women

In Portugal, men are used to women in positions of authority, and many women work outside the home in urban areas. There's currently a strong movement toward Portuguese women in business.

With that said, however, traditionally conservative attitudes toward women's place in society have prevailed.

- While Portuguese men treat foreign businesswomen fairly and respectfully, they're nevertheless still macho, especially outside the cities. Be prepared for sexist behavior.
- It's best for a foreign woman to invite a Portuguese man to a business lunch. If a dinner invitation is necessary, it should include his wife.
- The Portuguese frown upon a woman's going to a bar or nightclub alone. Doing so may bring her unwelcome attention.
- Gallantry won't permit a Portuguese man to let a woman pay for lunch or dinner, but it's acceptable for a woman to try to pay. If you insist on paying, arrange payment with the wait staff beforehand.
- Take a taxi after dark or when there aren't many people around.

Holidays and Festivals

January	New Year's Day (1)
February/March	Carnival (Shrove Tuesday)
March/April	Easter (Thursday–Sunday)
April	Liberation Day (25)
April/May	Feast of the Ascension (40 days after Easter)
May	Labor Day/May Day (1)
June	Corpus Christi (60 days after Easter) National Day (10)
August	Feast of the Assumption (15)
October	Republic Day (5)
November	All Saints' Day (1)
December	Independence Restoration Day (1) Feast of the Immaculate Conception (8) Christmas (24–25)

Note: Some regions and cities celebrate their own unique festivals and holidays. Check for local celebrations before planning a trip.

ROMANIA*

Greetings from Romania

Greetings from the land where the women are beautiful, the men are smart, and the brandy is strong.

Myths about Romania abound. Greek mythology claims that Jason and the Argonauts traveled the Romanian shoreline while searching for the Golden Fleece—perhaps because the Greeks believed that ours was a land of riches. Romania is also a legendary home of dragons, and the beasts are an important part of Romanian folklore.

Perhaps our best-known—and most infamous—historical figure is Wallachian prince Vlad Tepes (the Impaler). The prince was also known as Dracula, the son of Vlad Dracul (Dragon), so called because of his membership to the Order of the Dragon, an organization that fought the Ottoman Empire. Despite Dracula's penchant to impale his enemies and subjects, he was a hero during the struggle against the Ottoman Empire in the mid-fifteenth century. Of course, he was also the inspiration for Bram Stoker's 1897 novel *Dracula*.

Romanians descended from Latin-speaking Romans who settled in the area in the second and third centuries AD. Although other cultures—most notably, Slavic—gained control of our land, the Roman influence prevailed. Today, we consider ourselves Roman; we are not Slavic! While the Slavic culture (among others) has influenced our vocabulary, Romanian is a Romance language (as are Italian and French), and many believe it is more closely related to Latin than any other living language.

Historically, Romania has been divided into the principalities of Moldavia, Wallachia, and Transylvania. Wallachia and Moldavia were part of the Ottoman Empire for centuries. They became free of the Empire's control in 1856, united in 1859, adopted the name "Romania" in 1862, and achieved recognized independence in 1877. Transylvania became part of Romania after World War I. Today, each of us strongly identifies with his or her home principality.

After World War II, Romania became a Communist country based on the Soviet model. But starting in the 1960s, the country began to chafe under what it considered the Soviets' intrusiveness.

* This country's name has no conventional long form.

In 1965, Nicolae Ceausescu became Romania's leader, and his totalitarian Communist regime intruded more deeply into citizens' lives than ever before. He exported most of Romania's agricultural and industrial production, leaving Romanians to cope with extreme shortages of food, fuel, medicines, and basic necessities. Under Ceausescu's orders, thousands of Romanian villages were bulldozed and their inhabitants forced to move into apartment blocks.

Unlike other formerly Communist countries, who peacefully and jubilantly welcomed the transition of government, our nation's break from Communist control was quick and violent. On December 16, 1989, a massive protest erupted in Timisoara. The focus was the forced removal of Laszlo Tokes, a Lutheran minister of the Hungarian Reformed Church who had earlier criticized the regime. Enraged, Ceausescu sent army units into the city. More than a hundred protesters were massacred, and the nation reacted violently—it was the beginning of the revolution.

> While in the past the world may have equated Romania with Dracula, today you may expect to see celebrities like Nicole Kidman, Renée Zellweger, and Donald Sutherland roaming Romanian cities instead. American and European filmmakers are flocking to Romania and finding the country a favorite destination for their projects.

On December 22, the Romanian army defected to the protesters, and Ceausescu and his wife, Elena, tried to flee Bucharest. They were captured, and after a hasty trial by a military tribunal, they were shot by firing squad on December 25.

Today, Romania is a republic. Modernization is occurring rapidly, and although many Romanians are being left behind, we are working to catch up. We are eager to put our past behind us and move our society into the new millenium. We joined the North Atlantic Treaty Organisation (NATO) in 2004 and hope to join the European Union (EU) in 2007.

Romanian history and culture makes ours a terrific nation to visit. Folklore festivals are frequent and wonderful. Ask your Romanian friends to recommend some of the more authentic ones. Also visit the Bucovina monasteries, whose beautiful exterior frescos (illustrating biblical scenes, prayers, and sacred hymns and themes) have survived since the fifteenth century.

The Carpathian Mountains offer excellent hiking and skiing. They are home to Europe's second largest bear population, about a third of the wolf population, and the densest lynx population. Other wildlife is also abundant there, and the mountains have some of the most pristine forests on the continent.

As a people, we are very well educated in technology and the sciences. (Most of us who leave the country do so to pursue technology jobs.) We celebrate being the best educated people in Central Europe.

While our infrastructure and bureaucracy are still challenging to deal with, we hope our beautiful, unspoiled landscapes and our low costs will make us competitive for many years. Come and see for yourself—we welcome you!

Vital Statistics

Population	22,329,977
Capital	Bucharest
Area	91,699 square miles, slightly smaller than Oregon
Government	Republic
Living Standard	GDP = US $5,080 per capita
Natural Resources	Petroleum (reserves declining), timber, natural gas, coal, iron ore, salt, arable land, hydropower
Agriculture	Wheat, corn, barley, sugar beets, sunflower seeds, potatoes, grapes, eggs, sheep
Industries	Textiles and footwear, light machinery and auto assembly, mining, timber, construction materials, metallurgy, chemicals, food processing, petroleum refining
Climate	Temperate; cold, cloudy winters with frequent snow and fog; sunny summers with frequent showers and thunderstorms
Member of the EU?	Applicant nation, hoping to join in 2007
Currency	On July 1, 2005, Romania changed its currency from Romanian lei (ROL) to Romanian new lei (RON). The old currency is valid until December 31, 2006, but old lei can be exchanged at banks indefinitely.

The People

Correct Name	noun: Romanian(s) adjective: Romanian
Ethnic Makeup	Romanian 89.5%, Hungarian 6.6%, Roma 2.5%, Ukrainian 0.3%, German 0.3%, Russian 0.2%, Turkish 0.2%, other 0.4%
Languages	Romanian (official), Hungarian, German
Religions	Eastern Orthodox (including all sub-denominations) 86.8%, Protestant (various denominations including Reformate and Pentecostal) 7.5%, Roman Catholic 4.7%, other (mostly Muslim) and unspecified 0.9%, none 0.1%

Meeting and Greeting

- Romanians introduce women before men, from eldest to youngest.
- If possible, have a third party introduce you to others. Try to avoid introducing yourself.
- Romanians shake hands upon meeting, even if they've already met earlier that day.
- Handshakes between men are robust, while handshakes between women or between men and women are gentler.
- Good friends may "air kiss" one another (first on the left cheek, then on the right).
- Women often say *bună* (BOO-nah), which means "good," as a greeting. Young men sometimes say *salut* (sah-LUTE), which means "salutation."
- An urban Romanian man may "air kiss" a woman's hand. Even men who don't may say, "*Sărut mâna*," (suh-root MUH-nuh), which means "I kiss your hand." Young people may also say this greeting to elders as a sign of respect. Foreigners, however, should avoid saying this greeting and should never attempt to kiss a woman's hand.
- Romanians believe it's bad luck to kiss or shake hands across a threshold.

Names and Titles

- Romanians use first names only among family and close friends. Don't use first names until your Romanian colleagues invite you to do so.

- Romanians always use professional titles.
- Romanians don't commonly use *Domnule*, *Doamnă*, and *Domnişoară* as titles in business. Rather, they address people by their work titles (for example, professor or engineer).

English	Romanian	Pronunciation
Mr.	*Domnule*	(DOHM-noo-lay)
Mrs.	*Doamnă*	(DWAHM-nah)
Miss	*Domnişoară*	(dohm-nee-soh-AH-rah)

Language

Romanian is the only Romance language that developed in the eastern half of Latin-influenced Europe. If you speak another Romance language (for example, French, Italian, or Spanish), you may be able to read and understand some basic Romanian.

Although Romanian vocabulary is mostly Latin based, the language's phonology and grammar developed differently from the other Romance languages—most likely due to the country's isolation from other Romance-speaking nations and its close contact with Slavic- and Hungarian-speaking nations.

Many Romanians are bi- and trilingual, speaking Hungarian, German, French, and/or English. Historically, French was the most common second language, but today English is rapidly replacing it. Many children learn English as a second language in school, and young people may have some ability to converse. Older Romanians, however, are unlikely to speak English.

Because Romania has a significant number of ethnic Hungarians as well as other minorities, state-financed schools teach ethnic minorities in their own languages.

Conversation

Romanians talk more openly than Americans do, and they may not always be politically correct. For example, they may ask you about your salary. If you'd rather not discuss the topic, politely say, "In the United States, that is a strange question!"

Also, be prepared for Romanian humor, which can be quite dark.

Acceptable topics

- Icebreaking subjects that are typical in the United States (for example, asking where someone is from, where he or she works, what he or she thinks of the weather, and so on)
- Your family
- Your Romanian colleague's family
- Romanian wine and food
- Romania's relationship with the United States: Romanians admire Americans and want a good, close relationship with them. (The only hard feelings toward Americans stem from their response to the Yalta Conference. Romanians dreamed for years that Americans would liberate Romania from Stalin's rule—and they never did.)

    Also, Romanians may be curious about life in the United States. They may believe the stereotypes of Americans portrayed on American television programs, but they'll welcome an authentic description of your life.

Unacceptable topics

- The Roma (Gypsies): The Roma aren't of Romanian heritage. They're originally from northwest India, although many settled in Romania before moving to other lands. Be aware that some Romanians are prejudiced against dark-skinned people like the Roma, Arabs, and Turks.
- Criticisms of Communism: Older Romanians may fondly remember parts of Communism (job security, for example). Even if your Romanian colleagues criticize Communism, don't join in.

Topics that require sensitivity

- Nicolae Ceausescu's brutal regime and execution
- Romania's struggles for democracy and prosperity
- Emigration of college-educated Romanians
- Romanian organized crime
- Romanian orphanages
- The AIDS epidemic in Romania

Body Language

- When conversing, Romanians maintain eye contact.
- Romanians may stand closer to one another than Americans do. Upon introduction, however, they stand farther apart.

- Friends hold hands or walk arm in arm.
- The "okay" sign (index finger and thumb making a circle) is vulgar. So is the thumbs-up sign. Avoid using either gesture.

Phrases

English	Romanian	Pronunciation
Hello/Good day	*Bună ziua*	(BOO-nah ZEE-wah)
Good morning	*Bună dimineața*	(BOO-nah dee-mee-NYAH-tsah)
Good evening	*Bună seara*	(BOO-nah SAY-ah-rah)
Please	*Vă rog*	(vah rog)
Thank you	*Mulțumesc*	(mul-tsu-MESK)
You're welcome	*Cu plăcere*	(kuh pla-CHEH-reh)
Yes	*Da*	(dah)
No	*Nu*	(noo)
Excuse me	*Scuzați-mă*	(skoo-ZAH-tsee-mah)
Goodbye	*La revedere*	(lah reh-veh-DEH-reh)
Pleased to meet you	*Mă bucur de cunoștință*	(mah booh-COOR deh COON-osh-teent-zah)
How are you?	*Ce mai faceți?*	(chay may FAH-cheh-tsee?)

Dining

Romanian cuisine is regional. Food in Moldavia and Wallachia has much in common with food in Greece and Turkey. Transylvania has dishes similar to those in Hungary.

Romanians eat a lot of soup, and they offer many delicious varieties. They also serve several delectable varieties of sausage and cured meat. (Pork is the most popular meat.)

Typical Foods

Mici: seasoned ground pork, barbecued and served with mustard

Zacuscă: roasted eggplant, bell peppers, onions, and tomatoes. Prepared and canned in the fall (every family has its own cherished recipe), Romanians serve it as a spread with bread.

Mămăligă: polenta

Sarmale cu mămăligă: cabbage rolls and polenta

Ciorbă: a sour soup made of blended vegetables and meats

Cozonaci: panettone (yeast cake made with candied fruit peels and raisins)

Drinking

- As Europe's fifth-largest wine producer, Romanians are very proud of their wines, which are among the world's finest. Be sure to try local varieties—some of which are quite ancient. (Romanians have produced wine since the seventh century BC.) Many French varieties of wines are also available.
- Homemade brandy is the most popular beverage. It's legal, and every village has its own recipe. Romanians drink it as the French drink wine.

    There are three levels of brandy. *Țuică* is distilled once and isn't strong. *Palinca* is distilled twice and is stronger. *Hornica* is distilled three times and is very strong. When trying this beverage, be careful: it can be very powerful!

- Tap water may not be safe outside urban areas. In fact, throughout the nation, tap water may have high lead levels. Bottled water is cheap and widely available.

Toasting

- The toast *noroc* (noh-ROKE) means "good luck," and *salut* (sah-LUTE) means "to your health." Romanians say either at formal and informal occasions.
- *Poftă bună* (POHFF-tah BOO-nah) means "enjoy the meal." Romanians often say it to one another before eating.
- Those who receive toasts should always reciprocate.
- During toasts, the giver and receiver maintain eye contact.

Tipping

Romanians generally don't tip, but they expect foreigners to tip. They greatly appreciate tips in euros or American dollars, but you may tip the equivalent in lei.

- Restaurants: The bill may include a 10 percent service charge. If the bill doesn't include a service charge, tip 10 percent of the bill.

- Taxis: Tip 10 percent of the fare.
- Porters: Tip two euros or dollars. If you have many bags, tip more.
- Bellhops: Tip one euro or dollar if escorted to the room; tip two euros or dollars if they handle your baggage.
- Cloakroom and washroom attendants: Tip one euro or dollar.
- Hair stylists and barbers: Tip 5 to 10 percent of the bill.

Manners

Romanians behave very formally and expect the same from others. Once they've developed a relationship, however, they may behave much more informally.
- Don't seat yourself. Let your host or hostess seat you.
- Don't begin eating until your host or hostess invites you to begin.
- Your hostess will urge you to take second and third helpings. It's a compliment to accept second helpings, so try not to stuff yourself with the first helping. You may decline second and third helpings, but you must do so with many compliments: "I wish I could eat more; it's so delicious, but I simply can't. Your hospitality has been too generous."
- If you're done drinking, keep your glass more than half-full. Romanians refill glasses that are less than half-full.
- It's impolite to eat in front of someone without food. Always offer to share.
- In a restaurant, address a waiter as *domnule* (DOHM-noo-lay) and a waitress as *domnisoară* (dohm-nee-soh-AH-rah).
- Don't keep your hands in your pockets while conversing with someone.
- Men always rise when a woman enters the room.
- Men remove hats when going inside a building.
- When strangers greet you, be sure to reciprocate.
- Ask permission before smoking.

Dress

- For business, women wear skirts, dresses, or tailored suits. Men wear conservative suits. In some offices, slacks and sweaters (with shirts and ties) are acceptable. Until you know the dress code, dress more formally than casually.
- For the theater or opera, men wear suits; women wear cocktail dresses.
- For dinner, men wear jackets and ties; women wear suits or dresses.

- For casual attire, men wear fashionable jeans with a stylish shirt. Younger, urban women may wear the same, although many Romanian women prefer to wear skirts or dresses.
- Before entering a church, women should cover their heads. Their shoulders and arms should be covered as well, and hemlines should fall below the knee.

Gifts

Romanians open gifts upon receipt. When visiting someone's home, bring candy or small toys for any children. The family will appreciate the gesture.

Hostess Gifts

Consider giving
- Flowers, wrapped and in an odd number (An even number of flowers is for funerals only.)
- Wine
- Cake or pastries
- Good-quality chocolates

Don't give
- Personal items
- Items that imply that consumer goods aren't available in Romania (cigarettes, chewing gum, and so on)

Business Gifts

Romanians don't routinely exchange business gifts at initial meetings, but you may give a small gift as a way to get acquainted. Romanians may exchange gifts at the conclusion of a deal if both parties got to know each other well.

But be aware: some Romanian companies disapprove of exchanging business gifts at an initial meeting and at the conclusion of a deal. They interpret such gifts as bribes. Ask a knowledgeable, trusted colleague whether giving gifts at these occasions is appropriate.

Giving small gifts to your Romanian colleagues at Christmas is acceptable but not expected.

Consider giving

- Small, useful office items (for example, pen and pencil sets)
- Foods and crafts from your home region
- Books about the United States, especially your region

Don't give

- Ostentatious gifts (may be considered bribes)
- Items made in Russia

Toilet Tips	
English	**Romanian**
Restroom	*Toalete*
Women's restroom	*Femei*
Men's restroom	*Bărbați*
Hot water (red dot)	*Cald*
Cold water (blue dot)	*Rece*

Helpful Hints

- Romania is steeped in history. Visit one or more of the country's 1,500 museums.
- Outside urban areas, shops and restaurants rarely accept credit cards.
- Avoid hailing a taxi from the curb; instead, have your hotel call one for you. Also ask your hotel concierge what a reasonable charge for the trip should be. If your taxi doesn't have a meter, agree on a price before getting inside the taxi.
- Don't confuse Romanians with Russians. Romanians don't like Russians and never considered the Soviet Union a friend. (They are, however, on good terms with Germans.)
- If you're sensitive to cigarette smoke, beware: It seems as though everyone smokes in Romania. They think prohibiting smoking is crazy.
- Along with birthdays, many Romanians celebrate the day of the patron saint for which they're named.
- A Romanian may wear a wedding ring on the right hand while engaged to be married, then move it to the left hand after getting married.
- Most Roman Catholics in Romania are ethnic Hungarians. There's generally at least one Roman Catholic church in any larger Romanian city.

- Most Romanians are Orthodox Christians and follow the Orthodox Christian calendar of fasting and abstinence before feast days, especially during Lent. In Romania, Orthodox Christian churches are older than the Roman Catholic churches.
- Orthodox Christians make the sign of the cross differently than do Roman Catholics. (Orthodox Christians touch the right shoulder first, then the left; Roman Catholics do the opposite.)

Punctuality

Romanians have a relaxed attitude toward time. They enjoy more free time and take more holidays (vacations) than Americans do. They value punctuality but don't always achieve it.
- For business occasions, be on time, but be prepared to wait. Romanians working in private industries are usually more punctual than those working in government or state-owned enterprises.
- Arrive on time for meals at restaurants, theater performances, and concerts.
- For social occasions, arrive about fifteen minutes after the stated starting time.

Corporate Culture

For more information on doing business with a formerly Communist country, see pages 17–18.

Structure
Romanian companies are very hierarchical. Make sure you deal with someone who's permitted to make decisions.

Meetings
- Let someone tell you where to sit.
- Meetings always begin with small talk.
- Make sure your presentations are simple to follow and include plenty of facts and figures.
- Men should never remove their jackets or ties unless the most senior Romanian present does so first.

Communication

- Decisions must filter through the levels of the organization, which takes time. Be persistent and keep working on a deal until either it's accepted or your Romanian colleagues specifically tell you that they reject the deal and don't want to pursue it further.
- Romanian businesspeople take pride in conducting themselves formally and properly at all times. Be sure to behave likewise to communicate that you're reliable.

Business Cards

- Business cards are common in Romania. Make sure to bring plenty of your cards.
- Have your information printed in English on one side and in Romanian on the other. Include your full title and any postgraduate degrees.
- If your company has been in business for more than fifty years, be sure to include the founding date on your card. Romanians believe that longevity conveys stability and reliability.

Be Aware

- Corruption in government and business remains a problem in Romania. Foreigners, however, should not—under any circumstances—try to bribe an official.
- Romania is a small country where everyone knows everyone else. Having a respected local contact introduce you to Romanian colleagues is important and will help establish relationships. Foreigners must prove their reliability and sincerity before Romanians will trust them enough to do business.
- Foreigners may find Romanian bureaucracy maddening. One official's sphere may overlap another's, complicating things even further. Be patient and persistent. Your local contact should help you navigate the bureaucratic channels.
- Romanians connect themselves to people, not companies. If your company replaces you with another representative, that person will have to build his or her own relationships. (If that happens, help your replacement by introducing him or her to your Romanian colleagues.)
- Romanians are eager to do business with foreigners, especially Americans.
- To Romanians, prestige comes from family and education, not wealth.

- Make appointments two or three weeks in advance, by letter if possible. Know that it's difficult to schedule appointments for July or August and for the two weeks before and after Christmas and Easter.

Socializing

- Business breakfasts aren't common.
- Some businesses may close for lunch.
- Romanians seldom invite others to their homes. If you receive such an invitation, know that it's a great honor.

Especially for Women

Most Romanian women work outside the home, yet are still responsible for domestic chores. Few Romanian women hold high-level positions in business or government.

- Romanians show foreign businesswomen respect. For example, Romanian men may feel obliged to defer to them in public.
- Foreign businesswomen shouldn't appear loud or aggressive. Such behavior repels Romanians.
- Women shouldn't make casual eye contact with Romanian men. They'll interpret such behavior as flirting.
- Romanian men won't let women pick up the check. Women who want to pay should make arrangements with the wait staff beforehand.

Holidays and Festivals	
January	New Year's Day (1–2)
April/May	Orthodox Easter and Easter Monday
May	Labor Day (1)
December	National Day (1)
	Christmas (25–26)

SLOVAKIA
SLOVAK REPUBLIC

Greetings from Slovakia

Greetings from the land where we Slovaks are glad to finally live in an independent, democratic country.

Our history has been turbulent. For nearly one thousand years, our land was part of the Hungarian empire and was known as Upper Hungary. During that time, Hungarian culture and language were forced on us, and our folk music helped keep our culture and language alive. (We continue our love of Slovak folk music today.)

After World War I, we united with the Czech and Moravian people to become the Czechoslovak Republic (Czechoslovakia). In March 1939, Slovakia declared its independence and allied itself with Nazi Germany—a fact that still inflames passions today. In 1944, an underground resistance movement gained strength and organized the Slovak National Uprising against the Nazi occupation.

After World War II, Czechoslovakia was united once again—this time under Soviet Communist influence, although Slovakia supported the government less than did the Czech lands.

During the 1970s and 1980s, Czechoslovakians began to oppose the Communist regime. While the Czechs' dissent was political, Slovaks used their Catholic faith to express their opposition. Several mass pilgrimages and religious celebrations drew large numbers of people, effectively becoming nationalist demonstrations. In November 1989, Slovaks joined Czechs in massive protests against the Communist government; in less than a month, Czechoslovakia was no longer under Communist rule.

The next few years were difficult for Czechoslovakia. The transition to a market economy proved easier for the wealthy Czech lands than for poorer Slovakia, and agreeing on economic reform and on a constitution became increasingly difficult.

The split between the two areas grew wider, and on January 1, 1993, Czechoslovakia disbanded its federation—peacefully and upon mutual agreement—into the Czech Republic and Slovakia.

Since independence, we have been eager to move our country forward. Our fear of Hungarian expansionism still strains our relations with Hungary and ethnic Hungarians, but we are working toward a peaceful resolution. We are proud members of the North Atlantic Treaty Organisation (NATO), and we gladly joined the European Union (EU) in 2004.

Slovakia is a great place to do business. To become more competitive, in 1991 we started reforming fiscal and monetary policies and privatizing state industries. The strategy has paid off. In 2003, Steve Forbes of *Forbes* magazine said, "The Slovak Republic is set to become the world's next Hong Kong or Ireland, [that is], a small place that's an economic powerhouse. Foreign investors are already taking note."

In 2004, the World Bank named Slovakia the fastest-transforming business environment. We improved our investment climate and joined the world's top twenty economies for ease of doing business. New business registrations went up 12 percent after we simplified entry procedures.

We are quickly becoming the world's largest per capita automobile manufacturer. Volkswagen, Peugeot-Citroen, Kia Motors, Ford Motor, and Hyundai are—or soon will be—building vehicles in Slovakia.

Slovakia is also a great place to visit for outdoor activities. People from around the world come to the High Tatras to ski and to hike the mountains' more than 600 kilometers (373 miles) of trails. We love to play football (soccer) and ice hockey just as much as we love to go mushrooming and tend our gardens (even many city dwellers have country gardens). In addition, we have wonderful caves to explore. The Domica Cave in the Slovak Red Mountains is one of the world's largest. It is very colorful and has massive onion-shaped stalactites.

> Juraj Jánošik has been a Slovak folk hero for three hundred years. Known as the Slovak Robin Hood, Jánošik's gang robbed from wealthy noblemen, landowners, and merchants and gave to the poor. He was caught and executed at the age of twenty-five. Jánošik became a symbol of the Slovak national revival in the eighteenth century.

Our spas are world famous. Each spa is located near mineral springs and specializes in alleviating different ailments and complaints.

We welcome visitors, especially Americans. There are nearly a million Slovak Americans, and every Slovak has a relative, neighbor, or friend living in the United States. Come see us soon!

Population	5,431,363
Capital	Bratislava
Area	18,859 square miles, about twice the size of New Hampshire
Government	Parliamentary democracy
Living Standard	GDP = US $11,280 per capita
Natural Resources	Brown coal and lignite; small amounts of iron ore, copper and manganese ore; salt; arable land
Agriculture	Grains, potatoes, sugar beets, hops, fruit, pigs, cattle, poultry, forest products
Industries	Metal and metal products, food and beverages, electricity, gas, coke, oil, nuclear fuel, chemicals and manmade fibers, machinery, paper and printing, earthenware and ceramics, transport vehicles, textiles, electrical and optical apparatus, rubber products
Climate	Temperate; cool summers; cold, cloudy, humid winters
Member of the EU?	Yes, since 2004
Currency	Slovak koruna (SKK); working toward converting to the euro by 2009

The People

Correct Name	noun: Slovak(s) adjective: Slovak
Ethnic Makeup	Slovak 85.8%, Hungarian 9.7%, Roma 1.7%, Ruthenian/Ukrainian 1%, other and unspecified 1.8%
Languages	Slovak (official) 83.9%, Hungarian 10.7%, Roma 1.8%, Ukrainian 1%, other or unspecified 2.6%
Religions	Roman Catholic 68.9%, Protestant 10.8%, Greek Catholic 4.1%, other or unspecified 3.2%, none 13%

Meeting and Greeting

- Slovaks shake hands firmly upon meeting and departure.
- Close friends may kiss one another on the cheek upon departure.
- Men should wait for women to extend a hand before attempting to shake it.

Names and Titles

- Don't use first names until your Slovak colleagues invite you to do so.
- When addressing someone, use the title on his or her business card.

English	Slovak	Pronunciation
Mr.	*Pán*	(pahn)
Mrs.	*Pani*	(PAH-nyih)
Miss	*Slečna*	(SLETCH-nah)

- After getting married, a Slovak woman usually takes her husband's last name, but often changes the last letter to *a* if the name ends with a vowel sound, or adds *ová* if the name ends with a consonant sound.

     Examples: Iveta Prosbikova (husband: Martin Prosbik)

                      Helena Gyurovska (husband: Rastislav Gyurovsky)

  Some Slovak women are resisting this tradition. Only recently have Slovak women been allowed to legally hyphenate their maiden and married names.
- Slovaks may add *ová* to a foreign woman's last name to indicate gender (for example, Madeleine Albrightová).

Language

Slovak belongs to the West Slavic group of languages, along with Czech, Polish, and the Sorbian languages of eastern Germany. Although the Slovak languages began to distinguish themselves in the tenth century AD, Latin had been the territory's administrative, liturgical, and literary language for centuries. By the mid-nineteenth century, the Slovak languages had consolidated and written Slovak became standardized. Today, Slovak has important regional differences.

In former Czechoslovakia, both Slovak and Czech were official languages. Media broadcasts were in both languages. The Czech and Slovak languages share many similarities, and speakers of one language could converse on a basic level with speakers of the other. Today, however, younger speakers of one language don't interact with speakers of the other as much as had earlier generations, and thus can't understand the other language as readily.

Slovaks do speak other languages. English and German are the most popular second languages studied in Slovak schools. (Russian was a mandatory subject under Communism, but today it's studied minimally.) Ethnic Hungarians near the Hungarian-Slovak border speak Hungarian. In this area, city limit signs printed in Slovak and Hungarian are common.

Slovaks appreciate any attempt foreigners make to speak a few words in Slovak. Foreigners should never speak Czech to Slovak colleagues. Doing so is very rude.

Phrases

Please note that the Slovak language has diacritical marks that aren't used in English. The phrases below have been simplified for North American readers.

English	Slovak	Pronunciation
Hello/Good day	*Dobrý deň*	(DOH-bree dyien)
Good morning	*Dobré ráno*	(DOH-brair RAH-noh)
Good evening	*Dobrý večer*	(DOH-bree VEH-cher)
Please/You're welcome	*Prosím*	(PROH-seem)
Thank you	*Dakujem*	(dya-KUH-yem)
Yes	*Áno*	(AH-noh)
No	*Nie*	(NYEE-eh)
Excuse me	*Prepáčte*	(pray-PAHCH-tyeh)
Goodbye	*Do videnia*	(doh vee-DEH-NYEE-ah)
Pleased to meet you	*Teši ma*	(teh-SHEE-mah)
How are you?	*Ako sa máš?*	(AH-ko-SAH-mash)

Conversation

Slovaks are formal and reserved upon introduction, but they warm up as a relationship develops. Bragging, however, is never acceptable, and Slovaks may interpret assertiveness in conversation as self-centeredness.

Acceptable topics

- Praise of anything Slovak: Slovaks want to know what the world thinks of their nation, but they're very sensitive to criticism.
- Sports, especially ice hockey: Slovaks are big hockey fans and love to discuss Slovak players in the National Hockey League.

Unacceptable topics

- The Roma (Gypsies): Many Slovaks are prejudiced against this group.
- Topics that confuse or compare Slovakia with Slovenia or the Czech Republic: Slovaks fiercely protect their national identity.

Topics that require sensitivity

- Politics: Listen to your Slovak colleagues and ask questions, but don't offer opinions.
- The Communist era and the subsequent revolution: Some Slovaks are happy to tell extraordinary stories about this time. Simply listen to them without making judgments.
- The Slovak government's relationship with Hungary

Body Language

- Slovaks stand closer to one another than Americans do.
- Beckoning someone with an index finger is a rude gesture.
- Making a fist and tucking the thumb under the fingers means "good luck."
- When conversing, Slovaks maintain eye contact. Doing so conveys sincerity.

Dining

Austrian and Hungarian dishes have heavily influenced Slovak cuisine, which includes *štrudla* (strudel) as well as dishes seasoned with very spicy paprika.

Many Slovak dishes have cryptic names that don't describe the ingredients. For example, *Španielský vtáčik* means "Spanish birds," but it's a dish of beef rolled with bacon and gherkins, served with rice and sauce.

Slovakia is rapidly offering international cuisine. In Bratislava, there are restaurants serving Chinese, Mexican, German, Italian, and Jewish food.

Slovaks eat their main meal at midday, and they usually eat a light supper of cold cuts, cheese, and bread.

Typical Foods

Bryndzove halušky: gnocchi-like dumplings with melted sheep's milk cheese and fried bacon sprinkled on top (It's the national dish.)

Kapustnica: hearty cabbage soup with smoked pork sausage and sometimes mushrooms or even plums

Lokše: thin, round potato and flour bread (like a tortilla)

Hranulky: spicy potato puffs

Plnená paprika and *plnená kapusta*: peppers and cabbage stuffed with rice and ground pork or beef, often served with a spicy tomato sauce

Liptauer: a cheese named after the Liptov region in central Slovakia

Živánska: pork roasted with onion, garlic, bacon, and potatoes (Pork is the most popular meat.)

Vypražany bravčovy rezen: breaded pork cutlet (like schnitzel)

Freshwater fish, especially carp and trout

Medovníky: honey cakes with ginger

Palacinky: crepes filled with jam, ice cream, chocolate sauce, sweet cheese, fruit, or other filling

Drinking

- Slovaks enjoy wine (*vino*) and prefer it to beer (*pivo*). Be sure to try the local varieties, including sparkling wine.
- Other popular alcoholic beverages in Slovakia include *slivovica* (plum brandy), *borovička* (juniper berry brandy), and *Demänovka* (bittersweet liqueur sweetened with honey).
- Slovaks believe that water from mineral springs is medicinal. Depending on the mineral content, the taste varies among springs.

Toasting

- The toast *dobrú chuť* (DOH-broo koot) means "*bon appétit*," and *na zdravie* (nahs-DRAHV-ee-eh) means "cheers." Slovaks say either at formal and informal occasions.
- When giving or receiving a toast, always maintain eye contact. When clinking glasses with someone, look directly into his or her eyes. Not doing so is terribly rude.
- It's acceptable for women to propose toasts.

Tipping

- Restaurants: The bill may include a 5 to 10 percent service charge. If the bill doesn't include a service charge, most Slovaks round up the bill to the next SKK10, but foreigners should tip 10 percent. Give the tip to your server; don't leave it on the table.

- Taxis: Round up the fare to the next SKK10.
- Porters: Tip the equivalent of fifty cents to one euro per bag.
- Bellhops: If they show you to your room, tip the equivalent of one euro. If they handle your luggage, tip fifty cents to one euro per bag.
- Hair stylists and barbers: Tip 5 to 10 percent of the bill.

Manners

- When entering someone's home, be sure to remove your shoes. (Your host won't ask you directly to do so.) Leave your shoes on only if your host does. Your host may provide slippers.
- Don't admire any specific item in someone's home. He or she may feel obligated to give it to you. Instead, make general compliments.
- It's polite to refuse refreshments when first offered, then accept when offered again. It's insulting, however, to refuse refreshments altogether. (Keep these manners in mind when you offer guests refreshments.)
- Hosts may serve guests refreshments but not eat the meal themselves.
- Asking for seconds compliments the host.
- Don't yawn in front of anyone. Slovaks consider doing so impolite.
- Slovaks always treat the elderly with great respect.
- Slovak men always enter a bar before women.

Dress

Slovaks dress more fashionably in urban areas, but more conservatively in rural areas.

- For business, men wear dark suits and ties; women wear tailored suits or dresses. The higher a person's title, the more formal the attire.
- For formal occasions or for theater or opera performances, men wear dark suits; women wear cocktail dresses.
- Casual dress is always smart casual. (See page 45.)
- T-shirts and jeans are popular to wear at an informal party or gathering. If you wear either, make sure they're stylish and neat.
- If you're unsure about what attire is appropriate for a particular situation, ask your Slovak colleague or the hotel concierge. In general, it's always better to dress more formally than casually.

Gifts

Slovaks generally open gifts upon receipt. When visiting someone's home, bring a small gift for any children. The family will appreciate the gesture.

Hostess Gifts

Consider giving
- Flowers, except chrysanthemums (for funerals only), unwrapped and in an odd number
- Fine chocolates
- Liqueur

Don't give
- Dried flower arrangements (for funerals only)
- Personal items

Business Gifts

It's acceptable to exchange small gifts at first meetings, at the conclusion of a deal, or at holidays. Slovaks are very proud of their folk arts, and your Slovak colleagues may give you pottery, wood carvings, or other traditional gifts. If they do, be appreciative.

Consider giving
- Books about or folk art from your home country or region
- Good-quality pens
- Small electronic items
- Wine or liquor

Don't give
- Very expensive items (may be considered bribes)

Helpful Hints

- Always remember that Slovaks are linguistically and culturally distinct from Czechs.
- Menus often list the meal's weight in grams to help diners know the portion size.
- At restaurants, the price of the main course usually doesn't include side dishes; you must order them separately.

- Many restaurants, especially outside Bratislava, don't accept credit cards. Be prepared to pay in cash.
- Be sure to visit Bratislava's Old Town, where residents are revitalizing its scenic streets and Gothic buildings.

Toilet Tips

English	Slovak
Restroom	*Záchody/WC/Toalety*
Women's restroom	*Ženi*
Men's restroom	*Muži*
Hot water (red dot)	*Horúca*
Cold water (blue dot)	*Studená*

Corporate Culture

Slovakia is working hard on economic reforms to make itself competitive and attract investment; however, an entrenched bureaucracy and quickly changing laws and rules make doing business in Slovakia difficult. Foreigners will need a trusted local contact to help them through regulatory and bureaucratic mazes.

For more information on doing business with a formerly Communist country, see pages 17–18.

Structure

Slovak companies are hierarchical. Decisions are made from the top down, and decision making is a time-consuming process that can frustrate foreigners. Patience is necessary.

Meetings

Meetings begin with small talk, and they may end with participants drinking a shot of liquor. While this latter process is less common today than it once was, it's insulting to refuse if offered.

Communication

- Subordinates may have a difficult time giving feedback to superiors, and Slovak managers generally won't seek out such feedback.
- Don't publicly confront people about problems; doing so will hurt their pride. Always approach people privately.

- When dealing with your Slovak colleagues, be honest and sensitive—and don't brag!
- Language in the workplace is extremely polite. Slovaks frown upon cursing.

Business Cards

Have your information printed in English on one side of your business card and in Slovak on the other. Don't have your information printed in Czech.

Be Aware

- Slovaks won't do business with someone until a relationship has been developed.
- Slovaks may view entrepreneurs as opportunists and carpetbaggers.
- Slovaks value education and experience highly. What you know is more important than whom you know.
- Slovaks believe deadlines are important, and missing them shows inefficiency and disrespect.
- Customer service may be slow and unhelpful—a remnant of Communism. Be patient.
- Most businesses are closed on Sundays.
- Some rural businesses and small shops close for lunch.

Socializing

- Slovaks usually do business entertaining in restaurants.
- Doing business over lunch or coffee is acceptable, but wait for your Slovak colleagues to bring up business topics.
- Dinners are largely for socializing.

Especially for Women

Women make up over half the Slovak labor force. Although discrimination against women in the workforce is against Slovak law, it's still fairly common. Women are underrepresented in government office and in upper management.

Slovak women play a more traditional role than American women do. While more men are helping with housework and childcare, women handle the majority of these duties.

- Traditionally in Slovakia, women didn't eat with men, but this tradition is disappearing. A foreign woman may invite a Slovak man to a business dinner. If she wants to pay for the meal, she should arrange payment with the wait staff beforehand.

- Women should always graciously accept chivalrous gestures (like when a man opens a door for a woman) and speak quietly and evenly.

Holidays and Festivals	
January	New Year's Day (1) Epiphany (6)
March/April	Easter (Friday–Monday)
May	Labor Day (1) National Day (8)
July	Saints Cyril and Methodius Day (5)
August	National Uprising Day (29)
September	Constitution Day (1) Our Lady of the Seven Sorrows (15)
November	All Saints' Day (1) Day of Freedom and Democracy of the Slovak Republic (17)
December	Christmas (24–25) Boxing Day (26)

SLOVENIA
REPUBLIC OF SLOVENIA

Greetings from Slovenia

Greetings from the sunny side of the Alps, where we Slovenes are happy to be independent.

Our journey to independence was long and tumultuous. In the seventh and eighth centuries AD, our ancestors pledged allegiance first to the Slavic kingdom, then Frankish rule. In the fourteenth century, Slovenia became part of the Hapsburg Empire. Napoleon Bonaparte gained control briefly in the early nineteenth century before rule returned to the Hapsburg Empire.

After World War I, Slovenia became part of the Kingdom of Serbs, Croats, and Slovenes, renamed Yugoslavia in 1929. As a part of Yugoslavia, Slovenia's autonomy was restricted to mainly cultural affairs. As the wealthiest area, it was taxed more heavily than other regions in the kingdom.

In World War II, some Slovenians allied themselves with Germany and Italy, some joined the Communist-led Slovene National Liberation Front, and still others joined splinter factions. Atrocities were committed on all sides, too often against innocent civilians accused of collaboration with whomever one faction was battling. There were mass reprisals after the war. Soon, we became part of the Communist Federal People's Republic of Yugoslavia.

During the next two decades, Slovenia achieved greater economic prosperity than the southern Yugoslav regions by operating under a "socialist self-management" system. Although Slovenes made up less than a tenth of the Yugoslav population, Slovenia accounted for a third of all exports.

In the 1970s, liberalization prompted several autonomy movements, and by the 1980s, as Yugoslavia's economy fell into inflation and debt, even Slovenian Communists wanted Slovenia to break from the Yugoslav kingdom.

In June 1991, Slovenia was the first republic to secede. Shortly afterward, the Yugoslav army attacked, but Slovene militiamen defeated them in what became known as the Ten-Day War, a battle that saw very little bloodshed. Less than four months later, the last of the Yugoslav military left Slovenia, and we at last became an independent nation.

After achieving independence, Slovenia designed its economy and political system to match those of the Western European countries. Over the next decade, our economy grew quickly, and we enjoyed political stability. We proudly joined the North Atlantic Treaty Organisation (NATO) and the European Union (EU) in 2004.

Our lovely nation borders both the Alps and the Adriatic Sea. You can ski in the morning and swim in the afternoon. Our nearly thirty miles of coastline are pristine and breathtaking. We are also the third-most forested nation in Europe. More than half our land is covered with forests, which are home to bears, wolves, and lynx. If the

Slovenia has a long democratic tradition. For centuries, Carantania, an ancient Slovenian state, used an investiture ceremony that many consider a milestone in the development of democracy. Upon the death of a ruling duke, the Carantanian nobility elected a successor, and the common people participated in an investiture ceremony.

The ceremony was so famously unique, it reportedly influenced Thomas Jefferson when he was drafting the democratic ideals for the fledging United States.

mountains and coast were not enough to attract visitors, the mammoth Postojna caves are a popular tourist attraction.

While in Slovenia, visitors must try our excellent wines and enjoy our folk arts, especially our lace. For centuries, people from around the world have sought our uniquely patterned *cipka* lace.

Our standard of living is very high, higher than some of the older EU countries and dramatically higher than some of the new EU countries. We are proud to be very well educated. Many of us speak several languages.

We are not a developing country; we are European oriented and modern. For example, Slovenes are among the highest cell phone users in Europe. You will see ten-year-olds riding bikes while chatting on cell phones.

We say that we have a German work ethic and a Slavic soul. In truth, our culture is much like Austria's; we are Slavic in language only. We are not Balkan or Eastern European—we are Central European.

Visit our beautiful land and experience our burgeoning economy!

Vital Statistics

Population	2,011,070
Capital	Ljubljana
Area	7,827 square miles, slightly smaller than New Jersey
Government	Parliamentary democratic republic
Living Standard	GDP = US $18,470 per capita
Natural Resources	Lignite coal, lead, zinc, mercury, uranium, silver, hydropower, forests
Agriculture	Potatoes, hops, wheat, sugar beets, corn, grapes, cattle, sheep, poultry
Industries	Ferrous metallurgy and aluminum products, lead and zinc smelting, electronics (including military electronics), trucks, electric power equipment, wood products, textiles, chemicals, machine tools
Climate	Mediterranean climate on the coast; continental climate with mild to hot summers and cold winters in the plateaus and eastern valleys
Member of the EU?	Yes, since 2004
Currency	Tolar (SIT); working toward converting to the euro by 2007

The People

Correct Name	noun: Slovene(s) adjective: Slovenian
Ethnic Makeup	Slovene 83.1%, Serb 2%, Croat 1.8%, Bosniak 1.1%, other or unspecified 12%
Languages	Slovenian (official) 91.1%, Serbo-Croatian 4.5%, other or unspecified 4.4%
Religions	Catholic 57.8%, Orthodox 2.3%, other Christian 0.9%, Muslim 2.4%, unaffiliated 3.5%, other or unspecified 23%, none 10.1%

Meeting and Greeting

- Slovenes shake hands upon meeting and departure. They shake hands with women first.
- Slovenes always smile upon greeting and expect others to do so as well.
- Friends kiss one another on each cheek as a greeting and a farewell.

Names and Titles

English	Slovenian	Pronunciation
Mr. (Sir)	*Gospod*	(gos-POD)
Mrs./Ms. (Madam)	*Gospa*	(GOS-pah)
Miss	*Gospodična*	(gos-poh-DEECH-nah)

- Don't use first names until your Slovenian colleagues invite you to do so. Some Slovenes use first names only after many years of friendship.
- Slovenes always use professional titles.
- Slovenes say "hello" only among friends in informal situations. In formal situations, they say "good morning/day/evening." (See table on page 382.)

Language

Slovenian is related to Serbo-Croatian and is a very phonetic language; each letter makes only one sound. Slovenian also has a rare linguistic characteristic: the dual noun form, used when speaking of two things or people.

Many people believe the Freising Manuscripts are the oldest surviving documents in what eventually became Slovenian. This collection of confessions and sermons dates from about 1000 AD.

Italian and German are the most common second languages, although many Slovenes speak English. Most businesspeople speak English and German fluently.

Slovenes strongly believe that their language kept their culture alive throughout centuries of foreign occupation. They warmly receive any attempts foreigners make to speak the language.

Conversation

Before speaking to someone, Slovenes greet him or her formally—even when asking a stranger for the time. Before beginning a conversation, they formally greet everyone present.

Slovenes have traditionally used formal and informal forms of the pronoun *you*: *vi* (vee) and *ti* (tee), respectively. Today, younger people use the formal form less often than did previous generations.

Acceptable topics
- Hiking and other outdoor activities
- Sports: Marathon swimmer Martin Strel is a national hero. He has set records swimming the Danube, Mississippi, and Yangtze Rivers.
- Gardening
- Music

Unacceptable topics
- Comparisons between Slovenia and other countries
- Status of the Roma (Gypsies) in Slovenia

Topics that require sensitivity
- World War II and its aftermath
- Politics: Even though Slovenia is relatively homogeneous (unlike the rest of the former Yugoslavia), approach this topic carefully.

Body Language

- Slovenes beckon someone by curling an index finger, palm up and other fingers folded.
- Girls and women may walk together arm in arm or holding hands.
- Slovenes believe that good posture is important.

Phrases

Please note that Slovenian uses diacritical marks that aren't used in English. The Slovenian phrases below have been simplified for North American readers.

English	Slovenian	Pronunciation
Hello (used in informal situations)	*Zdravo*	(ZDRAH-voh)
Good day	*Dober dan*	(DOH-bar dahn)
Good morning	*Dobro jutro*	(DOH-broh YOO-troh)
Good evening	*Dober večer*	(DOH-brow veh-CHER)
Please/You're welcome	*Prosim*	(PROH-seem)
Thank you	*Hvala*	(HWAH-la)
Yes (formal)	*Da*	(dah)
Yes (informal)	*Ja*	(yah)
No	*Ne*	(nah)
Excuse me	*Dovolite mi, prosim*	(doh-VOH-lee-teh mee, PROH-seem)
Goodbye	*Nasvidenje*	(nahs-WEE-den-yeh)
Pleased to meet you	*Me veseli*	(may vay-SAY-lee)
How are you?	*Kako ste*	(kah-KOH steh)

Dining

Slovenia doesn't have a national cuisine. Each region has its own traditional foods, influenced by its neighbors. Food in the north is similar to that of Austria, and food in the west has Italian influences.

Slovenes gather at *gostilnas* (inns) to eat and enjoy one another's company. They're usually family owned and have a warm, welcoming atmosphere.

Typical Foods

In the north:

Klobasa: sausage

Njoki: gnocchi

Zavitek: strudel

Dunajski zrezek: Wiener schnitzel

In the west:

Rizota: risotto

Zlikrofi: ravioli

Throughout Slovenia:

Golaz: goulash

Paprikas: chicken or beef stew

Struklji: dumplings stuffed with cheese, meat, or vegetables

Seafood: including shellfish and Adriatic bluefish, abundant along the seacoasts

Buckwheat flour dishes

Potica: spiral-shaped paper-thin pastry filled with walnuts, butter, cream, and vanilla

Gelato: numerous stands on city streets

Drinking

- Since ancient times, Slovenia's climate and location has allowed for the production of unique wines, and Slovenes are proud of their excellent wines. Numerous wineries offer tastings; be sure to try *Cvicek* (a light red) and *Teran* (a hearty red), among others.
- Mixed fruit drinks are very popular. Fruit-based aperitifs are especially excellent—they're not syrupy or overly sweet. Slovenes make pear aperitif by tying a bottle over a pear blossom on the tree, letting the pear grow inside the bottle.
- When at restaurants, order local wine, beer, or *zganje* (a strong local brandy).

Toasting

- The toast *Na zdravje* (nah-ZDRAHV-yeh) means "to your health." The toasts *Živijo* (zhee-VEE-yo) and *Živijli* (zhee-VEE-lee) both mean "good life." Slovenes say the first to a group in general, and the second to specific people. Slovenes say any of these toasts at formal and informal occasions.
- The toast *Dober tek* (DOH-ber tehk) means *"bon appétit."*

Tipping

- Restaurants: The bill may include a service charge. If the bill doesn't include a service charge, tip 10 percent of the bill (15 percent for exceptional service).

- Taxis: Tip 10 percent of the fare.
- Bellhops: For showing you to your room, tip the equivalent of one euro. Also tip the equivalent of one euro for each bag handled.
- Porters: Tip the equivalent of one euro for each bag handled.
- Doormen: Tip the equivalent of one euro.
- Hair stylists and barbers: Tip 10 percent of the bill.

Manners

Slovenes are very welcoming and friendly. Their manners are much like those of Austrians. See page 78 for more information on Austrian manners.
- When entering someone's home, ask whether you should take off your shoes.
- Slovenes always serve guests first, but no one begins eating until the host begins.
- The evening ends after coffee. Guests take care not to stay too late.
- Don't talk to people with your hands in your pockets.
- When complimented, Slovenes smile and reply, "*Hvala, kaj piješ?*" (HWAH-la, KYE PEE-yesh), an expression that gracefully accepts the compliment. It means "Thanks, what do you want to drink?" (But don't expect a drink—it's just a polite expression.)

Dress

European styles are popular in Slovenia. Slovenes dress fashionably but not loudly.
- For business, men wear suits or sport coats with ties; women wear tailored suits or dresses.
- At the theater, opera, or other formal occasions, men wear dark suits; women wear cocktail dresses.
- Casual wear is always smart casual (see page 45). Young people in urban areas wear jeans. If you choose to wear jeans, make sure they're neat and stylish.
- Slovenes wear furs in the winter.

Gifts

Slovenes open gifts upon receipt. When visiting someone's home, bring small gifts or sweets for any children. The family will appreciate the gesture.

Hostess Gifts

Consider giving
- Flowers, in an odd number only
- High-quality wine

Don't give
- Any item that implies modern consumer goods aren't available in Slovenia (cigarettes, chewing gum, and so on)
- Personal items

Business Gifts

Slovenes don't normally exchange business gifts, but it's a good idea to have a small wrapped gift in your briefcase in case you're given one.

Consider giving
- Pen and pencil sets
- High-quality wine
- Photo book about your home region

Don't give
- Any item that implies modern consumer goods aren't available in Slovenia (cigarettes, chewing gum, and so on)
- Very expensive gifts (may be considered bribes)

Toilet Tips

English	Slovenian
Restroom	*WC/Sanitarije*
Women's restroom	*Ženske*
Men's restroom	*Moški*
Hot water (red dot)	*Toplo*
Cold water (blue dot)	*Hladno*

Helpful Hints

- Most shops close at noon on Saturdays and are closed Sundays.
- You can purchase anything in the cities, especially items from Italy or Austria.
- Slovenes are very health conscious. They smoke less than people in many other European countries, and they value physical fitness. Skiing and bicycling are popular sports.
- If you have the opportunity, visit the over-seven-hundred-year-old capital, Ljubljana. In the first century BC, it was the Roman town of Emona, and today there are traces of ancient Rome throughout the city.
- You may also want to visit the Soca Valley. During World War I, the valley was the site of the bloody Soca Front, which killed an enormous number of people, an event commemorated in Ernest Hemingway's novel *A Farewell to Arms*.

Punctuality

For business meetings, Slovenes are generally punctual and expect foreigners to be so as well. For social occasions, they arrive on time or up to fifteen minutes late. They never arrive early.

Corporate Culture

Slovenes are familiar with Western economic practices. When part of the former Yugoslavia, Slovenia operated businesses on a self-management system, which allowed some local autonomy and thus was more market oriented than a completely centralized system.

For more information on doing business with a formerly Communist country, see pages 17–18.

Structure

Slovenes make decisions at the top. Never consider a deal final until the senior manager has authorized it.

Meetings

- Slovenes run meetings fairly efficiently.
- Meetings open with some small talk.

- To persuade Slovenes, facts are more important than emotion.
- Slovenes may take their time to make decisions, so be patient.

Communication
- Many businesspeople, especially younger ones, speak English. You may not need an interpreter, but check in advance.
- Slovenes appreciate frequent contact by phone, e-mail, fax, and letter.
- Don't call Slovenian colleagues at home unless it's an emergency.

Be Aware
- Slovenes exchange business cards at the beginning of meetings, after shaking hands.
- For business success in Slovenia, you'll have to build relationships. Establishing personal contacts and maintaining correspondence are crucial.
- Confirm all appointments in advance and in writing.
- Slovenes take long vacations, usually five weeks.

Socializing
- Slovenes do most business entertaining in restaurants. They invite people to their homes only after a personal relationship has developed. If someone has invited you to a restaurant or to their home, be sure to reciprocate with a similar invitation.
- Business breakfasts aren't as common as in the United States.

Especially for Women

For economic reasons, both parents work outside the home in most Slovenian families, although women still take care of the majority of domestic duties.

Although Slovenian women dominate the teaching, culture (museums, festivals, and so on), and health care industries, the Slovenian government has initiated programs to train women for professional careers, improve their economic status, and ensure their equality in society.

Women are an important part of Slovenia's entrepreneurial movement. Many have reported that they prefer working for themselves because owning their own businesses gives them independence, personal achievement, and financial rewards.

- Although women may have an advantage in business—largely because many Slovenes consider women more trustworthy than men—businesswomen still must break into an old-boy network. Younger Slovenian men, however, accept foreign businesswomen better than their older peers do.
- A foreign woman may invite a Slovenian man to a business dinner. If she wants to pay, she should arrange payment with the wait staff beforehand.

Holidays and Festivals

January	New Year's Day (1–2)
February	Day of Slovenian Culture (8)
March/April	Easter and Easter Monday
April	Resistance Day (27)
May	Labor Day (1–2)
June	Day of Slovenian Sovereignty (25)
August	Feast of the Assumption (15)
October	Reformation Day (31)
November	Remembrance Day (1)
December	Christmas (25) Independence Day (26)

SPAIN
KINGDOM OF SPAIN

Greetings from Spain

Greetings from what we think is the most beautiful, entertaining, and cultured place in the world. Other people must think so as well, because Spain welcomes more than fifty million visitors a year.

Everywhere you go in Spain, you see our stunning architecture: from nearly two-thousand-year-old Roman aqueducts, to Moorish palaces, to Gothic cathedrals, to the Guggenheim museum in Bilbao—an incredible feat of modern architecture.

Spaniards have always excelled in the arts. Any list of the world's greatest visual artists is disproportionately Spanish: El Greco, Velázquez, Goya, Picasso, Dalí, Gris, and Miró are all prime examples.

Cervantes' *Don Quixote*, published in 1605, is a treasure. In 1989, Camilo José Cela continued our tradition of literary mastery when he won the Nobel Prize in Literature.

We created the guitar, and we became guitar maestros, especially of classical and flamenco music. Flamenco is our signature music, and we have kept it fresh in the new century with flamenco-rock fusion.

Spaniards have their own sense of time. Unlike Americans, we are not always in a hurry. For us, time does not fly, it walks. If servers or clerks do not wait on you immediately, they are not rude; they just assume you want to take your time.

We do not like to hurry, and we do not understand why anyone would want to. For centuries, we traditionally stopped each workday for a few hours to rest. Our beloved siesta let us escape the afternoon heat and have long, late nights. We usually have dinner at 10:00 PM and stay up far past midnight. Even young children stay up late.

Unfortunately, the siesta has become a casualty of modernity. More people commute, air conditioning makes us more comfortable, and we must be in our offices when the rest of the business world is working. Furthermore, some of us worry about the serious health effects of late, sleep-shortened nights. As a result, in December 2005 our government abolished siestas in the workplace. Today, workers' lunch breaks are officially from noon to 1:00 PM, like the rest of Europe.

We remember that our country was once one of the most powerful in the world. But we also cannot forget the Spanish Civil War (1936–1939), which scarred our country and killed more than 350,000 Spaniards. After the war, more than another hundred thousand Republicans were executed or died in prison. During dictator Francisco Franco's reign, our country was isolated by sanctions and excluded from the United Nations and the North Atlantic Treaty Organisation (NATO). As a result, our economy stagnated.

Luckily by the 1970s, with rising tourism and improved international relations, we had the fastest growing economy in Europe. In 1986, we joined the European Union (EU), and today our gross domestic product (GDP) is growing faster than the Eurozone GDP as a whole. We also forecast that our very low budget deficits will become budget surpluses in the next few years.

While our economy has rebounded, our demographics have not. Spaniards are living longer but having fewer babies. We likely have one of the lowest birthrates in Europe, and our population is aging. Also, although emigration has slowed, our labor force has remained weak. As a result, Spain has a growing immigrant population.

Relationships with our fellow Spaniards are important to us, but we strongly identify with our home regions. Spain has seventeen autonomous regions, and each has its own culture, food, and history as well as it own rights, elected officials, justice system, and relationship with our capital, Madrid. Visitors need to be sensitive to our loyalties and should not compare regions.

We are conservative and traditional, and we value character, breeding, and modesty. While we strive to have our image project affluence and social position, we do not appreciate those who flaunt their superiority, intelligence, or ability.

When you visit us, our slower pace may enchant or irritate you. Our inability to keep our voices down may fascinate or annoy you, as may our propensity to smoke where and when we choose. But you will have to get used to our ways, because we are not going to change for you.

Nevertheless, we welcome the opportunity to meet new people. Come visit us soon!

Population	40,341,462
Capital	Madrid
Area	194,900 square miles, slightly more than twice the size of Oregon
Government	Parliamentary monarchy
Living Standard	GDP = US $27,790 per capita
Natural Resources	Coal, lignite, iron ore, uranium, mercury, pyrites, magnesite, sepiolite, fluorspar, gypsum, zinc, lead, tungsten, copper, kaolin, potash, hydropower, arable land
Agriculture	Grain, vegetables, olives, wine grapes, sugar beets, citrus, beef, pork, poultry, dairy products, fish
Industries	Textiles and apparel (including footwear), food and beverages, metals and metal manufactures, chemicals, clay and refractory products, pharmaceuticals, medical equipment, shipbuilding, automobiles, machine tools, tourism
Climate	Temperate in the north; more extreme in the center, with hot, dry summers and cold winters; Mediterranean climate in the south
Member of the EU?	Yes, since 1986
Currency	Euro (€)

The People

Correct Name	nouns: Spaniard(s), Spanish adjective: Spanish
Ethnic Makeup	Composite of Mediterranean and Nordic types
Languages	Castilian 74%, Catalan 17% (spoken mostly in the northeast), Galician 7% (spoken mostly in the northwest), Basque 2% (spoken mostly in the far north). Castilian is the official language nationwide; the others are official regionally.
Religions	Roman Catholic 94%, other 6%

Meeting and Greeting

- Spaniards shake hands firmly, with eye contact.
- As a greeting, men may embrace friends and family (male and female). Women may embrace other women and kiss one another on the cheek. Women may kiss men if neither has seen the other in a while or if the occasion is especially emotional.
- With that said, don't be surprised if a brand-new acquaintance hugs and kisses you—but never initiate a hug, kiss, or backslap, unless you know the person well.

Names and Titles

- A Spaniard's last name is a combination of the father's last name (family name) followed by the mother's family name (that is, her father's family name). After marriage, a Spanish woman doesn't take her husband's family name.

Example:	Father	Juan Sastre Sergovia
	Mother	Elena Valdez Sanchez
	Son	Jose Sastre Valdez
	Daughter	Maria Sastre Valdez

- In conversation and correspondence, use only the family name.

Example:	Name	Address
	Jose Sastre Segovia	*Señor* Sastre

English	Spanish	Pronunciation
Mr.	*Señor*	(sen-YOHR)
Mrs.	*Señora*	(sen-YOHR-ah)
Miss	*Señorita* (used for girls younger than age eighteen)	(sen-yohr-EET-ah)

- Spaniards use the titles *Don* (dohn) and *Doña* (DOHN-yah) to address older men and women, respectively, or to show respect. They also use the titles for high-level executives and in more formal relationships.

- Use *Don* and *Doña* with the first name only.

  Example: **Name**   **Address**

  Francisco Garcia-Mancha   *Don* Francisco

- Never use *Don* and *Doña* with your own name.

Language

Spain has four official languages: Castilian, Catalan, Galician, and Basque. The first three are Romance languages (descended from Latin). Castilian (*castellano*), the dominant language, is what Americans call "Spanish." It's used for business, and everyone speaks and understands it. Catalan and Galician are regional languages.

Basque is Europe's oldest language, dating back to the Stone Age. It's unlike any other language on earth, and many find it very difficult to learn.

While English is the most common second language, Spaniards speak it mostly in tourist centers only.

Spaniards will appreciate any attempt foreigners make to speak their language.

> According to legend, the devil once spent seven years with the Basques, trying to learn their language. He learned only three words and forgot those as soon as he left.

Conversation

Spaniards are animated when conversing; don't mistake their passion for anger. When you're speaking, expect to be interrupted. Spaniards say, "Do not talk while I am interrupting." They don't care for sarcasm, and because of their strong Catholic faith, they find taking the Lord's name in vain especially offensive.

Acceptable topics
- Your home country
- Travel
- Spanish art and architecture
- Spanish history (pre–twentieth century)
- Music
- Food and wine
- Sports
- Family (Let Spaniards talk about their families, too.)

Unacceptable topics

- Comparisons among Spanish regions
- Personal topics: health, salary, social position, and so on

Topics that require sensitivity

- The Basque movement, also known as Euskadi Ta Askatasuna (ETA): The ETA has waged a terrorist campaign for Basque separatism for more than thirty years; more than eight hundred people have been killed in attacks. A small minority of Basques agree with ETA tactics.
- The Spanish Civil War
- Francisco Franco
- Regional stereotypes
- The Catholic Church
- Gibraltar (British colony occupying a narrow peninsula of Spain's Mediterranean coast)
- Social attitudes toward women
- Bullfighting: Don't discuss unless you and your companions share the same views.

Body Language

Spaniards are formal and dignified in public, but relaxed in private. They do, however, publicly show affection to friends and family.

- Generally, Spaniards stand very close to one another. Don't back up—it's rude behavior.
- Spaniards interpret eye contact from a woman to a man as an expression of interest, but they commonly stare at foreigners without a reason. Don't let their staring unnerve you.
- Spaniards use a lot of hand gestures when they speak. Never mimic them.
- You may have to push to get service; Spaniards don't respect queuing (standing in line).

Phrases

English	Spanish	Pronunciation
Good morning/day	*Buenos días*	(bway-nohs DEE-ahs)
Good afternoon (until 8:00 PM)	*Buenas tardes*	(bway-nahs TAHR-dehs)
Good evening (after dark)	*Buenas noches*	(bway-nahs NOH-chehs)
Please	*Por favor*	(pohr fah-VOHR)
Thank you	*Gracias*	(GRAH-see-ahs)
You're welcome	*De nada*	(day NAH-dah)
Yes	*Sí*	(see)
No	*No*	(noh)
Excuse me	*Perdóneme*	(perh-DOHN-nay-may)
Goodbye	*Adiós*	(ah-DYOHS)
Pleased to meet you (said by a man)	*Encantado*	(en-ken-TAH-doh)
Pleased to meet you (said by a woman)	*Encantada*	(en-ken-TAH-dah)
How are you?	*¿Cómo está usted?*	(KOH-moh ehs-TAH oos-TEHD)

Dining

In Spain, lunch is the main meal, often including an appetizer, a main dish accompanied by a salad, bread (served without butter), and fresh fruit or dessert.

Dinner is late, often between 9:00 to 10:00 PM and later on weekends. It's usually a light meal: a sandwich, sweet bread, or crackers with tea or hot milk. Sometimes there are three courses, but with a light main course.

Unlike Tex-Mex food, Spanish food isn't hot and spicy. Meat, eggs, chicken, fish, vegetables, and fruit are staples of the Spanish diet. The main course often is an egg dish.

Typical Foods

Paella: saffron-flavored rice with clams, mussels, or squid, or any combination of the three

Carne al Horno: roast meats

Langosta del Pobre: monkfish

Gazpacho: cold vegetable soup

Huevos Fritos: fried eggs

Empanadas: meat-filled turnovers

Merluza en Salsa Verde: hake (the country's most popular fish) in green sauce

Tortilla: Spanish potato (sweet potato) omelet

Flan: caramel custard

Tapas: wide variety of appetizers, including chorizo (a spicy sausage), chicken, pork, and ham, served throughout the day

Olive oil: used to fry foods

Drinking

- Most northern Spaniards drink *vino* (wine) and *cerveza* (beer). Nearly all southern Spaniards drink *Jérez* (sherry), the national drink.
- *Sangría*—a mixture of wine, brandy, sugar, fruit juice, and soda water—is a popular summertime drink.
- Spaniards serve red, white, or rosé wine with both lunch and dinner.

Toasting

- The toast *salud* (sa-LOOD) means "health," and Spaniards use it at formal and informal occasions. (They also say it after someone sneezes.)
- After the host stands, says a few thoughtful words, and raises a glass, everyone stands and says, "*Salud*." In a small group, standing may not be necessary.
- You can make a toast at any time, but keep it brief.
- It's acceptable for women to give toasts.

Tipping

Tip everyone for everything. It's common to round up the bill to the nearest euro for any service rendered.

- Restaurants: The bill usually includes a 10 to 15 percent service charge (the bill will read *propina incluida*). If the bill doesn't include a service charge, leave a 5 to 10 percent tip. You can leave small change as an additional tip for good service; leave an additional 5 percent tip for exceptional service.
- Cafés: Leave small change.

- Bars: Leave small change whenever you've ordered a drink.
- Taxis: There are automatic surcharges for airport runs and trips with luggage. For any trip, tip 10 percent of the fare (including surcharges), and tip slightly more than 10 percent for long trips or if the driver helps with your luggage.
- Bellhops and porters: Tip 50 cents per bag (one euro for fancier hotels).

Manners

Spaniards base their manners on easy, relaxed formality.
- Spaniards seat women and older people first.
- Fruit knife and fork or dessert utensils may be placed above the dinner plate.
- Spaniards don't use bread plates. They set bread on the table, and they serve butter with bread at breakfast only.
- It's better to decline food rather than leave food on your plate. Don't ask to have your leftovers boxed to take with you.
- Spaniards won't be insulted if you refuse an alcoholic beverage.
- Stay until the guest of honor leaves.
- To summon a waiter (there are few waitresses in Spain), hold up an index finger, make eye contact, and say, "*Por favor*" (pohr fah-VOHR), which means "please."
- Compliment the food to anyone appropriate (hostess, waiter, and so on).
- Wait staff appreciate friendliness and compliments.
- When entering a shop or restaurant, greet the staff politely. When you leave, say, "*Adiós*" (ah-DYOHS), which means "goodbye."

Dress

Appearance is extremely important to Spaniards, and they will judge you on how you look. Wearing high-quality designer clothing and accessories will suggest professionalism and social standing. Spaniards dress well, and their casual attire is smart casual (see page 45).
- Dress conservatively and elegantly. Avoid wearing bright or flashy colors.
- Pay special attention to your shoes. Shabby shoes ruin a nice outfit—and your Spanish colleagues will notice. Never wear sneakers.
- For business, men wear jackets and ties, even in warm weather. (If the senior businessman takes off his jacket during a meeting, his subordinates may

do so, too.) Women wear well-cut dresses or blouses and skirts. In general, women dress modestly and femininely.

- In restaurants, men wear jackets and ties. (Better restaurants require them.) Women wear dresses, dressy pants, or pantsuits. Generally, dressier outfits are required for places in the cities, including fine restaurants.
- For most formal occasions, men wear dark suits and women wear cocktail dresses. Invitations will clearly state whether events are black tie.
- Always wear conservative clothing in churches.
- Spaniards wear swimsuits, beach attire, and shorts only in resort areas or at beaches. When off the beach, wear a cover-up over your swimsuit.
- Topless beaches are common, and there are nude beaches in remote areas.

Gifts

Spaniards open gifts upon receipt.

Hostess Gifts

Consider giving
- Pastries or cakes
- Chocolates
- Flowers in odd numbers (not thirteen—an unlucky number), except yellow roses (connote infidelity) or chrysanthemums and dahlias (for funerals only)

Don't give
- French or Italian wines

Business Gifts
Spaniards normally don't exchange gifts at business meetings, but exchanging small gifts may be appropriate at the successful conclusion of negotiations. It's acceptable to give a Christmas gift to a Spanish colleague, but it's not expected.

Consider giving
- Desk items
- Books
- Art
- Music

Don't give
- Obviously expensive gifts (may be considered bribes)

Toilet Tips

English	Spanish
Restroom	*Servicios*
Women's restroom	*Damas*
Men's restroom	*Caballeros*
Hot water	*C*
Cold water	*F*

Helpful Hints

- Spaniards seldom invite others to their homes. Consider such an invitation a compliment. Bring gifts for any children, and pay the children special attention.

- Beware of people (often Roma, also known as Gypsies) who hand a flower or gift to unsuspecting tourists. They'll demand payment.

- Don't carry packages or handbags on the arm that's next to the street. A thief on a motorbike could snatch them and zoom away.

Although not all Spaniards are bullfighting fans (some don't even like to attend bullfights), bullfighting is serious business. Spaniards consider it more an art than a sport.

When attending a bullfight, follow the proper protocol. Never be late, and never talk or shout at dangerous moments or when the kill is approaching.

- Be aware that Spaniards are heavy smokers.
- Restaurants generally charge for bread and individual rolls.
- Order only Spanish wines, which are very good. Spaniards are proud of them.

Punctuality

Be patient. Spaniards do nothing in a hurry. While they expect foreign visitors to be punctual for business meetings, they're lax about their own punctuality for social occasions or business appointments.

For social meetings, it's acceptable and common for southern Spaniards to be thirty minutes late and northern Spaniards to be fifteen minutes late. Foreigners may arrive a bit late for social events.

Corporate Culture

Structure

Conflict and stress exist in business between the old bureaucratic, authoritarian management style that managers over age fifty use and the new, more participative management style that younger managers use.

Spanish companies are run from the top down. The boss asserts authority and solves problems. Subordinates expect him or her to be strong and consistent, and view a willingness to share decision making as a weakness.

The real organizational structure, however, is social, not functional. People on the third or fourth level may have more actual power than those at the top.

While subordinates accept criticism from the boss, they're likely to resent criticism from colleagues or outsiders. When reprimanded, a person often won't admit fault.

Meetings

Spaniards don't often have meetings, except when necessary to communicate instructions or save time. Small talk precedes every meeting. Don't get frustrated when meetings don't immediately get to the point.

During negotiations, leave room for concessions, but don't haggle.

Communication

- Most large companies conduct business in English and Spanish, but Spanish is the dominant business language. You can't expect your colleagues to speak English. Check ahead to see whether you'll need an interpreter.
- Spaniards may hesitate to express disagreement to your face; they believe that open disagreement is disrespectful. Instead, they'll discuss their disagreement with others, who will eventually pass it on to you.
- Most Spaniards won't mind being called at home for important business. Expect small talk to start telephone conversations.

Business Cards
- Have your business card printed in Spanish and English.
- Present business cards at the end of meetings.

Be Aware
- Spaniards are very proud people. Don't mistake their self-reliance and sense of worth as intolerance. Never embarrass anyone.

- Expect delays and procrastination. Spanish bureaucracy means odd office hours, plenty of paperwork, seemingly random rules and regulations, and unhelpful staff.
- Spaniards' dismissal of rules and regulations produces a constant crisis atmosphere.
- Spaniards' loyalty lies with people, not institutions.
- Bankers are the business elite, but in recent years Spaniards admire entrepreneurs.
- Outside of work, Spaniards generally socialize with people of the same professional level.
- Spaniards don't do business during the lunch break (noon to 1:00 PM).
- Book appointments at least two weeks in advance.

Socializing
- Spaniards do most business entertaining in restaurants. You may receive an invitation to a home during the last days of meetings.
- Breakfast meetings are acceptable but not favored.
- While lunches and dinners are a vital part of establishing business relationships, don't discuss business unless your host initiates it (which may not happen). Spaniards believe doing business while eating causes indigestion.
- Spaniards invite spouses to dinners, but not always.

Especially for Women

Traditionally, by their thirties Spanish women had married and left the job market permanently. Today, most women keep working after marriage and return to work after having children. Furthermore, Spanish society is aggressively pursuing equality between the sexes. For example, the government must appoint an equal number of men and women to cabinet posts. There are also new laws against domestic violence.

Nevertheless, machismo persists. Few working women are on the fast track; female lawyers and doctors are extremely rare. In addition, society expects even working women to be the primary caretakers of the family and home.

Progress for professional women has been slow, but educationally qualified women (a recent phenomenon) are gradually gaining acceptance in the business community.

- While Spaniards accept foreign businesswomen, it's important that women immediately establish credentials and ability.

- Spanish men are charming, but women used to American men may find them too bold. Be especially careful of making eye contact with a Spanish man, who may interpret your gaze as flirting.
- Although it's rare (and very rude) to whistle at women, staring is common and acceptable. If someone stares at you, just ignore it.
- For dinner, don't dine alone in restaurants or bars. For lunch, dining alone is acceptable.
- It's acceptable for a foreign woman to invite a Spanish man to a business dinner, but she may have trouble paying for the meal. Spanish men expect to pay. If you want to pay, arrange payment with the wait staff beforehand.

Holidays and Festivals

January	New Year's Day (1)
	Epiphany (6)
March	Saint Joseph's Day/Father's Day (19)
March/April	Easter (Thursday–Monday)
May	May Day/Labor Day (1)
May/June	Whitsunday (Pentecost)
	Corpus Christi (60 days after Easter)
June	Feast of the King (24)
	Saint Peter and Saint Paul Day (29)
July	Feast of Santiago, the patron saint of Spain (25)
August	Feast of the Assumption (15)
October	National Day (12)
November	All Saints' Day (1)
December	Constitution Day (6)
	Feast of the Immaculate Conception (8)
	Christmas (25)

Notes: Carnival (Shrove Tuesday) isn't an official holiday, but several local festivals celebrate it in February or March.

Many Spaniards vacation between July 15 and September 15. Check your colleagues' availability before scheduling a trip during that time.

SWEDEN
KINGDOM OF SWEDEN

Greetings from Sweden

Greetings from the land where ecology is a passion. Sweden has ninety thousand pristine lakes and countless breathtaking vistas, and we intend to keep them that way.

We are a classless society and work to promote cooperation. We see ourselves as the perfect union of capitalism and socialism, and of progress and humanity. We support moderation, invention, performance, training, quality, compromise, teamwork, and workplace safety. Our high taxation makes becoming wealthy difficult, but we have one of the highest standards of living in the world.

We strive for reconciliation, individualism, collectivism, and equality. Women make up almost half of our workforce, and everyone has at least twenty-seven days' annual vacation. Men must serve thirty weeks' to twenty months' compulsory military service, and the government has considered making such service compulsory for women. Most couples have parallel careers.

Although almost all Swedes were born into the Lutheran faith, today most are agnostic. We generally attend church only for baptisms, confirmations, weddings, funerals, and even divorce ceremonies, which some of our churches offer.

We celebrate our soul through our music. Sweden has won the Eurovision Song Contest several times and has given the world Jenny Lind, Birgit Nilsson, and, of course, ABBA. (Although we disapprove of those who flaunt wealth, we accept fame if it glorifies Sweden.)

You may find some of our customs unusual. In winter, we run naked from hot saunas, roll in snow, then return to the saunas. Many of us swim nude. We are unencumbered by sexual taboos. We believe in easy, natural sex.

Despite our comfort with our sexuality, there is truth to the stereotypical cold, aloof, brooding, and self-absorbed Swede. (Swedish director and playwright Ingmar Bergman certainly portrayed his countrymen as such.) Even with generous parental leave, our birthrate is still below replacement level. Half our marriages end in divorce, and in the last two decades, the number of single-person households has been growing. Some attribute our melancholy to our high taxes and long, dark, cold winters.

Nevertheless, we know our country provides a wonderful lifestyle, and we are proud to be the conscience of the world. We have spoken out against apartheid and dictatorships. Although over a thousand years ago Vikings of the region used violence to attain their goals, we no longer care to project brutality to the world—just the opposite.

> Swedes are very fond of their royal family, who represent Sweden's egalitarian values. They were delighted when King Carl XVI Gustaf married commoner Silvia Sommerlath.

Today, we avoid conflict and attempt to broker peace whenever possible. (For example, spanking a child is against the law.) We believe in consensus and compromise. This strategy has kept our country officially out of war for the past two centuries.

Of course, to maintain peace, we must protect our country. We have an army, navy, air force, and an impressive defense industry to deter attacks.

When you visit us, know that our regional pride equals our national pride. We do not appreciate praise of regions other than our own. Furthermore, please recognize that Norway, Denmark, Finland, and Sweden are sov-

> Alfred Nobel was born in Stockholm. He invented dynamite, but he wanted to be remembered for peace and progress. Today, everyone knows about the prizes he established. Although Norway awards the Nobel Peace Prize, Swedish institutions select the winners of the physics, chemistry, medicine, and literature prizes.

ereign countries. While we share similarities with our Nordic neighbors, each has a unique language, history, and culture.

Our behavior may seem cold at first, but we will warm to you if you give us a chance. Come visit us soon!

Vital Statistics

Population	9,001,774
Capital	Stockholm
Area	173,700 square miles, slightly larger than California
Government	Constitutional monarchy
Living Standard	GDP = US $42,640 per capita
Natural Resources	Zinc, iron ore, lead, copper, gold, silver, tungsten, arsenic, feldspar, timber, uranium, hydropower

Agriculture	Barley, wheat, sugar beets, meat, milk
Industries	Iron and steel, precision equipment (bearings, radio and telephone parts, armaments), wood pulp and paper products, processed foods, motor vehicles
Climate	Temperate in south with cold, cloudy winters and cool, partly cloudy summers; subarctic in north
Member of the EU?	Yes, since 1995
Currency	Swedish krona (SEK); Sweden has chosen to use its own currency rather than converting to the euro.

The People

Correct Name	noun: Swede(s) adjective: Swedish
Ethnic Makeup	Indigenous population: Swedes, Finnish, and Sami minorities Foreign-born or first-generation immigrants: Finns, Yugoslavs, Danes, Norwegians, Greeks, Turks
Languages	Swedish, small Sami- and Finnish-speaking minorities
Religions	Lutheran 87%, small percentages of Roman Catholic, Orthodox, Baptist, Muslim, Jewish, Buddhist

Meeting and Greeting

- Swedes dislike casual introductions; they prefer third-party introductions. Always try to wait for someone to introduce you, but if waiting isn't possible, shake each person's hand and introduce yourself.
- Swedes introduce women first.
- Swedish men shake hands swiftly and firmly with other men. They shake hands more lightly with women, as do women with other women.
- Older people expect a handshake upon greeting or departure. Younger people generally don't shake hands when greeting or leaving friends.
- Swedes don't smile when shaking hands.

Names and Titles

- Swedes use professional and academic titles but generally only for very formal occasions.
- To address a Swede, use *Herr*, *Fru*, or *Fröken* + last name.
- After an introduction, Swedes quickly move to using first names with other Swedes. Wait for your Swedish colleagues to use your first name before using their first names.

English	Swedish	Pronunciation
Mr.	*Herr*	(hair)
Mrs.	*Fru*	(frew)
Miss	*Fröken* (used for girls under age eighteen, waitresses, and female teachers)	(FRUH-ken)

Language

- While Swedish is the official language, many Swedes speak English. It's a required second language in school.
- Swedes appreciate foreigners' attempts to speak Swedish.

Conversation

Swedes see themselves as extremely broadminded. They'll discuss any subject, including sex, money, religion, politics, incest, and euthanasia. With that said, although Swedes feel free to criticize their own country, they won't appreciate your joining in.

When conversing with Swedes, don't rush to fill pauses in conversation. Swedes appreciate silence. Also know that they find profanity especially offensive.

Acceptable topics
- Travel
- Ice hockey
- Politics and current events

- Music
- Philosophy
- Nature
- Sweden's accomplishments—its economy, high standard of living, sports, architecture, and so on
- Sweden's history: Swedes are especially proud that their country was one of the greatest European powers in the seventeenth century.

Unacceptable topics
- Personal topics (marital status, salary, social position, health, and so on)
- Praise of another city or area in Sweden: Swedes' regionalism is very strong.
- Complaints about the cost of items
- Superficial small talk
- Jokes about Norwegians: Swedes poke fun at Norwegians. Don't join in.
- Insincere compliments: Swedes consider them rude. When describing an event, object, or whatever, use *like*, not *love*. Also, don't brag or use superlatives when speaking. Swedes don't appreciate embellishments to the truth.

Topics that require sensitivity
- Swedish culture: Feel free to praise the culture, but never criticize the government, economy, the social welfare system, Swedish humor, sexual habits, suicide rate, or any other parts of Swedish culture.

Body Language
Generally, Swedes have reserved body language, and they dislike physical contact. Only family or close friends embrace, touch, or kiss—usually in private. Public displays of affection, however, are becoming increasingly common.
- Keep a distance of at least two arm's lengths between you and surrounding people.
- Maintain eye contact while talking with someone.
- Posture is important. Don't slouch or lean against walls or tables.
- Avoid talking with animated hand gestures. Swedes don't use them.
- Swedes don't queue (stand in line). Ticket dispensers, however, are common; you won't be served without a number.

Phrases

English	Swedish	Pronunciation
Good morning	*God morgon*	(goo MOHR-ahn)
Good afternoon/day	*God dag*	(goo dog)
Good evening	*God afton*	(goo AHF-tohn)
Hello (casual)	*Hej*	(hey)
Please	*Var vänlig*	(vahr VAHN-leeg)
Thank you	*Tack så mycket*	(tahk so MICK-et)
You're welcome	*Var så god*	(vahr so GOOD)
Yes	*Ja*	(yah)
No	*Nej*	(nay)
Excuse me	*Ursäkta mig*	(oor-SECT-uh may)
Goodbye	*Adjö* or *Hejdå*	(ahd-YOH) or (HAY-doh)
Pleased to meet you	*Det var trevligt*	(det vahr TREV-lickt)
How are you?	*Hur mår du?*	(hur more DO)

Dining

Swedish cuisine contains a lot of fish, cheese, vegetables, and fruit. It doesn't contain much fat or meat.

Swedes eat their food in a certain order: cold fish dishes, cold meats and vegetable salads, small hot dishes (meatballs, sausages), desserts (cheese, fruit, pastry).

In Sweden, a casual dinner has three courses:

* Meat or fish, potatoes, vegetables
* Salad
* Dessert followed by coffee

A formal or business dinner has four courses:

* Smoked salmon, caviar, marinated herring, or soup
* Meat or fish, potatoes, vegetables
* Salad
* Dessert followed by coffee

Typical Foods

Gravlax: salmon cured with dill

Lutefisk: lye-soaked, nearly gelatinous dried cod (Swedes love it, but it's definitely an acquired taste. Start with a small portion.)

Renkött: reindeer meat

Drinking

Swedes often drink the following beverages:

- *Vin* (wine) or *öl* (beer)
- *Absolut Renat Brännvin*: a popular brand of vodka
- Cocktails: vodka, Scotch, brandy, wine, gin, Campari (a bitter Italian aperitif)
- Aquavit: a strong liquor distilled from grain or potatoes and sometimes flavored with caraway seeds and other spices
- Coffee: Dinner without coffee, the national drink, would be unthinkable to a Swede.

Toasting

- Before drinking, let the host make a small speech and offer the first toast. Also, let those senior in age or rank propose toasts before proposing a toast yourself.
- The toast *Skål* (skohl) means "cheers," and Swedes use it at formal and informal occasions.
- Toasting protocol is often formal. During a toast, the toaster makes a few remarks, lifts his or her glass, meets the eyes of the person receiving the toast, and says, "*Skål.*" The recipient then nods and says, "*Skål*" in return. Then everyone takes a drink. Men must wait for women to put down their glasses before doing so themselves. Women should do so immediately out of courtesy.
- When toasting with aquavit, one traditionally drinks it in one gulp. Swedes don't expect foreigners to do so, but if you decide to follow suit, be careful: aquavit is very strong.
- Between the main course and dessert, the male guest of honor taps his glass with a knife or spoon and thanks the hostess on behalf of all the guests. If the guest of honor is female, she thanks the host.
- It's acceptable for women to propose toasts.

Tipping

- Restaurants: The bill always includes a 15 to 20 percent service charge, but it's common to round up the bill when paying. In five-star restaurants, leave a 5 percent additional gratuity on the table.
- Taxis: The fare usually includes a 10 percent tip, but it's common to round up the fare when paying.
- Bellhops and porters: Tipping isn't common, but SEK10 to SEK20 is appropriate.
- Gas station attendants, hair stylists, barbers, hotel maids, and doormen: No tip is necessary. All earn good salaries.

Manners

Swedes may behave very formally.
- Don't ask for a tour of your host's home unless you have a well-established relationship.
- Don't use a dinner knife for butter. Swedes usually provide a butter knife.
- When dining in a home, Swedes usually offer the main course twice.
- Don't eat fast. Swedes believe Americans shovel food into their mouths.
- Always leave some food on the serving platter. It's rude to take the last pieces of food.
- Try to eat everything on your plate, but if you're too full to finish, your hosts shouldn't be offended.
- Leave a dinner usually no later than 11:00 PM.
- The day after a party, call—or, preferably, write a note—to thank your host and hostess.
- To beckon wait staff, wave your hand and make eye contact.
- A man should tip his hat to women and remove his hat while talking to a woman.
- Don't be loud.

Dress

Swedes dress in warm, European-style clothing (see pages 44–45). Their attire is fashionable but casual and elegant. They are always dressed well in public.
- For business, men wear conservative suits and ties. Women wear dresses or pantsuits.

- Unless a restaurant allows casual attire, men wear suits and ties, and women wear dresses or elegant pants and blouses. If you're unsure what attire is appropriate, ask a knowledgeable colleague.
- For the opera or theater, men wear suits and women wear dresses or dressy pantsuits.
- For formal occasions, men wear tuxedos (called "smoking jackets"), and women wear cocktail dresses.
- Traditionally, Swedes wore furs during the day and evening. An increasing number of anti-fur demonstrations, however, have reduced the number of furs in Sweden.

Gifts

Swedes open gifts upon receipt.

Hostess Gifts

Consider giving
- Flowers (unwrapped)
- Wine (very expensive in Sweden)
- Chocolates
- Books
- Recordings of music

Don't give
- Crystal
- Any items made in Sweden

Business Gifts
Swedes generally don't exchange gifts in business, but it's common to exchange small gifts with Swedish colleagues at Christmas.

Consider giving
- Any item that relates to the business itself (for example, if you work for a technology firm, a computer item like a laptop case)

Don't give
- Any items made in Sweden

Toilet Tips	
English	**Swedish**
Restroom	*Toalett/WC*
Women's restroom	*Damer*
Men's restroom	*Herrar*
Hot water	*Varmvatten*
Cold water	*Kallvatten*

Helpful Hints

- Swedes say, "*Hallå*" (hall-LOW) to get someone's attention, not as a greeting.
- Swedish women may practice their English with strangers. Foreign men shouldn't mistake their conversation as flirting.
- Remember to thank someone for dinner or a gift upon next meeting.
- Swedes are comfortable with nudity. Some people sunbathe in the nude. Don't be surprised to see people changing clothes on the beach—with or without using a towel as cover.
- Swedes' patience may test Americans'. Be patient in lines for buses, trains, and so on. Don't cross a street against a red light.
- As always, never drink and drive. Sweden strictly enforces its drunk-driving laws.
- It's easiest to get a taxi at a cab stand or hotel.
- If you touch it, you bought it. If you pick up produce in a food market, you must buy it.
- It's difficult to return items unless they're flawed.

Punctuality

Swedes take punctuality for business meetings seriously and expect that you'll do likewise; call with an explanation if you're delayed.

Swedes insist on punctuality for social occasions. It's better to arrive early at someone's home for a party and wait outside than risk being a few minutes late. Swedes often serve dinner immediately at dinner parties. There may be no cocktail hour.

Corporate Culture

Structure

The structure of most Swedish companies is horizontal and functional, with middle- and lower-level managers making most decisions. Competence earns authority, and senior managers regularly delegate key decisions.

The decision-making process is time consuming, but once made, decisions are implemented rapidly.

Meetings

Meetings begin and end punctually, and agendas are clearly set. Meetings can be for briefing, discussion, or decision making. Swedes usually get right down to business after brief small talk. They're factual, practical, and precise, and get to the point quickly; they expect the same of you. Swedes are tough negotiators.

Presentations are important. They should be clear, to the point, and detailed. You must back them with numerous facts, figures, tables, and charts.

Communication

Swedes commonly use English in business, and you'll rarely need an interpreter. (Check in advance, however, to be safe.) When communicating with Swedes, be clear and concise; they'll be equally clear with you.

Don't call a Swedish colleague at home, unless the matter is urgent and you have a well-established relationship.

Business Cards

- Swedes exchange business cards, but they don't have a specific protocol for doing so.
- Business cards in English are acceptable.

Be Aware

- The pace of Swedish business is slow and relatively relaxed—don't rush people.
- When you first meet them, Swedes may appear stiff or aloof. But when they get to know you, strong personal relationships can develop. Keep in mind, though, that Swedes tend to keep their business and social relationships separate.
- Coffee breaks and lunches are long in Sweden.

> Sweden is famous for its *smorgasbord* (large buffet) at parties and special occasions. Guests help themselves to the hot and cold foods placed on a large table.

- In summer, many businesses close by 3:00 or 4:00 PM.
- Avoid scheduling appointments for around February 20 to March 1 (school holidays).

Socializing

- Swedes do most business entertaining in restaurants.
- Business breakfasts are acceptable, but not as common as in the United States.
- Business lunches are common, and business discussions are acceptable. In fact, you can discuss business at any time during a meal.
- Swedes include spouses in business dinners.

Especially for Women

Sweden is a good place for women to do business. In Sweden, women make up roughly half of the workforce—one of the highest percentages in the world.

With that said, while Swedes widely accept foreign businesswomen, they have more conservative attitudes toward their own businesswomen.

- A foreign woman won't have a problem inviting a Swedish man to a business dinner and paying for the meal.
- A woman may eat alone in the better restaurants (including restaurants of major hotels) and bars without hassle.
- Women are usually safe walking alone at night, but use common sense.

Holidays and Festivals	
January	New Year's Day (1)
	Epiphany (6)
March/April	Easter (Friday–Monday)
April/May	Feast of the Ascension (40 days after Easter)
May	Labor Day (1)
May/June	Whitsunday (Pentecost) and Whitmonday (day after Pentecost)
June	National Day (6)
	Midsummer Day (*Midsommardagen*)—celebrations commence on Midsummer Eve and can last for a week
November	All Saints' Day (1)
December	Christmas (24–25)
	Boxing Day (26)
	New Year's Eve (31)

SWITZERLAND
SWISS CONFEDERATION

Greetings from Switzerland

Greetings from the land of diversity. Although our ethnic mix may make it difficult to define the Swiss people, we are proud of our diverse country.

Our nation is remarkably cohesive despite our language differences and localized governments. "Unity, yes; uniformity, no" is our motto. We have maintained hundreds of years of peaceful neutrality, harmony, stability, and prosperity.

Those who are shortsighted might deduce that Switzerland should be an economic and political disaster. Ours is a landlocked country with a small home market (mostly agriculture and no heavy industry), no former colonies, few natural resources, four national languages, and no desire to join the European Union (EU). Yet we are anything but a disaster.

While we are an old country—the Swiss Confederation formed in 1291—we have become one of the world's richest through efficiency, hard work, and consensus building. Our economy is very sound, and our currency is strong. We thrive on the vast income of our ski resorts.

We prize our independence and neutrality, but we work hard to promote world peace. Despite our refusal to join the EU, we want to work with our neighbors to improve the world. Recently, we agreed to levy a withholding tax on any savings that EU members earn in our banks, and we agreed to deposit a lump sum each year into the EU's social cohesion funds, used to support the economies of poorer areas. (We refuse, however, to reveal our banking system's secrets.)

Furthermore, although Switzerland has only recently (in 2002) become a member of the United Nations (UN), for years Geneva has been the headquarters of the European Fair Trade Association (EFTA), World Trade Organization (WTO), World Health Organization (WHO), and many other international agencies.

As a people, we are staunchly conservative and serious. We value cleanliness, honesty, sobriety, thrift, tolerance, punctuality, and responsibility. We strongly respect saving and material wealth. We are proud of our environment. We recycle everything, and Switzerland was the first European country to require catalytic converters in all new cars.

We care deeply about how foreigners view us. In *The Third Man*, Orson Welles (as Harry Lime) dismisses the Swiss, saying our peaceful way has produced nothing more than the cuckoo clock. We resent that image. We are the first to admit that rules and regulations preoccupy us.

But we have a lighthearted side. We love circuses (you will find many in towns all over Switzerland), and we are great collectors. Because we all live within an hour's drive of a mountain, many of us could ski before we could walk.

In the end, you may find us boring or too serious, but our way has worked very well for us, and we see no reason to change. We have had years of continued prosperity and peace, and we hope you will find working with us prosperous, too.

Vital Statistics

Population	7,489,370
Capital	Bern
Area	15,940 square miles, slightly less than twice the size of New Jersey
Government	Similar in structure to a federal republic
Natural Resources	Hydropower potential, timber, salt
Living Standard	GDP = US $53,400 per capita
Agriculture	Grains, fruits, vegetables, meat, eggs
Industries	Machinery, chemicals, watches, textiles, precision instruments
Climate	Temperate, but varies with altitude: cold, cloudy, rainy/snowy winters; cool to warm, cloudy, humid summers with occasional showers
Member of the EU?	No
Currency	Swiss franc (CHF)

The People

Correct Name	noun: Swiss adjective: Swiss
Ethnic Makeup	German 65%, French 18%, Italian 10%, Romansch 1%, other 6%
Languages	German (official) 63.7%, French (official) 20.4%, Italian (official) 6.5%, Serbo-Croatian 1.5%, Albanian 1.3%, Portuguese 1.2%, Spanish 1.1%, English 1%, Romansch (official) 0.5%, other 2.8%
Religions	Roman Catholic 41.8%, Protestant 35.3%, Orthodox 1.8%, other Christian 0.4%, Muslim 4.3%, other 1%, unspecified 4.3%, none 11.1%

Meeting and Greeting

- The Swiss shake hands firmly, with eye contact.
- Switzerland is a multilingual verbal society; greetings vary according to region. If you don't know any French, German, or Italian greetings (see pages 167, 182, and 237), an English greeting is acceptable.
- At parties, let the host introduce you.

Names and Titles

- The Swiss use academic and professional titles frequently, and they use first names only for very close friends and family.
- Address people according to region:

  French region   *Monsieur* and *Madame* (see page 168)

  German region   *Herr* and *Frau* (see page 182)

  Italian region   *Signor* and *Signora* (see page 238)

Language

- German, French, Italian, and Romansch are the national languages, but the Swiss speak French and German most often. Many speak English.
- Each canton (political subdivision) has chosen the language it uses, and the Swiss honor that choice. For example, each Parliament member speaks in his or her canton language.

- Italian Swiss, French Swiss, and German Swiss differ from standard Italian, French, and German. The dialects can be difficult even for other Italian-, French-, and German-speaking people to understand.
- The Swiss appreciate any effort foreigners make to speak the canton language.

Conversation

Conversation protocol varies according to the region. See pages 169, 183–84, and 239 for more information on conversation protocol in France, Germany, and Italy, respectively.

Even though the Swiss from each region converse like people from neighboring countries, always remember that they aren't French, German, or Italian—they're Swiss, and they're very proud of it.

Acceptable topics
- Football (soccer)
- Skiing
- Switzerland's natural beauty

Unacceptable topics
- Jokes: Also, never tease or mock.
- Personal issues: Never ask about anyone's occupation, age, marital status, religion, or health.

Topics that require sensitivity
- Switzerland's neutrality, especially during World Wars I and II
- Money and Swiss banks
- Switzerland's universal military service

Body Language

The Swiss are private people. They may appear reserved, detached, and standoffish. Body language depends upon the region. See pages 170, 184, and 240 for French, German, and Italian body language rules. Here are some general rules:
- Don't point your index finger to your head. The Swiss consider the gesture an insult.
- The Swiss frown on poor posture; don't stretch or slouch in public.
- Expect pushing and shoving in queues (lines), especially ski lift lines.
- Never put your feet on a desk, chair, or table.

Use phrases in the language spoken in the region. See French, German, and Italian phrases on pages 170, 185, and 240, respectively.

Dining

The Swiss take great care in preparing and serving excellent fresh food. Dining habits and food vary according to the region. See pages 171, 185–86, and 241 for more information on dining habits and food in France, Germany, and Italy, respectively.

Lunch is the main meal of the day. It may be a light meal if you have a dinner party that evening. (A dinner party serves the day's main meal.)

Typical Foods
Sausages
Leek soup
Fish
Cheese fondue: bread dipped in melted cheese (accompanied by white wine)
Meat fondue: pieces of meat dipped in hot oil or broth, served with sauces
    (accompanied by red wine)
Raclette: cheese melted in front of a fire or under an electric warmer, served
    with onions and baked or boiled potatoes (accompanied by white wine)
Roesti: sliced, roasted potatoes
Horse meat

Italian Swiss
Polenta: cornmeal porridge
Ossobucco: braised veal shank

French Swiss
Similar to French food; see page 171.

German Swiss
Geschnetzeltes: veal (minced) with thick cream sauce
Bernerplatte: sauerkraut and/or string beans with smoked pork chops, bacon,
    ham, and pork sausages
Birchermuesli: oat flakes soaked in milk, with fresh fruit, berries, and nuts
    (as breakfast, light lunch, or light dinner)

Drinking

- The Swiss seldom drink cocktails before meals; instead, they may drink white wine or champagne. They may also serve Campari (a bitter Italian aperitif), *Cynar* (artichoke extract), *blanc-cassis* (blackberry liqueur and white wine), *pastis* (anise liquor), vermouth, sherry, or white wine.
- The Swiss serve beer, hard cider, white wine, and red wine during the meal. They serve hard liquor and cordials or coffee after the meal. The Swiss make some of the world's best coffee.
- The Swiss like to serve these specialties: *grappa* (Swiss-Italian brandy), *marc* (Swiss-French brandy), *Pflümliwasser* (plum brandy), *apricotine* (apricot brandy), *Poire Guillaume* (pear brandy), kirsch (cherry liqueur).
- Although Swiss water is excellent, nobody drinks tap water—only mineral water. Generally, the Swiss believe tap water is for external use only.

Toasting

- The host proposes the first toast. Lift your glass and clink glasses when others invite you to do so. Don't drink until after the host has taken a drink.
- It's polite to propose a toast to thank your host. To do so, look at him, raise your glass, and say, "To your health," or give a toast in French, German, or Italian (see pages 172, 186–87, or 242).
- It's acceptable for women to propose toasts.

Tipping

Tipping isn't common in Switzerland. By law, all hotel, restaurant, café, bar, taxi, and hairdressing services include a 15 percent service charge. Locals, however, usually round up restaurant bills. Feel free to do so as well, if the service is exceptional.

For bellhops and porters, tip the equivalent of one euro, but always in Swiss francs.

Manners

- Use utensils to eat almost all foods, even fruit and sandwiches.
- Cut potatoes, soft foods, and salads with a fork, not a knife.

- Eat white asparagus with your hands.
- Break bread with your hands, not a knife.
- If salt and pepper aren't on the table, don't ask for them.
- It's polite to try a little of everything you're offered. The hostess especially appreciates guests who take second helpings.
- When dining in someone's home, try to eat everything on your plate. It's impolite to leave food on your plate.
- Smoke at the table only if others do. Even then, ask permission before lighting up.
- Leave a party no later than midnight.
- You may seat yourself in most pubs and inexpensive restaurants. If you're uncertain whether you should, ask the wait staff.
- Greet clerks when entering and leaving shops.
- In the German region, never wave your hand to beckon wait staff. Instead, say, *"Herr Ober"* (hair OH-burr) or *"Fräulein"* (FROY-line) to summon a waiter or waitress.
- In general, show courtesy—the Swiss highly value courtesy. Also, show great respect for the elderly.
- Never litter; the Swiss will scold you if you do.

Dress

The Swiss dress conservatively. Your attire should always be clean and neat.
- For business, men wear suits and ties. Women wear pantsuits, skirts and jackets, or dresses.
- In restaurants, men wear trousers, shirts, and sweaters. Women wear sweaters and skirts or dress pants. Better restaurants usually prefer elegant attire. Check in advance whether a restaurant requires men to wear a coat and tie.
- For formal occasions, men wear dark suits or tuxedos (invitations will specify). Women wear cocktail dresses.
- Jeans are acceptable for casual occasions if they're stylish, clean, and neat.
- When visiting a church, never wear shorts or any clothing that exposes your knees or shoulders.

Gifts

The Swiss open gifts upon receipt. When visiting someone's home, bring a small gift for any children. The family will appreciate the gesture.

Hostess Gifts

Always bring a small, attractively wrapped gift for the hostess. It's polite to send flowers to her on the morning of a large party or the next day with a thank-you note.

Consider giving
- Good-quality candy
- Pralines
- Unwrapped flowers (odd number), except chrysanthemums or white asters (for funerals only)
- Pastries

Don't give
- Personal items
- Large, expensive gifts (The Swiss consider such gifts vulgar.)

Business Gifts

The Swiss normally don't exchange gifts at business meetings; however, pack a small gift in your briefcase in case your colleagues give you one. It may be appropriate to exchange small gifts at the successful conclusion of negotiations. It's acceptable to give a gift to a Swiss colleague at Christmas, but it's not expected.

Consider giving
- Liquor: whiskey, cognac, bourbon, very good wine
- Attractive coffee-table books
- Desk accessories

Don't give
- Items with a sharp point

Toilet Tips

See pages 175, 189, and 245 for French, German, and Italian Toilet Tips.

Helpful Hints

- Don't expect quick friendships. A personal relationship develops only after a business relationship has been established. When, however, the Swiss offer their friendship, it's for life.
- Follow all the rules. Ask if you're uncertain.
- Never bargain anywhere in Switzerland, including markets.
- Payment in euros may be acceptable in major cities, but you'll receive change in Swiss francs.
- At pubs and inexpensive restaurants, expect strangers to sit at your table. You don't need to talk with them.

Punctuality

The Swiss insist on punctuality for social and business occasions. They consider tardiness an insult. Call with an explanation if you'll be delayed.

Corporate Culture

The Swiss business climate is very conservative, and company culture can vary depending on region. (See pages 176–77, 190–92, and 246–48 for more information on French, German, and Italian company culture, respectively.)

Structure
Swiss companies' structure is traditional and vertical.

Meetings
The Swiss make brief small talk before doing business. Meetings, like other activities in Swiss companies, are impersonal, brisk, orderly, well planned, and task oriented. Presentations must be orderly, well prepared, thorough, and detailed. (Always remember that the Swiss dot every *i* and cross every *t*.)

You must be patient; discussions are detailed, cautious, and sometimes pessimistic. Decision making is slow and methodical. The Swiss are hard but fair bargainers, not hagglers.

Communication

- Generally, the Swiss speak English during business transactions with foreigners, but it's a good idea to check in advance whether you'll need an interpreter.
- The Swiss keep information close and communicate it only upon request.
- It's not acceptable to call a Swiss colleague at home unless it's an emergency.

Business Cards

- Bring a good supply of business cards. Give a card to each person you meet.
- Business cards in English are acceptable.
- At meetings, hand your business card to the receptionist upon arrival.

Be Aware

- The Swiss are formal and courteous. They're also hard working, thrifty, and reliable. They're known for excellent quality and craftsmanship.
- In Switzerland, unemployment and inflation are low and labor relations are good.
- It's essential to schedule appointments ahead of time; never "drop in" on a Swiss colleague.
- Every town and village has its own food, customs, and culture. There's intense rivalry among Swiss towns.

Socializing

- The Swiss do most business entertaining in restaurants. They seldom invite visitors to their home. Know that an invitation to someone's home is an honor.
- Business breakfasts aren't common.
- Business lunches are more common than business dinners, but dinners are becoming popular.
- The Swiss generally include spouses in business dinners. They don't discuss business if spouses are present, but they generally do if spouses aren't.

Especially for Women

While the Swiss view women's role in society conservatively (women have been able to vote only since 1971), they treat both foreign and native business-women fairly and professionally.

Men, however, dominate the banking and finance fields, and Swiss women must have better qualifications than their male counterparts to get to the top. A relatively small number of Swiss women hold top jobs, but slowly more women are becoming involved in business and public service.

- Swiss men are very conservative; many would be embarrassed if a foreign businesswoman invited them to dinner. If possible, invite a Swiss man to a business lunch instead. Expect Swiss men to insist on paying for a meal. If you want to pay, arrange payment with the wait staff beforehand.
- It's generally safe for a woman to go out alone at any hour, but use common sense.

Holidays and Festivals	
January	New Year's Day (1)
March/April	Easter (Friday–Monday)
April/May	Feast of the Ascension (40 days after Easter)
May/June	Whitsunday (Pentecost) and Whitmonday (day after Pentecost)
August	National Day (1)
December	Christmas (25)
Note: Some cantons observe additional holidays.	

TURKEY
REPUBLIC OF TURKEY

Greetings from Turkey

Greetings from the traditional gateway between the East and West. Turkey straddles two continents, and the Bosporus strait symbolically divides Asia from Europe.

Turkey is an extremely ancient land. In the 1960s, archaeologists discovered the remains of Çatalhüyük, a city in south-central Turkey that dates back to 6700 BC. Near the Dardanelles strait, people can still visit the ruins of ancient Troy, the city made famous in Homer's epic poem *Iliad*.

Our ancestors hailed from various lands and ruled great empires in the area for sixteen centuries. Our Turkic ancestors were warriors that entered the region from Central Asia as early as the tenth century AD. During the reign of the mighty Byzantine Empire, Constantinople (now İstanbul) was the heart of Eastern Christianity. Around the beginning of the fourteenth century, the Ottoman Empire began controlling the region, establishing the Islamic faith and laying the foundation of our culture today.

The Ottoman Empire's influence continued for over the next six hundred years. In the early twentieth century, however, the empire began to fall apart; in 1923 our nation became the Republic of Turkey.

The republic's leader, Mustafa Kemal—known as Atatürk, which means "Father of the Turks"—envisioned a modern Turkish state, and modernization for Turkey came quickly. During his fifteen-year presidency, Atatürk's accomplishments were astounding. He successfully changed our legal and political systems, our government, our language and alphabet, even our music and dancing. Women were no longer required to wear veils and were given rights equal to men's. Civil marriage was introduced and polygamy was outlawed. Citizens were free to practice whatever religion they chose, and the Western calendar replaced the Islamic calendar.

As a result of Atatürk's changes, today we are a modern secular country. (Many Turks even celebrate a secular Christmas holiday.) Turkish law separates religion and state, and continued modernization is still one of our main goals. We have become steadily more westernized, and our economy is developing. A growing number of multinational companies are successfully doing business in our country.

Despite the fact that only about three percent of Turkey lies in Europe, we strongly believe we should be allowed to join the European Union (EU). We feel our geographic position as well as our religious and cultural differences would be assets to the EU.

We are extremely patriotic, and we are as proud of our history as we are of our modern society. Our combination of traditional and modern attitudes is easy to observe. For example, BMWs and donkey carts share our streets.

In Turkey, the family is the most important social unit. Everyone depends upon and is loyal to his or her family. Households almost always include unmarried adult children and sometimes married sons and families. Many of our businesses are family owned and operated.

Turks are famous for their hospitality, which is generous, sincere, and almost overwhelming. Our guests believe they cannot refuse our abundant offerings of food and drink without hurting our feelings.

We follow current affairs, and you will find us very well informed. We love football (soccer) and avidly support our favorite teams. We are opinionated and will not hesitate to share our opinions with you.

We ask that foreigners remember that although the majority of us are Muslims, we are Turks—not Arabs. Our language is Turkish, not Arabic. We are astute businesspeople and want to build relationships before doing business. We are not in a rush, so be patient and do not pressure us.

Come visit us. You will find Turks welcoming and friendly and Turkey a great place to expand your business into Europe and/or Asia.

Vital Statistics	
Population	69,660,559
Capital	Ankara
Area	116,196 square miles, slightly larger than Texas
Government	Republican parliamentary democracy
Living Standard	GDP = US $4,810 per capita
Agriculture	Tobacco, cotton, grain, olives, sugar beets, legumes, citrus, livestock
Industries	Textiles, food processing, autos, mining (coal, chromite, copper, boron), steel, petroleum, construction, lumber, paper
Climate	Temperate; hot, dry summers with mild, wet winters; harsher in the interior
Member of the EU?	Applicant nation, hoping to join in 2015
Currency	New Turkish lira (YTL)

The People

Correct Name	noun: Turk(s) adjective: Turkish
Ethnic Makeup	Turkish 80%, Kurdish 20%
Languages	Turkish (official), Kurdish, Arabic, Armenian, Greek
Religions	Muslim 99.8% (mostly Sunni), other 0.2% (mostly Christians and Jews)

Meeting and Greeting

- Turks firmly shake hands with everyone (including children) upon greeting and departing, beginning with the eldest or most senior person.
- As a display of humility, devout Muslims may avoid looking into someone's eyes (especially if the person is of the opposite sex). Also, some Muslims may not shake hands with people of the opposite sex.
- Close friends may kiss one another on each cheek as a greeting.
- As a mark of respect in business, men should extend a handshake to women.

Names and Titles

English	Turkish	Pronunciation
Sir (Mr.)	*bey*	(bay)
Madam (Mrs. and Miss)	*hanim*	(HAH-num)

- Turks use first names when addressing one another, and they quickly move to using first names with foreigners. Foreigners, however, should use last names and appropriate titles until their Turkish colleagues invite them to use first names.
- Many Turks are familiar with Western professional titles like *doctor* and *professor*, but the more polite way to address professionals—as well as elders and superiors—is by first name + *bey/hanim*.

    Examples: Dennis Alkan   Dennis *bey*
    Suzan Alkan   Suzan *hanim*

- Among friends, Turks may address one another by title + first name. Less commonly, Turks may informally address professionals by title + *bey/hanim*.
    Example: Dennis Osman is a lawyer (*avukat*).
        Avukat Dennis or *Avukat bey*

Language

Until the 1920s, Turks spoke Ottoman Turkish, which uses the Arabic alphabet. In 1928, the Turkish republican government oversaw the modernization of the Turkish language. Modern Turkish uses the Roman (Latin) alphabet and is more direct and concise—as well as simpler to read, spell, and print—than Ottoman Turkish.

The change in language has greatly increased literacy in Turkey. Today, only scholars and people who learned to read before 1928 can read Turkish in the Arabic alphabet.

German and English are popular second languages. A Kurdish minority speaks Kurdish and Turkish.

Conversation

Turks make every effort to converse, despite any linguistic barriers. They appreciate any effort foreigners make to speak their language.

Outside the business environment, Turkish women generally don't converse with men until formally introduced.

Acceptable topics
- Sports, especially football (soccer)
- Your family (but don't ask about your Turkish colleagues' families unless they bring up the subject)
- Turkey's historical and geographical importance
- Turkey's excellent cuisine
- Your home region

Unacceptable topics
- Problems or bad news (when a guest in someone's home)
- Personal topics: But after securing a friendship, discussing personal topics may be acceptable. With this said, however, Turks ask even casual acquaintances personal questions (age, salary, and so on). If you'd rather not answer such questions, simply reply, "In my country, that would be a strange question."

Topics that require sensitivity
- Atatürk: Although he remains a beloved hero to many (and there are laws against insulting him), some Turks are ambivalent about his legacy.
- Relations with Cyprus and with the Kurds: Don't bring up these topics, and if your Turkish colleagues bring them up, just listen to them. Turkey is working very hard to resolve these issues.
- Islamist political parties

Body Language
- Turks generally stand closer to one another than Americans do.
- Tilting your head downward slightly means "yes." Tilting your head upward slightly while making a dental click with your tongue (*tsk*) means "no."
- Turks don't show affection in public.
- Turks often rub worry beads to relieve tension or as a nervous habit.
- Placing the thumb between the index and middle fingers is a rude gesture. It's equivalent to raising a middle finger in the United States.
- Making a V with the index and middle fingers means "two." Turks usually use the gesture to signify the number of sugar cubes they want in tea or coffee.
- Turks commonly jump to the front of a line—queuing isn't respected.

Phrases

English	Turkish	Pronunciation
Good morning	*Günaydın*	(gewn-EYE-duhn)
Good day	*İyi günler*	(ee-yee-GEWN-lar)
Good evening	*İyi akşamlar*	(ee-AH ack-shahm-LAHR)
Please	*Lütfen*	(LEWT-fahn)
Thank you	*Teşekkür ederim*	(TEH-sheh-kewr EH-der-em)
You're welcome	*Bir şey değil*	(beer shay DEEL)
Yes	*Evet*	(EH-vet)
No	*Hayır*	(hire)
Excuse me	*Affedersiniz*	(ah-fed-AHR-sen-eez)
Goodbye (said by one who's leaving)	*Allaha ısmarladık*	(ah-LAHS-mahr-lah-dik)
Goodbye (said by one who's staying)	*Güle Güle*	(gew-LEH gew-LEH)
How are you?	*Nasılsınız*	(NAH-sil-sih-niz)
Pleased to meet you	*Taniştiğmiza*	(tan-ish-TOOHR-mooz-ah)
Pleased to meet you (when shaking hands only)	*Memnun oldum*	(MEM-nun OLD-um)

Dining

Turkish cuisine is rich, quite lavish, and among the world's finest. Bread and other carbohydrates are an essential part of Turkish fare. Devout Muslims don't eat pork, and even secular Turks don't eat it.

Typical Foods

Meze: hors d'oeuvres of astonishing variety and abundance (It's the first course when alcoholic beverages are served.)

Yufka: a thin, flaky dough—common in many Turkish dishes

Pilav: rice pilaf

Patıcan Salatası: salad made of roasted eggplant that's puréed and mixed with yogurt and lemon

Kebap: sliced pieces of red meat, roasted or skewered

Şiş Kebap: lamb shish kebabs

Börek: phyllo filled with feta, spinach, or meat

Deniz Ürünleri: seafood

Zeytinyağı Fasulye: green beans, tomatoes, and olive oil served at room temperature

Baklava: phyllo with honey syrup and ground nuts

Muhallebi: milk pudding

Drinking

Drinking alcohol is a personal preference. Some Muslims drink alcohol, but devout Muslims never do. Westernized Turks may host cocktail parties.

- *Rakı* is a very strong anise liqueur. (Never drink it on an empty stomach.) Turks usually serve it with hors d'oeuvres.
- *Ayran* is a beverage made of yogurt, water, and salt.
- Turks drink *bira* (beer) and *şarap* (wine) occasionally.
- *Kahve* is thick, Turkish coffee that's served in very small cups after lunch and before dinner (not with a meal). It comes *totlı* (TATH-lee), *orta* (ORE-tah), or *sade* (SAH-day), which mean "sweet," "medium," and "without sugar," respectively.

> Turkey's first coffeehouse opened in 1554. Ever since, coffeehouses have been the places for intellectuals, artists, political dissidents, and the unemployed to play chess, recite poetry, or denounce the government—all over fragrant cups of Turkey's famous coffee, which is thicker and stronger than espresso.

Toasting

- The informal toast *Şerefe* (shay-ray-FAY) means "to the honor." The formal toast *Şerefinize* (shay-ray-fay-NEH-zeh) means "to your honor."
- Hosts may say *buyrun* (BUOY-run) as an invitation to begin eating at formal and informal occasions.
- An important Turkish ritual is to say *ziyade olsun* (zee-YAH-day OHL-suhn), which means "wishing plentitude," to the hostess after the meal. The hostess usually responds with *afiyet olsun* (AH-fee-yet OL-suhn), which means "wishing good health."

Tipping

- Restaurants: Except in expensive restaurants, the bill usually doesn't include a service charge. If the bill does include a service charge, *servis dahil* will appear at the bottom of the bill. If it doesn't, *hizmet dahil* will appear, and you should leave a 10 to 15 percent tip. You may leave small change as an additional gratuity for exceptional service. Leave the tip on the table.
- Taxis: Turks usually don't tip, but many drivers have come to expect a 15 percent tip from foreigners. (Tips in dollars or euros produce big smiles!)
- Bellhops and porters: Tip the equivalent of one euro per bag.
- Hair stylists and barbers: Tip 10 percent of the bill.
- Cloakroom and washroom attendants: Tip the equivalent of 25 to 50 euro cents.
- Ushers: Tip the equivalent of one euro.
- Service people may decline the first and even second offers to tip. If they refuse three times, they won't accept your tip and you should stop trying to give it.

Manners

- Upon entering a home, most Turks remove their shoes. Guests should follow their hosts' lead.
- The hostess usually serves food at the table—first to guests, then the elderly, children, and finally other adults.
- Don't eat anything with your fingers unless your host does so.
- Hosts may expect you to eat a lot and may be offended if you don't. Try not to leave any food on your plate. If a serving is too large, let your host know you've eaten all you can, then take a few more bites. Doing so will appease your host.
- When finished eating, place your knife and fork side by side on the plate.
- An important Turkish ritual is to compliment the host or hostess at the end of the meal, saying, "*Çok lezetli*" (choke LEZ-et-lee), which means "very tasty," or "*Elinize sağlik*" (EL-in-iss-eh SAH-lick), which means "God bless your hands" and is more sophisticated.
- Speak quietly when in public.

- Show great respect for elders. Rise when an older person enters a room and offer him or her your seat.
- Never point the sole of your foot toward someone. Be especially careful to not do this when crossing your legs. In fact, never cross your legs at a business meeting.
- When talking to others, especially older people or superiors, don't stand with your hands on your hips or in your pockets.
- It's rude to pass anything with the left hand.
- To beckon wait staff, raise your hand and wave if necessary.
- If you invite someone to dine, you pay the bill. Dutch treat doesn't exist in Turkey.
- During the Turkish national anthem, stand quietly and show respect. Don't chew gum or move around. Doing either will get you into big trouble.
- Ask permission before taking photos of anyone, especially in a mosque.
- Always remove your shoes before entering a mosque.

Dress

Turks most often wear conservative, modest clothing in Western styles; however, they also tend to dress up and accessorize a lot, especially for evening events.

- For business, men wear conservative suits or sport coats and ties. In very warm weather, men may forgo jackets, but still wear ties. Women wear tailored suits or dresses, with heels.
- At restaurants, men should check whether coats and ties are required. Women wear dresses or dress pants and blouses.
- For formal events, men wear dark suits; women wear cocktail dresses.
- Casual attire is smart casual (see page 45). Men wear stylish shirts and pants; women wear tailored pants or skirts (never denim) and blouses.
- Neat, fashionable jeans are acceptable for shopping or running errands, but never for business.
- A sun hat and sunglasses are necessary, especially in summer.
- Women should cover their heads, arms, and legs when visiting a mosque. They should avoid wearing short skirts, low-cut blouses, and shorts except at the beach. Although you may see some young urban women scantily dressed, American women should always dress modestly.

Gifts

Turks don't open gifts in the giver's presence. Upon receiving a gift, thank the giver and set it aside to open later.

When visiting the home of someone you know well, bring a small gift for any children. The family will appreciate the gesture.

Hostess Gifts

Consider giving
- Roses or carnations
- Candy
- Chocolates
- Wine (if your hostess drinks)

Don't give
- Alcoholic beverages, if you're unsure whether the host's family drinks
- Any gift that's overly lavish

Business Gifts

Turks may exchange business gifts. Exchanging gifts at Christmas is rare, but exchanging gifts at New Year's is quite common.

Consider giving
- American-made gift items that aren't overly expensive
- Desk accessories
- Pens
- Calendars

Don't give
- Overly personal items

Toilet Tips

English	Turkish
Restroom	*Tuvalet*
Women's restroom	*Bayanlar*
Men's restroom	*Baylar*
Hot water	*Sıcak su*
Cold water	*Soğuk su*

Helpful Hints

- Be sure to review the Muslim information on pages 65–67.
- Despite its conservative people, Turkey has nude beaches. Don't be surprised to see them.
- Don't bargain in big, modern stores, but be sure to bargain at bazaars or markets. These shopkeepers expect bargaining, and you'll love the expressions you'll encounter while doing so!
- Expect your host or colleague to offer a light cologne to refresh yourself (more common in rural areas than in big cities).
- Turks strictly forbid exporting antiques. They require proof of purchase to transport a new carpet or anything that looks antique out of Turkey. For older items, they require a museum export certificate from a museum directorate.
- If cigarette smoke bothers you, be warned: Smoking is virtually the national pastime in Turkey.

Punctuality

Turks take punctuality for business meetings very seriously and expect foreigners to arrive on time. Be aware that traffic is heavy in large cities; give yourself plenty of time between appointments, and call with an explanation if you're delayed.

Turks insist on punctuality for social occasions. For a dinner party, a 7:00 PM start time means 7:00 PM. Arriving a little late for a cocktail party, however, is acceptable.

Corporate Culture

Turkey is more industrialized and more educated than many other Muslim countries.

Structure
In most Turkish companies, the chairman or general manager is the boss. The organization is strictly vertical, and decisions are made at the top.

Workers give ideas and input to their immediate supervisors, who then pass the ideas on to the next level of management. "Jumping rungs" on the corporate ladder isn't acceptable, and low-level workers might not get credit for their ideas or input.

Meetings

Turks generally engage in brief small talk before discussing business.

Communication

- Many Turkish businesspeople speak English, but ask beforehand whether an interpreter is needed. Turkish companies that do international business most likely will have someone who understands English.
- If absolutely necessary, it's acceptable to call a Turkish colleague at home at a reasonable hour.
- Turks may have difficulty criticizing their supervisors or giving them feedback.

Business Cards

- Business cards in English are acceptable.
- Give a business card to each person upon introduction or at the beginning of a meeting.

Be Aware

- Consideration, politeness, respect, and courtesy are very important to Turks. When visiting an office or factory, shake hands with everyone upon arrival and departure.
- Schedule business appointments well in advance. Confirm appointments immediately by letter and confirm them by phone a couple of days before the scheduled dates.
- It may be difficult to make appointments for Friday afternoons, when devout Muslims meet to pray.
- June, July, and August are vacation months. Many businesspeople aren't available. Be sure to also check for the numerous regional and local holidays and festivals.
- It's best not to schedule appointments during Ramazan (Ramadan— thirty days of praying and fasting during daylight hours) or during Seker Bayrami (Candy Festival), the three-day festival after Ramazan.
- Turks take deadlines seriously. They expect people to work late and on weekends if necessary.

Socializing

- Traditionally, Turks did most business entertaining in restaurants. Entertaining in homes, however, is becoming popular.
- Business breakfasts are rare.

- Turks may discuss business any time during the meal, but foreigners should let them initiate such discussion.
- Turks may include spouses in business dinners.

Especially for Women

In Turkey, attitudes toward women are generally conservative (especially in rural areas), but men tend to be very respectful. In cities, women frequently work outside the home. Many Turkish women are highly educated and have careers. Turkey offers excellent maternity leave, but many mothers choose to stay home to supervise their children's education.

- Turks welcome foreign businesswomen.
- A foreign woman may invite a Turkish man to a business dinner, and she'll have no trouble paying for the meal.
- Women should avoid traveling alone. They should arrange to travel with a friend, if possible.
- During the day, women may eat in most restaurants alone without hassle. In the evening, they should go to restaurants in a group.
- Women shouldn't walk alone at night. In fact, groups of two or three women shouldn't walk alone in certain urban areas. Subways in Ankara and İstanbul are modern and safe, but still use common sense. Take a taxi everywhere after dark.
- Beware of pickpockets. Especially in İstanbul, women should carry purses on the arm farthest from the street. A thief may grab a purse while driving by a woman, possibly dragging her along while stealing the purse.

Holidays and Festivals	
January	New Year's Day (1)
April	National Independence and Children's Day (23)
May	Youth and Sports Day (19)
August	Victory Day (30)
October	Republic Day (28–29)

Notes: Islamic holidays vary with the Islamic calendar. Check to see when they're observed for the year you're traveling.

Kurban Bayrami (Sacrifice Festival) is a four- to five-day public holiday. Many businesses close early during these days, if they're open at all.

UNITED KINGDOM
UNITED KINGDOM OF GREAT BRITAIN AND NORTHERN IRELAND

Greetings from the United Kingdom

Greetings from the nation that comprises four separate countries. England, Scotland, Wales, and Northern Ireland make up the United Kingdom (UK).

The formation of the UK took the better part of a millennium. England was unified in the tenth century, and Wales formally united with it in the six-teenth century. Scotland joined the union in 1707. In 1801, the Act of Union allowed the UK to annex Ireland; however, the majority of Ireland became an independent republic in 1922. Six counties in northern Ireland remained part of the UK, and the union became known by its current formal title: United Kingdom of Great Britain and Northern Ireland.

Today, we are a single European Union member state, and we consider our nation a commonwealth—that is, four countries working together toward a common good. During our heyday in the nineteenth century, our influence and power encircled the globe. Over the decades, immigration from many of our former colonies gave our culture a worldwide flavor.

A prime example of the UK's diverse culture is its growing Muslim population. Roughly 1.6 million Muslims currently live in the UK.

Although Muslims account for a small percentage of the UK population, they hold significant positions in British society. Five members of the House of Lords are Muslim, as are two members of the House of Commons, over two hundred local council members, and a dozen city mayors. Imams serve as chaplains in British hospitals, prisons, the armed services, and even Eton, the elite boarding school. The Islamic Bank of Britain opened in London in 2004 and is run according to Islamic banking principles.

The recent violence stemming from radical Muslim militant groups has affected all UK citizens, regardless of heritage. Regarding terrorism, Lord Nazir Ahmed, a member of the House of Lords, said, "An attack on Britain is an attack on us (British mainstream Muslims)—we live here."

As a result, today the UK is culturally and ethnically diverse. We value tolerance, and any form of discrimination is taboo here.

As citizens of the UK, we call ourselves British, yet many of us are also English, Scottish, Welsh, or Northern Irish. We prefer that foreigners recognize each of our home countries individually. Please remember that the UK is *not* England, which doesn't include Scotland, Wales, or Northern Ireland. Nor is the UK Great Britain, which includes only England, Scotland, and Wales.

We are a terrific place to visit and to do business, and we welcome visitors and potential business colleagues. Our tradition of trade and commerce is old and distinguished. Come experience the diversity and civility the UK offers!

Note: This chapter discusses both the UK and the countries that make up the UK. The information presented in the discussion of the UK also applies to each of the countries. Additional information about each country appears in the discussion of that country.

Vital Statistics

Population	60,441,457
Capital	London
Area	94,526 square miles, slightly smaller than Oregon
Government	Constitutional monarchy
Living Standard	GDP = US $38,860 per capita
Natural Resources	Coal, petroleum, natural gas, iron ore, lead, zinc, gold, tin, limestone, salt, clay, chalk, gypsum, potash, silica sand, slate, arable land
Agriculture	Cereals, oilseed, potatoes, vegetables, cattle, sheep, poultry, fish
Industries	Machine tools, electric power equipment, automation equipment, railroad equipment, shipbuilding, aircraft, motor vehicles and parts, electronics and communications equipment, metals, chemicals, coal, petroleum, paper and paper products, food processing, textiles, clothing, and other consumer goods
Climate	Temperate; moderated by prevailing southwest winds over the North Atlantic Current; more than half of the days are overcast.
Member of the EU?	Yes, since 1973
Currency	British pound (GBP, £). The UK has chosen to use its own currency rather than convert to the euro.

The People

Correct Name	nouns: Briton(s), Brit(s), British (collective plural) adjective: British
Ethnic Makeup	English 83.6%, Scottish 8.6%, Welsh 4.9%, Northern Irish 2.9%, African 2%, Indian 1.8%, Pakistani 1.3%, mixed 1.2%, other 1.6%
Languages	English, Welsh (speakers total about 26% of the population of Wales), Scottish Gaelic (about 60,000 speakers in Scotland)
Religions	Christian (Anglican, Roman Catholic, Presbyterian, Methodist) 71.6%, Muslim 2.7%, Hindu 1%, other 1.6%, unspecified or none 23.1%

Meeting and Greeting

- The British say "How do you do?" upon meeting. They shake hands lightly.
- Not everyone offers a hand to shake; men should wait for women to extend a hand before offering a handshake.
- People who meet regularly generally don't shake hands upon meeting.
- Upon first meeting, the British are informal but reserved, which may make them appear cool, indifferent, or (ironically) overly formal. In truth, they're very friendly and helpful to foreigners.

Names and Titles

- After introductions, British businesspeople commonly use first names. Foreigners, however, should wait to use first names until their British colleagues do so.
- The British use *Mr, Mrs, Ms* (all without periods), and *Miss* to address one another.

    They don't commonly use academic titles, but they do use honorary titles like *Sir, Dame,* and *Lord.*

> Understanding titles and forms of address in the UK can be complex and confusing. An excellent resource is *Debrett's Correct Form,* published by Debrett's Limited. It explains in detail the British system of titles and forms of address.

    Example: Brits address a knighted man as Sir + first name; that is, Sir George Thomas is called Sir George.

- The British use *Doctor* to address medical doctors except surgeons; they use *Mr* and *Ms* to address surgeons.
- Ask people how you should address them.

Language

- Nearly everyone in the UK speaks English. The British generally don't speak other languages, but many younger Brits may speak French or German.
- The British business world once preferred everyone to speak with the "Oxford accent" or "BBC accent"—that is, pronouncing words in the way that has been passed down from one educated generation to the next. Today, speaking with this accent is a bit out of fashion. Regional accents are accepted—even on the BBC.
- Most Brits can tell exactly where someone hails within the UK by listening to his or her regional accent.
- Americans will quickly see that some British spellings differ distinctly from American spellings (for example *waggon* instead of *wagon*). The British spellings may be distracting, but most meanings are obvious.

Conversation
- Keep in mind that Brits are very friendly but may be uncomfortable conversing with strangers. Don't try to chat with a Brit while standing in a queue (line) or riding the tube (subway).
- The British appreciate quiet conversation. Boisterous conversation or behavior embarrasses them. Don't gush or praise excessively, and avoid making glib, insincere comments such as "Have a nice day." Speak clearly without using slang.
- The British don't use superlatives. "We're quite pleased," means they're extremely happy.
- Brits aren't politically correct. They may be blunt and direct, especially when doing business. Don't be offended by British humor or banter.
- Don't assume anything about a Brit's education, background, or ethnicity. The UK is so diverse that making assumptions is bound to insult someone.
- Pay attention to Brits' tone of voice and facial expressions. The British are polite and may not tell you that you've offended them.
- Lastly—and perhaps most importantly—never mimic the British accent or try to sound British. If you do, you'll appear disrespectful and foolish.

Acceptable topics

- British contributions to literature: The British revere language and have given the world the works of William Shakespeare, John Milton, Lord Byron, Beatrix Potter, and J. K. Rowling, to name just a few.
- The weather (a safe yet popular topic)
- Travel
- Current affairs
- Sports—but avoid talking about football (soccer) rivalries

Unacceptable topics

- Topics that confuse one UK nation with another or imply that they're all the same
- The location of someone's home: The British joke that if two Brits were stranded on an island, they'd divide it into a good and bad side.
- Someone's job or profession
- Money
- Jokes about British culture: Brits find savage, self-deprecating humor about their culture and nation hilarious—but a foreigner should absolutely never join in.

Topics that require sensitivity

- Northern Ireland
- Religion
- The monarchy: The British believe that the royal family has held them together through difficult times. While they may criticize them, you should not join in.
- The European Union or the euro
- Class systems
- Race and immigration

Body Language

- The British don't display affection in public and prefer a distance between themselves and others. They don't slap another's back or put an arm around another's shoulder.
- Brits reserve any hugging, kissing, or affectionate touching for family members and very close friends.
- Brits interpret crossing your arms during a meeting as boredom or lack of interest.

- Rubbing your nose is a rude gesture.
- Queuing is mandatory. The Brits are fanatical about waiting your turn in line. Never violate this rule.

Phrases

Don't assume that understanding the language means understanding the culture. Foreigners who mistake the meanings of words and phrases make many gaffes. Just imagine the misunderstandings that could arise when the meanings of these words and phrases are misunderstood:

British English	American English
Chemist	Pharmacist
Boot	Trunk of car
Pants	Underwear
Surgery	Doctor's office or practice
Bomb	Dazzling success
Braces	Suspenders
Rubber	Eraser
Fanny	Female genitalia
Fag	Cigarette
Hoarding	Billboard
Pissed	Intoxicated
Strike out	To go after an opportunity
To knock up	To wake up or to telephone
To shag	To have a sexual encounter
To table something	To bring an issue forward for discussion

Note: Several good American/British dictionaries are available and will come in handy when working extensively with Brits. If you're unsure of a word's meaning, always ask for clarification.

Dining

British cuisine was once thought (at best) bland or (at worst) unappetizing—but no longer. The UK now boasts some of the world's best restaurants. British meals feature scrumptious fare that will satisfy anyone feeling "peckish" (hungry). Brits love to share a meal with others, and you're more likely to receive an invitation to dine in someone's home in the UK than any other place in Europe.

British meals

- Breakfast: A light breakfast consists of cereal, toast, coffee, or tea. An English breakfast consists of juice, cereal, bacon, sausage, eggs, toast, fried mushrooms, and fried tomatoes.
- High tea: Usually, hotels serve this light meal to tourists between 3:30 and 4:30 PM. It consists of small sandwiches, biscuits, pastries, cakes, and scones with jam and clotted cream.
- Tea: Brits serve this light supper between 5:00 and 7:00 PM.
- Dinner: This more substantial meal consists of cocktails, appetizers, soup, meat or fish, potatoes, vegetables, salad, dessert, and cheese and crackers. Brits serve it between 7:00 and 8:00 PM.
- The Sunday joint: This is a traditional Sunday meal, featuring a roast, Yorkshire pudding, and other traditionally British dishes.

Drinking

- The British serve alcoholic beverages before dinner.
- Tea is the national drink, but coffee is becoming increasingly popular. Coffee shops are opening all over the UK.
- Always buy a round of drinks when in a pub.

Toasting

- "Cheers" is a common informal toast.
- "To the queen" is a formal toast that Brits make after the main course at formal dinners.
- At formal dinners, the host or hostess always initiates the first toast.

Tipping

- Restaurants: The bill may include a 10 to 15 percent service charge. If the bill doesn't include a service charge, leave a 10 to 15 percent tip. You may leave small change as an additional gratuity for exceptional service.
- Taxis: Tip 10 to 15 percent of the fare.
- Bellhops and porters: Tip £1 per bag.

- Cloakroom and washroom attendants: Tip £1.
- Hair stylists and barbers: Tip 10 to 15 percent of the bill.
- Catering staff: In the UK, wages for catering staff are deliberately low. Workers expect tips to compensate for the pay deficiency. When using a caterer, tip the staff 10 percent of the bill; tip 15 percent for exceptional service.

Manners

The British admire good manners, especially at the table.
- Phone ahead to arrange a visit to a Brit's home. Never drop in unexpectedly!
- When visiting a Brit's home, don't wander through rooms or the garden (the yard) without your host.
- To eat the last spoonfuls of soup, always tip the soup bowl away from you.
- When finished eating, leave a little food on your plate.
- The host folds his napkin to signal the end of the meal.
- The guest of honor should be the first to leave a party or dinner. All other guests should leave shortly after him or her.
- Be sure to send the host and hostess a handwritten thank-you note the day after a dinner or party. Also, always send a thank-you note when you receive a gift or when anyone does a favor for you.
- In restaurants, the person who extended the invitation pays the bill.
- To summon wait staff, simply raise your hand. Don't wave or shout.
- Always let someone of a higher rank enter a room or building first.
- Men show politeness to women. They open doors for women, stand when a woman enters the room, and offer their seats to women on public transportation.
- Women should cross legs at the ankles, not at the knees.
- Always hold the door open for the person following you.
- Always stand during the national anthem, "God Save the Queen."
- Say "please" and "thank you" whenever the occasion calls for it.
- Respect Brits' desire for privacy. Never ask anyone personal questions, and never stare at anyone.

> Always behave civilly in every situation. Civility is an important British value.

Dress

The British prefer to wear conservative attire in brown, black, and other dark colors. Fashion is less important than the quality of clothing. In general, people in larger cities, especially London, dress more formally than those in more rural areas.

Men's clothing often expresses affiliation rather than style. School, military regiment, university, or club ties are particularly important. The British are expected to know what a tie represents, but foreigners may ask about a tie's meaning. Foreigners should avoid wearing striped ties that symbolize British regimentals.

Brits enjoy dressing up. They like wearing uniforms for social occasions, and they love costume parties.

- For business, men wear dark suits and ties. White, striped, or colored shirts are appropriate. They don't wear tweeds, which are considered casual wear. Women wear tailored suits or dresses, with heels. Women in Britain wear slacks less often than do women in the United States.

- For casual occasions and at pubs, men and women wear wools or tweeds. Slacks, sweaters, and jackets are appropriate.

- At restaurants, women wear dressy pantsuits, dresses, or skirts and blouses. For men, jackets are always appropriate, but dark suits are best for better restaurants. Some restaurants require ties.

- At theaters and concerts, people wear anything from jeans to formal attire. To be safe, women should wear dresses and men should wear dark suits. For the opera, men may be expected to wear tuxedos.

- For formal occasions, men wear business suits, black tie, morning coats, or tails. (Ask your British colleagues or the hotel concierge which attire is required.) Women wear formal dresses or extremely elegant jackets and pants or skirts. You can easily rent formal attire in the UK.

  Women often wear hats at formal occasions: weddings, garden parties, formal luncheons, formal race meets (horse races), and so on. Local meets require more casual attire.

- Only tourists and young people in cities wear shorts.

- Designer jeans have become common and acceptable for casual events. Even the Duchess of Cornwall, Camilla Parker Bowles, wears jeans for casual occasions.

Gifts

The British open gifts upon receipt.

Hostess Gifts

Present your gift to the hostess upon arrival.

Consider giving

- Flowers, except white lilies and chrysanthemums (connote death) or red roses (connote romance): Sending flowers the morning of a dinner party is an appropriate gesture.
- Chocolates
- Wine or champagne
- Books
- Gifts from your home state or region

Don't give

- Scotch, bourbon, or other liquor, unless you know your host's favorites: Brits' preferences for alcoholic beverages are firm.

Business Gifts

The British normally don't exchange gifts at business meetings or at the conclusion of negotiations. It's acceptable—but not expected—to give gifts to British colleagues at Christmas; they probably won't have gifts for you.

Consider giving

- Ties
- Pens
- Books, diaries, or leather notebooks
- Desk accessories (for example, paperweights)

Don't give

- Obviously expensive gifts (Brits may consider them vulgar.)
- Tacky knickknacks

Helpful Hints

- Some banks in Scotland, Northern Ireland, the Isle of Man, Jersey, and Guernsey issue their own bank notes (backed by British pounds). Shops in other parts of the UK may choose not to accept them.

- Some restaurants don't accept credit cards. Be sure to carry enough cash to pay the bill.
- Don't be surprised to see "no children, no dogs" signs in some restaurants. Many restaurants, however, do allow dogs. Brits love animals, especially dogs and horses.
- Be aware that thirteen is a very unlucky number in the UK.

Punctuality

For business meetings and for meals in restaurants, the British expect punctuality, but foreigners should prepare to wait at least ten minutes for British colleagues.

For social occasions at someone's home, punctuality is impolite. Guests should arrive at least ten to twenty minutes after the start time stated on the invitation. They should never arrive early.

Be aware that traffic and mass transportation schedules in major cities may extend travel times. Allow time for delays.

Corporate Culture

Structure

British company organization traditionally is multilayered, with a vertical chain of command. The leader is responsible for making important decisions and implementing major plans. The board of directors is the central power in many companies, and most decisions require the board's endorsement.

A network of formal and informal committees exists in larger companies. Organizations prefer consensus to individual initiative; nonetheless, groups are reluctant to take responsibility for errors.

In older companies, the old-boy network thrives. They may hire employees because they attended the right school (like Eton) or university (like Oxford or Cambridge) or come from a prestigious family.

Newer companies, however, tend to have more progressive hiring and promotion policies.

Meetings

Brits schedule meetings well in advance with a clearly defined purpose—that is, to reach a decision or an agreement, or to formulate a plan or implement a plan or decision.

At meetings, participants usually begin to discuss business after a few moments of polite conversation. People may voice their opinions; however, not all participants will be well prepared to do so. Agreement may be slow to come, and decision making can be adversarial.

Presentations should be detailed and understated.

Communication

Expect your British colleagues to observe formalities and protocol in business, especially in London.

It's unacceptable to call British colleagues at home, unless you have their permission or it's an emergency.

Business Cards

Most British businesspeople exchange business cards; bring plenty of your own. There isn't a specific procedure for exchanging cards with the British.

Be Aware

- "The City" is the London business community that consists primarily of banks, brokerage firms, insurance companies, and other financial institutions. London is one of the world's major financial centers.
- Contacts are important in the UK. It's best for foreigners to have a well-connected third party initiate business relationships.
- Relationships among different levels in companies are generally distant and guarded.
- Company loyalty is less common today than in the past.
- Make initial business appointments well in advance. British businesspeople will meet colleagues or clients on short notice, but they don't appreciate cold calls.

Socializing

- Business lunches in restaurants or pubs are most common. During the meal, Brits discuss business, but they don't carry out negotiations.
- Once considered a bad North American habit, breakfast meetings are now acceptable in the UK.
- Brits commonly include spouses in dinners for socializing or for thanking a customer. Guests don't discuss business at dinner in someone's home unless the host initiates the conversation.
- The British appreciate dinner invitations, and they're excellent dinner companions. But don't try to impress British guests with an extravagant dinner; they prefer understatement.

- A British colleague may invite you to watch a cricket match or a regatta. Both are prestigious events, and dress is elegant.

Especially for Women

Although the UK offers negligible maternity benefits and expensive childcare facilities (compared to other Western European nations), women make up nearly half of the UK workforce. The old-boy network is alive and well in the UK, but women are more commonly holding managerial positions, especially in the public sector and in the service industries.

- A foreign woman may invite a British man to a business dinner, but she should extend the invitation to his wife as well. If she wants to pay for the meal, she should say so when giving the invitation, and arrange payment with the wait staff beforehand.
- Women may go to pubs alone without hassle; however, they may prefer the lounge section, which is often more comfortable and has a more mature clientele.
- A woman shouldn't be insulted when a Brit calls her "love," "dearie," or "darling." These terms of endearment are common, acceptable addresses in the UK.

Holidays and Festivals	
January	New Year's Day (1) Second January (2—or closest working day)*
March	Saint Patrick's Day (17)**
March/April	Easter (Friday–Sunday) Easter Monday***
May	Early May Bank Holiday (first Monday) Spring Bank Holiday (last Monday)
July	Battle of the Boyne (12)**
August	Summer Bank Holiday (last Monday)
December	Christmas (25) Boxing Day (26—or closest working day)

* Scotland only
** Northern Ireland only
*** England, Wales, and Northern Ireland only

ENGLAND

Greetings from England

Greetings from the largest country in the UK. For centuries, many have considered our capital, London, the crossroads of the world. The onetime capital of the British Empire and a major world port, London has grown into a cosmopolitan, multicultural city.

Men, women, and children from all over Europe, the United States, Latin America, Asia, and Africa have made London their home. People of all races have exchanged ideas and goods here for centuries. Today, nearly one third of Londoners are ethnic minorities. We believe that the city's diversity gives us strength and proves that globalization can work.

For many countries that were once British colonies, London continues to be the business center. By developing modern business centers in "The City" and new business centers at the Docklands, we've successfully kept our economic infrastructure growing and current.

Of course, there's more to England than London, and Londoners constitute just a part of the English. Accents and loyalties change over every hill, and each region of our beautiful country is distinct and contributes to our economy. The West Midlands is the place for manufacturing, and the East Midlands boasts England's best farmland. East Anglia is home to new high-technology industries, and the North West is famous for its textiles. Humberside has its steel industry, and the North has its engineering and pharmaceutical industries. Finally, the South West's tourism industry is booming.

We English adore animals, especially horses and dogs, and we love gardening. Our cities work to maintain a natural quality to urban life by providing large, open green spaces. London's Hyde Park, the Green Park, and the Regent's Park are just a few famous examples.

We admire politeness, reserve, and restraint; we strive for courteous, unassuming, and gracious behavior. That said, we are competitive, as shown by our passion for football (soccer), Rugby, and our national pastime, cricket. We believe in fair play and champion the underdog. We like being with our fellow fans; we feel comfortable with those with whom we have a great deal in common.

Our strong sense of history makes us value our traditions and customs, and we often prefer the old ways to the new. Over time and through wars and terrorism, we've tried to maintain our values. After the attacks on London's transportation system on July 7, 2005, our quiet determination to resume ordinary life exemplified our philosophy of keeping a "stiff upper lip."

Our ways don't always support multiculturalism perfectly, but with continued tolerance and civility, we believe our country—especially London—is an excellent model for today's global world.

Please visit us. We welcome you, but ask that you always show respect for our traditions and customs.

Vital Statistics

Population	50,093,100 (83% of the UK population)
Capital	London
Area	50,363 square miles, about the size of New York state

The People

Correct Name	nouns: British, English adjectives: British, English
Ethnic Makeup	English, Scottish, Irish, Welsh, West Indian, Indian, Pakistani (More than 85% of English residents identify their ethnic heritage as white British.)
Language	English
Religions	Anglican, Roman Catholic, Muslim, Sikh, Hindu, Jewish

Dining

Typical Foods

Fish and chips: deep-fried, breaded fish and French fries

Spicy foods, including Indian and Chinese dishes

Ploughman's platter: cheese, bread, meats, butter, and relishes

Bubble and squeak: leftover potatoes and cabbage fried together (supposedly named for the sound it makes while cooking)

Meat pies: most notably, steak-and-kidney pie

Cornish pasties: turnovers filled with meat, potatoes, and vegetables

Black pudding: sausage made from pig's blood

Roast beef with Yorkshire pudding (The pudding resembles popovers.)

Bangers and mash: mashed potatoes with sausages

Scones with clotted cream: biscuit-like teacakes served with a thick
   butter-like cream
Trifle: layers of cake, fruit, pudding, sherry, and cream

Drinking

- Popular alcoholic drinks in England include:
    * various beers, the most traditional called "bitter"
    * wine: becoming especially popular with young people
    * gin and tonic
    * vodka and tonic
    * vodka and cola
    * Pimm's Cup: gin-based tonic mixed with lemonade
    * shandy: beer with lemonade (that is, lemon-lime soda)
    * cider (or *scrumpy*): tart beverage with a high alcohol content,
      made from fermented apples
- If you don't drink alcohol, be polite and order a drink anyway, then sip it
  or pretend to drink it.
- In England, if you order whiskey, you'll get Scotch. If you want whiskey,
  you must order by its brand name (for example, Jack Daniel's).
- The British may serve drinks without ice. If you want ice, you must
  ask for it.
- The British serve coffee and tea after meals.

Manners

- Especially in England, never insult the royal family or show an undue
  interest in their private lives.
- Never handle fruits or vegetables at a produce market. Let the vendor give
  you the item.
- Don't be too casual, especially with the English language.
- Don't jump a queue (cut in line). Such behavior is an outrage to the English.

Helpful Hints

- Especially in London, it's best to call the people "British." Use *English* only when you're sure of a person's English heritage.
- The English inject all forms of humor—self-deprecating, sarcastic, and even sexist—into their daily lives. Don't let their humor offend you.
- A car is an important status symbol in England. Having a chauffeur is a definite sign of success.
- Learn cricket etiquette. The British expect quiet behavior at matches, and they always clap for a good play by either team.
- The English view themselves as natural leaders. They say, "God is an Englishman."
- It's acceptable for a foreign woman to invite an Englishman to a business dinner, but he may misinterpret her intentions. It's best for women to invite Englishmen to lunch.

In England, "the South" refers to the area within a couple hours' drive south of London. It conveys an image of wealth, sophistication, and social status. "The North" refers to the rest of the country.

Some northern residents consider the North the "real" England, when compared to the hodgepodge of nationalities, cultures, and languages in the South.

SCOTLAND

Greetings from Scotland

Greetings from one of the world's most breathtakingly gorgeous countries. From the Highlands and fjords to the mountains and firths, Scotland's natural beauty is unparalleled.

We Scots passionately love our country and feverishly guard our uniqueness. While we value our long, successful union with England, we refuse to adopt English attitudes. We're determined to stay Scottish.

Most Scottish traditions come from our centuries-old clans (families with the same name and common ancestors). Each clan has its own tartan, a unique plaid design that appears on ties, kilts, and other clothing. We're extremely sentimental about our country and our clans.

Just like the rest of the European Union, we struggle with immigration issues, but we've always offered shelter to those fleeing oppression. We recently launched a campaign to stop racism and discrimination in our country. "One Scotland Many Cultures" hopes to raise awareness and celebrate Scotland's cultural diversity, while challenging racist attitudes and behavior.

We strongly believe in equality, respect, and fairness for all. A shopkeeper's child and a Member of Parliament's child are classmates with the same opportunities to compete.

Our educational system is excellent. The royal family send their sons to Scotland for their education. Tony Blair, our Edinburgh-born prime minister, was also educated in Scotland. Many believe that one of Blair's goals is to raise the English school system to the level of Scottish education.

Our small nation paved the way for modernity. We firmly believe that Scots invented almost everything that has led to today's world, including the steam engine, telephone, and television.

We also invented capitalism. In 1776, Scotsman Adam Smith produced one of the great achievements in intellectual history: *An Inquiry into the Nature and Causes of the Wealth of Nations*. Most of Smith's observations of a free market are put into practice today.

To look into our soul, read our beloved Robert Burns, whom United Nations Secretary-General Kofi Annan described as "a poet of the poor, an advocate for political and social change, and an opponent of slavery, pomposity, and greed." Today, Scots and admirers from around the world celebrate his

birthday to honor his contributions—and also to have a
grand party!

Scots live in Scotland, speak Scottish, and drink Scotch. Scotch is whiskey, but it's also a mist (that is, a persistent drizzling rain).

We value hard work, and
our hard work has paid off.
Scots have very quietly (and modestly) achieved high success in international
finance. Our financial services industry accounts for one in ten Scottish jobs.
From 1998 to 2004, employment in financial services rose by almost a third,
while our economy as a whole grew less than 10 percent.

Although our behavior may seem cool and aloof at first, we're eager to do
business with you. Come visit us and our spectacular land!

Vital Statistics

Population	5,078,400 (8% of the UK population)
Capital	Edinburgh
Area	30,405 square miles, approximately the size of South Carolina

The People

Correct Names	nouns: Scot(s), Scotsman(-men) adjective: Scottish
Ethnic Makeup	Celtic; very small minority groups from England, Ireland, India, Pakistan, and Hong Kong
Languages	English and Scottish Gaelic
Religions	Church of Scotland, Roman Catholic, less than 1% Muslim, and very small numbers of Buddhists, Hindus, Jews, and Sikhs (More than a quarter of the population doesn't identify with any religion.)

Meeting and Greeting

- Scots welcome strangers kindly and very civilly—so much so that upon
  introduction, Scots may appear reserved, noncommittal, and in no hurry
  to impress. They'll warm up once you've developed a relationship.

Language

- Scots speak English with a soft, almost musical accent.
- Scottish Gaelic (GAL-lick) differs from Irish Gaelic (GAY-lick) in vocabulary, spelling, and grammar. Fewer than sixty thousand people speak Scottish Gaelic, a steep decline in recent years; however, there are some hopeful signs that the decline is reversing.

Body Language

- To ask for the bill in a restaurant, motion to your server as if signing your name.
- Scots respect queuing. Never jump ahead in a queue (line).

Dining

Scottish cuisine is simple and delicious.

Typical Foods

Lamb stew: Scottish lamb is world famous.

Scotch egg: hard-boiled egg wrapped in sausage

Haggis: famous national dish of sheep or calf heart, liver, and lungs, chopped with suet and oatmeal, and stuffed like a sausage in the animal's stomach

Kippers: smoked herring

Salmon: smoked, grilled, or poached

Crawachan: oatmeal laced with whiskey, cream, and lots of sugar

Drinking

Scots prefer Scotch before dinner. Most drink it without water or soda.

Toasting

- The toast *shlante* (SHLAHN-tay) means "to your health." Scots use it at formal and informal occasions. Foreigners may say "cheers" or "good health" instead of *shlante*.

Dress

- At formal occasions (black-tie events, weddings, and so on), women wear evening gowns; men wear kilts. For the premiere at Edinburgh Festival, however, men wear tuxedos.
- Smart casual attire (see page 45) is appropriate for most occasions. Very few hotels or restaurants require jackets and ties.
- Dressy jeans are acceptable for some casual occasions, but T-shirts rarely are.
- If you're unsure about what attire to wear, ask your Scottish colleagues or your hotel concierge.

Helpful Hints

- You may call Scots "British," but they dislike "Brit."
- Never joke about kilts or ask a Scot what he wears under his kilt.
- Respect Scots' privacy. Never stare at anyone.
- Scots are always polite and courteous. Make sure you always behave in kind, and never be loud in public.
- Be prompt. Scots are punctual for social and business meetings.

Corporate Culture

Scots pride themselves on being internationalists; they interact well with foreigners, but are suspicious of go-getters. They're determined, thorough, and respect success only when achieved over time.

Scots are skilled businesspeople who begin negotiating from the outset. Fortitude and resilience are Scottish trademarks.

WALES

Greetings from Wales

Greetings from the land of castles and King Arthur. While we've been part of the United Kingdom for centuries, we've kept our own language, literature, and traditions.

The Welsh name for our country is *Cymru* (KUM-ree), which means "land of the comrades." The word *Wales* is Germanic and means "land of the foreigners."

Our history shows our enduring battle for independence. King Arthur allegedly led his Welsh countrymen against Saxon invaders in the sixth century. Then we repelled Viking raiders between the ninth and eleventh centuries. During nearly the same time, we began resisting the Normans. But in 1282, the last Welsh crown prince died, and within a year our nation came under English rule.

We didn't give in easily. In the early fifteenth century, Owain Glyndwr (Owen Glendower) led a brief rebellion against the English—he failed. Consequently, the English didn't allow the Welsh to hold administrative posts for several centuries.

We finally lost our battle for political independence under Henry VIII, who passed an act that asserted Wales had always been part of England. By the mid-sixteenth century, we formally united with England (although we believe that England absorbed us). Nevertheless, we hung on fiercely to our language, literature, and traditions.

The Welsh language (*Cymraeg*) is one of the oldest living languages in Europe. Although Welsh is Celtic, please don't confuse it with Gaelic. We're very proud of our language, which we managed to keep alive through centuries of suppression. The 1993 Welsh Language Act was the culmination of a revival that began in the 1960s. Today in Wales, Welsh and English are used equally in public business and the administration of justice.

In 1998, the Government of Wales Act established the National Assembly for Wales. Our country remains a part of the UK, and there are still Welsh Members of Parliament. But since July 1, 1999, the Assembly determines policies on Welsh education, housing, environment, and other areas.

Today, we still struggle to maintain our traditions and values. We also face challenges in our farming and industrial sectors. Our steel and coal industries have collapsed, causing widespread unemployment.

Despite our troubles, we know how to enjoy ourselves. We love family life; we spend most of our evenings at home with our families. Sports are important to us; our favorite is Rugby. We also love to sing and talk—especially in pubs, where we sometimes burst into song spontaneously. Our male choirs and glee clubs are famous.

Every year, we celebrate our culture at the National Eisteddfod of Wales, the largest traveling festival in Europe. It features competitions in singing, reciting, and dancing. There's also plenty of food and football (soccer). The tradition is ancient; the first *eisteddfod*, which was a gathering of bards, dates back to 1176. Since 1880, the festival alternates every year between sites in North and South Wales.

Come listen to our music, watch seabirds on our coasts, and hike or bike through our gorgeous land. We're confident, fiercely independent, and nonconformist—and we're determined to remake ourselves while maintaining our history and traditions. Although we're a work in progress, don't count us out of your business plans. We have much to offer!

Vital Statistics

Population	2,952,500 (5% of the UK population)
Capital	Cardiff
Area	8,019 square miles, slightly larger than New Jersey

The People

Correct Name	noun: Welsh adjective: Welsh
Ethnic Makeup	Celtic and Anglo-Saxon; small percentages of other ethnicities, but fewer than 10% identify themselves as non-white British
Languages	English and Welsh
Religions	Largely Christian (about 70%), with small communities of Jews, Muslims, Buddhists, Hindus, and Sikhs (Roughly 20% of Welsh don't identify with any religion.)

Language

- Official notices appear in both Welsh and English. The number of Welsh speakers has grown in recent years; more than 20 percent of the population speak Welsh.
- Welsh words are famously difficult for native English speakers to pronounce. Although the language is strictly phonetic, some consonants differ in sound from English consonants. For example, *dd* is pronounced like "th" in *them*. Some Welsh sounds don't exist in English.

Dining

Welsh food is simple. Generally, lunch is the main meal. Some restaurants and pubs serve only lunch.

Typical Foods
Leeks: This onion-like edible plant is also a national emblem.
Lamb: perhaps the most popular meat in Wales
Sewin: Welsh trout
Mutton stew
Welsh rarebit: melted cheese and butter with beer, served on toast
Bara laver: vegetable dish made with seaweed
Cawl: meat and vegetable soup

Toasting

The toast *lechyd da* (YEH-hid day) means "good health." The Welsh use it at formal and informal occasions.

Dress

Welsh dress is generally informal. In cities, some people dress more formally for dinner. Because of the rainy climate, always take a raincoat and umbrella when going outdoors.

Gifts

Welsh lovespoons are famous and are gifts for almost any occasion.

Helpful Hint

Never call the Welsh "English"; "British," however, is acceptable.

A number of celebrities that many assume are English are actually Welsh. Famous Welsh-born actors include Richard Burton (whose first language was Welsh), Anthony Hopkins, and Catherine Zeta-Jones.

Corporate Culture

- Before doing business with the Welsh, it's necessary to establish a personal relationship.
- The Welsh believe that rank and age are important in business. Older, senior-ranked people will be accepted quickly; others will have to work to prove their competence.
- The Welsh make decisions slowly. You must be patient.
- The Welsh do most entertaining in restaurants or homes. Make sure you entertain anyone who has entertained you.

NORTHERN IRELAND

Greetings from Northern Ireland

Greetings from the UK's smallest country—or, as one of our writers described Northern Ireland, "a great country, just pretending to be small."

As a country, Northern Ireland is very young, but our people have a long, turbulent past. For centuries, we were simply part of Ireland (including when Ireland was part of the UK). But in 1921, most of our island formally seceded and became the (largely Catholic) Republic of Ireland. Six of Ulster's nine counties in the north chose to remain part of the UK, becoming (largely Protestant) Northern Ireland.

Since the partition of our island, there has been an ongoing debate about whether the two countries should reunite. Unionists (and the more extreme Loyalists) support Northern Ireland's remaining part of the UK. Nationalists (the minority) favor Northern Ireland's becoming part of the Republic of Ireland.

The debate has often escalated into violence. The Irish Republican Army (IRA), a paramilitary organization determined to expel the British and reunite Northern Ireland with the Republic of Ireland, has used terrorist tactics to advance its agenda. In support of Northern Ireland's union with the UK, the Ulster Defence Association (a Unionist organization) and the Ulster Volunteer Force (an illegal Protestant paramilitary organization) have responded in a similarly violent manner.

From the late 1960s to the late 1990s, Northern Ireland suffered a period of brutal conflict—often called "the Troubles." During that time, more than three thousand people were killed, mostly civilians.

In April 1998, the British and Irish governments took a major step forward to establish peace by signing the Good Friday Agreement, fostering hope that the Troubles—although still unresolved—may soon come to a nonviolent end. Since 1998, violence in Northern Ireland has decreased, and hope for peace and reconciliation continues.

Although we've lived with intolerance and radicalism for decades, Northern Ireland isn't the dangerous place that the media depicts. In 2000, the United Nations' International Crime Victims Surveys determined that we had the lowest crime rate of the nations surveyed. 2002 statistics from the World Health Organization show that Northern Ireland had a lower rate of violent death than the rest of the UK, as well as Germany, Denmark, and the United States.

Most Northern Irish don't support the radical political and religious movements in our country. We want the same things everyone else wants: family, home, good jobs, safety and security, and most of all, peace.

Our country is a great place for businesses. Over 640 foreign-owned companies have set up operations in Northern Ireland. Seagate, DuPont, Caterpillar, Microsoft, and Citigroup are just a few examples. Between 1990 and 1999, Northern Ireland had the largest gross domestic product (GDP) growth in the UK, and we expect that growth to continue. Unemployment levels are at a twenty-five-year low and are currently lower than those of the EU as a whole. Our telecommunications are advanced; we were the first nation in the UK to develop a fully fiber-optic infrastructure. By 2005, we had 100 percent broadband coverage.

Tourism is also enjoying great growth, as more people discover our attractions. The Botanic Gardens in Belfast are renowned, as is the Grand Opera House. Many people from England and the Republic of Ireland visit Belfast to shop and to dine in the city's excellent, chic restaurants. The coastal road going north from Belfast is exceptional for bicycling through quaint fishing villages as well as the small towns hidden in the green countryside.

We eagerly await visitors to enjoy our hospitality. Stop in a pub for a drink and a chat. We value friendliness, sincerity, and honor—we dislike pretentious behavior. Before coming to visit, please learn a bit about us. We greatly appreciate any knowledge visitors show of our history and culture.

Vital Statistics	
Population	1,710,300 (3% of the UK population)
Capital	Belfast
Area	5,452 square miles, about the size of Connecticut

The People

Correct Name	noun: Northern Irish adjective: Northern Irish
Ethnic Makeup	Celtic and Anglo-Saxon (The Chinese, the largest ethnic group, compose only about 0.2% of the population.)
Languages	English, Irish (about 10% of the population)
Religions	Protestant (slightly more than 45%, mostly Presbyterian, Church of Ireland, and Methodist) and Roman Catholic (slightly more than 40%) (Only 0.4% identify themselves with a non-Christian religion.)

Language

Northern Irish have an affinity for poetry. In 1995, Seamus Heaney, an Ulster writer and poet, won the Nobel Prize in Literature. Paul Muldoon, Medbh McGuckian, and Ciaran Carson are other Northern Irish poets of note.

When conversing with your Northern Irish colleagues, avoid talking about religion and politics, if possible. These topics have created conflict for many years.

Dining and Drinking

Northern Irish food is simple, but the country offers numerous ethnic restaurants. Pubs are an important part of social life.

Helpful Hints

- Northern Irish may be called "British," but never "English."
- Northern Irish work hard, but have a slower pace than North Americans.
- Be aware that Northern Ireland has one of Europe's youngest populations—nearly 60 percent are younger than age thirty-five.
- If in Belfast, be sure to take a "black taxi tour" to see the political murals. Also, if possible, go to Ballycastle to enjoy the beach.
- The name of Northern Ireland's second-largest city is the subject of an ongoing dispute. Some Nationalists call it "Derry," and some Unionists call it "Londonderry." To avoid causing the most offense, call the city "Derry" unless someone insists on calling it "Londonderry."

- Although Northern Ireland is often called "Ulster," this term isn't technically correct. All of Northern Ireland lies in Ulster, but not all of Ulster lies in Northern Ireland. Six of Ulster's nine counties are in Northern Ireland, and the remaining three are in the Republic of Ireland.

RESOURCES

The demographic data for the countries I discuss in this book are current as of its publication date. I've included these figures for comparison's sake. The Central Intelligence Agency's (CIA) World Factbook is a free online resource with a wealth of statistical information. To learn the most current information, visit http://www.cia.gov/cia/publications/factbook before planning a trip. You may also want to visit the European Union's official website, http://www.europa.eu.int/index_en.htm, to learn more about EU countries.

Before visiting Europe, obtain the addresses and telephone numbers of the American Embassies in the nations you'll be visiting. Here are some other numbers to help you plan your trip:

U.S. Department of State
Hotline for American Travelers: 888-407-4747, 202-647-5225 (from overseas)
http://www.travel.state.gov

Centers for Disease Control and Prevention
Traveler's Health Hotline: 877-FYI-TRIP
http://www.cdc.gov/travel

World Health Organization
http://www.who.int/ith/en

INDEX

A

Academic titles, 238
Act of Union (1801), 224, 441
Addresses, envelope, 31
Administration, EU membership and, 8
Affection, displaying. See Hugging; Kissing
Agriculture
  in Austria, 72
  in Belgium, 86
  in Bulgaria, 98
  in Cyprus, 109
  in the Czech Republic, 120
  in Denmark, 132
  in Estonia, 144
  in Finland, 154
  in France, 166
  in Germany, 181
  in Greece, 196
  in Hungary, 211
  in Ireland, 225
  in Italy, 236
  in Latvia, 253
  in Lithuania, 267
  in Luxembourg, 278
  in Malta, 288
  in the Netherlands, 301
  in Norway, 315
  in Poland, 327
  in Portugal, 340
  in Romania, 353
  in Slovakia, 367
  in Slovenia, 379
  in Spain, 391
  in Sweden, 405
  in Switzerland, 416
  in Turkey, 428
  in the United Kingdom, 442
"Air kiss," 121, 237, 354
Albania, European Union and, 7
Alcoholic beverages
  in Austria, 77
  in Belgium, 90
  in Bulgaria, 102
  in Cyprus, 113
  in the Czech Republic, 124
  in Denmark, 136
  in England, 456
  in Estonia, 148
  in Finland, 158
  in France, 171
  general information on, 39
  in Germany, 186
  in Greece, 200
  in Hungary, 216
  in Ireland, 228–29
  Islam and, 67
  in Italy, 241
  in Latvia, 258
  in Lithuania, 270
  in Luxembourg, 282
  in Malta, 292
  in the Netherlands, 305
  in Norway, 319
  in Poland, 331
  in Portugal, 339, 345
  in Romania, 358
  in Slovakia, 371
  in Slovenia, 383
  in Spain, 396
  in Sweden, 409
  in Switzerland, 420
  in Turkey, 433
America/Americans
  France and, 165, 166
  ignorance of, about other countries, 19
  Luxembourgers on, 278
  "the ugly," 4
American style (eating), 38
Andorra, 10

Anglo-Irish Treaty (1922), 224
Aquavit, 319
Architecture, 339, 389
Art and culture. See also Dance; Literature; Music
  of the Czech Republic, 119
  of Hungary, 209
  of Latvia, 251
  of Norway, 314
  of Poland, 326
  of Portugal, 339–40
  of Slovenia, 338
  of Spain, 389
  of Sweden, 403
Ash Wednesday, 63
Atatürk (Mustafa Kemal), 427
Atheism, 12
Attire. See Dress
Auschwitz, 325
Austria, 71–83
  body language in, 75–76
  common phrases spoken in, 76
  conversation in, 75
  corporate culture in, 81–83
  dress in, 79
  drinking in, 77
  European Union and, 8
  foods of, 77
  gift-giving in, 79–80
  greetings used in, 73
  helpful hints for traveling in, 80–81
  holidays and festivals of, 83
  Hungary and, 210
  language spoken in, 33, 74–75
  manners in, 78
  names and titles used in, 73–74
  overview of, 71–72
  people of, 73
  punctuality in, 81
  tipping in, 78
  toasting in, 77
  toilet tips for traveling in, 80
  vital statistics on, 72
  women in, 83
Austrian State Treaty, 71
Austro-Hungarian Empire, 71, 210

B

Balkans, 29. See also Bulgaria; Greece
Balls, 72, 79
Basque language, 393
Battle of the Bulge, 277
Beer, 77
  Czech, 124
  Estonian, 148
  Finnish, 158
  German, 186
  Irish, 229
  Latvian, 258
Belgium, 85–95
  body language in, 89
  conversation in, 88–89
  corporate culture in, 93–94
  dress, 91
  European Union and, 7
  greetings used in, 86
  helpful hints for traveling in, 93
  holidays and festivals in, 95
  language spoken in, 33, 88
  names and titles in, 87
  overview of, 85
  people of, 86, 87
  punctuality in, 93
  toilet tips for traveling in, 92
  vital statistics on, 86
  women in, 94
Benelux Economic Union (1958), 277
Beverages. See Alcoholic beverages; Drinking
Blair, Tony, 458
Body language
  of Austrians, 75–76

  of Belgians, 89
  of Bulgarians, 100
  of Cypriots, 111–12
  of Czechs, 123
  of Danes, 134
  of the Dutch, 303–4
  of Estonians, 146
  of Finns, 156
  of the French, 170
  general rules on, 34–35
  of Germans, 184
  gestures and, 36
  of Greeks, 198–99
  of Hungarians, 214
  of the Irish, 227
  of Italians, 239–40
  of Latvians, 256
  of Lithuanians, 269
  of the Maltese, 291
  of Muslims, 66
  of Norwegians, 318
  of Poles, 329
  of the Portuguese, 343
  during presentations, 56
  of Romanians, 356–57
  of Scots, 4607
  of Slovaks, 370
  of Slovenes, 381
  of Spaniards, 394
  of Swedes, 407, 418
  of the Swiss, 418
  touching and, 35
  of the Turks, 431
  in the United Kingdom, 445–46
Body odors, 175
Bokmål dialect (Norwegian language), 316
Bosnia-Herzegovina, European Union and, 7
Brussels (Belgium), 85, 86
Budapest (Hungary), 210, 211
Bulgaria, 97–105
  body language in, 100
  conversation in, 100
  corporate culture in, 104
  dress in, 103
  drinking in, 102
  European Union and, 7, 8
  foods of, 101
  gift-giving in, 103–4
  greetings used in, 99
  holidays and festivals in, 105
  language spoken in, 33, 99–100
  manners in, 102
  names and titles in, 99
  overview of, 97–98
  people of, 99
  punctuality in, 104
  tipping in, 102
  toasting in, 102
  toilet tips for traveling in, 104
  vital statistics of, 98
  women in, 105
Bulgarian language, 99–100
Bullfighting, 340, 399
Burdick, Eugene, 3
Burgenlandian, 71
Business communication
  in Austria, 82
  in Belgium, 94
  in Cyprus, 116–17
  in the Czech Republic, 129
  in Denmark, 140
  in Finland, 162
  in France, 176–77
  in Germany, 191
  in Greece, 205
  in Hungary, 220
  in Ireland, 233
  in Italy, 247
  in Latvia, 262
  in Lithuania, 275

in Luxembourg, 285
in the Netherlands, 310
in Norway, 322
in Poland, 335
in Portugal, 349
in Romania, 363
in Slovakia, 374–75
in Slovenia, 387
in Spain, 400
in Sweden, 413
in Switzerland, 424
in Turkey, 438
in the United Kingdom, 452
Businesses. *See also* Business communication;
    Corporate culture; Meetings, business;
    Socializing, business
in former Communist countries, 16–18
Business gifts, 49–50
given to Austrians, 80
given to Belgians, 92
given to Bulgarians, 103
given to Cypriots, 115
given to Czechs, 127
given to Danes, 138
given to Estonians, 150
given to Finns, 160–61
given to Germans, 189
given to Greeks, 203
given to Hungarians, 219
given to Italians, 245
given to Latvians, 260–61
given to Lithuanians, 273
given to Luxembourgers, 283
given to Norwegians, 321
given to Poles, 333
given to Romanians, 360–61
given to Slovaks, 373
given to Slovenes, 385
given to Spaniards, 398
given to Swedes, 411
given to the British, 450
given to the Dutch, 308
given to the French, 174
given to the Irish, 231
given to the Maltese, 294
given to the Portuguese, 346
given to the Swiss, 422
given to Turks, 436
Byzantine Empire, 427

C

Čapek, Karel, 122
Capital city
of Austria, 72
of Belgium, 86
of Bulgaria, 98
of Cyprus, 109
of the Czech Republic, 120
of Denmark, 132
of England, 455
of Estonia, 144
of Finland, 154
of France, 166
of Germany, 181
of Greece, 196
of Hungary, 211
of Ireland, 225
of Italy, 236
of Latvia, 253
of Lithuania, 267
of Luxembourg, 278
of Malta, 288
of the Netherlands, 301
of Northern Ireland, 467
of Norway, 314
of Poland, 327
of Portugal, 340
of Romania, 353
of Scotland, 459
of Slovakia, 367
of Slovenia, 379
of Spain, 391
of Sweden, 404
of Switzerland, 416
of Turkey, 428

of the United Kingdom, 442
of Wales, 463
Carinthian, 71
Castilian (Spanish) language, 393, 395
Catalan language, 393
Catholic Church. *See* Roman Catholic Church
Ceausescu, Nicolae, 352
Cell phone use, 93, 37815
Central Europeans, 29
Christianity, 12, 62–63
Climate
of Austria, 72
of Belgium, 86
of Bulgaria, 98
of Cyprus, 109
of the Czech Republic, 120
of Denmark, 132
of Estonia, 144
of Finland, 154
of France, 167
of Germany, 181
of Greece, 196
of Hungary, 211
of Ireland, 226
of Italy, 237
of Latvia, 253
of Lithuania, 267
of Luxembourg, 278
of Malta, 289
of the Netherlands, 301
of Norway, 315
of Poland, 327
of Portugal, 341
of Romania, 353
of Slovakia, 367
of Slovenia, 379
of Spain, 391
of Sweden, 405
of Switzerland, 416
of Turkey, 428
of the United Kingdom, 442
Closings, in correspondence, 30
Clothing. *See* Dress
Coffee
in Cyprus, 113
Czech, 124
in Finland, 153, 158
Greek, 200
in Hungary, 216
in the Netherlands, 305
in Sweden, 409
in Turkey, 433
Coffeehouses, 77, 433
Communication. *See also* Body language; Business
    communication; Conversation; Language
using regional terms for, 28–29
written, 29–32
Communion, 62
Communist rule. *See also* Former Communist countries
in Bulgaria, 97–98
in the Czech Republic, 119
in Hungary, 210–11
in Latvia, 251–52
in Lithuania, 266
in Poland, 325
in Romania, 351–52
in Slovakia, 365
Continental style, eating, 38
Conversation
acceptable topics for, 27
in Austria, 75
in Belgium, 88–89
body language used in, 239–40
in Bulgaria, 100
in Cyprus, 111
in the Czech Republic, 122–23
in Denmark, 134
in Estonia, 146
in Finland, 156
in France, 169
general rules on, 26–29
in Germany, 183–84
in Greece, 198
in Hungary, 213
in Ireland, 226–27

in Italy, 239
in Latvia, 255–56
in Lithuania, 269
in Luxembourg, 280
in Malta, 290
in the Netherlands, 303
in Norway, 317
in Poland, 329
in Portugal, 343
in Romania, 355–56
in Slovakia, 369–70
in Slovenia, 381
in Spain, 393–94
in Sweden, 406
in Switzerland, 418
topics requiring sensitivity for, 28
in Turkey, 430–31
unacceptable topics for, 27
in the United Kingdom, 444–45
Copenhagen criteria, 7–8
Corporate culture
in Austria, 81–83
in Belgium, 93–94
in Bulgaria, 104
the business card and, 54–55
in Cyprus, 116–17
in the Czech Republic, 129
in Denmark, 139–40
in Estonia, 151
in Finland, 162–63
in France, 176–77
general guidelines on, 52–53
in Germany, 190–92
in Greece, 204–6
in Hungary, 220–21
in Ireland, 232–33
in Italy, 246–48
in Latvia, 262–63
in Lithuania, 274–75
in Luxembourg, 285–86
in Malta, 295–96
meetings and, 55–56
names/titles and, 54
nervousness and, 52
in the Netherlands, 310–11
in Norway, 322–23
in Poland, 334–35
in Portugal, 348–49
in Romania, 362–63
in Scotland, 461
in Slovakia, 374–75
in Slovenia, 386–87
socializing and, 56–57
in Spain, 400–401
of Sweden, 413–14
in Switzerland, 423–24
in Turkey, 437–38
in the United Kingdom, 451–53
in Wales, 465
Correspondence, 30–32
Council of the European Union, 9
Court of Auditors, 9
Court of Justice, 9
Credit cards, 37, 361, 374, 451
Cricket, 453, 457
Crime, 13, 467
Croatia, European Union and, 7
Culture preservation, 9
Currency
of Austria, 72
of Belgium, 86
of Bulgaria, 98
of Cyprus, 110
of the Czech Republic, 120
of Denmark, 132
of Estonia, 144
the euro, 10
of Finland, 154
of France, 167
of Germany, 181
of Greece, 196
of Hungary, 211
of Ireland, 225
of Italy, 237
of Latvia, 253

of Lithuania, 267
of Luxembourg, 278
of Malta, 289
of the Netherlands, 301
of Norway, 315
of Poland, 327
of Portugal, 341
of Romania, 353
of Slovakia, 367
of Slovenia, 379
of Spain, 391
of Sweden, 405
of Switzerland, 416
of Turkey, 428
of the United Kingdom, 442
Cutlery. *See* Utensils, table
Cypriot Greek dialect, 110–11
Cypriot Turkish language, 111
Cyprus, 107–18
    body language in, 111–12
    conversation in, 111
    corporate culture in, 116–17
    dress in, 114
    drinking in, 113
    the euro and, 10
    European Union and, 8
    foods of, 112
    gift-giving in, 114–15
    helpful hints for traveling in, 115
    holidays and festivals in, 118
    language spoken in, 33, 110–11
    manners used in, 113–14
    names and titles in, 110
    overview of, 107–9
    people of, 110
    punctuality in, 116
    tipping in, 113
    toilet tips for traveling in, 115
    vital statistics on, 109–10
    women in, 117
Cyprus Problem, the, 107–8
Cyrillic (Russian) alphabet, 99
Czechoslovakia, 119, 365, 368. *See also* Czech
        Republic; Slovakia
Czech Republic. *See also* Former Communist countries
    body language in, 123
    common phrases spoken in, 123
    Communist rule and, 15
    conversation in, 122–23
    corporate culture in, 129–30
    dress in, 126
    drinking in, 124
    the euro and, 10
    European Union and, 8
    foods of, 124
    gift-giving in, 126–27
    greetings in, 121
    helpful hints for traveling in, 128
    holidays and festivals in, 130
    language spoken in, 122
    manners used in, 125–26
    names and titles used in, 121
    people of, 120
    punctuality in, 128
    tipping in, 125
    toasting in, 124–25
    toilet tips for traveling in, 127
    vital statistics on, 120
    women in, 130

D

Dance, 3, 153, 156
Dates, writing, 31
Denmark, 131–41
    body language used in, 134
    conversation in, 134
    corporate culture in, 139–40
    dining in, 135
    dress in, 137–38
    drinking in, 136
    the euro and, 10
    European Union and, 7, 8
    foods of, 135
    gift-giving in, 138
    greetings used in, 133

helpful hints for traveling in, 139
holidays and festivals in, 141
language spoken in, 33, 133
manners in, 137
names/titles used in, 133
overview of, 131–32
people of, 133
punctuality in, 140
tipping in, 136
toasting in, 136
toilet tips for traveling in, 139
vital statistics on, 132
women in, 140–41
Dialects, regional, 24
Diet. *See also* Food
    Hindu, 64
    Jewish, 65
    of Muslims, 66–67
Dining. *See also* Drinking; Food; Meals,
        women paying for; Toasting
    in Austria, 78
    business socializing and, 56
    in the Czech Republic, 125
    in Denmark, 137
    entertaining European guests, 40–41
    in Finland, 159
    formal, 38–39
    in France, 172–73
    general rules on, 36
    in Germany, 187–88
    in Greece, 199–200, 201–2
    in Hungary, 217
    in Ireland, 228–29, 230
    in Italy, 241, 242–43
    in Latvia, 257
    in Lithuania, 270, 272
    in Malta, 291, 293
    in the Netherlands, 305–6
    in Norway, 320, 323
    in Poland, 330, 332
    in Portugal, 345–46
    in Romania, 359
    in Slovakia, 370–71
    in Spain, 395, 397
    in Sweden, 410
    in Switzerland, 420–21
    table manners for, 37–38
    in Turkey, 434, 435
    in the United Kingdom, 446–47, 448
Dogs, 81
Dress
    in Austria, 79
    in Belgium, 91
    in Bulgaria, 103
    in churches, 62
    in Cyprus, 114
    in the Czech Republic, 126
    in Denmark, 137–38
    Estonian, 149
    Finnish, 160
    in France, 173
    general guidelines on, 44–45
    in Greece, 202
    Hungarian, 218
    Irish, 230
    in Italy, 243–44
    in Latvia, 259
    in Lithuania, 272
    in Luxembourg, 283
    in Malta, 293
    in the Netherlands, 307
    in Norway, 320
    in Poland, 332, 334
    in Portugal, 346
    for presentations, 55
    in Romania, 359–60
    in Scotland, 461
    in Slovakia, 372
    of Slovenia, 384
    in Spain, 397–98
    in Sweden, 410–11
    in Switzerland, 421
    in Turkey, 435
    types of, to avoid, 45–46
    in the United Kingdom, 449

in Wales, 464
Drinking
    in Austria, 77
    in Belgium, 90
    in Bulgaria, 102
    in Cyprus, 113
    in the Czech Republic, 124
    in Denmark, 136
    driving and, 93, 412
    in England, 456
    in Estonia, 148
    in Finland, f158
    in France, 171
    general information and rules on, 39
    in Germany, 186
    in Greece, 200
    in Hungary, 216
    in Italy, 241
    in Latvia, 258
    in Lithuania, 271
    in Luxembourg, 282
    in Malta, 292
    in the Netherlands, 305
    in Norway, 319
    in Poland, 331, 337
    in Portugal, 345
    in Romania, 358
    in Scotland, 460
    in Slovakia, 371
    in Slovenia, 383
    in Spain, 396
    in Sweden, 409
    in Turkey, 433
    in the United Kingdom, 447
    while driving, 412
Driving, 15
    drinking and, 39, 412
    in Hungary, 219
    safety guidelines on, 60
Drug use, in the Netherlands, 300
Dublin, 225
Dutch language, 85, 87, 303, 304

E

Eastern Europeans, 29. *See also* Czech Republic;
        Hungary; Poland; Slovakia; Slovenia
East Germany, 180
The Economist, 53
Economy
    of Cyprus, 117
    of Estonia, 143–44
    EU membership and, 8
    of the former Communist countries, 16–17
    of Germany, 180
    of Hungary, 210
    of Italy, 236
    of Luxembourg, 278
    of the Netherlands, 299
    of Poland, 334
    of Portugal, 340
    of Slovakia, 366
    of Slovenia, 337
    of Spain, 389
    of Switzerland, 415
Electronic communication, 29, 30
England, 454–57. *See also* United Kingdom, the
    drinking in, 456
    foods of, 455–56
    manners in, 456
    overview of, 454–55
    people of, 455
    vital statistics on, 455
English as a second language, 23–24
English language
    British versus American, 446
    spoken in Austria, 75
    spoken in Cyprus, 111
    spoken in Denmark, 133
    spoken in Finland, 156
    spoken in France, 166, 168
    spoken in Hungary, 213
    spoken in Ireland, 226, 227
    spoken in Luxembourg, 277
    spoken in Malta, 290
    spoken in Norway, 316

spoken in Poland, 328
spoken in Portugal, 342
spoken in Romania, 355
spoken in Slovakia, 368
spoken in Slovenia, 380
spoken in Spain, 393, 400
spoken in Sweden, 406
spoken in the Netherlands, 299, 303
spoken in the United Kingdom, 444
spoken in Turkey, 430
Envelope addresses, 31
Environmental problems, in Malta, 288
Estonia, 143–52. *See also* Former Communist countries
body language in, 146
conversation in, 146
corporate culture in, 151
dress in, 149
drinking in, 148
the euro and, 10
European Union and, 8
foods of, 147
gift-giving in, 149–50
greetings in, 145
helpful hints for traveling in, 151
holidays and festivals in, 152
language spoken in, 33, 145–46
manners in, 149
names and titles used in, 145
overview of, 143–44
people of, 144
popular phrases used in, 147
punctuality in, 151
tipping in, 148
toasting in, 148
toilet tips for traveling in, 150
vital statistics on, 144
women in, 152
Estonian language, 145, 147
Ethnic makeup
in Austria, 73
in Belgium, 86
in Bulgaria, 99
in Cyprus, 110
in the Czech Republic, 120
in Denmark, 133
in England, 454
of England, 455
in Estonia, 145
in Finland, 155
in France, 167
in Germany, 181
in Greece, 196
in Hungary, 211
in Ireland, 225
in Italy, 237
in Latvia, 252, 253
in Lithuania, 266, 267
in Luxembourg, 279
in Malta, 287–88, 289
in the Netherlands, 301
in Northern Ireland, 468
in Norway, 315
in Poland, 327
in Portugal, 341
in Romania, 354
in Scotland, 459
in Slovakia, 367
in Slovenia, 379
in Spain, 391
in Sweden, 405
in Switzerland, 417
in Turkey, 429
in the United Kingdom, 443
in Wales, 463
Ethnic Russians, 266
Etiquette. *See* Manners
European Atomic Energy Community (Euratom), 8
European Coal and Steel Community (ECSC), 8
European Commission, 9
European Community (EC), 7, 195
European countries. *See also* Europeans; individual country names
American ignorance about, 19
Balkan, 29
Baltic, 29

basic facts to know about, 19–20
being the ugly American and, 3–4
cultural preservation of, 9
showing consideration and respect for, 5–6
Slavic, 28
ten commandments of travel in, 6
European Court of Human Rights, 108
European Economic Community (EEC), 8
European Fair Trade Association (EFTA), 415
European Parliament, 9
Europeans
avoiding generalizations about, 3
entertaining, 40–41
letter gathering comments from, x–xii
European Union (EU)
Belgium and, 85
challenges facing, 11–15
Cyprus and, 108
Estonia and, 144
France and, 165
history of, 7
Lithuania and, 266
Luxembourg and, 277
multilingualism and, 26
the Netherlands and, 299
newest nations in, 15–18
objectives of, 8–9
Poland and, 326
population of, 8
qualifications for membership in, 7–8
Romania and, 352
Slovakia and, 366
Slovenia and, 338
Switzerland and, 415
timeline on, 8
Turkey and, 427–28
Euro, the, 10, 14
Euskadi Ta Askatasuna (ETA), 13, 394
Exchange Rate Mechanism (ERM II), 10
Eye contact
in Austria, 75
in Czech Republic, 123
in Finland, 156
in Latvia, 258
in Lithuania, 269
in Romania, 356, 358, 364
in Slovakia, 370, 371
in Spain, 394, 402
in Turkey, 429

F

Family
in Italy, 235
in Turkey, 428
Fasting periods, 63
Federal Republic of Germany. *See* Germany
Festivals. *See* Holidays and festivals
Filmmaking, in Romania, 352
Financial Times, 53
Finland, 153–64
body language in, 156
common phrases spoken in, 157
conversation in, 156
corporate culture in, 162–63
dress in, 160
drinking in, 158
European Union and, 8
foods of, 157
gift-giving in, 160–61
helpful hints for traveling in, 161
holidays and festivals in, 164
language spoken in, 33, 156
manners in, 159
overview of, 153–54
people of, 155
punctuality in, 161
tipping in, 159
toasting in, 158
toilet tips for traveling in, 161
vital statistics on, 154
women in, 163
Finno-Ugric languages, 213
First impressions, 20. *See also* Greetings
First names, using, 21, 22
Flanders, 85

Flemings (Belgium), 85, 87
Flemish companies, 93
Flirting, behavior interpreted as, 337, 364, 402, 412
Floor numbers, 32, 284
Florentine Italian language, 239
Flowers, giving, 48–49, 79, 103, 150, 160, 244, 260, 273, 283, 320, 450
Food
Austrian, 76–77
Belgian, 89
Bulgarian, 101
Cypriot, 112
Czech, 124
Danish, 135
Dutch, 304–5
English, 455
Estonian, 147
Finnish, 157
French, 171
German, 185–86
Greek, 200
Hungarian, 215–16
Irish, 228
Italian, 241
kosher, 65
Latvian, 257–58
Lithuanian, 271
Luxembourg, 281
Maltese, 291–92
Muslim, 66–67
Norwegian, 318
Polish, 330–31
Portuguese, 344–45
Romanian, 357–58
Slovakian, 370–71
Slovenian, 382–83
Spanish, 395
Swedish, 408–9
Swiss, 419
Turkish, 432–33
Welsh, 464
you do not like, 38–39
Forest Brothers, the, 266
Formal dining, 38–39
Former Communist countries. *See also* individual country names
challenges facing the European Union and, 15–16
economies of, 16–17
EU membership of, 15–16
religion and, 12
tips for doing business in, 17–18
France, 165–78
body language in, 170
common phrases spoken in, 170
conversation in, 169
corporate culture in, 176–77
dress in, 173
European Union and, 7
foods of, 171
gift-giving in, 174–75
helpful hints for traveling in, 175
holidays and festivals in, 178
language spoken in, 33, 168
manners in, 172
names and titles in, 168
overview of, 165–66
tipping in, 172
toasting in, 172
toilet tips for traveling in, 175
vital statistics on, 166
women in, 178
Freising Manuscripts, 380
"French kiss," 199
French language, 33, 168
spoken in Belgium, 85
spoken in Luxembourg, 279
spoken in Portugal, 342
spoken in Romania, 355
spoken in Switzerland, 417–18
titles in, 87
used in Luxembourg, 279
French Republic. *See* France

G

Galician language, 393

Generalizations, avoiding, 3
Geneva (Switzerland), 415
German language
    spoken in Austria, 74–75
    spoken in Luxembourg, 279–80
    spoken in Slovakia, 368
    spoken in Slovenia, 380
    spoken in Switzerland, 417–18
    spoken in Turkey, 430
Germany, 179–93
    body language in, 184
    common phrases used in, 185
    conversation in, 183–84
    dress in, 188
    drinking in, 186
    foods of, 185–86
    gift-giving in, 188–89
    greetings used in, 182
    helpful hints for visiting, 190
    holidays and festivals in, 193
    language spoken in, 33, 183
    Lithuania and, 265
    manners in, 187–88
    names and titles in, 182
    overview of, 179–80
    people of, 181
    tipping in, 187
    toasting in, 186–87
    toilet tips for traveling in, 189
    vital statistics on, 181
    women in, 193
Gestures, 36
    in France, 170
    in Germany, 184
    in Greece, 198
    in Hungary, 214
    in the Netherlands, 304
    rude, in Cyprus, 112
    in Turkey, 431
Gift-giving
    in Austria, 79–80
    in Belgium, 91–92
    in Bulgaria, 103–4
    in Cyprus, 114–15
    in the Czech Republic, 126–27
    in Denmark, 138
    in Estonia, 149–50
    in Finland, 160–61
    in France, 174
    general guidelines on, 46–50
    in Germany, 188–89
    in Greece, 203
    in Hungary, 218–19
    in Ireland, 231
    in Italy, 244–45
    in Latvia, 260
    in Lithuania, 273
    in Luxembourg, 283–84
    in Malta, 294
    in the Netherlands, 308
    in Norway, 319–20
    in Poland, 333
    in Portugal, 346–47
    in Romania, 360–61
    in Slovakia, 373
    in Slovenia, 385
    in Spain, 398
    in Sweden, 411
    in Switzerland, 422
    in Turkey, 436
    in the United Kingdom, 450
    in Wales, 465
Gifts. See also Business gifts; Hostess gifts
    to avoid giving, 48
    business, 49–50
    to consider giving, 47–48
    general guidelines on, 46
    given to Jews, 65
    Hindu religion and, 64
    hostess, 48–49
    for Muslims, 67
    receiving, 46–47
Glendower, Owen, 462
Good Friday, 63
Good Friday Agreement, 466

Goulash, Hungarian, 215
Government
    of Austria, 72
    of Belgium, 86
    of Bulgaria, 98
    of Cyprus, 108, 109
    of the Czech Republic, 120
    of Denmark, 132
    of Estonia, 144
    of Finland, 154
    of France, 166
    of Germany, 181
    of Greece, 196
    of Hungary, 211
    of Ireland, 225
    of Italy, 236
    of Latvia, 253
    of Lithuania, 267
    of Luxembourg, 278
    of Malta, 288
    of the Netherlands, 299, 301
    of Norway, 314
    of Poland, 327
    of Portugal, 340
    of Romania, 353
    of Slovakia, 367
    of Slovenia, 378, 379
    of Spain, 391
    of Sweden, 404
    of Switzerland, 416
    of Turkey, 428
    of the United Kingdom, 442
Grand Duchy of Luxembourg. See Luxembourg
Great Britain, Malta and, 287, 288. See also England;
        Scotland; Wales
Greece, 195–207
    body language in, 198–99
    common phrases used in, 199
    conversation n, 198
    corporate culture in, 204–5
    dining in, 199–200
    dress in, 202
    drinking in, 200
    European Union and, 7, 8
    gift-giving in, 203
    greetings in, 197
    helpful hints for traveling in, 204
    holidays and festivals in, 207
    language spoken in, 33, 197
    manners in, 201–2
    names and titles in, 197
    overview of, 195–96
    people of, 196
    punctuality in, 204
    tipping in, 201
    toasting in, 201
    toilet tips for traveling in, 203
    vital statistics on, 196
    women in, 206
Greek Cypriots, 107–8, 118
Greetings
    in Austria, 73
    in Belgium, 86
    in Cyprus, 110
    in the Czech Republic, 121
    in Denmark, 133
    in Estonia, 145
    in Finland, 155
    general rules about, 20–21
    in Germany, 182
    in Greece, 197
    in Hungary, 212
    in Ireland, 225–26
    in Italy, 237
    in Latvia, 254
    in Lithuania, 268
    in Luxembourg, 279
    in Malta, 289
    in the Netherlands, 302
    in Norway, 315
    in Poland, 327
    in Portugal, 341
    in Romania, 354
    in Scotland, 459
    in Slovakia, 367

    in Slovenia, 380
    in Spain, 392
    in Sweden, 405
    in Switzerland, 417
    in the United Kingdom, 443

H

Hand shaking
    in Austria, 73
    in the Czech Republic, 120
    in France, 167
    general guidelines on, 42
    general rules about, 20–21
    in Lithuania, 268
    in Poland, 327
    in Portugal, 341
    in Romania, 354
    in Slovakia, 367
    in Slovenia, 380
    in Spain, 392
    in Sweden, 405
    in Switzerland, 417
    in Turkey, 429
Havel, Václav, 119
Health, general guidelines on, 60
Hellenic Republic. See Greece
Helpful hints
    about Austria, 80–81
    about Belgium, 93
    about Cyprus, 115
    about the Czech Republic, 128
    about Denmark, 139
    about England, 456, 457
    about Estonia, 151
    about Finland, 161
    about Germany, 190
    about Greece, 204
    about Hungary, 219
    about Ireland, 231–32
    about Italy, 246
    about Lithuania, 274
    about Luxembourg, 284
    about Malta, 295
    about Northern Ireland, 468–69
    about Norway, 321
    about Poland, 334
    about Portugal, 347
    about Romania, 361–62
    about Scotland, 461
    about Slovakia, 373–74
    about Slovenia, 386
    about Spain, 399
    about Sweden, 412
    about Switzerland, 423
    about Turkey, 437
    about the United Kingdom, 450–51
Hinduism, 63–64
History
    of Austria, 71
    of Belgium, 85
    of Bulgaria, 97
    of the European Union (EU), 7
    of Germany, 180
    of Hungary, 209–10
    of Ireland, 224
    of Lithuania, 265–66
    of Luxembourg, 277
    of Malta, 287
    of Northern Ireland, 466
    of Poland, 325
    of Romania, 351–52
    of Slovakia, 365–66
    of Slovenia, 337–38
    of Spain, 390
    of Turkey, 427
    of the United Kingdom, 441
    of Wales, 462
Holidays and festivals
    in Austria, 83
    in Belgium, 95
    in Bulgaria, 105
    in Cyprus, 118
    in the Czech Republic, 130
    in Denmark, 141
    in Estonia, 143, 152

in Finland, 164
in France, 178
general guidelines on, 61
in Germany, 193
in Greece, 207
in Hungary, 222
in Ireland, 234
in Italy, 249
in Latvia, 263
in Lithuania, 276
in Luxembourg, 286
in Malta, 297
in the Netherlands, 312
in Norway, 323
in Poland, 337
in Portugal, 350
in Romania, 364
in Slovakia, 376
in Slovenia, 388
in Spain, 402
in Sweden, 414
in Switzerland, 425
in Turkey, 439
in the United Kingdom, 453
Holland, 309
Holocaust, the, 12
Hostess gifts, 48–49
    for Austrians, 79–80
    for Belgians, 92
    for the British, 450
    for Bulgarians, 103
    for Cypriots, 114
    for Czechs, 126–27
    for Danes, 138
    for the Dutch, 308
    for Estonians, 150
    for Finns, 160
    for the French, 174
    for Germans, 188–89
    for Greeks, 203
    for Hungarians, 218
    for the Irish, 231
    for Italians, 244–45
    for Latvians, 260
    for Lithuanians, 273
    for Luxembourgers, 283
    for the Maltese, 294
    for Norwegians, 320–21
    for Poles, 333
    for the Portuguese, 345–46
    for Romanians, 360
    for Slovaks, 373
    for Slovenes, 385
    for Spaniards, 398
    for Swedes, 411
    for the Swiss, 422
    for Turks, 436
Hotel safety, 60
Hugging
    in the Netherlands, 304
    in Spain, 392
    in the United Kingdom, 445
Hungarian language, 33, 213, 214–15, 368–69
Hungary, 209–22
    body language in, 214
    common phrases spoken in, 214–15
    Communist rule and, 15
    conversation in, 213–14
    corporate culture in, 220–21
    dress in, 218
    drinking in, 216
    the euro and, 10
    European Union and, 8
    foods of, 215–16
    gift-giving in, 218–19
    greetings in, 212
    helpful hints for traveling in, 219
    holidays and festivals of, 222
    language spoken in, 33, 213
    manners in, 217
    names and titles used in, 212–13
    punctuality in, 220
    Slovakia and, 365–66
    spas in, 221
    tipping in, 216

toasting in, 216
toilet tips for traveling in, 219
women in, 221–22
Hus, Jan, 119

I

Iceland, 33
Immigrants/immigration
    in Austria, 71
    European Union facing challenge of, 11–12
    Germany and, 180
    in Ireland, 224
    in Latvia, 252
    in the Netherlands, 300
Industry
    in Austria, 72
    in Belgium, 86
    in Bulgaria, 98
    in Cyprus, 109
    in the Czech Republic, 120
    in Denmark, 132
    in Estonia, 144
    in Finland, 154
    in France, 167
    in Germany, 181
    in Greece, 196
    in Hungary, 211
    in Ireland, 225
    in Italy, 236
    in Latvia, 253
    in Lithuania, 267
    in Luxembourg, 278
    in Malta, 288
    in the Netherlands, 301
    in Norway, 315
    in Poland, 327
    in Portugal, 340
    in Romania, 353
    in Slovakia, 367
    in Slovenia, 379
    in Spain, 391
    in Sweden, 405
    in Switzerland, 416
    in Turkey, 428
    in the United Kingdom, 442
Interfaith etiquette, 61–67
Inventions, Hungarian, 209
Ireland, 223–34
    body language in, 227
    conversation in, 226–27
    corporate culture in, 232–33
    dining in, 228
    dress in, 230
    drinking in, 228–29
    European Union and, 7, 8
    foods of, 228
    gift-giving in, 231
    greetings used in, 225–26
    helpful hints for traveling in, 231–32
    holidays and festivals in, 234
    immigration and, 11
    language spoken in, 226
    manners in, 230
    overview of, 223–24
    people of, 225
    punctuality in, 232
    tipping in, 229
    toasting in, 229
    vital statistics on, 225
    women in, 233–34
Irish (Gaelic) language, 226
Irish Republican Army (IRA), 466
Islam. See Muslims/Muslim faith
Italian language, 33, 238–39, 380, 417–18
Italian Republic. See Italy
Italy, 235–49
    body language in, 239–40
    common phrases spoken in, 240
    conversation in, 239
    corporate culture in, 246–48
    dining in, 241
    dress in, 243–44
    drinking in, 241
    European Union and, 7
    foods of, 241

gift-giving in, 244–45
greetings in, 237
holidays and festivals of, 249
language spoken in, 33, 238–39
manners in, 242–43
name and titles used in, 238
overview of, 235–36
people of, 237
punctuality in, 246
toasting in, 242
toilet tips for traveling in, 245
vital statistics on, 236–37
Itinerants, 232

J

Jánošík, Juraj, 366
Judaism, 64–65

K

Kalanta, Romas, 266
Kaszubs, the, 328
Kemal, Mustafa, 427
Kepel, Gilles, 13
Kingdom of Belgium. See Belgium
Kingdom of Denmark. See Denmark
Kingdom of Norway. See Norway
Kingdom of Spain. See Spain
Kingdom of Sweden. See Sweden
Kissing, 35. See also "Air kiss"
    in Austria, 73
    in the Czech Republic, 121
    in France, 167
    in Greece, 199
    in Italy, 237
    in Latvia, 254
    in Lithuania, 268
    in Poland, 328
    in Slovakia, 367
    in Slovenia, 380
    in Spain, 392
    in Turkey, 429
Kosher foods, 65
Kosovo, 10

L

Language. See also Body language; Phrases, common
    corresponding country with, 33–34
    importance of one's native, 24
    learning, 23
    pronunciation and, 24
    speaking the English, 23–24
    spoken in Austria, 73, 74–75
    spoken in Belgium, 85, 86, 88
    spoken in Bulgaria, 99
    spoken in Cyprus, 110–11
    spoken in the Czech Republic, 120, 122
    spoken in Denmark, 133
    spoken in Estonia, 145–46
    spoken in Finland, 155
    spoken in France, 167, 168
    spoken in Germany, 181, 183
    spoken in Greece, 196, 197
    spoken in Hungary, 209, 211, 213
    spoken in Ireland, 223, 225, 226
    spoken in Italy, 237, 238–39
    spoken in Latvia, 253, 255
    spoken in Lithuania, 267, 268–69
    spoken in Luxembourg, 277, 279–80
    spoken in Malta, 289, 290
    spoken in the Netherlands, 299, 301, 302–3, 303
    spoken in Northern Ireland, 468
    spoken in Norway, 315, 316
    spoken in Poland, 327, 328–29
    spoken in Portugal, 341, 342
    spoken in Romania, 354, 355
    spoken in Scotland, 460
    spoken in Slovakia, 367
    spoken in Slovenia, 379, 380–81
    spoken in Spain, 391, 393
    spoken in Sweden, 405, 406
    spoken in Switzerland, 417
    spoken in the United Kingdom, 443, 444
    spoken in Turkey, 429, 430
    spoken in Wales, 463, 464
    translation of, 26

using an interpreter and, 25
  willingness to make mistakes with, 4
Latvia, 251–63
  body language in, 256
  common phrases spoken in, 256
  dining in, 257
  dress in, 259
  drinking in, 257
  the euro and, 10
  European Union and, 8
  foods of, 257–58
  gift-giving in, 260–61
  helpful hints for traveling in, 261
  holidays and festivals of, 263
  language spoken in, 33, 255
  manners in, 259
  name and title usage in, 254–55
  nationalism and, 14
  people of, 253
  punctuality in, 261
  tipping in, 259
  toasting in, 258
  toilet tips for traveling in, 261
  vital statistics of, 253
  women in, 263
Lederer, William J., 3
Lines. See Queuing
Literature
  of Denmark, 131
  of Portugal, 339–40
  of Scotland, 458–59
Lithuania, 265–76
  body language in, 269
  common phrases spoken in, 270
  conversation in, 269
  corporate culture in, 274–75
  dress in, 272
  drinking n, 271
  the euro and, 10
  European Union and, 8
  foods of, 271
  gift-giving in, 273
  holidays and festivals in, 276
  language spoken in, 33, 268–69
  manners in, 272
  overview of, 265–66
  people of, 267
  punctuality in, 274
  tipping in, 272
  toasting in, 271
  toilet tips for traveling in, 273
  vital statistics on, 267
  women in, 275–76
Lithuanian language, 268–69
Living standard. See also Economy
  in Austria, 72
  in Belgium, 86
  in Bulgaria, 98
  in Cyprus, 109
  in the Czech Republic, 120
  in Denmark, 132
  in Estonia, 144
  in Finland, 154
  in France, 166
  in Germany, 181
  in Greece, 196
  in Hungary, 211
  in Ireland, 225
  in Italy, 235, 326
  in Latvia, 253
  in Lithuania, 267
  in Luxembourg, 278
  in Malta, 288
  in the Netherlands, 301
  in Northern Ireland, 467
  in Norway, 314
  in Poland, 327
  in Portugal, 340
  in Romania, 353
  in Slovakia, 367
  in Slovenia, 379
  in Spain, 391
  in Sweden, 404
  in Switzerland, 416
  in Turkey, 428

in the United Kingdom, 442
London (England), 454
Luxembourg, 277–86
  body language in, 280
  common phrases spoken in, 281
  corporate structure in, 285–86
  dress in, 283
  drinking in, 282
  European Union and, 7
  foods of, 281
  gift-giving in, 283–84
  greetings in, 279
  helpful hints for traveling in, 284
  holidays and festivals in, 286
  language spoken in, 33, 279–80
  manners in, 282–83
  names and titles in, 279
  overview of, 277–78
  punctuality in, 284
  tipping in, 282
  toasting in, 282
  toilet tips for traveling in, 284
  vital statistics on, 278
  women in, 286
Luxembourgish language, 279, 281

M
Maastricht Treaty, 7, 8
Macedonia, European Union and, 7
Machismo, 401
Magyar language, 213
Magyars, 209
Malta, 287–97
  body language used in, 291
  common phrases spoken in, 291
  conversation in, 290
  corporate culture in, 295–96
  dress in, 293
  drinking in, 292
  the euro and, 10
  European Union and, 8
  gift-giving in, 294
  greetings used in, 289
  helpful hints for traveling in, 295
  holidays and festivals in, 297
  language spoken in, 33, 290
  names and titles used in, 289
  overview of, 287–88
  punctuality in, 295
  tipping in, 292
  toasting in, 292
  toilet tips for traveling in, 294
  vital statistics on, 288–89
  women in, 296
Maltese language, 290
Manners
  in Austria, 78
  in Belgium, 90–91
  British, 448, 456
  in Bulgaria, 101
  in Cyprus, 113–14
  in the Czech Republic, 125–26
  in Denmark, 137
  Dutch, 306–7
  in Estonia, 149
  in Finland, 159
  in France, 172
  general guidelines on, 42–43
  in Germany, 187–88
  in Greece, 201–2
  in Hungary, 217
  in Ireland, 230
  in Italy, 242–43
  in Latvia, 259
  in Lithuania, 272
  in Luxembourg, 282–83
  in Malta, 293
  in Norway, 320
  in Poland, 332
  in Portugal, 345–46
  in Romania, 359
  in Slovakia, 372
  in Slovenia, 384
  smoking and, 43
  in Spain, 397

in Sweden, 410
  in Switzerland, 420–21
  table, 37–38
  Turkish, 434–35
McAleese, Mary, 233
Meals. See Dining; Food
Meals, women paying for
  in Ireland, 234
  in Italy, 248
  in Latvia, 263
  in Lithuania, 276
  in Luxembourg, 286
  in Malta, 296
  in Norway, 323
  in Portugal, 350
  in Romania, 364
  in Slovakia, 376
  in Slovenia, 388
  in Spain, 402
  in Switzerland, 425
  in Turkey, 439
  in the United Kingdom, 453
Medications, 60
Meetings, business
  in Austria, 82
  in Belgium, 93–94
  in Cyprus, 116
  in the Czech Republic, 129
  in Denmark, 139–40
  in Finland, 162
  in France, 177
  general guidelines on, 55–56
  in Germany, 191
  in Greece, 205
  in Hungary, 220
  in Ireland, 232
  in Italy, 247
  in Latvia, 262
  in Lithuania, 274–75
  in Luxembourg, 285
  in the Netherlands, 310
  in Norway, 322
  in Poland, 335
  in Portugal, 348
  in Romania, 362
  in Slovakia, 374
  in Slovenia, 386–87
  in Spain, 400
  in Sweden, 413
  in Switzerland, 423
  in Turkey, 438
  in the United Kingdom, 451–52
Merger Treaty, 8
Metric conversion chart, 32
Military service, 403
Moldavia (Romania), 351
Monaco, 10
Montenegro, 7, 10
Multilingualism, 26
Music
  Hungarian, 209
  Irish, 223
  of Latvia, 251
  of Lithuania, 265, 274
  of Portugal, 340
  in Wales, 463
Muslims/Muslim faith, 12–13
  alcoholic beverages and, 433
  body language and, 66
  dietary restrictions and, 66–67
  food and, 432
  gift-giving and, 67
  overview on, 65–66
  in the United Kingdom, 441

N
Name day celebrations, 62, 219, 334, 361
Names and titles
  in Austria, 73–74
  in Belgium, 87
  in Bulgaria, 99
  corporate culture and, 54
  in Cyprus, 110
  in the Czech Republic, 121
  in Denmark, 133

in Estonia, 145
in Finland, 155
in France, 168
general rules on, 21–22
general rules on using, 21–22
in Germany, 182–83
in Greece, 197
in Hungary, 212–13
in Ireland, 226
in Italy, 238
in Latvia, 254–55
in Lithuania, 268
in Luxembourg, 279
in Malta, 289
in the Netherlands, 302
in Norway, 315–16
in Poland, 328
in Portugal, 341–42
in Romania, 354
in Slovakia, 368
in Slovenia, 380
in Spain, 392–93
in Sweden, 406
in Switzerland, 417
of Turkey, 429–30
of the United Kingdom, 443–44
National Agency for Latvian Language Training
    (NALLT), 255
National Eisteddfod of Wales, 463
Nationalism, 14, 179
Natural resources
    of Austria, 72
    of Belgium, 86
    of Bulgaria, 98
    of Cyprus, 109
    of the Czech Republic, 120
    of Denmark, 132
    of Estonia, 144
    of Finland, 154
    of France, 166
    of Germany, 181
    of Greece, 196
    of Hungary, 211
    of Ireland, 225
    of Italy, 236
    of Latvia, 253
    of Lithuania, 267
    of Luxembourg, 278
    of Malta, 288
    of the Netherlands, 301
    of Norway, 313, 314
    of Poland, 327
    of Portugal, 340
    of Romania, 353
    of Slovakia, 367
    of Slovenia, 379
    of Spain, 391
    of Sweden, 404
    of Switzerland, 416
    of the United Kingdom, 442
Nature
    in Norway, 314
    in Romania, 353
    in Slovakia, 366
    in Slovenia, 338
Netherlands, the, 299–312
    body language used in, 303–4
    common phrases spoken in, 304
    conversation in, 303
    corporate culture in, 310–11
    dress in, 307
    drinking in, 305
    European Union and, 7
    food and meals in, 304–5
    gift-giving in, 308
    greetings used in, 302
    holidays and festivals in, 312
    language spoken in, 33, 303
    manners in, 305–6
    names and titles in, 302
    overview of, 299–300
    people of, 301
    punctuation in, 309
    toasting in, 305–6
    toilet tips for traveling in, 309

vital statistics on, 301
    women in, 311–12
Nicosia, 115
Nobel, Alfred, 313, 404
Nobel prizes, 209, 313, 326, 389, 404, 468
Nonverbal communication. See Body language
Nordic countries, 29, 53. See also Denmark; Finland;
    Iceland; Norway; Sweden
North Atlantic Treaty Organisation (NATO), 85, 98
    Luxembourg and, 277–78
    the Netherlands and, 299
    Romania and, 352
    Slovakia and, 366
    Slovenia and, 337–38
Northern Europeans, 29. See also Denmark; Finland;
    Norway; Sweden
Northern Ireland, 224, 466–69. See also United
    Kingdom, the
Norway, 313–23
    body language in, 318
    common phrases spoken in, 318
    conversation in, 317
    corporate culture in, 322–23
    drinking in, 319
    foods of, 318
    helpful hints for traveling in, 321
    holidays and festivals of, 323
    language spoken in, 33, 316
    overview of, 313–14
    punctuation in, 322
    toasting in, 319
    toilet tips for traveling in, 321
    vital statistics on, 314–15
    women in, 323
Norwegian language, 316, 318
Nudity, 45
    in Denmark, 138
    in France, 173
    in Spain, 398
    in Sweden, 403, 412
    in Turkey, 437
Numbers, writing, 31
Nynorsk dialect (Norwegian language), 316

O

Olympic games, 195
Orthodox Christians, 63, 362
Orthodox Jews, 64
Ottoman Empire, 97, 351, 427
Ottoman Turkish language, 430
Outdoors, the. See Nature
Overtipping, 41

P

Pace, 51–52
    in Luxembourg, 284
    in Spain, 389
    in Sweden, 413
Passport, 59
People, the
    of Austria, 73
    of Belgium, 87
    of Bulgaria, 99
    of Cyprus, 110
    of the Czech Republic, 120
    of Denmark, 133
    of Estonia, 145
    of Finland, 155
    of France, 167
    of Germany, 181
    of Greece, 196
    of Hungary, 211
    of Ireland, 225
    of Italy, 237
    of Latvia, 253
    of Lithuania, 267
    of Luxembourg, 279
    of Malta, 289
    of the Netherlands, 301
    of Norway, 315
    of Poland, 327
    of Portugal, 341
    of Romania, 354
    of Scotland, 459
    of Slovakia, 367

of Slovenia, 379
    of Spain, 389
    of Sweden, 405
    of Switzerland, 417
    of Turkey, 429
    of the United Kingdom, 443
    of Wales, 463
Personal space
    in Denmark, 134
    in Italy, 240
    in Lithuania, 269
    in the Netherlands, 303–4
    in Portugal, 343
    in Romania, 356
    in Spain, 394
    in Sweden, 407
    in the United Kingdom, 445
Phrases, common
    in British versus American English, 446
    in Czech, 123
    in Dutch, 304
    in Estonian, 147
    in Finnish, 157
    in French, 170
    in German, 185
    in Italian, 240
    in Latvian, 256
    in Lithuanian, 270
    in Luxembourgish, 281
    in Maltese, 291
    in Norwegian, 318
    in Polish, 330
    in Portuguese, 344
    in Romanian, 357
    in Slovak, 369
    in Slovene, 382
    in Spanish, 395
    in Swedish, 408
    in Turkish, 432
Poland, 325–37
    body language in, 329
    common phrases spoken in, 330
    Communist rule and, 15
    conversation in, 329
    corporate culture in, 334–35
    dining in, 330
    dress in, 332
    the euro and, 10
    European Union and, 8
    foods of, 330–31
    gift-giving in, 333
    greetings in, 327–28
    helpful hints for traveling in, 334
    holidays and festivals in, 337
    language spoken in, 33, 328–29
    Lithuania and, 265
    manners in, 332
    names and titles in, 328
    overview of, 325–26
    people of, 327
    punctuality in, 334
    tipping in, 331–32
    toasting in, 331
    toilet tips for traveling in, 333
    vital statistics on, 327
    women in, 336–37
Polish language, 328
Politics, EU membership and, 7
Population
    of Austria, 72
    of Belgium, 86
    of Bulgaria, 98
    of Cyprus, 109
    of the Czech Republic, 120
    declining, 14–15
    of Denmark, 132
    of England, 455
    of Estonia, 144
    of the European Union, 8
    of Finland, 154
    of France, 166
    of Germany, 181
    of Greece, 196
    of Hungary, 211
    of Ireland, 225

of Italy, 236
of Latvia, 253
of Lithuania, 267
of Luxembourg, 278
of Malta, 288
of the Netherlands, 300, 301
of Northern Ireland, 467
of Norway, 314
of Poland, 327
of Portugal, 340
of Romania, 353
of Scotland, 459
of Slovakia, 367
of Slovenia, 379
of Spain, 391
of Sweden, 404
of Switzerland, 416
of Turkey, 428
of the United Kingdom, 442
of Wales, 463
Portugal, 339–50
  body language in, 343
  common phrases spoken in, 344
  conversation in, 343
  corporate culture in, 348–49
  dress in, 346
  drinking in, 345
  European Union and, 7, 8
  food of, 344–45
  gift-giving in, 346–47
  greetings in, 341
  helpful hints for traveling in, 347
  holidays and festivals of, 350
  language spoken in, 33, 342
  manners in, 345–46
  tipping in, 345
  toasting in, 345
  toilet tips for traveling in, 347
  vital statistics on, 340–41
  women in, 349–50
Portuguese language, 342, 344
Portuguese Republic. See Portugal
Presentations
  general guidelines on, 55–56
  in Italy, 247
  in Lithuania, 275
  in the Netherlands, 310
  in Sweden, 413
Professional titles, 238
Prostitution, 300
Public transportation
  in Austria, 80–81
Punctuality
  in Austria, 81
  in Belgium, 93
  in Bulgaria, 104
  in Cyprus, 116
  in the Czech Republic, 128
  in Denmark, 139
  in Estonia, 151
  in Finland, 161
  in France, 176
  general guidelines on, 50–51
  in Germany, 190
  in Greece, 204
  in Hungary, 220
  in Ireland, 232
  in Italy, 246
  in Latvia, 261
  in Lithuania, 274
  in Luxembourg, 283
  in Malta, 295
  in the Netherlands, 309
  in Norway, 322
  pace and, 51–52
  in Poland, 334
  in Portugal, 348
  in Romania, 362
  in Slovenia, 386
  in Spain, 399
  in Sweden, 412
  in Switzerland, 423
  traffic and, 51
  in Turkey, 437
  in the United Kingdom, 451

ways of expressing time and, 51

Q
Questions, asking
  about host country, 5–6
  by Greeks, 198
  in Romania, 355
Queuing
  in Austria, 76
  in England, 456
  in Germany, 184
  in Greece, 198
  in Italy, 240
  in Scotland, 460
  in Turkey, 431

R
Ramadan, 65
Ramazan, 438
Regional dialects, 24
Regionalism
  European Union facing challenges regarding, 13–14
  in Germany, 179
  in Italy, 236
  in Spain, 389
Regional terms, 28–29
Religion
  in Austria, 73
  in the Baltic nations, 29
  in Belgium, 86
  in Bulgaria, 99
  in Cyprus, 110
  in the Czech Republic, 120
  in Denmark, 133
  in England, 455
  in Estonia, 145
  European Union facing challenges with, 12
  in Finland, 155
  in France, 167
  in Germany, 181
  in Greece, 196
  in Hungary, 211
  interfaith etiquette and, 61–67
  in Ireland, d225
  in Italy, 237
  in Latvia, 253
  in Lithuania, 267, 274
  in Luxembourg, 279
  in Malta, 289
  in the Netherlands, 301
  in Northern Ireland, 468
  in Norway, 315
  in Poland, 326, 327
  in Portugal, 341
  in Romania, 354, 361–62
  in Scotland, 459
  in Slovakia, 367
  in Slovenia, 379
  in Spain, 391
  in Sweden, 403, 405
  in Switzerland, 417
  in Turkey, 427, 429
  in the United Kingdom, 443
  in Wales, 463
Republic of Austria. See Austria
Republic of Bulgaria. See Bulgaria
Republic of Cyprus. See Cyprus
Republic of Finland. See Finland
Republic of Hungary. See Hungary
Republic of Ireland. See Ireland
Republic of Latvia. See Latvia
Republic of Lithuania. See Lithuania
Republic of Malta. See Malta
Republic of Slovenia. See Slovenia
Republic of Turkey. See Turkey
Restaurants. See also Meals, women paying for
  in Austria, 78
  in Belgium, 90
  in Germany, 185, 188
  in Greece, 201
  in Hungary, 217
  in Luxembourg, 281, 284
  in Slovakia, 373–74
  in Spain, 397, 399
  in Switzerland, 423

in Turkey, 434
in the United Kingdom, 447, 448, 451
Restrooms, 61. See also Toilet tips
Riga Motormuseum, 261
Robinson, Mary, 233
Rock music, 274
Roma (Gypsies), 356
Roman (Latin) alphabet, 145, 430
Roman Catholic Church, 62–63, 326, 361
Romania, 351–64
  body language in, 356–57
  common phrases spoken in, 357
  conversation in, 355–56
  corporate culture in, 362–63
  dress in, 359–60
  drinking in, 358
  European Union and, 7, 8
  foods of, 357–58
  gift-giving in, 360–61
  greetings in, 354
  helpful hints for traveling in, 360–61
  holidays and festivals in, 364
  language spoken in, 33, 355
  manners in, 359
  names and titles in, 354–55
  overview of, 351–52
  people of, 354
  punctuality in, 362
  tipping in, 358–59
  toasting in, 358
  toilet tips for traveling in, 361
  vital statistics on, 353
  women in, 364
Romanian language, 355
Royalty
  in Norway, 313
  in Sweden, 404
Russian language
  spoken in Estonia, 145, 146
  spoken in Latvia, 255
  spoken in Poland, 329
Russia/Russians
  Estonia, 146
  Latvia and, 252
  Lithuania and, 265, 266
  Romanians and, 361

S
Safety
  general guidelines on, 59–60
  for women, 178, 312
Salazar, António, 339
Salutations, 30
Sami, the, 313
Samizdat, 266
San Marino, 10
Saunas, 45, 143, 153, 163
Scandinavian countries, 29. See also individual
  country names
Scandinavian languages, 133
Scotland. See also United Kingdom, the
  body language in, 460
  food and drink in, 460
  greetings in, 459
  language spoken in, 460
  overview of, 458–59
  people of, 459
  toasting in, 460
  vital statistics on, 459
Scottish Gaelic, 460
Serbia, European Union and, 7
Shaking hands. See Hand shaking
Shoes, taking off, 125, 217, 259, 372, 384, 434, 435
Siestas, 389
Silesians, the, 328
Silverware. See Utensils, table
Slovakia, 365–88
  body language in, 370
  common phrases spoken in, 369
  Communist rule and, 15
  conversation in, 369–70
  dress in, 372
  the euro and, 10
  European Union and, 8
  gift-giving in, 373

greetings in, 367
  helpful hints for traveling in, 373–74
  holidays and festivals in, 376
  language spoken in, 33, 368–69, 371
  manners in, 372
  names and titles in, 368
  overview of, 365–66
  tipping in, 371–72
  toilet tips for traveling in, 374
  vital statistics on, 367
  women in, 375–76
Slovak language, 369
Slovak Republic. See Slovakia
Slovene language, 380–81
Slovenia, 377–88
  body language in, 381
  conversation in, 381
  corporate culture in, 386–87
  dining in, 382, 384
  dress in, 384
  drinking in, 383
  the euro and, 10
  European Union and, 8
  foods of, 382–83
  gift-giving in, 385
  helpful hints for traveling in, 386
  holidays and festivals of, 388
  language spoken in, 33, 380–81
  manners in, 384
  names and titles in, 380
  overview of, 337–38
  people of, 379
  punctuality in, 386
  tipping in, 383–84
  toasting in, 383
  toilet tips for traveling in, 385
  vital statistics on, 379
  women in, 387–88
Smiling, 34
  in the Czech Republic, 121
  in France, 170
  in Hungary, 214
  in Latvia, 256
  in the Netherlands, 304
  in Slovenia, 380
  in Sweden, 405
Smith, Adam, 458
Smoking
  in Denmark, 141
  in Ireland, 231
  in the Netherlands, 307
  in Poland, 334
  in Romania, 359, 361
  in Switzerland, 421
  in Turkey, 437
  while dining, 38
Smorgasbords, 162, 413
Socializing, business. See also Conversation; Dining
  in Austria, 83
  in Belgium, 94
  in Cyprus, 117
  in the Czech Republic, 130
  in Denmark, 140
  in Finland, 162–63
  in France, 177
  general guidelines on, 56–57
  in Germany, 192
  in Greece, 206
  in Hungary, 221
  in Ireland, 233
  in Italy, 248
  in Latvia, 263
  in Lithuania, 275
  in Luxembourg, 285–86
  in the Netherlands, 311
  in Norway, 323
  in Poland, 336
  in Portugal, 349
  in Romania, 364
  in Slovakia, 375
  in Slovenia, 387
  in Spain, 401
  in Sweden, 414
  in Switzerland, 424
  in Turkey, 438–39

in the United Kingdom, 452–53
Soviet Union. See also Communist rule
  Finland and, 154
Spain, 389–402
  body language in, 394
  common phrases spoken in, 395
  conversation in, 393–94
  corporate culture in, 400–401
  cultural preservation and, 9
  dining in, 395
  dress in, 397–98
  drinking in, 396
  European Union and, 7, 8
  eye contact in, 394
  foods of, 395–96
  gift-giving in, 398
  greetings in, 392
  helpful hints for traveling in, 399
  holidays and festivals of, 402
  language spoken in, 33, 393
  manners in, 397
  names and titles in, 392–93
  overview of, 389–90
  people of, 391
  punctuality in, 399
  tipping in, 396–97
  toasting in, 396
  toilet tips for traveling in, 399
  vital statistics on, 391
  women in, 401–2
Spanish language, 342, 393, 395
Spas
  Hungarian, 221
  in Slovakia, 366
Staring, 76, 394, 402
Strel, Martin, 381
Styrian, 71
Sweden, 403–14
  body language in, 407
  common phrases spoken in, 408
  conversation in, 406–7
  corporate culture in, 413–14
  dress in, 410–11
  drinking in, 409
  the euro and, 10
  European Union and, 8
  foods of, 408–9
  gift-giving in, 411
  greetings in, 405
  helpful hints for traveling in, 412
  holidays and festivals of, 414
  language spoken in, 33, 406
  manners in, 410
  names and titles in, 406
  overview of, 403–4
  people of, 405
  punctuality in, 412
  tipping in, 410
  toasting in, 409
  toilet tips for traveling in, 412
  vital statistics on, 404–5
  women in, 414
Swedish language, 406
Swiss Confederation. See Switzerland
Switzerland, 415–25
  body language in, 418
  conversation in, 418
  corporate culture in, 423–24
  dress in, 421
  drinking in, 420
  European Union and, 8
  gift-giving in, 422
  greetings in, 417
  helpful hints for traveling in, 423
  holidays and festivals in, 425
  language spoken in, 34, 417–18
  manners in, 420–21
  names and titles used in, 417
  overview on, 415–16
  people of, 417
  punctuality in, 423
  smoking in, 421
  tipping in, 420
  toasting in, 420
  vital statistics on, 416

women in, 425–26

T

Table manners, 37–38. See also Manners
Tap water, 358, 420
Tarnovo Constitution (1879), 97
Taxi, taking a, 60, 80, 128, 361
Ten-Day War (1991), 377
Terrorism, 13
Thank-you notes, 30, 37
Time. See also Pace
  punctuality and, 51
  recorded in written communication, 31–32
Tipping
  in Austria, 78
  in Belgium, 90
  in Bulgaria, 101
  in Cyprus, 113
  in the Czech Republic, 125
  in Denmark, 136
  in Estonia, 148
  in Finland, 159
  in France, 172
  general rules on, 41–42
  in Germany, 187
  in Greece, 201
  in Hungary, 216
  in Ireland, 229
  in Italy, 242
  in Latvia, 259
  in Lithuania, 272
  in Luxembourg, 282
  in Malta, 292
  in the Netherlands, 306
  in Norway, 319
  in Poland, 331–32
  in Portugal, 345
  in Romania, 358–59
  in Slovakia, 371–72
  in Slovenia, 383–84
  in Spain, 396–97
  in Sweden, 410
  in Switzerland, 420
  in Turkey, 434
  in the United Kingdom, 447–48
Titles. See Names and titles
Toasting
  in Austria, 77
  in Belgium, 90
  in Bulgaria, 101
  in the Czech Republic, 124–25
  in Denmark, 136
  in Estonia, 148
  in Finland, 158
  in France, 172
  general rules on, 40
  in Germany, 186–87
  in Greece, 201
  in Hungary, 216
  in Ireland, 229
  in Italy, 242
  in Latvia, 258
  in Lithuania, 271
  in Luxembourg, 282
  in Malta, 292
  in the Netherlands, 305–6
  in Norway, 319
  in Poland, 331
  in Portugal, 345
  in Romania, 358
  in Scotland, 460
  in Slovakia, 371
  in Slovenia, 383
  in Spain, 396–97
  in Sweden, 409
  in Switzerland, 420
  in Turkey, 433
  in the United Kingdom, 447
  in Wales, 464
Toilet tips
  for traveling in Austria, 80
  for traveling in Belgium, 92
  for traveling in Bulgaria, 104
  for traveling in Cyprus, 115
  for traveling in the Czech Republic, 127

for traveling in Denmark, 139
for traveling in Estonia, 150
for traveling in Finland, 161
for traveling in France, 175
for traveling in Germany, 189
for traveling in Greece, 203
for traveling in Hungary, 219
for traveling in Italy, 245
for traveling in Latvia, 261
for traveling in Lithuania, 273
for traveling in Luxembourg, 284
for traveling in Malta, 294
for traveling in the Netherlands, 309
for traveling in Norway, 321
for traveling in Poland, 333
for traveling in Portugal, 347
for traveling in Romania, 361
for traveling in Slovakia, 374
for traveling in Slovenia, 385
for traveling in Spain, 399
for traveling in Sweden, 412
for traveling in Turkey, 436
Tokes, Laszlo, 352
Touching, general rules on, 35. *See also* Hugging;
    Personal space
Traffic, 15
    Greek, 204
    punctuality and, 51
Transylvania (Romania), 351
Travelers, 232
Treaties of Rome, 8
Treaty of Paris, 8
Treaty of Trianon (1920), 210
Treaty on European Union, 7
Turkey, 427–39
    body language in, 431
    common phrases spoken in, 432
    conversation in, 430–31
    corporate culture in, 437–39
    dress in, 435
    drinking in, 433
    European Union and, 7
    foods of, 432–33
    gift-giving in, 436
    greetings in, 429
    helpful hints for traveling in, 437
    holidays and festivals of, 439
    language spoken in, 34, 430
    manners in, 434–35
    names and titles in, 429–30
    overview of, 427–28
    people of, 429
    punctuality in, 437
    tipping in, 434
    toasting in, 433
    toilet tips for traveling in, 436
    vital statistics on, 428
    women in, 439
Turkish coffee, 113, 124, 433
Turkish Cypriots, 107–8, 118
Turkish language, 111, 430, 432
Turkish Republic of Northern Cyprus (TRNC),
    108, 109, 110, 117
Tyrolese, 71

U

The ugly American, 3–4
Ulster, 469
United Kingdom, the, 441–53
    body language in, 445–46
    conversation in, 444–45
    corporate culture in, 451–53
    Cyprus and, 107
    dining in, 446–47
    dress in, 449
    drinking in, 447
    England, 454–57
    the euro and, 10
    European Union and, 7, 8
    gift-giving in, 450
    greetings in, 443
    helpful hints for traveling in, 451
    holidays and festivals in, 453
    language spoken in, 34, 444
    manners in, 448

Muslims in, 441
names and titles used in, 443–44
Northern Ireland, 466469
overview of, 441–42
people of, 443
punctuality in, 451
Scotland, 458–61
tipping in, 447–48
toasting in, 447
vital statistics on, 442
Wales, 462–65
women in, 453
United Nations (UN), 108, 415
United States. *See* America/Americans
Utensils, table
    formal dining and, 38
    in Sweden, 410
    table manners and, 37
    used in France, 172
    used in Italy, 242
    used in Portugal, 346
    used in Spain, 397
    used in Switzerland, 420

V

Vatican City, 10, 63
Vegetarianism, 40
Velvet Revolution (1989), 119
Viennese Ball season, 72
Vike-Freiberga, Vaira, 263
Vital statistics
    on Austria, 72
    on Belgium, 86
    on Bulgaria, 98
    on Cyprus, 109–10
    on the Czech Republic, 120
    on Denmark, 132
    on England, 455
    on Estonia, 144
    on Finland, 154
    on France, 165–66
    on Germany, 181
    on Greece, 196
    on Hungary, 211
    on Ireland, 225
    on Italy, 236–37
    on Latvia, 253
    on Lithuania, 267
    on Luxembourg, 278
    on Malta, 288–89
    on the Netherlands, 301
    on Northern Ireland, 467
    on Norway, 314–15
    on Poland, 327
    on Portugal, 340–41
    on Romania, 353
    on Scotland, 459
    on Slovakia, 367
    on Slovenia, 379
    on Spain, 391
    on Sweden, 404–5
    on Switzerland, 416
    on Turkey, 428
    on the United Kingdom, 442
    on Wales, 463

W

Wales, 462–65. *See also* United Kingdom, the
Wałęsa, Lech, 325–26
Wallachia (Romania), 351
Wallonia, 85
Walloon companies, 93
Walloons (Belgium), 85, 87
Wedding rings, 58, 361
Welsh language, 462
West Germany, 7, 180
Wine, 77
    Czech, 124
    of Malta, 292
    of Portugal, 39
    Romanian, 358
    of Slovenia, 383
    of Spain, 396
Women. *See also* Meals, women paying for
    attitudes toward business, 57–58

in Austria, 83
in Belgium, 94
in Bulgaria, 105
covering their heads, 63
in Cyprus, 117
in the Czech Republic, 130
in Denmark, 140–41
in Estonia, 152
in Finland, 163
in France, 178
general guidelines about/for, 58–59
in Germany, 193
in Greece, 206
hand shaking and, 20
in Hungary, 221–22
in Ireland, 233–34
in Italy, 248
in Latvia, 263
in Lithuania, 275–76
in Luxembourg, 286
in Malta, 296
in the Netherlands, 311–12
in Norway, 323
in Poland, 336–37
Portugal in, 349–50
in Romania, 364
in Slovakia, 368, 375–76
in Slovenia, 387–88
in Spain, 401–2
in Sweden, 414
in Switzerland, 424–25
in Turkey, 439
in the United Kingdom, 453
Work hours
    in Germany, 191
    in Latvia, 262
    in Spain, 389, 401
    in Sweden, 414
World Health Organization (WHO), 415
World Trade Organization (WTO), 415
World War I, 71, 277
World War II
    Austria and, 71
    Bulgaria and, 97
    Czechoslovakia and, 119
    Denmark and, 131
    Hungary and, 210
    Latvia and, 251
    Lithuania and, 265
    Luxembourg and, 277, 278
    Malta and, 287
    Norway and, 314
    Poland and, 325, 326
    Slovakia and, 365
    Slovenia and, 337
Written communication, 29–32

Y

Yugoslavia, 377

IF YOUR COMPANY DOES INTERNATIONAL BUSINESS, YOU CAN'T AFFORD TO IGNORE THESE BOOKS.

Doing business abroad? If so, you must read this engaging series of travel guides created especially for business travelers by Mary Murray Bosrock. These books capture the nuances of business cultures around the world and help you achieve your best while working in unfamiliar territories.

EUROPEAN BUSINESS CUSTOMS & MANNERS
PUT YOUR BEST FOOT FORWARD: ASIA
PUT YOUR BEST FOOT FORWARD: MEXICO/CANADA
PUT YOUR BEST FOOT FORWARD: RUSSIA
PUT YOUR BEST FOOT FORWARD: SOUTH AMERICA
PUT YOUR BEST FOOT FORWARD: USA

Ask about discounts and pricing.

Corporate Leaders Are Saying...

"As the business opportunities in Asia grow, so does the competition. In Asia, perhaps more than any other region in the world, being competitive means understanding the local cultures. Mary Bosrock provides a helpful guide to understanding Asia."
—Walter F. Mondale, former Vice President of the United States and Ambassador to Japan,
on *Put Your Best Foot Forward: Asia*

"No matter how sophisticated we think we've become as global citizens, basic courtesy from one person to another is still the primary language of business. Mary Bosrock's books are excellent examples of how to relate to our global neighbors."
—Michael R. Bonsignore, Director, Medtronic, Inc. (former Chairman and CEO, Honeywell International, Inc.)

"In today's global marketplace it is essential for business travelers to have well-developed international communication skills. Mary Bosrock provides valuable guidance to savvy travelers who want to get it right the first time."
—Harvey Golub, Chairman of the Board, Campbell Soup Company
(former Chairman and CEO, American Express Company)

www.meadowbrookpress.com

Meadowbrook Press • 1-800-338-2232 • 5451 Smetana Drive • Minnetonka, MN • 55343